THE MASTER KEY

THE de LAURENCE-SCOTT CO.

CHICAGO, ILL., U.S.A.

Dr L W D Laurence

The Master Key

by

Dr. L.W. de LAURENCE

de LAURENCE, SCOTT & COMPANY
CHICAGO, ILLS. U.S.A.

The Master Key

by

Dr. L.W. de LAURENCE

de LAURENCE, SCOTT & COMPANY
CHICAGO, ILLS. U.S.A.

The Master Key

Teaches

Scientific Concentration

SECOND EDITION

The Master Key

By L. W. de LAURENCE

Teaches
Scientific Concentration

MIND TRAINING. WILL CULTURE. THOUGHT - CONTROL. MENTAL DISCIPLINE. ATTENTION. OBSERVATION. MEMORY. THINKING. PUBLIC SPEAKING. CONVERSATION. READING. IMAGINATION. THE CULTIVATION OF THE SENSES. CONTROL OVER MIND AND BODY. CONTROL OVER THE ACT OF BREATHING. CONTROL OVER BAD HABITS. WILL-POWER IN ALL ITS TYPES AND MANIFESTATIONS. THOUGHT - CONTROL (IN PUBLIC PERFORMANCES, SUCH AS SPEAKING, SINGING, PLAYING) SELF-CONSCIOUSNESS. PERSONAL MAGNETISM. TO DEVELOP A STRONG PERSONALITY. TO ACQUIRE POISE AND DISTINCTION. RATIONAL AND MORAL EDUCATION ETHICALLY DIRECTED. INDIVIDUAL MENTAL EFFICIENCY. THE PSYCHOLOGY OF FAITH AND DOUBT. CONCENTRATION APPLIED TO HEALTH AND DISEASE. CONCENTRATION APPLIED TO FEAR AND DISEASE. EXPECTANCY AND ATTENTION. CONCENTRATION DURING THE PERIOD OF GESTATION. THE SECRET OF ABUNDANCE. THE POVERTY CURE. THE ART OF GETTING RICH. "OPPORTUNITY" IN A NEW LIGHT. REAPING AND SOWING.

What The Master Key Contains

HE MASTER KEY is divided into *Six Parts:* contains *Thirty-seven* full *Chapters* embracing *Thirty-five Lessons* of graduated difficulty covering *Forty* individual numbered *Exercises* in which the fundamental principles, and the various aspects of *Concentration* and *Mental Discipline* are fully explained.

"The Master Key"

It contains *abundant material* for the student, material which will last him a long time, and thus keep his interest in the subject of *Concentration* keen and progressive.

Preface to the Second Edition

CONCENTRATION AND MENTAL DISCIPLINE.

N no branch of human knowledge has there been a more lively increase of the spirit of research during the past few years than in the study of Psychology, Concentration and Mental Discipline. Many points of "mental doctrine" have been passing afresh through the crucible; plain instruction is a popular cry, and, in some directions, a real requirement of the age; the requests for authentic lessons in Thought Control, Mental Discipline and Concentration have never before been so great as in recent years.

¶ Students seeking knowledge in this field have advanced with the fuller possibilities provided by the constant addition of reliable teachings and more data for comparative study. Thousands of students of Concentration have received the reward of diligent, skillful and devoted study.

¶ Scholars in Psychology and Mental Discipline have specialized to so great an extent that many conclusions are less speculative than they were, while many more are thus available for arriving at a general judgment; and, in some directions at least, the time for drawing such conclusions, and so making practical use of such specialized research seems to have come, or to be close at hand.

¶ Many people, therefore, including the large mass of men and women employed in the many avenues of commercial life, as well as those suffering from mental maladies and bad mental habits, desire to have in an accessible form instruction that would throw a flood of light on these heretofore supposed esoteric studies that are of living and vital interest to the faith; and at the same time, "practical" questions by which is really denoted the application of "faith in one's self" to life and to the needs of the day.

¶ It thus seems an appropriate time for the issue of a treatise, which shall aim at presenting a general study for the student of the present application of Concentration in various branches of the wide field which is included in the study of Psychology and Mental Habits.

¶ This volume is designed to supply such work, and seems to be well liked by men of known reputation as thinkers and scholars, teachers and divines, who are, one and all, firm upholders of the law of Concentration, Faith and Mental Discipline.

¶ It is an indisputable fact that about every scrap of information or instruction given out personally, by books or by the circulation of literature by schools of mental science have declared as the foundation of its success its association with some supernatural power, cult or creed—proclaiming that the student's success was entirely dependent upon his acceptance of some particular mystical doctrine or belief.

¶ The author desires it to be distinctly understood that the Lessons, contained herein, have no conclusions of this nature; neither has he any connection with any creed or person who expresses these peculiar views, as he never felt that it came within the scope of an author's work, in a book of this kind, to interfere with the personal views of the student regarding religion, creed or cult.

¶ Shades of opinion and differences of judgment must exist, if thought is not to be at a standstill—petrified into an unproductive fossil; but while neither the author nor all of his readers can be expected to agree with every point of view in the details of the discussions in all the various books published on the subject of New Thought, Christian Science, Magnetism and divers "isms" and "mental fads," he is convinced that the principles, so conservatively enunciated in this Volume, are such as must conduce to the strengthening of the student's "Concentration," and "faith in himself," as these are essential requisites in every avenue of human endeavor.

¶ The object of this work is to provide an introduction to the study of *"thought"* as it has developed itself within the confines of the Practical Psychology. Interest in Concentration, Mind, Mental Discipline, the intelligent treatment and moral management of Mental Maladies, has in recent times become so pronounced and widespread that it is hoped that, even amongst the various and excellent works which have appeared in response to that interest, room may perhaps be found for an attempt to present the subject in its logical sequence, and in such a form as may best meet the wants of the interested student.

Dr. L. W. de Laurence.

CONTENTS

CONTENTS

A HIGH-GRADE SYSTEM OF
Mind Training
FOR PROFESSIONAL MEN
BUSINESS MEN AND BUSINESS WOMEN

THE MASTER KEY, by *Dr. de Laurence*, teaches *"Scientific Concentration,"* and is the only High-Grade Course on Mind-Training in existence.

It is *sound, scientific, authoritative, practical,* and is right now being studied by thousands of people in all walks of life in every part of the civilized world.

Scientific Concentration and Mind-Training, as taught herein, aims at the unfolding of one's individuality to the full. It makes *Intellectually, Emotionally, Volitionally well-balanced men and women.*

"Scientific Concentration" is the finest drill for the development of mental discipline you can undertake. It gives you *control* over distraction and worry; a cultivated *power of inhibition, mental poise, decision* of character, and a quiet sense of power.

THE MASTER KEY gives you a complete *Memory Training,* and shows you how to cultivate to the full your powers of *Attention* and *Observation.*

It shows you how to work or study with the *minimum of fatigue,* and teaches you how to think on original lines, and how to speak well *(especially in public).* You are safe in studying *"Scientific Concentration"* as taught in this book. Eminent men and women commend it.

Here is a book that teaches how to concentrate on thoroughly *common-sense, practical, and strictly scientific lines.* It really gives you a splendid all-round *mental training*—one that will be eminently useful in any department of life, as a close perusal of its contents will show.

THE PUBLISHERS.

xiv

The Master Key

CHAPTER I.

INTRODUCTION.

MENTAL EQUILIBRIUM.

Thought, our manner of thinking and self-control, or mental discipline are important factors in life's achievements. On these depend our power of concentration and the mental equilibrium that must be maintained by those who wish to advance. It lies within the earnest student to create a world of thought wherein he may weather with calm fortitude the storms of mental life, for disappointment and sorrow pass no one by, and suffering is the loom in which character is made.

Mind can be so powerful a defensive arm in the battle of earthly existence, that, in behalf of his interests and welfare, the student should learn to measure its force, understand its almost limitless power, and educate himself to employ it judiciously. The student must learn to appreciate at its true value this force, given to him that he may be able to meet and conquer, not only exterior difficulties, but even greater and more subtle enemies from within.

Thought is a product of the mind, a mental vibration, and therefore, a force which penetrates even into the physical body and worldly affairs of mankind.

It is thought that slowly and unerringly builds up or tears down the whole moral fabric of our being. Consciously or unconsciously it acts upon everyone with whom you have near or remote contact. The great discoveries of science, the mechanical inventions, the master-pieces in music and art; all these, being achievements due to the patient and tireless efforts of the intellect, are but the results of concentrated thought.

If your thinking is inspired by high ideals, nourished by the practice of virtue and honesty, and is submissive to a will that

1

sincerely directs it to its highest end, it will achieve moral, intellectual, and even material results of a positive character, as surely as sound seed planted in good soil will blossom and bear fruit following the natural law of its growth.   Through the same certain process do evil results follow upon evil and sordid lines of thought, and hence the employment of this faculty for unworthy ends in any circumstances is a disintegrating action, morally disastrous to the individual, even though the material or intellectual aim has been accomplished.

Thought is a creative force—a fact that the student must always bear in mind.   Every thought, be it good or evil, creates corresponding conditions.   There is, however, a species of mental activity—if I may call it activity at all—which is akin to the flapping of canvas in the ill-trimmed sails of a vessel.   It occupies some to the extent that they fancy they are thinking, but in reality they are floating aimlessly on the tide.   Unless thought be employed for specific accomplishment, and guided and controlled by the will, it follows the line of least resistance and spends itself in idle dreaming.   This dissipation of a great force weakens our mental and moral, and even our physical, faculties. It is in no wise different from the atrophy that follows upon non-use of our muscles in the work for which they were designed.

If we can say that any faculty of the human compound is more important than the faculty of thought—that one must be the will.   It is the Divine part of man.   Our most elementary concept of a successful man or woman is the concept of a compelling force—a great urging towards a result—and this is will, and everyone of us possesses in a greater or less degree this faculty as an essential constituent of our individuality.

If we are to seek peace and moral strength in the highways of achievement the will must focus on worthy aims—our end must be work well done rather than selfish advancement for.its own sake.   When the human will is directed by truth, honesty and confidence, man is guided and directed by an unerring vision of right, and even though failure should await his efforts, his whole moral nature has been strengthened by disinterested endeavor, and the way is prepared for some greater achievement with more telling results.

Reason is the *mentor of the will—thoughts are its workmen*.   Reason plans the spiritual or material edifice; will is the foreman who controls and directs, keeping order and industry in the ranks of the workmen until the structure is complete. Thoughts, in other words, must be absolutely controlled by the will and directed by it into proper channels.

With the larger part of humanity, thoughts, like wayward, spoiled children, run hither and thither, seeking distraction and fair fields where no mental effort is required. The moment concentration is demanded—and this is speaking generally—they rebel, scamper off, and only a firm will can bring them back. At first they sulk; the mind remains inactive, and all that has been gained apparently is a restless obedience on their part and a certain moral and mental strength, the result of persistent effort. But as thought was created subject to will, repeated and persistent effort on the part of this faculty reduces thought to docile and absolute obedience.

When you accomplish this, anarchy has been uprooted in the mental kingdom; a sensation of peace and strength is experienced in the re-establishment of order under the reign of reason and will. Infinite patience and untiring perseverance are important factors in the accomplishment of this result. The student of *psychology* and *mental discipline* must have no illusions concerning the arduous task that lies before him, and he must bring to it, not only courage and the determination to conquer, but a vigilance that never sleeps.

Few of today sufficiently realize the power of a thought; its danger and its creative potency. The minds of average human beings run riot. The majority of people even in this era of *psychology* and *mental culture* take little thought of what and how they think.

Actions are regarded to be the prime objects of consideration in their relation to the established order of things—they are learning only now, that if they would influence their actions with unquestioned certainty, they must cultivate the field in which their actions spring up and grow into actualities—and this field is the field of thought.

Many believe because their thoughts are their own and unknown to others, they imagine they can harbor all sorts of unworthy sentiments and feelings so long as they do not actually allow these feelings to betray themselves in corresponding actions. They do not realize that every bad mental habit indulged in against precept of perfection, not only inclines them to the act, but it lowers the ideal, and weakens their moral nature and power of resistance.

The Catholic Church recognizes how effective is thought in producing conditions since she requires her children to confess their sins of thought, and imposes penance for any deliberate evil intention, even though the act was never committed.

It follows, then, that our true worth or unworthiness lies in our manner of thinking, no matter how seemingly just or unjust we máy outwardly appear. In the fortress of the mind alone is peace or unrest to be found, and in this the immutable law of compensation is made manifest.

The man who possesses all that life has to offer, who seems calm, prosperous, and upon whom fate apparently smiles, may be in a tumult of interior unrest and dissatisfaction. His outer life appears well ordered, while inwardly he is unforgiving, grasping and self-seeking. The apparently unfortunate being, on the contrary, who is generous, honest and distinterested in his thoughts, no matter how great may be his suffering, his privation, his unhappiness, possesses moral strength and clearness of vision, unknown to his prosperous brother; he has interior mental peace which gives content even in suffering. His life is pure at its fountain head—which is his world of thought—and this clear limpid stream runs through it in acceptance, resignation and the uplifting that comes from perfect harmony between his thoughts and his actions. Into such a life the whole world can gaze.

Thoughts are as important, and even more so, than words. Many are careful what they say, being fully alive to the disastrous or beneficent consequences of speech. It is equally important, therefore, to realize that although subtle and invisible in their efforts, thoughts are more potent than words. Words can be so empty, so feeble, while thought is always vital. We can say things we neither think nor mean, and such words carry no weight, but we must think things to feel them. Therefore the results of wrong thinking are much more harmful to the individual than anything he can say. They also pass on to others, in that subtle emanation which we call moral atmosphere, as a strengthening or disturbing influence, sometimes vaguely felt, sometimes imperceptible, but at all times positively active.

We must guard our thinking with the same circumspection we apply to speech, and could we realize this fact; and think as discreetly as we choose our words, believing it to be of equal importance, we would greatly simplify the task of thought control. There would be fewer regrets and anxious moments in life. A realization of what thought can accomplish will bend our energies toward learning how to employ this force, in order to attain the results they were meant to accomplish when properly controlled.

The discipline of the mind is hard and painful work, but its conquest more than compensates for the mental stress and earnestness it costs. Until mental control has restored order in the mind the thoughts that one would deny entrance to, struggle, clamor and batter on the door of the mind; while the thoughts that right reason urges one to entertain strain at the leash, seeking freedom to run where they will and give place to the discordant, idle brood that claim their habitual abiding-place.

The peculiar feature of this chaotic mental condition is that thought only becomes refractory when commanded. When free to sweep across the mind at will and according to mood, its strength is not perceived. If your thoughts be gloomy, unkind or bitter, the natural result is depression and bad temper. Should this mood persist, these discordant thoughts dwell peacefully and unmolested in the mind. Here you have a vicious circle—indulgence in discordant thoughts producing the mood; indulgence in the mood keeping the mind filled with these weakening and depressing thoughts.

Never lose sight of the fact that what you fear you attract. What you hope for and believe in you create; for mind is magnetic and attracts to itself whatever it frequently thinks about. It is fatal ever to parley with a thought one does not wish to entertain. Instantly it must be replaced by a concept, good and encouraging. Should the mind be filled with fear and dread—usually unfounded—of some impending danger, the picture should be reversed instantly, the mind forming an image of a happy successful issue to the situation. Even should the trend of your thinking be strongly and persistently in an evil vein, its seeming strength is fictitious and yields before a resolute act of the will. Here I am speaking not only of normal but undisciplined minds. Those suffering from neurasthenia, a disease in which the will is attacked, have neither the mental nor the moral force to expel fixed ideas, which are one of the symptoms of the malady.* Those same neurasthenics, however, can be cured by being taught to watch and control their

*See *Chapter XXXII, Lesson Thirty,* Individual Mental Efficiency.

thoughts, practising mental control for one minute at a time at first, until to reassert its authority becomes a habit of the mind.

How common it is to see people worrying about things that may never happen, mentally turning over situations that can be neither changed nor altered. This mental habit is demoralising to both body and soul, for such indulgence begets irritability and unrest; it weakens the nerves by the strain this manner of thinking puts upon the whole nervous system.

It is often necessary to entertain worrying, depressing and sad thoughts. Every situation must be looked at bravely and squarely if you are to know what strength and resource you must bring to bear upon it. You entertain such thoughts deliberately with the object of solving the problem, and such thinking is a deliberate act of the will. The introspection is normal and wholesome, and is accompanied by exterior activities directed to restoring happiness and peace of mind.

When sorrow comes, and death robs us of our loved ones, it is human and natural to grieve. Nature demands—within measure—the outward expression of grief which relieves the burdened heart, else sorrow eats within, and undermines the whole being. But in this legitimate indulgence in grief, if, instead of turning over in our minds the why and wherefore of our bereavement, or of dwelling upon the void in our lives, we strive manfully to fulfil the simple duties of our station in life, fixing the mind upon the task on hand, the mental and moral strength acquired through keeping the thoughts where the mind and hands are working, would give courage to bravely bear afflictions until time lays its healing hand upon our wounds. In the words of JOUBERT, *"Dieu a ordonne au temps de consoler les Malheureux."*

We have all known moments when we were besieged by worrying thoughts we really did not wish to entertain. Reason told us these thoughts were fruitless and depressing, and we knew full well they were demoralizing both to character and well-being. Notwithstanding this fact, we allowed these thoughts to harass our minds, dislodging them only temporarily in seeking some exterior distraction that enabled us to forget for the moment. This left them still master of the situation, for the distraction was but a weak surrender, not a firm and conquering *act of will* prompted by the realization that such thoughts were useless and harmful. The will is the sole, sure guardian of the mind, and when will acts in harmony with reason the mind is secure not only against these troublesome invaders, but is free to concentrate itself upon what is good, productive and useful. Furthermore, our happiness and peace of mind would not then be at the mercy of thoughts we do not wish to entertain and yet are powerless to banish completely.

Each student can prove to his own satisfaction that once having accomplished thought control, intellectual and moral qualities, and even material conditions, can be created by persistently holding the thought of that which one wishes to achieve.

By your manner of thinking you can entirely change your feelings in regard to others, and even help others to correct the faults that created your resentful attitude towards them.

As a student of *Concentration* and Mental Discipline, you must not forget that good is positive and evil is negative, and evil, being negative in its nature, should not be dwelt upon. To correct grave faults of character or disposition *the mind must fix itself, not conspicuously upon uprooting these faults, but upon acquiring the opposite virtues.* Should thoughts of bitterness and resentment for an injury done occupy the mind, it is not always possible to forgive the person simply because you believe it is Christian to do so. The mind inclines naturally to dwell upon the wrong done and the destestable character of the person who has done it. Each time these thoughts are indulged in, even though seemingly justifiable in the eyes of the injured party, hatred of the guilty person increases, and you see him only in his relation to yourself; all else in his life is ignored, however praiseworthy it may be. Nothing can bring about a change of heart save to resolutely dwell upon the one or more good qualities of that person or the good actions he has done in his life.

At first the evil inherent in many people rebels at this lenient attitude of mind, for their own evil tendencies grow and strengthen in thoughts of *ill-will.* A hard battle must now be fought, for your wrongs seem to fill up the whole horizon, and the poor sinner's one redeeming quality appears but a trivial thing to consider. If these bitter and disturbing thoughts are instantly replaced by good thoughts each time they occur, be it one hundred times a day, one hundred times the moral nature has been strengthened, the mind disciplined; and when the battle seems to last beyond your strength to endure, suddenly all

resentment disappears, giving place to feelings of pity and com-
passion towards your enemy.   The mollification of your resentment at once relieves the tension in your moral nature, peace
abides within, and you are once more free: for in yielding to
evil sentiments you become their slaves.   Students of Psychology can make it a habit to see only the good in people, by
refusing to dwell upon their faults, however glaring they may
be.   If you are to accomplish this, it can be only by instantly
turning the mind from the faults of your neighbor to the
good qualities or virtues he may possess.

The man who labors to see only what is good in others,
who remembers only the kind actions done to him, even though
these kind actions may have been followed by much selfishness,
neglect and ingratitude, is a man who eliminates from his life
all mental friction.   This must be so because good-will and indulgence towards the weaknesses of others, fill his heart to the
exclusion of unkind feelings, and a consciousness of his own
failings, and a determination to correct them, arrests the tendency to criticise and condemn the faults of his neighbor.

This most desirable condition of soul can be brought about
by our manner of thinking.   Once we realize that the workings
of the mind are according to psychological laws, we know that
in learning these laws, and in acting in harmony with them,
we inevitably arrive at self-control, happiness and interior peace,
independent of place and condition.

In order to bring these truths home forcibly to himself the
student must first realize that thought is creative: that by persevering in a certain manner of thinking he can, not only create
qualities, sentiments and even conditions, but through thought
he can also transform that which already exists.   This being
the case distressing and morbid thoughts should never be indulged in, save when the situation that begot them must be
studied with a view to its removal.   Should there be no remedy
for the evil, no exit from the unhappy mental state, then it is
the height of folly to dwell upon it.   Depressing, anxious
thoughts are powerless to change a situation, they only vitiate
one's mental, moral and physical vitality.

The mind must be turned to the few blessings, or perhaps
the sole blessing one has; we must see only this blessing, and
resist bravely the inclination to dwell upon the privations and
disappointments in our lives.   In so doing, the natural result
is entire acceptance of the unhappy condition, and once accept-

ance enters the heart, peace comes with it to dwell within and sweeten our lives. Sometimes, in after years, we see the wisdom of not having obtained that for which we wept, and for which we uselessly cast a shadow over our lives by our grief and repining. This should teach us that a great unmutable power for right is behind our lives, ordering them to the accomplishment of the highest good. This highest good is ever and always our own ultimate peace and happiness.

The creative power of thought, resides in every human being in like measure, and was given to man to aid him to attain his full development and consequent happiness. The degree to which it can be taken advantage of depends upon individual effort and *true faith in one's self.*

Our moral, intellectual, or material ideal must be chosen according to reason; that is, not attempting, save in the moral order, to accomplish results beyond our individual talents and capacities. We must nourish and strengthen the ideal by persistent thought of it, and persistent thought requires an act of the *will,* a combination which finds us in the harmonious employment of all our faculties towards a desired end. When this end or object is worthy and righteous, the powers of *right* are with the one who strives, and the efforts of men are fruitless to frustrate his work.

In whatever line creation is sought along—circumstances, health, mental virility, efficiency, or what not, *Concentration, Faith, Belief, Realization* and *Mental Discipline* will be factors that are indispensable. Everywhere in nature Concentration and Crystallization are necessary to the formation of matter in its various forms. It would be almost impossible for water to become ice if it were kept in constant motion. If one could see the activities of the mind rushing and whirling about first in one direction, then in another, they would gain some idea of the steadying effect of *Mental Discipline.* Concentration is like the provision of a channel to a quantity of water which is running over here and there, in twenty different directions, wasting, having no effect, but the placing of a deep channel would attract all the water, and its force would be sufficient to drive a mill.

Personal power is the desideratum of most people, for without it little headway in any direction can be made. He who would possess it must concentrate on it, though to possess it means that preparation for it should be made. No force is worth anything unless it is understood.   A cheque for a thousand dollars would be useless to a South Sea islander or a native in the heart of a desert, so an influx of power would be out of place where a man had not learned the use of that power, where he had not created beforehand in himself some purpose to which power could be put when it was there.

Let *character come first* in all self-development, and there is no better way of employing Concentration than by applying it to this end; by building *day by day a strong, evenly balanced character*, all development afterwards will be sane. Whatever virtue a man would possess let him dwell on it in thought, meditating so to speak—not in the morbid sense, but—seeing and realizing himself as already the possessor of it, *as he indeed is in his innermost center,* and the longer he keeps this *thought and belief* before him the more indissolubly will it weave itself into his being until he is that virtue personified.

With a strong character gained by *Will Culture, Scientific Concentration* and *Mental Discipline* personal power is assured, and living on the superior side of life, on the highest side of the soul, as taught herein, the student gradually develops a power of mind that will enable him to cope with the vicissitudes of life.   If to know oneself is one of the most important things a man can do there is nothing which will so help him as this practice of concentrating on those things one would have knowledge on, and after knowledge comes wisdom—before which all else pales into nothingness.

The training of the mind requires: *first,* a vigilant surveillance of thought in order to discover our failings in this regard; *second,* Concentration upon what is good, useful and true; and lastly, a directing of thought to the accomplishment of that which we desire.

Courage of the student to face the truth about himself, and the *will to persevere* in the work of reform in his world of thought, lead unquestionably to peace, to mental strength, and to the adjusting of his life to conditions however difficult the conditions may be.

This is the secret of true content, the content the world is unconsciously seeking, even when pursuing pleasure and vain gratifications that ever elude its grasp, or, when attained, are found to be *Dead Sea fruit.*

The Master Key

Part One

CHAPTER II.

LESSON ONE.

LOGICAL THINKING AND ETHICAL ORDER.

Franklin was asked one day how he happened to be so lucky as to see clearly into problems of physical science. *"By always thinking of them,"* he replied. It is the same with ethical order; we only come near the ideal by always thinking or concentrating on it.

Scientific Concentration, which summed up is *"Logical Thinking"* intelligently applied, illuminates the student's path, prevents his making mistakes and, eventually leads to success.

Those mistakes made by the student are never quite regrettable if, recognizing the wrong road, he seeks to return to the right one. *The beginning of success is the knowledge of one's faults.* Many suffer today through faulty concentration as a close perusal of this work by the intelligent student will show.

Of the many faculties with which the human mind is possessed not one has been less utilized and brought intelligently under mental discipline and used to further and better one's physical, mental and moral well being than that of Concentration. Scarcely a thought is given to it by many, as it does not seem to merit any particular attention. People have got on very well without it, some say, so why bother about it? The question is on a par with *"What's the good of anything?"* and would be put by the same kind of an individual. There was not the same need for it in the past that exists today. Not that our ancestors were altogether idle, or had no brains, but that pres-

11

sure was not so great, that their avocations were largely pastoral, and did not demand the focusing and intelligent concentrating of the powers of the mind for long together.   Warring with each other certainly demanded watchfulness, and resourcefulness, but impulse and a ready wit supplied it to a great extent.   Times have changed since then, and man has become a much more mental creature, though from one standpoint he has never been anything else, but the life he has led has been more bosomed in mentality. By the very character of his make-up he has become more diverse in his talents; he has branched out in a thousand directions, as the unfolding life within sought expression.   If he led the nomadic life today he would sink back to the animal.   He may seek simplicity, because it permits the higher faculties of the mind their rightful expression, but it will not be the simplicity our forefathers associated with the word.   A man may enjoy to the utmost the beauties of Nature and yet realize the joy of living in our complex civilization. Complexity cannot be avoided now, even were it desirable, which it is not, but to thoroughly extract the best from it a man must be able to adapt his mental faculties to the life lived. This cannot be done unless he has a knowledge of *Scientific Concentration*, because it is the gateway to the other powers of the mind.   It should come almost first in the training of the mind, in the growth of the mentality, in brain-getting or growing.   It is inseparably connected with success, of whatever that success may consist.

Its need, in fact, is much greater today than ever before, not only on account of the greater complexity to which reference is made above, but because evolution as a factor in life has modified and changed our nature and powers to some extent. Writers, noting the restlessness which is running through every stratum of society, attribute it to the education act passed in England in 1870 and also in this country, because prior to compulsory education illiteracy was very common, and the masses were not able to think as those who have benefited by it.   No doubt there is a modicum of truth in the contention, but it does not explain all.   Dissatisfaction with things was bound to be one result of education among the people, and the nonsensical teaching that it was the right of the brainless to confiscate the fruit of those gifted with initiative and push was certain to be a popular one.   Changes of this character are necessarily slow, when measured by the life of an individual, and they might even be questioned, but that this force of evolution is operative will not be doubted by thinking people.

Students of history will be struck when making a comparison with the mental life of the nation of today with that of five hundred years ago. While all the great levers which function in the moving of man's nature are as manifest today, there is a very different mentality seen and this suggests an idea which must have been increasingly apparent to everyone during the last decade—man is after all a mental and spiritual creature. That is to say, he is more mind than body. In prehistoric times when the physical vehicle was the all-important part of his being, when outward form was being fashioned to fit in with the life then lived there was no room for mind: the need for it had not been felt. Man's varied wants were few and simple, and the mental principle could well be ignored. Today writers speak of man as being all mind; they affirm most emphatically that mind is all, that whatever form life may take it is only an expression of the mind or mental part of man. This view of life alters one's whole outlook of it; the holding of such a theory gives more weight and power to the mind as the arbiter of man's happiness. The view obtains more and more among thoughtful people that consciousness or life is imprisoned in the early ages of the earth in rock and stone, and as later times dawn passes into forms which permit a freer play of expression. Through the kingdom of Nature this life passes in turn, vitalizing, pulsing through the various forms which each kingdom provided for the purpose. When the human kingdom is reached more mentality is expressed, and it then becomes more evident that mind is at the base of all manifestation, and that man is the highest expression of this truth. The presence of the animal in man is too patent to question, but it is equally plain that man has the choice of allying himself with the lower or higher principles within him. In so far as he recognizes the basis of his being as mental and ignores the animal will he more fully realize within himself the truth of the assertion that man is nothing but mind and soul in expression.

It is because man is a mental creature that he so widely diverges from the animals. Unlike them he has a part of his nature which merely physical wants will not satisfy, save in the case of some very aboriginal tribes, and they scarcely count at the moment, for the higher animals are above them in intelligence. Man recognizes this difference, but he does not understand the full import of it. He does not as yet see in himself the highest expression of the Law, nor does he understand what the Law is. He obeys the law of his being, however, little dreaming the real causes and effects expressing themselves through him. It is clear to him that mind holds a dominating place in the world. He knows that it is the thinkers, the scientists, the philosophers who stand at the head of the race, because they have developed the highest part of their nature. He recalls what a vast space separates the amoeba from him. That tiny creature, the first form of sentient life, minus the five senses, no limbs, no ears, no head, no eyes, no stomach even. No wonder it is a popular starting point with all authors when comparing man as we now know him and from what he sprang first. It is a long way down the vistas of time since that period; every step in the upward path of man has been in the direction of mind, and today the Law is beginning to be understood which will lift man entirely out of the rut of unconsciousness, in which he has trudged all these aeons. The animals do not know why they are here, what the object of evolution is, the purpose of life; many men are in the same position, but here and there men have penetrated into the mysterious chasms and awe-inspiring laboratories of Nature, which yields her secrets reluctantly to the seeker after knowledge. Right along the ages growth has been insistent, but unconscious, and man has reached a point now where it should cease to be unconsious any longer.

Why? Because the physical growth has now reached its climax. There is no particular in which the human form could be improved. All that is necessary for its perfect functioning has been provided. Some writers think that man's strong desire to fly will result in his providing his body with wings, but this desire for the conquest of the air without adventitious aids like aeroplanes and balloons does not necessarily require the sprouting of organs which would decidedly be in the way in many cases. Man has no fins, yet he can swim, so there is no need to imitate the birds. Indeed, among the Hindus and more than one Eastern race levitation has been known for thousands of years, and it is accomplished by counteracting the law of gravitation. The writer is acquainted with a disciple of Eastern philosophy who got to the point of discovery of the secret of levitation without having come in contact with Easterns, having worked out the theory from his own con-

sciousness, but his brain refused to carry the discovery through. It is axiomatic that no question can be asked which cannot be answered, so that provided man was really in earnest and desired strongly enough to raise his own body without any outside agency he would indubitably accomplish it.

No, the human body is scarcely likely to alter in shape, or that other physical organs will be grafted on to it, but it is extremely probable that man will enlarge his conceptions of the kosmos, will demand to know why he is here, what his destiny is, how he may control it, how enjoy a wider use of power. All this is natural, because it is in the nature of mind to be unsatisfied with theories and explanations which are obviously not founded on truth. Truth is really what man seeks, though he may not always be aware of it. The desire to know is to know what IS, and what is can only be truth. I am constantly reminding students that the words good, beautiful and true are practically all the same, as Plato long ago taught. Some think that they will depreciate in the eyes of people if they openly confess to their neighbors or announce that they are searching for the truth. They fear the world will laugh at them, or take them for mere' visionaries; then truth often seems to be so abstract, so diaphanous, so filmy, unreal, breathing of mysticism or the occult. Man has been searching for it, as a matter of fact, since he was first launched on this chain of globes, and the quest of the holy grail is no legend.

The desire for knowledge of "self" is apparent on every side, and it will no longer be satisfied with the old-time answers to its questionings. He must *know;* authority no longer carries any force or weight, for it has so often been found lacking in truth, and each man can only assimilate that portion of truth which he is able to make his own. To gain this knowledge, or even the lower knowledge, if I may divide knowledge in this way, man must possess the tool by means of which he can delve within himself for it, and what faculty of the mind can so materially assist him in either this work or the exploration of that vast territory of man's being—the *Subconscious*—than *Concentration.*

Most writers have been content to dismiss the subject with a few words and the setting of some exercises; its difficulties have been carefully veiled, and its simplicity been delightfully described. With some people this is a sure way to get them to study a thing. Few are built like Browning's *Grammarian*, who said:

> "Let me know all! Prate not of most or least
> Painful or easy."

In reality, Concentration is not a power which can be readily gained, one of the chief reasons being that it should be taken up after mind-training generally rather than precede it. Of course, to train the mind even Concentration to some extent is necessary, but it can only be practiced properly when we know something of the laws of thought and the possibilities of the soul, hence the failure of so many students to be able to concentrate after the perusal of a book or article professing to deal with it. It is no use telling a person that all he has to do is to get interested in a thing and he will be able to concentrate on it. This applies to a very limited area; it does not help one much with the varied duties of life, or the attitude of the mind and other faculties. Concentration can only be said to be satisfactory when we can apply it at any moment of our lives to whatever subject or problem we desire. Something more must be known concerning consciousness and its modes of action.

For his first lesson, then, the student must seek to gain some knowledge of the factors which constitute his mind, to see how best to train them, to eliminate from his mentality that which destroys the power to concentrate, how to direct and govern his feelings and emotions so that they shall bring about the formation of those elements so essential to the power to fasten the fangs of the mind deeply into any point and keep them there until he gives it permission to relax its hold. This is only a portion of the problem, but it leads directly to the path of Concentration, the end of the student's goal in this course. The true and sincere student will not mind the spade work, for he gains a prize worth all the most brilliant jewels the world can offer him: he has gained *The Master Key!* After it study, the acquirement of learning, the acquisition of wisdom, the royal road to truth, power, self-culture in the widest sense are his. The deepest secret that Nature holds can be wrested from her by it, for the penetrative power of Concentration pierces the most impenetrable—or apparently so—veil.

Brains are necessary as a preliminary to Concentration, and

the sluggish materials which bear that name must be cultivated, as I have pointed out in this work.   They are not the prerogative of the few, though by the negative evidence offered we might imagine that they were most sparingly doled out by Nature.   While they may be plentiful, however, they are used to so small an extent that their owners might often get on as well without them.   No one knows how *lethargic* people are in regard to study or any mental work better than teachers. Those who have been many years in the teaching of Psychology can testify how difficult it is to get faithful students, no matter what advantages may be offered.   The fact of education having to be enforced by law offers as striking a testimony as any to the mental apathy, the failure to see the advantages which spring from the cultivation of one's mental powers and faculties.   The cry that parents in the old days got on all right without education and they did not see why their minds could not do the same was very common at one time, and even today may be heard from time to time.   There is almost a premium on ignorance among the working class in this country and also in other English-speaking countries, for in spite of the alluring facilities offered in cheap textbooks and free schools and institutions not twenty per cent of them speak their language grammatically.   Self-culture is extremely distasteful to the great bulk: a football match or a baseball game would be more to the taste of the modern youth and a novelette to the modern maid.   Anything which requires the exercise of the mind is given a wide berth.   Even among the middle classes the shrinking from mental work is almost as marked, unless it have some connection with the avocation followed.

There is no disguising this tendency of the age, and before the student can profitably practice Concentration he must make up his mind that he is going to overhaul his mental stock-in-trade—gather the material together before he sets it to work on some task.

Many may regard their brains as being overtaxed; a very small portion of the brain-area has been used so far, though one may be sixty or seventy years old, unless he has passed his life in purely sedentary work, and only then when the work has been of a very varied description, a working journalist providing an example.   The writer will admit that this is a busy age, an age of hustle and bustle, but it does not follow that we are overworked mentally, even if our work may be mental.

There is a great fear of overtaxing the brain, and suffering from nervous breakdown, but none need overwork, provided he obtain sufficient sleep. A break in work is decidedly desirable, and those whose work is purely sedentary may obtain relaxation, even by taking up the study of another subject, because another portion of the brain will be employed thereby. Remember that just as water continually trickling down a hillside makes a channel for itself before long, so repeating certain trains of thought, or doing the same thing with the brain repeatedly, like a bookkeeper adding up columns of figures, makes a channel in the brain. If the convolutions of the brain were spread out they would be found to make a good sized area, and would satisfy the most ardent devotee of knowledge.

Mental Discipline must be begun now, and to do this light, sensational reading should be lessened almost to the point of extinction, because reading three lines on one subject is to commence a definite train of thought, which is broken the next minute, or often less than half a minute, by the intrusion of another subject. This diffuses or scatters the thought, and if those who are guilty of the habit only knew the amount of harm done their mental mechanism the writer feels sure they would abandon the habit at once. The custom of seeking to extract the pith from everything may be commendable in itself, but it works out with disastrous effects to the average mind, just as efforts to subsist on essences and concentrated foods in tabloid form do with regard to the body. The desire to get at the pith of a subject at the very commencement arises from a wish to avoid study, and this is not the right attitude of those who seek to acquire the faculty of concentration. In conversation, too, a thought should be kept until all concerning it of an interesting nature has been extracted, which does not mean wearing it threadbare. Diffusion essentially means surfacing things only, and Concentration means getting into the depths, a going to the center of a thing.

By *Mental Discipline* is meant the assertion of the "I" over the mind, which may strike some readers as odd, because they have generally associated themselves with their mind. They unthinkingly say *"my mind,"* showing that the mind is not themselves, but something possessed by the real man, and that is really the fact. This course of Mental Discipline will not venture to define what the real man is, as it would take the student too far out of his way, but it is essential that he understand that the mind is only an instrument, just as the body is. Some people know from experience—often painful—that they do things at times that they really do not wish to do, possibly partaking of something which has up to now acted injuriously to them, or followed some course that they do not approve, yet felt, through their lack of Mental Discipline, that they had to follow. Begin to regard this mind, then, *as something amenable to the will,* to the true self, and being amenable it must of necessity be lower. Being lower it is the servant, *and not the master as it really seems to be to most people.* There is in reality not the slightest excuse for your shortcomings, your *"little weaknesses,"* though you like to think there is, because it seems to exculpate you, and make you greater than you are. In truth, it only lowers you, weakens you, makes you less capable of bringing out the powers and principles within you, and the object of this course is to strengthen, to evolve.

It will be well to remind yourself daily that you are not your mind, that you are something infinitely far higher, and that in proportion as you recognize this truth you shall be able to subjugate the mind, and learn to concentrate, because if you are obsessed with the idea that you are at the mercy of your own mind you will accomplish nothing. I happened to state at a lecture I gave recently that anyone could control his thought if he wished, and in the discussion which followed a gentleman challenged the statement, because he had been trying for thirty years to do so and had not succeeded. On such a principle, if a man who had been trying to learn to play the piano for thirty years and had not succeeded, it might be laid down that no one could learn to play the instrument. The absurdity is apparent, yet almost as absurd objections are brought against the New Psychology. Because one man has not contacted his higher self he denies the existence of it. I grant the idea may be strange; there may be more evidence to support the popular theory that a man is his mind, or that he is *"mind, body and spirit,"* which is a half truth. The fact is, many are all so strongly under the domination of the everyday mind that the illusion seems quite natural, and mankind is all pretty much alike. It has taken some people twenty years to realize it, but they have done so eventually, and possibly some people have been even longer than this.

The Master Key

CHAPTER III.

LESSON TWO.

THE HURRY HABIT.

If the student wishes to get his mind under control he should cultivate the habit of avoiding hurry, which is one of the first things to undermine the growth and expansion of its powers. Some people do not come under the category of hurry, but they worry, which is almost as bad. Where Concentration is aimed at the mind should be like the surface of a lake, which permits reflection, but both worry and hurry ruffle its surface, so that it can no longer fulfil its proper function, which is to hold and meditate upon. Hurry and worry cause a ceaseless agitation, a turning back of the mind upon itself, a going over the same chain of thought in the endeavor to find a solution to some pressing question. It is well known that in such cases the solution is rarely forthcoming by such a method, any more than a name or a fact which escapes the memory for the moment is recalled by intense thinking. It is when the mind is relaxed, when it has gone along another line that the missing information is ushered into the consciousness, or brought forth from the inner recesses of the mind to the objective portion of it.

Different temperaments find different methods appeal to them for the stilling of the mind. The phlegmatic, slow-moving mind is not touched by a devotional attitude, nor is the devotional temperament attracted by the purely intellectual, whilst the active type does not find comfort in either intellectual or devotional ways.

How can the hurry habit be most effectively checked? Not always by trying to induce a state of peace within the mind, but by the removal of one of the potent causes of it—the attempt at doing too much and *the undue or exaggerated im-*

portance we attach to things. It has been noted that when even
a great man passed away the world did not come to a standstill, but went on its way as before. The work was not interrupted, but proceeded again. The man might be missed, but
not for long, so that the average man need not fear that if he
omits to do this or that dire consequences will result. He will
know by experience what he can accomplish, and he will be
unwise if he set himself more to do than that. It may be
that he has duties set for him which have to be got through.
Much of this could be avoided by refusing to undertake more
responsibilities than he knew he could fulfil. Many wish to
be helpful, to give no offence, to be willing to give a fellow
being a lift—excellent intentions, but there are limits to everything, and a line has to be drawn. Better decline things than
have to leave unfinished or badly done tasks. We see on every
hand the botched, slipshod work, and not only does it make
trouble for others, but it makes the creator of it slipshod in
character: it prevents his rising, prevents his bringing forth
and giving, as he should do, his very best to the world. The
world is always looking for the best, and will pay the highest
price for it, but the markets are glutted with the second-rate
things, which no one wants but those who cannot afford to
buy better. On them it has a demoralizing effect, as well as
their makers, and therefore the habit is bad all round.

Thoroughness Re-acts Beneficially on the Mind.

By attempting less whatever is taken up will be done more
thoroughly, and this thoroughness will re-act on the mind, and
the thinking will be more thorough. When there is no need
to hurry, the thought can act more effectively, more clearly,
and it will, as a matter of fact, act more rapidly as time goes
on, so that the fancied giving up of things it was deemed to
be our duty to perform will be seen to have resulted in adding
to our efficiency. Method and system will be inculcated, and
these in themselves will be invaluable adjuncts to the gaining of
Concentration and Will Culture. By system one can learn
that priceless art of economizing time, because the stilling of the
mind will result in your seeing more clearly where you can
save time, and how things may be more effectively performed
and fit in with other things. Thus you will eventually be in a
position to take up things which you had laid aside, thinking

you could not squeeze in the necessary time for their accomplishment. Merely reading the rules, systems and methods laid down in this work will do little unless they be followed up by actual practice.

It is evident that once the mind is stilled it is more easy to concentrate it on one subject and keep it there, and when this can be accomplished you may be said to have reached the consummation of your desires.

There are few more inspiring ideas to a man than that *"he can who thinks he can."* Is this really true, it may well be asked? Does the mere fact of thinking we can accomplish a certain thing, attain a cherished goal really enable us to do it? The simplicity of it seems alluring, but at the same moment so repellent, because so improbable. It is one of the twentieth century aphorisms of New Psychology, a statement that even a Smiles might question, or the most bigoted optimist entertain a doubt about, yet it is thoroughly scientific. Let us examine the assertion a little. A man would prove it just as he would a theorem in Euclid. He would have to admit what all living psychologists now admit, i. e., that the mind does not express a quarter of what it might do; that beneath the threshold of consciousness there reside extensions of the powers exhibited in part; that consciousness as we know it is a very complex thing, and not the simple phase of mental activity it once was supposed to be. Experimental psychology has disclosed the fact that "There are a million energies in man. What may we not become when we learn to use them all?" This is the work which lies before us at the present time, and which the coming ages will see immensely advanced. *The merest tyro knows that if a man thinks he cannot do a thing he rarely does it, or if he does, it is not done brilliantly. It is obvious that when a man doubts his own powers he does not make the fullest use of them.* Confidence in oneself has always been considered indispensable for success in whatever direction a man might seek it, for the diffident man does not really put forth his abilities, therefore he naturally only evokes part of his abilities.

The first idea arising from the statement is that if a man can only think in a certain manner he will be able to do more, and this is because thoughts running in a particular direction endow one with more force, just as the studying of a difficult problem causes a rush of more blood to the brain than when conversation or light reading is being engaged in. It is a law of nature that where there is the demand there is the supply. By the entertaining the idea that we can we direct the attention into a particular channel, the conception of possibility arises, and with this the latent power that is coiled up in everyone is stirred up. It is the call of the mind for something, and an immediate response is made to the demand.

If there is more power, then more ability must be the result, and with ability it is possible to double one's usefulness. Concentration demands ability to keep the mind one-pointed, and by a study of the laws of mind we are able to focus the mind upon whatever we desire. Seeing that the mind is made up of innumerable mental actions, for any change of a decided nature to take place there must be a predominant tendency of the mind, so that this belief in ourselves can only become really alive by its over-riding all other thoughts in the mind.

Now this is the attitude that must be taken up by the man who would concentrate successfully. He must believe that he can, and by so doing he will impregnate his mentality with the force of the idea until it becomes a fixed thought. Then it is that he will awaken the power that will render it possible for him to do what he has set his mind upon. Remember, that it is the power you are to evoke that will enable you to do, not the mere thinking that you can, and this is a point which needs bearing in mind. Too many people imagine they have only to think and their power is finished.

With the power which belief brings to one a rearrangement of mental atoms takes place and the efforts to control the mind gain perceptible strength from day to day. It is only he who thinks he can concentrate who can feel that he can concentrate; there must be feeling and thought brought into line before much will be accomplished, and this emphasizes the necessity of preliminary training: it is a course of preparation which the mind undergoes, quite prior to the actual practice of Concentration. Why should *Belief* bring power? *For one thing it has supplanted Doubt,* and a whole volume might be written on the part which this mental nightmare (doubt) has played in the evolution of man, casting him back into darkness every time he has endeavored to step towards the light. In my work entitled *The Immanence of God—"Know Thyself"* I have placed before the reader the evil it has wrought in man. It is so subtle, so insidious in its workings that its presence is frequently not suspected.

The Master Key

LESSON THREE.

DOUBT BARS THE WAY.

We all know what glamor means, but it is one of the most difficult things conceivable to find it in ourselves; it is like turning the mind upon itself. One has read of persons trying to record the impressions made upon them after having used opium; a study in madness, in which the victim portrays the changes in consciousness as he began to pass out of the realm of·sanity, illustrates this difficulty. *Edgar Allen Poe* pictures the same idea in a wonderful manner. It is so different to set to work on a material which is outside the worker to working on the worker himself. We use our eyes to see what is round about us, what is really outside them; if we could conceive turning the eye on itself—not another person's eye—and subjecting it to a minute anatomical dissection we should get some notion of the task. Yet we sharpen a knife by bringing it in contact with another, so that though both blades were blunt before being brought together they are so no longer.

This glamor of the mind is regarded by some as a wise provision of Nature to hide from us our deficiencies and short-comings from ourselves, to soften and assuage the pain which the discovery would awaken, but only the weak now would ever be content to accept such an anodyne. Its action, like that of all anodynes is to deaden, to stupefy, to stunt and dwarf, and therefore to lead to involution instead of evolution.

Glamor may be necessary at certain stages in the growth of the ego, but it decidedly is not so when a man begins to take himself in hand, and the man who is anxious to know how to concentrate does not usually rest there: it is a means to an end, and that end is the bringing forth of all the powers latent in man and using them to the fullest extent.

THE OLD MAN OF THE SEA.

Doubt possesses in a remarkable degree this quality of glamor; it is like *"The Old Man of the Sea"* in one sense: we carry it about on our backs, even when we know we have it, deluding ourselves with the idea that we must always bear the burden. But at a prior stage the excrescence is there, and we know it not. This constitutes the insidiousness of the thing.

We really entertain this mental visitor, this alien (doubt) without knowing it; we start a movement, so to speak, and, as everyone knows, once a thing is set going one never knows where it will stop. In fact, once begun a thing acquires a momentum of its own. When we deal with forces it is not like dealing with dead things. A stone thrown from the hand will travel until the force which actuated it is spent, and it falls to the ground. It is mechanical; it lacks the life which force possesses, though even a stone has life, only not sufficiently developed to the point we find in the case of a vital force. A force contains the elements of self-initiation; that is to say, it has potentialities. It has, as it were, life behind it, so that when we start it off it has the faculty of going on through its own volition. We get some idea of this in the problem of perpetual motion, which has exercised the minds of the greatest thinkers in all ages. They have tried to create some device which, once set going, would continue to move for all eternity. As a result some clever mechanical apparatus have been invented, things which would wind themselves up when they had run down, showing the idea of a something existing in the universe which pulsed with the primeval life. It does exist, too; the atom is an example of it. It is a vortex of perpetual force, of movement, which cannot be destroyed, but which may be altered as regards direction.

And this is the practical bearing it has for us. So long as the mind exists it must work. True, we can cease thinking for brief spaces of time, but they are very brief indeed. Whether we like it or not the mind will go on functioning, and if we do not provide it with work it will find work for itself.

In this way Doubt will be accepted as something for the mind to pit itself against, and Doubt bars the way to accomplishment. To seek to concentrate a mind in which Doubt has a state, is like trying to extract the maximum worth and brightness from a fire grate which is choked with ashes and piled up with rubbish as well. What avail is the best coal when put on such a fire? If we give the fire time all the rubbish will probably be burnt up, but this will require too long a period, and we cannot get the best out of our fire whilst it is in this state. A mind which harbors Doubt is a mind which is confused, and this confusion is not always apparent to its possessor. You can only secure the fullest use of a power by its being unfettered by others and only by the fullest use, by using one hundred per cent, do you achieve anything worth while. When forces are divided there is leakage in power, and one force neutralizes another. When in a big crowd of people, one-half wants to go in just the opposite direction to what the other half is going, many times the power is necessary in pushing through, this power is utterly thrown away. It leaves the man with less power for whatever purpose he may need it.

If you would concentrate with ease you must clarify the mind first; you must throw overboard much which you deemed essential to its well-being. Doubt, for one thing, must be shown the door. The ructions created in a mind by this soul-destroying negative, which is really a reflection, and has no solid existence, are gigantic, and accounts for many people having such average minds. Many will find much in their mental makeup that is only a useless burden, and they should drop it. The student should dwell from time to time on the idea that because he thinks and actually believes he can improve his power of Concentration he really can.

While engaged in clarifying the mind he will do well to consider some of the laws of the mind, its mode of working, the character of thought.

The mind is like a bottled up volcano, full of immense forces, only, unlike its physical prototype, it is under lock and key, or under control; the control is unconscious, however, just as the mind's powers usually are. The lid comes off when the mind is unhinged, when there is a want of balance, and the most brilliant genius has paid the penalty of not understanding the forces he has created or developed. If we would control it we must seek to understand it. I have referred to the intense activity of the mind, the fact that it is never still, but always moving like a large crowd, a number of which wish to go in various directions. Why do not people train the forces of their mind so that they will all work in one direction, and thus ensure harmony, a oneness of goal, thereby avoiding much needless friction and waste of brain energy, of which such a a large amount is generated?

One might imagine a juggler endeavoring to keep twenty balls in the air at one time. So long as he had each ball in his hand he would have full control of it, but as soon as it left his hand he would be unable to alter its course. He would simply have to wait till it returned to his hand, and sometimes it would not even do this, but fall to the ground. The man who had never practiced juggling would find it would take him all his time to keep three balls in the air at one time, and this illustration will exemplify to some extent the problem we are considering.

The balls would well stand for the tendencies of the mind. These tendencies would be absolutely under our control while lying inert, but once we set them going they would be out of hand till the force endowing them had been spent. By one of the laws of the mind a tendency has a faculty or leaning to multiply itself, just as a snowball when set rolling gathers more snow and thus becomes a huge globe. Undesirable tendencies must, therefore, be controlled, checked, directed, when they will help instead of hindering our growth.

Reverting to glamor once more we see it has its constructive side. It enables us to view with equanimity the pin-pricks of daily life, as well as the really great troubles, the disappointments and trials which make so large a part of the lives of some people. When one lives in squalid surroundings, in dirty dark manufacturing districts, where beauty is a stranger, with people who do not embody many of the virtues in their composition, we may transform as by magic, the disharmonious elements, seeing everything through a rose-tinted atmosphere. The sting is thereby removed, and we look with complacency on circumstances and people alike. Such an attitude helps much to gain the upper hand of hurry, to which reference has been made. It is the investing of the daily life with romance, which has no need to be less in evidence than it was in the past when chivalry and the idealizing tendency were so largely in evidence. Every adjunct which leads to the raising of the mind, which takes it from so-called realities of existence aids us in our task of learning to concentrate.

The Master Key

CHAPTER V.

LESSON FOUR.

THE GREAT GOSPEL OF OPTIMISM.

There may spring up an objection that we are deluding ourselves by regarding things in this fashion. We see an emaciated, stooping figure, painfully crawling along one of our busy streets breathing with difficulty, the limbs trembling as with ague, and almost giving way with each step; the eyes seek the ground, the figure shrinks as though striving to escape notice. Drink, want, disease and vice have each imprinted their marks upon the creature. When we think of man and the marvellous things he has done in art, invention, science, literature, philosophy, commerce, engineering, transforming wilderness and deserts into beautiful cities, with stately architecture, the forces of Nature ministering to his numerous wants quickly and quietly—when we regard such a creature and identify him with man, are we honest? The tottering, shrinking wretch is real, but it would be a libel on humanity to admit him into the same class. While it is true that man is higher than the beasts it is equally true that he has the power to sink below them. The ideal man is as real as the despicable wreck we have been dealing with, and it only remains for the student to ask himself: Is it more common sense to take this poor wretch as an exemplar or the highest man history places before us? Which will give rise to the loftiest conceptions of humanity? It is obvious that if the mind becomes that on which it dwells and the majority of the slum dwellers in any city prove it by their features, bearing and gait—*then we should ignore the caricature as such.*

If surroundings do not count why seek to abolish ugliness? Why lay out parks, provide art galleries, luxurious buildings, if refinement is not an adjunct to existence and somewhat above

28

that lived by the masses, if it does not conduce to more happiness, a fuller life, then one might as well fall back into the slough of the submerged. We all recognize tacitly, it may be in many cases, that education and a civilized environment tend to the upliftment and betterment of humanity.

More and more writers and teachers advocate the viewing of life through rose-tinted glass, and naturally, for it is the kernel of *The Great Gospel of Optimism*, which is being whole-heartedly preached in the United States, and in a lesser degree in England. Adopt the same habit; idealize everything in which you come into contact. Do not pay attention to the negative part of anything, and as you succeed in doing this you will see everything with an extended vision, to say nothing of being the happier for it. Happiness and True Faith in one's self has more to do with Concentration than one would willingly admit at first sight. If we are happy we regard things in a different light, and we take an interest in them.

It is difficult to concentrate on anything in which you are not interested, and it is difficult to be interested in anything you do not like. Students must as a consequence begin their exercises in Concentration with those things they like, that they feel deep interest in, and the deeper the interest the easier will it be for them to give themselves up whole-heartedly to it. The want of a real live interest in a subject has had more to do with the failure to concentrate than is generally imagined. The girl or youth who does not learn or grasp her or his lesson has not had the interest in it which allows the finer part of the mind to be employed in absorbing and assimilating the knowledge placed before it. Concentration on columns of figures would seem to the bulk of people as distasteful a piece of mental work which could be given a human being, hence it would be approached with positive dislike or loathing. Statistics is another form which most people shun because, as in figures, there is nothing to take an interest in, yet these things have an actual attraction for many people, who really devour these disconnected facts and figures, deriving a satisfaction from them which is lent by the Concentration expended on them. That is to say, the very effort to concentrate evokes a condition which not only enables things to be accomplished before with infinite labor, but a liking for the practice is engendered.

Putting the mind in this state, in which you find you have a real interest in a thing, you have not to invoke the will to keep the mind one-pointed. The will has a part to play in Concentration, and what that part is will be fully considered in its proper place further on in the work.

To create an interest in a thing find where it concerns us most. It often happens you have to do something you do not like, and if that *"task"* calls forth repugnance it is certain that you shall concentrate on it in a very imperfect manner. You will, in addition, use a far larger amount of vital energy in doing the work that you are justified in doing. All mental force must be conserved, for the student will find that he needs every ounce he possesses. Some spend nearly one-half—many people much more—what they generate uselessly, and the reader will bear this in mind.

It is possible to cultivate not merely an indifference to a thing you do not like, but to transmute that feeling of dislike utterly. If it be our work, and we have been put to this work against the grain, there may not appear to be any great virtue in trying to like it, but the fact of hating it creates a disharmony in the mind that we find quite inimical to mental growth and to all creative thought. Whatever be the duties we find we have to do they must always be done with grace, with love, with the feeling that it is due to our higher conception to dignify a thing and not let it degrade us. When it is repulsive to us our attitude should be to carry it out as well as we can, and this spirit will lead us to cease to be worried by the feeling of distaste. The task will become less uncongenial; if it is a piece of work requiring mechanical skill we will not paralyze our best energies by the idea that we are incompetent to do it.

It may be that you fail to perform it satisfactorily to your employer or yourself at first, but by calling to your aid the determination that you are not going to let the work be clumsily or inadequately done you will invoke the co-operation of the best that is in you and do the work well. This will especially be the case later when the mind has grown by the exercises given later in the work.

Much of the so-called incompetency of people does not proceed from stupidity, want of apprehension or inferiority in mind powers, but in the low estimate they have always placed upon themselves and their work. It has well been said that you are here to do something which no one else can do, save yourself. What that work may be no one would pretend to dogmatize upon, but one thing is clear: every human being is

an individual, and no two are alike, so that although the goal
of humanity be a common one no two people will reach it in
the same way. Evolution is not merely an unfolding, but as
Bergson has shown, a creating, so that the "new" is an actual
fact in nature, and things are not a re-hash.

"What man has done man can do" is no empty platitude,
but a matter of exact science, so that any man who wishes to
become a painter, a writer, an orator, a military leader, or anything else, may do so, provided he follows the laws of mind.
It is so easy to forget the potentialities within each of us because
we never see them, and people usually only believe in those
things that they see. That is why they are now and then
dumbfounded when they hear of someone whom they knew
well doing something really clever, or something for which they
have never given any hint that they possessed. If a man gets
the idea that he is only common clay, that he is not clever like
people he knows or has read about, he closes the avenues of the
mind wherein lie the same powers that the men he envies or
stands in awe of. Many men go through life for years before
waking up to their possibilities, and then they suddenly discover
the Great Within and the riches which respose therein, and they
are no longer the poor creatures they were. History is full of
these instances, of men who were absolute dunces at school, or
idle, dissipated, utterly aimless. The great bulk of mankind
goes through life in this blind fashion, though there are plenty
of signs now that it is waking up, that the general level is being
raised all round.

If you induce other trains of thought—and this is quite
possible—you come to regard unpleasant duties in a new light.
We see them as opportunities, opportunities to show the mettle
you are made of. You begin to learn that you are greater than
you supposed, and that knowledge alone warms you to your
work, quickens the intellectual powers, awakens the inventive
areas of the brain, lends dexterity to the fingers or limbs, calls
forth care and precision in whatever be the work. A well
known teacher of dancing avers that the art of dancing is in
the head, not the feet. This is one reason why a teacher in any
subject is so useful. In it not that he himself does the work,
but he shows that it is possible to be done, and the fact of
seeing it done, or knowing that it can be, provides the necessary
stimulus to induce the tyro to make the attempt by arousing
his faith. It further gives him the encouragement and sym-

pathy to try to accomplish it, and this putting forth of efforts increases in power and ability each time. Briefly, it is in the *doing* of a thing that we grow, not the mere theorizing about it.

The writer has used above the illustration of a piece of work, but it is equally applicable in the gaining of a mental faculty, in any phase of character-building, and readers should regard it in that light. It is practically immaterial to what purpose we apply the principle: it holds good in everything.

Examine every unpleasant thing which you are called upon to do, and see if there is not some aspect about it which appeals to you, some good point that merits commendation. In many cases this will be found, and your interest will at once be awakened. Once aroused you will see unsuspected features which will render it less irksome to fasten the attention on, and when this is so Concentration has been attained.

The student who would learn to concentrate successfully must utterly reverse the methods which are generally taught, just as the East adopts exactly the opposite system to that applied in the West in regard to science, the former seeking to perfect the instrument by which knowledge of the universe is possible—the mind, or the subjective method, the West beginning with the universe and ending with man, or the objective method, so he must not commence with the *without*, but with the *within*. One must be serene; serenity is the positive aspect and worry, to which I have referred in *Chapter Five*, is the negative. It is not sufficient not to worry, but one must cultivate a deep, quiet, *peace-compelling atmosphere*. Such an atmosphere of poise gives birth to forces awaiting our recognition. The usual conception of hustle and bustle being essential to accomplish anything is founded like so much else in the world upon appearances. The cult of striving in order to achieve enters into nearly every aspect of existence, because there underlies every effort that principle which is eating the heart out of hundreds and thousands—*competition*—a much misunderstood principle, which has its place in the order of things when rightfully understood. The universal urge, the *cosmic whip* which eggs the individual on and on, promotes growth, makes for evolution when it is properly apprehended. It differentiates the *thinking* from the *non-thinking* portion of humanity; it takes the jelly-fish, backboneless, colorless, inchoate, vacillating creature, and makes an individual of him. When the notion of life being a battle gains ascendency in the consciousness then

enmity towards all outside ourselves is generated—fighting is the dominating idea—*"the struggle for existence, the weakest go to the wall, survival of the fittest,"* are three classical phrases which well exemplify the spirit of the age, and define the attitude taken by so many. Individuality is what evolution or the principle of unfoldment aims at, but it is the gaining of a strength to help not to crush. Strength of body and strength of mind are the desiderata of weary men and women, because a strong character is the normal outcome of eternal progress; strength is evoked not to enable one to walk over those less strong than ourselves, but for the purpose of helping them; teacher and pupil must ever make up humanity, however high up the ladder of existence we mount; there are always those above the highest and noblest of us, as there are always those whose feet are as yet on the bottom rung of the ladder. The very phrase the brotherhood of humanity, which is so much in the air today, and which finds more expression now than in any epoch of which we have any record, means that equality is impossible; "brother" carries inherently in it one elder or younger than another member of a family, and who dare deny the duty of the elder to help the younger? Even among animals, with certain exceptions, this is a recognized principle, therefore how much more should it be so among human beings.

So we have to abandon the idea of striving to attain, of violent effort. Energy is necessary, so is ambition, zeal, faith and belief, but none of these things are to be used in the ordinary fashion. The spirit of serenity is the antithesis of strenuousness, and it is the strenuous life that is attempted by so many, and which yields so little in the bulk of cases. It is only as one learns to be serene that one knows that there are finer forces within us, and it is only by the co-operation of those finer forces that we can make the best use of our mental powers.

It is supposed by many that this quality is possessed by successful business men, but it is only partially practiced, because it is the surface of the mind which is used. Ask a successful business man if he could keep his mind on one thing for ten minutes, even money-making, or his business, or his favorite and most familiar thought, he would find it a tax. He might take half a dozen aspects of his business and think of each in turn, but this would be a very different matter to taking, as is often done in the East, a flower, focussing the mind on it to the exclusion of every other thought for twenty minutes or more. That is Concentration, and the value of its acquisition is that the tentacles of the mind can be dug into any problem, however abstruse, when its nature is understood, and all that it contains will be given up, because it is impossible to withhold it.

I have elsewhere cited the case of a judge who knew positively whether a witness was telling the truth or not, and he acquired this marvellous and desirable faculty by concentrating on truth as a virtue. He actually *"thought up"* all there was of truth, till he became truth itself. A lie to him set his nerves jangling, just as a drink-sodden man carries with him an atmosphere extremely obnoxious to any sensitive man, or wild animals in their natural state. *Bostock*, the well-known animal trainer, knew this and he found that a tamer in the habit of drinking was disliked very much by the animals, and his control over them was much slighter in consequence.

To keep the mind on one point for two minutes is too arduous for many, and so long as there is this lack of serenity this will be so. Business or professional men who can concentrate and who yet do not live the serene life simply force themselves to keep their minds on whatever they want, and they waste their forces and become prematurely old and worn out. You often hear such people say at the end of the day that they are "fagged out"; they have had a "hard day"; they have had many trying things; they may have got "worked up" about one or other matter.

Work, it should be borne in mind, never tires one. It is the spirit in which it is done that wearies. Even laborious work, when adequate rest is permitted, does not make one tired. Have you never heard people say they were "tired of doing nothing?" Have you not yourself experienced a feeling of tiredness spending a wet day at home, or in very tedious company? All of us have at some point or other of our lives felt thus. Invalids who make no greater physical effort than turning over in bed, complain of being tired out. What have they done to be fatigued? Well, the fact of being invalids to start with is proof positive of their not living according to law, so they may well be tired. Misused emotions, ill-governed feelings, bitterness of spirit, critical or other negative states, including worry, inharmony, fear, nervousness, hurry, all produce fatigue, and the fatigue which springs from mental causes is always more keenly felt than from physical effort.

The "born tired" type is no illusion; these people *do* genuinely feel tired, whether they work or not, and they are not confined to the masses either. If we did but know it energy in an unending stream is pouring into us every hour of the twenty-four, and few of us need be weary. I know the statement seems extreme, but students of Mental Discipline have proved it now for some time. A writer, who has produced several books, in five years, to say nothing of writing for one or two monthly magazines, says: " I can now endure almost anything without feeling tired or worn, and my working capacity has more than doubled during the last few years; still I consider myself simply in the very beginning of this phase of the subconscious field." If one is a sedentary worker he need not feel tired by poring over his work several hours in succession; all he needs is change, but this is a question we must not pause over at present, fascinating though it be. It is only introduced here as it has a distinct bearing upon the matter under consideration.

It is not the *"hard day,"* then, that tires, but the spirit in which the work is done, and this frame of serenity introduced into the daily life will give a zest for what was once considered irksome, difficult, or even repulsive. The idea of fighting for one's living must be banished, and the idea of coming into one's own, of daily unfoldment, daily growth must be substituted. The notion of being overworked has got more common nowadays because things seem to have moved more quickly of late years. This has arisen through so many more interests being introduced into life; the attention is necessarily more divided as a result. In this way one can see how imperative it is to grow out of this misconception and gradually substitute harmonizing thought. Jangled nerves must be straightened out; you must not permit yourself to be put out by others or affected by what goes on in your own immediate environment.

That it is unnatural attitudes of mind that cause weariness of body and not work anyone may prove for himself. If you have certain work to do which seems distasteful or difficult—it may be only looking for a missing receipt or letter, or turning out on a wet night to visit some one living a mile or two away— you maybe feel irritable. This feeling may lead to headache or even a sense of irritation, and irritation sets up molecular changes in the cells of the body. These changes are translated into "that tired feeling," which advertisers of patent medicines are so fond of quoting to push their wares, and the whole body feels it. So, a sleepless night, though the body lie eight or ten hours, will tire one on account of the toxins created in the tissues.

Tiredness, in many cases, is simply fatigue poisons generated in the body and has not the slightest reference to the amount of labor performed.

The Master Key

CHAPTER VI.

LESSON FIVE.

THE ABOLITION OF WORRY.

THE ACQUISTION OF SERENITY AND MIND POWER.

The *mental picture-making* faculty which most minds possess should always be pressed into service where it is desired to either create any new faculty in the mind or to strengthen a weak one. Direction is the one thing that is lacking in regard to our forces. Our heart beats *"of its own accord"* we say; the lungs act similarly, and we suppose that thought processes can initiate themselves and do their work without our interfering with them, but this is not so. Where energies are vigorously functioning every moment of the twenty-four hours they need direction, otherwise being highly imitative they copy whatever actions they may have just performed. That is what constitutes worry. It is going round and round in the vicious circle, coming to the same spot each time, so that no problem is ever solved by worry, because the solution lies outside the circle. We do not come across anything new, and it is the new we want when endeavoring to get out of a difficulty, or to solve a perplexing problem. Life seems largely made up of these problems, and it is because of our want of success in removing them from one's path that so many stay where they are. Many pursue the same course year after year, following in the same old groove. They are conscious of not making headway; they feel that they are only marking time, yet however much they may desire to strike out they are thwarted by these problems, and they move once more in the circumscribed orbit.

The mental picture-making faculty must be set to work. If the student wants to learn how to concentrate, he must get hold of the tools needed in preparing the way for it. If a man does not know that he possesses a thing he cannot expect to achieve something only to be accomplished by the aid of that something. Thus we have men and women who could be brilliant, if they would, who could be clever if they wished, who could be much more than they are, but if they think that all they are is present in their consciousness now they cannot use the auxiliary which would help them so wonderfully. A man who wanted to be wealthy might, by working long hours, existing on the barest necessaries of life, wearing his clothes to rags, never having a holiday, never helping anyone or anything, content to live in a garret, being miserly in the extreme, amass, after many years, a big sum of money. He could accomplish the same thing, with infinitely less labor, no privation, enjoy himself thoroughly, widen out his character instead of cramping it, and give pleasure and profit to many. The strenuous and toiling path always has its counterpart.

The student has been shown here the need for a wholesome state of mind before he can do much. The abolition of worry, the acquisition of serenity, the lessening of the number of activities, the tendency of the simple life, has severally been brought under notice, and as one wheel cogs into another so this practice of sketching out the mentality as he would like it will help him or her considerably. By seeing it as he would like it he gives less attention to the actual state of the mind, so that whatever weaknesses there may be by not being emphasized, as they are in the daily life, will gradually pass from the consciousness. As this takes place, the conditions which the student would like to see in his mind will slowly become established, and here one mental law will be of service to him. Mental matter is always in the state of building: something is always being constructed, and it is invariably modelled on the pattern set it by the image-making proclivities of the mind. As the mind dwells on one set of images by another great psychological law the energies surge to the center thus created for the moment. Thinking always sets up increased activity in the consciousness, and as the mind pictures what it needs, what it would like, more and more energizing factors come along. These energies seek to build up the pictures furnished, and provided those pictures are not altered and modified repeatedly they will become concrete: that is to say, they will set in motion those forces which will externalize the ideas

The Master Key

CHAPTER VI.

LESSON FIVE.

THE ABOLITION OF WORRY.

THE ACQUISTION OF SERENITY AND MIND POWER.

The *mental picture-making* faculty which most minds possess should always be pressed into service where it is desired to either create any new faculty in the mind or to strengthen a weak one. Direction is the one thing that is lacking in regard to our forces. Our heart beats *"of its own accord"* we say; the lungs act similarly, and we suppose that thought processes can initiate themselves and do their work without our interfering with them, but this is not so. Where energies are vigorously functioning every moment of the twenty-four hours they need direction, otherwise being highly imitative they copy whatever actions they may have just performed. That is what constitutes worry. It is going round and round in the vicious circle, coming to the same spot each time, so that no problem is ever solved by worry, because the solution lies outside the circle. We do not come across anything new, and it is the new we want when endeavoring to get out of a difficulty, or to solve a perplexing problem. Life seems largely made up of these problems, and it is because of our want of success in removing them from one's path that so many stay where they are. Many pursue the same course year after year, following in the same old groove. They are conscious of not making headway; they feel that they are only marking time, yet however much they may desire to strike out they are thwarted by these problems, and they move once more in the circumscribed orbit.

The mental picture-making faculty must be set to work. If the student wants to learn how to concentrate, he must get

87

hold of the tools needed in preparing the way for it. If a man does not know that he possesses a thing he cannot expect to achieve something only to be accomplished by the aid of that something. Thus we have men and women who could be brilliant, if they would, who could be clever if they wished, who could be much more than they are, but if they think that all they are is present in their consciousness now they cannot use the auxiliary which would help them so wonderfully. A man who wanted to be wealthy might, by working long hours, existing on the barest necessaries of life, wearing his clothes to rags, never having a holiday, never helping anyone or anything, content to live in a garret, being miserly in the extreme, amass, after many years, a big sum of money. He could accomplish the same thing, with infinitely less labor, no privation, enjoy himself thoroughly, widen out his character instead of cramping it, and give pleasure and profit to many. The strenuous and toiling path always has its counterpart.

The student has been shown here the need for a wholesome state of mind before he can do much. The abolition of worry, the acquisition of serenity, the lessening of the number of activities, the tendency of the simple life, has severally been brought under notice, and as one wheel cogs into another so this practice of sketching out the mentality as he would like it will help him or her considerably. By seeing it as he would like it he gives less attention to the actual state of the mind, so that whatever weaknesses there may be by not being emphasized, as they are in the daily life, will gradually pass from the consciousness. As this takes place, the conditions which the student would like to see in his mind will slowly become established, and here one mental law will be of service to him. Mental matter is always in the state of building: something is always being constructed, and it is invariably modelled on the pattern set it by the image-making proclivities of the mind. As the mind dwells on one set of images by another great psychological law the energies surge to the center thus created for the moment. Thinking always sets up increased activity in the consciousness, and as the mind pictures what it needs, what it would like, more and more energizing factors come along. These energies seek to build up the pictures furnished, and provided those pictures are not altered and modified repeatedly they will become concrete: that is to say, they will set in motion those forces which will externalize the ideas

contained in the mind, for as so frequently pointed out the
outcome of all thought is action, the bringing to the surface
what has previously gone on underneath it. It is the result
of the thought. Just as all we see around us in the universe is
the effect of a cause, and not that cause, so all physical actions
are the effects of causes set up in the mental and spiritual
worlds. Seeing that it takes little more labor to image the
mentality as we should like it we might as well idealize our
images, however far short of such ideals our minds may be at
the present moment. Let us see ourselves performing those
things we habitually do in the most perfect manner possible;
if we are not able to concentrate let us see ourselves keeping
our mind uninterruptedly on the point we wish to consider.
There is a difference in seeing ourselves do this and actually
doing it, and this will be understood later, but this preliminary
practice will contribute its quota to the success we seek. The
mind can only work to patterns; it cannot produce something
on which the thought has not been working, so that the more
clearly and more frequently the mind can be impressed with
mental pictures of what is desired the more certain the outcome, the more sure that we shall realize what we set out to
realize.

And here it would be well to decide what is best for the
time being. So many want this and that and the other, and
think about each in succession that one set of mental pictures
or ideas neutralizes the other. The habit of having a lot of
unfinished work about is common on the physical plane, and
the muddle it causes to all around is obvious; in the mind it is
even more fatal, for it destroys the efficiency of the mechanism
of the mind. No two people may feel the same need, so each
should decide for himself as to what will most help him at the
particular point of his success. Generally speaking, it is wisest
to take the weakest trait and strengthen that by the laws
enunciated herein.

A common fault with the beginner in applied metaphysics
is the desire to accomplish too much. When he learns the
possibilities of mind, what he can become, what he can do, he
wants to be everything all at once, and the forces of the mind
tumble over each other in their eagerness to obey his desires.
He rouses things up within the circumference of his mental
powers, and great activity is manifest for some time. Often as
a result a new idea crops up unexpectedly, and if he is wise he

will act on it, but this should only be done when he sees clearly ahead the legitimate result of the action. This the habit of making images will do, and though he may make mistakes in his deductions at first he will mature his judgment, and later will rarely need advice from others as to the best course to pursue under given circumstances. The encumbering mental material must be got out of the way, a definite plan must be sketched, and then adhered to. By taking the weakest trait, refusing to see it as at all weak, but rather the highest state of efficiency you can conceive you begin a policy of constructive thought, and therefore strengthen it at the outset. Of course, if action is part of plan you must see that it is not lacking, otherwise you become a mere theorist, a dreamer. Action is nearly always concerned, it will be found, and however unpleasant it may be—and it nearly always is in these cases, because that is why it was not performed before, it must be resolutely carried out. The other faculties of the mind must co-operate with the desire to amend the weakness. If the action has an unpleasant aspect or character it must be looked at from quite another standpoint and thus rendered innocuous. It has this side, be sure, and it is for you to find it out. *We give life to errors and then take the errors for truth itself, and therefore think we cannot get away from the result.*

Mental or soul forces frittered away in a hundred different directions accomplish nothing, any more than the sun's rays do, but focus them by Scientific Concentration, and we know how intensified is the power that is expressed thus. If there is a weakness in the character and the mind pictures the op-. posite virtue, strong and radiant, the gaps between where you now stand and the place you aim to be at will the sooner be filled up. Having materially strengthened the weakness, so much so that scarcely a trace of it remains one can then turn one's attention to other sides of the character which need development, or the building in any side that will help us to secure this wider power of Concentration. Till we have that we shall content ourselves with repairing breaches, with strengthening our ordinary mentality, and leave the creative aspect of the new psychology for future experiments.

Knowing what you want will indeed be a great gain, as it will conserve force, and that force can be turned into channels where it will accomplish our purpose more effectively than it would if diverted into first one channel and then into another.

This knowing what you want is one of the most tantalizing things in the world. Man being so much a creature of moods, unlike a rock or animal whose wants are few and therefore no ambition, he has a thousand and one activities, all of which call for expression at some point, and he spends most of his time in gratifying them. All the five senses demand gratification, and there are other physical activities which do not come in the five-fold division which quite as urgently seek gratification. Add to these the energies of the mind which are so much more numer-ous, though in the early stages of the life are not so articulate and insistent, and one begins to understand how complex and marvellous is man's composition.

The greater part of the lives of many is spent in a more or less aimless manner. There is no plan laid down at the com-mencement, except in a very general way. Possibly the first thing that occurs to a youth after leaving school is that he must be successful in whatever calling he is to follow. Then later he may marry and assume family responsibilities, when a broad division occurs in the plan, and those dependent upon him claim his care. These two divisions, however, make up the ideal of his life, a hobby coming in as an additional energy of the man.

But apart from these natural "wants" numerous others arise from time to time. These are largely due to impressions from the without, what we call "circumstances." Hopes, fears, desires, chase each other in quick succession, and all these alternatives although giving rise to a certain amount of activity do not educe a definite plan.

Nearly all these moods are of the surface of the mind, and it is one reason why one so seldom knows what one wants. This is not an enviable condition, and so long as mental action is confined to the surface so long will there be a blankness as to definite plans. The true mind can never work thus; there must be depth, and to secure depth one must try to feel the finer side of the mind. All thought must have an objective, and it is not by passing from one thing to another that this is gained. What might be called the metaphysical attitude must be adopted, because in that attitude do we perceive what we really want.

This attitude is concerned only with those actions which take place in the depths of mind, which are detached from the outer, from the everyday side of existence, and as those states of the mind are contacted the man comes to know what is the real mind. He learns to know what he really wants, what it is he is capable of enjoying, of understanding, but so long as he lives and thinks like the majority so long is he shut out from those depths of finer mentality. As soon as they are contacted thoughts and action become complimentary in the true sense, and the thinker is enabled to secure what he really wants.

Even the student of metaphysics is not exempt from the weakness of not knowing what he wants. He sees, perhaps twenty things he believes he wants, and works ardently at one —then another for a time, but through misapplied energy and want of knowledge he does not secure definite results. He does not perceive that only by knowing how the mind works, the order in which the various faculties of the mind are to be evoked and developed can he realize what he seeks. Trying to stimulate first this, then that faculty, with spasmodic prods here and there, may result in increased activity of the faculties involved, but this is not what one should seek, for as soon as the result of the prod or stimulus has been exhausted they sink back to their normal level. By co-ordinating the forces and activities powers are awakened that are practically self-acting, and once worked they continue the work begun.

The Master Key

CHAPTER VII.

LESSON SIX.

SELF-CONTROL AND SELF-RELIANCE.

MOTIVES CREATE INTEREST.

It is true that what each seeks will differ, but it is possible that one might plunge about for years before finding out just what he did really want, and under such circumstances there is one course which is safe. It is more than this: *It is wise,* and will appeal strongly to the earnest student because it will develop great *Self-Reliance, Poise* and a feeling of *Power.*

It is this: Practice *Thought-Control* and *Concentration* several times a day until you become possessed of *Calm Confidence,* and are thoroughly convinced of the reality of *Control* of yourself, and of others.

The fact that you have enrolled as a student of *Concentration* and *Will-Culture* clearly indicates that your desire for a stronger *Will* is earnest. Therefore, let this earnest desire form the basis of the first exercise.

(a) On a sheet of note paper write out a list of the reasons why you are taking up these lessons, also the benefits you hope to derive from them. Call this your *List of Motives.* These Motives must not be in any way general motives, but should be concerning matters in which you have a deep absorbing interest, in fact, *motives which will move you.* Write with the greatest care. Put Strong Will into your writing. *Feel* that you are engraving these desires *upon your Will,* as indeed you are.

As you doubtless know from experience, resolutions though easily made are not so easily continued; but this List, by being frequently reviewed, will be found to form an excellent incentive. This method of reminding oneself of one's pledges is wonderfully effective, and when performed in the proper

43

spirit—*with the earnest desire for Strong Will-Power*—is one which can scarcely fail. Even one reading of the List will spur you on to greater effort should at any time your interest lag. By repeatedly reviewing these motives you will soon get to know them by heart, and so be able to recall them at will. As time goes on new motives will come to you. These, of course, should be added to the original List, as this will do much towards keeping your interest alive and fresh.

To serve you as a guide I have mapped out a *Specimen List* of Motives.

This List is by no means complete—as it is impossible to tell the whole of anyone's private interests—but it will furnish you with sufficient material to make a beginning.

Make it in the form of a resolution somewhat as follows:

I (*here write your name in full*) hereby firmly and solemnly resolve to do my utmost to strengthen and increase my present *Concentration and Will-Power* for the following reasons:

I shall gain greater Strength of Character, so that my every thought, word, and action will be characterized with more power and purpose.

I shall become more able to help those around me (*mention the names of definite individuals,* as this will make your motive more interesting and personal; besides, having thought of others will keep your exercising from becoming a self-centered practice).

I desire to create for myself an independent position* in life (mention definite position).

I shall gain greater Self-Control and Self-Reliance.

I shall be able to exercise greater control over others.

My personal appearance will be greatly improved; my mouth and jaw will be stronger and firmer, and my whole bearing will denote greater Self-Confidence and Strength of Character.

My powers of Concentration will be enormously developed.

To the foregoing motives add others which touch you more personally, and about which you alone know. Always bear in mind that your motives must be powerful ones—regarding affairs which constantly engage your attention, and in which you take an engrossing and vitalizing interest. Use your own

---

*Let the student read carefully the section *"The Art of Getting Rich,"* *"Opportunity in a New Light,"* in Chapter XXXVII, Lesson Thirty-five.

words in writing out the List, but let them be forceful words. Infuse them with all the power and enthusiasm you can command. *Write with the thought firmly in mind that your success in Concentration, Mental Discipline and Will-Culture largely depends upon the strength and earnestness of your motives.*

Never be guilty of base or mean motives. Motives create Interest; Interest invigorates the Attention; the Attention is the life-blood of the Will; therefore, the purer and nobler your motives are, the healthier and stronger shall be your Will.

(b) *The Will,* like the muscles, can only be developed by exercise, and the development obtained depends very largely upon the amount of *"consciousness"* thrown into the exercising.

You know that when the arm is flexed in a purposeless fashion the biceps remain quite soft, but when the same action is performed with *"will,"* the muscles are made to stand out hard and firm. You are also aware that regular practice of this exercise in this manner will quickly develop the muscles used.

Similarly, when any daily duty is carried out in a listless manner it lacks vigor and force, but when performed with Attention, strongly *willed,* the action is characterized with a strength and purposefulness which makes it as vastly different from the carelessly performed act as the firm muscle is from the flabby one. Moreover, continued practice of this *willed* Attention assuredly develops the Will, because in summoning and holding the Attention to the task the Will is exercised, and thereby increases in strength and flexibility. *Therefore, development of the Attention means development of the Will.*

In everyday life you have a never-failing supply of opportunities for practice of *willed* Attention, *viz.,* when you are working, or perform any similar act of the daily routine. Instead of performing these acts in the usual perfunctory manner, you should infuse them with "life" by calling forth the Will to focus the Attention steadily and strongly upon them, at the same time earnestly affirming, "I WILL to do this act quickly yet carefully."

Interest is the key to Attention, so should any of these seemingly unimportant acts fail to possess Interest you must create it by surrounding the act with thoughts which are of interest to you. Thus, say to yourself, "By attending stead-fastly to this act I am strengthening and increasing my Will-Power and Concentration." Recall and apply any of your other motives, and your interest and attention in the task are certain to increase.

(c) You are possessed of a power which is invaluable—namely, *Calm Confidence.* By *Calm Confidence* is meant the power of performing every act in a calm, confident manner, so that you are able to accomplish with ease that which was formerly well-nigh impossible to you. You can experience this *Mood of Calm Confidence* by experimenting with exercises given herein.

Be seated; close the eyes, and let there come flowing into your mind peaceful, inspiring thoughts, such as—*"I feel much happier," "I am confident that I can accomplish any task," "Why, life is so good, so grand, so glorious and beautiful that I cannot feel other than confident and perfectly happy."*

Repeat these and similar affirmations, each time with re-newed earnestness, and you will find that, as the thoughts take hold, your eyes will brighten, you will sit up, draw in a deep, full breath, and bring the shoulders back. Your whole body will seem vitalized and tingling with a new-found strength, and you will feel capable of accomplishing any undertaking. You will experience the *Mood of Calm Confidence.*

Lay aside everything else and give this exercise a fair trial. Perform it earnestly and conscientiously, and you will experience that buoyancy of mind and body which comes only when you feel thoroughly confident of success.

Now, this power of Calm Confidence is *within you,* for it can be brought forth, and persistent practice is all that is re-quired to make it permanently one of the features of your per-sonality. Cultivate this state of mind assiduously, and you will be repaid a thousandfold for the time expended upon it.

(d) When feeling depressed and out-of-sorts you have doubtless noticed your breathing is shallow, short and jerky —just sufficient to keep the lungs supplied with as much oxygen as will keep you *existing.* But when you feel capable of accomplishing any task, when certain of success, or when elated over some specially good news, notice how the breath-ing is affected—it becomes fuller, deeper, more rhythmical, and more invigorating. Now, while it is true that your state of mind has this wonderful effect upon your breathing, *it is also true that your breathing exercises a remarkable influence over your state of mind.* Proper breathing is one of the greatest aids to Strong Will, because better breathing means better health, and one's Will-Power depends very largely upon one's state of health. In this connection the following breathing exercise is simply invaluable for its all-round benefits:

Breathe in deeply, quietly, unhurriedly, and rhythmically through the nostrils, affirming, while doing so, "I am inhaling health-giving oxygen and greater Will-Power." Hold the breath, and affirm, "I am *absorbing* Health and Will-Power." Now exhale *fully*, with the earnest affirmation, "I am breathing out all bodily weakness and weak Will." Do not go through this exercise in a casual, matter-of-fact manner else you will lose its undoubtedly great benefits. Live the thoughts you are suggesting to yourself. Let yourself *feel and realize* the sensations which the thoughts are bound to create, and very soon you will be the possessor of an increased supply of the powers upon which you have concentrated.

Practice this exercise *at least* twice a day—in the morning when you wake and at night before going to sleep. It can also be practiced any spare moments you have during the day, and will be found to possess great health value, apart from its immense value as a Will-Power builder.

(e) In the development of Will a certain amount of energy is expended; therefore, in order to avoid unnecessary fatigue, economy of energy is essential. This is achieved through the practice of Muscular Relaxing, which removes the possibility of overstrain and also enables you to perform more work with less fatigue than formerly. Try the effect of the following simple exercise:

Be comfortably seated. Inhale a deep, rhythmical breath which will vitalize your whole body. Now exhale fully and *very slowly.* As you exhale let the body thoroughly relax, the head drop forward, the arms fall listlessly to the sides, the fingers lose the stiffness, and the face be free from all tension so that you look and feel *thoroughly limp.* Close the eyes, as this will help you to realize more fully the sensation of sleep and rest. Hold before the mind a picture of Perfect Quietness. Carry the thought, "I am receiving and absorbing Power from this delightful peace." Again inhale, but do not change the body from this limp position. Relax even more fully than before. Inhale and relax a third time, after which, again inhale, but, in so doing, bring the body up and the shoul- ders back as in the original position.

As is obvious, the foregoing exercise, to be performed cor- rectly, requires the privacy of your own room, but quite an amount of small practices can be had any time throughout the day without their being noticed. Thus, during your spare moments, cultivate the habit of *slightly relaxing*. You cannot, of course, become limp as in the Relaxing Exercise proper; just let yourself become *less tense* all over.

Besides being great helps in the economizing of energy, these relaxing exercises possess exceptional value as tonics for jaded and overwrought nerves, and will do much towards de- veloping the *Mood of Calm Confidence.*

The foregoing comprises the student's exercises for this lesson, and they should be performed daily until results are obtained.

Perform the exercises as follows:

First, read over your List of Motives three times every morning and evening (see par. A).

Second, perform throughout the day four or five acts with Willed Attention (see par B).

Third, summon the Mood of Calm Confidence several times every morning and evening (see par. C).

Fourth, perform throughout the day several acts with Calm Confidence.

Fifth, perform Breathing Exercise several times every morning and evening (see par. D).

Sixth, perform Relaxing Exercise five times every morn- ing and evening (see par. E).

Before commencing each Exercise earnestly affirm—"I WILL to gain Strong Will-Power."

The performance of one exercise will, of course, indirectly help the performance of the others, but when you have got- ten well along you must consciously endeavor to *blend* the ex- ercises, that is, when performing one, try to embrace all the others. Thus, when reading your List of Motives, inhale deeply, and summon Calm Confidence and Attention. When exhaling, slightly relax.

While going through the Attention and Calm Confidence Exercises inhale fully, and at the same time recall a strong Motive. Perform the acts with the *Moods of Calm Confidence* and *Willed Attention* held strongly to the fore.   Slightly relax each time you exhale.

In the *Breathing Exercise* inhale deeply and rhythmically, while affirming some strong motive.   Inhale, absorb, and exhale with Confidence and Attention.   Exhale *very fully* and relax slightly.

During the Relaxing Exercise inhale deeply.   Recall strong Motive. *Feel* you are relaxing with Confidence and Attention.

Perform these exercises the same number of times as during the first fortnight.

As you develop the knack of performing the exercises conjointly as above, you will experience a growing feeling of Power.   You will *infuse* Will into every act.   The thought— "I WILL to gain Strong Will-Power," by being kept persistently before the Mind will come to *possess and dominate* the Mind, thus enabling you to perform every action with ease and grace, whilst imbuing them with greater Intelligence, Vigor, and Will-Strength.

By regular practice of the exercises in this *Lesson,* your thinking powers will be greatly quickened, and your power of Observation wonderfully developed.   Consider the important part observation plays in your life.   Your actions depend upon it, because before you can act you must desire; before you can desire you must be aware of the things to desire, and in becoming aware you must use your powers of Observation.

Besides giving your face an added appearance of Strength of Character and Will-Power, the practice of this exercise will undoubtedly develop your Self-Reliance.   It will make you feel more master of yourself, and able to judge matters in a much clearer, calmer and more collected manner.

By conscientiously practicing the Exercises in this course of Lessons, you are certain to develop Will-Power and Self-Control.   With *increased* Self-Control and Will-Power comes *greater control of others,* because, in conquering and training the latent and oftentimes rebellious faculties of your mind, you are creating that Strength of Character, and that Personality which hold such great influence with others.

Your thoughts will be imbued with greater strength, your speech characterized with more convincing forcefulness, and your actions fuller of confidence, vigor and purpose.   Thus, others will be made to recognize your Power so that they will give you their respect, esteem and confidence, and will seek your co-operation and aid. It is most gratifying to experience the development of this Power of Personality, and you shall find this one of your greatest encouragements and incentives to continue the study of *Concentration, Mental Discipline and Will-Culture* throughout life.

The Master Key

THE PSYCHOLOGICAL MOMENT.

The student has now arrived at the point where he can consider Scientific Concentration more closely, and the lessons contained in Part Two will show its practical application in self-development and Mental Discipline. The necessity of harmony, freedom from worry and all negative conditions of the mind, the creation of interest have cleared the way somewhat. There is a very prevalent opinion that there will not be much success unless we screw up the will and literally force ourselves to keep our mind on whatever it is that we seek; for this reason the efforts of so many have been fruitless. *For one thing the will is scarcely developed in many people; then they do not know how to rouse or use it, while the exercises practiced have been ill-chosen.*

The first fact necessary to emphasize about Concentration is that thousands of attempts are essential to perfectly succeed in it. This statement looks appalling at first, but it need not deter any sincere student who has made up his mind to master the subject. If it were like taking lessons in some subject, and the student had only one lesson a day or every other day, the time required to become proficient in the subject would require many days, involving innumerable hours of work. If one remembers one's early attempts to master Euclid or algebra one knows how hopeless the task seemed of ever grasping the principles underlying them. Yet eventually the obstacles were, by the earnest worker, successfully surmounted, and so it is with Scientific Concentration and Will Culture. No earnest student of it ever fails to obtain the Master Key, but with some the efforts require a longer period than with others.

It is not easy to find a more apt simile of the human mind

51

than the eastern one which regards it as a wild, restless horse, ever seeking to go its own way rather than the way its rider desires it to take. Persuasion accomplishes more than force on more plans than one, and this is very true of the mind. *Keeping ever at the back of the mind what it is we seek we say to ourselves, "I am not going to think of anything else." Of course, mind rebels; it has always been accustomed to have its own way till now, and cannot understand the curb placed upon it. It rears, kicks against the fetters imposed upon it, but that which is now for the first time almost opposing it is steadfast —has a definite purpose in view and is not to be lightly turned aside from it.*

When the mind finds itself thwarted it calls upon the senses to help it to overthrow the restraint placed upon it, and hearing, seeing, feeling, become suddenly preternaturally alert. The man becomes very much alive; he knows that within him a *titanic struggle is being waged,* and he decides that he will not relax for a moment or so, keeping the idea before him that he will let his mind go its own way, not because it wants, but because he, the real master of the mind, thinks the lesson has been learnt. He knows that though he could break its spirit he would have broken all there was in it, just as in the case of the restive steed. *The mind is there not to break, but to train, which is very different.* So he takes his attention off the subject he has been holding the mind to, but the lesson is not ended yet. He merely turns the thought to another subject for a couple of minutes, a subject chosen previously. When he has calmly considered this to the exclusion of any alien idea he drops it, and then permits the mind to go its own course.

This will be done daily, and despite any shortcomings on the part of the student in the initial stages he will certainly find he is getting some control of his mental mechanism.

Going back to what has been said regarding serenity, absence of fear and worry, the harmony, the lessening of activities, knowing what is really being aimed at, a feeling of confidence is certain to be born, and as this slowly possesses one there will begin to be created a mental atmosphere quite different to any experienced in the past.

Rhythm runs through all Kingdom of Nature, the mental part no less than the physical, and the automatism of the mind which was responsible for the want of ability to concentrate will first of all be broken up and then re-grouped in accordance with the pattern presented to it. New vibrations will be set up, Will Culture begins to take place, and if the reader can manage to set apart a certain hour daily for Concentration practice all the better. *Children and animals get sleepy at certain periods, so that one might set one's watch by them, just as flowers open and close their petals at exact times. Even adults know meal times without the aid of clocks and watches, and plenty of functions are quite automatic in themselves.* We are constantly reminded to take the path of least resistance, and in any training of the mind *regularity counts very much.* The busy man well understands this in the pleasant hours spent at home after business, every care thrown off, and the mind at ease, contented. This does not apply to all, I know, and it is a pity it does not, because it so easily could. But, all the same, there are many men and women to whom it does, and *they will understand what I am endeavoring to show—that rhythm unconsciously enters into one's daily life.* When the student has commenced to practice he finds that each time afterwards he takes it up or repeats it it becomes easier, because all the faculties concerned in it get ready for it, *look forward to it, so to say.*

Further than this, new interests will almost inevitably arise; ambition will be strengthened, and Concentration will come quite naturally. When any new ambition, or a new conception arises in the mind desire at once comes to the front, and when desire is awakened in us all the forces of the mind are increased and become more alert. Just as a football enthusiast would throw more energy into a game than would be expended in a day's work, and yet not feel as tired, so when strong desires can be aroused in a man he has little difficulty in concentrating.

It is a psychological law that the use of a faculty to its utmost increases its capacity, and so we find once more that after the steady daily application the mind rests easily on whatever subject we place before it. This does not mean that we shall abuse it, and practice gazing at black spots on the wall for twenty minutes at a stretch, as taught by so-called professors of New Thought, Hypnotism, etc., etc. This will lead to a wearying of the mind's forces, because the mind would not voluntarily take up gymnastic stunts of the above nature. *Where there is no real objective, where the mind is not legitimately fulfilling its function there is a sense of the mental powers being forced, and where this is the case the true forces are diverted into unnatural channels, and they work against the grain. This tends to a disruption, a disorganization of the mental mechanism.*

Success in Concentration is dependent upon the *attitude* which the mind takes up. There may be a praiseworthy attempt to feel that it is an admirable experiment to gaze fixedly at a spot with the mind fastened on it like a leech, but behind this there is the consciousness that it is only an experiment, *a means to an end,* and the utter artificiality of it creates an antagonism which will use up a certain amount of force and defeat the object we have in view. *A doubting or dissatisfied attitude will positively bar success,* and tend to produce either a feeling of indifference or disgust for Concentration or Will Culture, and this if allowed to go on will put the student back a long way. This is a form of *conscious* Concentration.

The Master Key

CHAPTER IX.

LESSON EIGHT.

UNCONSCIOUS CONCENTRATION.

If you would make Concentration and Mental Discipline not only a success but a positive pleasure then *carry it into every act of your life*. This explains what was said above about its being necessary to make thousands of attempts to master the art. If *Scientific Concentration* is put into *every* act of the day then one would concentrate a thousand times in six weeks or less, and if one could practice it perfectly in a year it would be an immense gain. This is what might be termed *Unconscious Concentration*.

Will Power can be used now, but not in the way so many advocate, in the helping of the mind on all subjects on which it is necessary. It will have been noticed that the words *"The Master Key"* figure in the title of this work, and no student will have had any difficulty in connecting the title with the mastery of "self" and things outside of "self," such as circumstances. Thus it is that the *human will*, in common with the other faculties of the mind, must share in the work of raising and transmuting the lower nature by a study of *Will Culture and Mental Discipline*.

At this juncture (unless previously dealt with in the earlier part of these studies) the student will be wise in deciding what he is going in for, what his aim is, what he intends to do with his possibilities, what faculties he particularly desires to train or evolve, and use the will to stir and prompt him to action— to keep him up to the mark. It will supplement his enthusiasm, it will steady too much zeal, too much one-sidedness, help him to keep a mental and moral balance, as the reins in the hands of a skillful horseman prevent the animal from stumbling. It is no light thing coming to a decision with regard to one's ideals; it takes time to *grow* to the point where one's future becomes an ideal, which is something ahead of the average mind. An ideal is too frequently associated in the mind with something visionary, something all very well for the dreamer, the poet, but of no use to the practical hard-headed business man or the intelligent woman, or even the average individual. Therefore with too many people we get no ideals, unless we apply the term to "making provision for the future," and paying one's debts—not a bad thing in its way. No one can go very far, however, without ideals of some kind, but it is not for the writer to lay down to the student of *Mental Discipline, Will Culture and Scientific Concentration* what these should be. Everyone must form his own. It is almost certain when he has dipped into the New Psychology a little he will be fired by the same enthusiasm, the same keenness to progress, to widen his outlook, to aim higher, to cultivate ambitions he dare scarcely have whispered to himself a short time before. It is a rule, in fact, for those coming in touch with *Mental Discipline and Will Culture* to have kindled within them what almost amounts to a new sense, a desire to express themselves along new lines. It is as though they had suddenly discovered a new sensation, or unexpectedly come upon a country whose existence they had never imagined before. What frequently happens in these instances is that the interior depths of the mind have been touched and they give rise to vibrations that shake the whole of the mental vehicles and initiate changes that lead to an almost new life.

To find out what your strong points are go back to your childhood and see in what direction your tastes lay. It may require a few moments daily to get the retrospective habit working smoothly, but it can be got to work in this direction, and each day will find recollection of one's early days more vivid. It has often been remarked by people that they can remember trivial incidents that occurred twenty or thirty years ago, whilst they have great difficulty in recalling matters that are really of importance that have only taken place a few days before. One reason for this is that in childhood *impressions being naturally fewer are deeper.*

When the tastes of early life have been re-discovered the student may see if they still lie in that direction, and if so he can set to work by constructive thinking to get the new vibrations to work.

The mind is always churning something over, hence if allowed to go its own way it invariably thinks injurious and useless thoughts. From these we get tendencies, many of them of a negative character, and from this we see the creation of destructive forces. *It is just as easy to turn these forces to constructive work as the reverse.*

To get the whole power of the mind it is necessary to get rid of the idea that the mind must work along the lines that it has always gone, because by thinking of the mind in this fashion we limit its possibilities.

If you were exploring a strange country and instead of going into the interior you contented yourself by sitting down on the shore and looking round, surmising that the interior would not differ much from the littoral, then you would be limiting your knowledge of that country.

It would only be by actively traversing the domain that you would gain a knowledge of the region. So, in the region of the mind's mental domain, if you wish to work with the whole force of the faculties, powers and tools of the mind, they must all be brought under way. The mind being a creature of habit, and, as just said, perpetually churning thought as the cow chews the cud, it must have something on which to operate. If we become enthusiastic over the work in hand, as we rationally ought to do, we shall find no obstacles to the employment of all its powers in the art of Will Culture and Mind Training, as taught further on in this work.

The mind can never do its best, however, so long as there is any underlying current of dissatisfaction, any factor which can in any way vitiate it. *There must be perfect tranquillity, for one thing; then there must be an intense and deep desire to gain the end in view, whatever it be.*

In this way do we obtain the co-operation of the various forces of the mind, which, while being one is composed of various parts; the interest of each aspect of the mechanism of consciousness is enlisted, and where the interest of all is concerned all move in one direction. This means harmony, and all harmonious movement is easy and rhythmical. There is no strain, one force does not move in opposition to another, and as a general result WILL POWER is generated. The whole of the force of the mind is engaged and there can consequently only be one direction in which it can move—*forward.*

This is the psychological moment in which to practice *Con-*

centration and Will Culture. An idea given to the mind in such a condition will be gripped as by an octopus; it will be absorbed. By one of the laws of the *New Psychology* a thought placed in front of the consciousness, so to speak, is photographed upon it; it is carried automatically to the sub-conscious, and by another law whatever once enters the realm of the sub-conscious, be it strong or weak, positive or negative, good or bad, is beyond the control of the will even. *The conception or thought must work out in the external life.* It cannot lie forgotten in some dark recess of the human mind, but it takes its turn, and affects the normal mind. Here is the secret of "moods." People regarded as level-headed and sane do things which astonish those who know them best. During some unguarded moment they have given way to some impulse and entertained an inimical thought, which they have fructified unwittingly with will, desire, and Concentration, and the result has been appalling. *Remorse for these "lapses" brought out by ignorance of the laws of the mind only too realistically brings home the danger.*

The bearing of these laws on one's affairs of life is to make the reader the more careful as to what thoughts he entertains. Knowing something of the apparatus of the mind, he will be careful to avoid admitting conceptions which are destructive. The mind at times seems filled with activity, and at such moments he will convert such conceptions into constructive ideas. He will know that if he wants *"inspiration"* to do a certain piece of work now is the time to take the opportunity. Shutting out everything but the idea on which he is intent he will close all the senses, wherever he is, hold down the mind to the one theme with which he is dealing, and it will fill the channel thus prepared.

The practicality of *Concentration* and *Will Culture* in daily life will be obvious. Every human being, however humble the niche he may fill in the great social scheme, has some duty or service to perform, and only as it is perfectly fulfilled does he honestly discharge it. But it does not end with this perfect fulfilment. *The performing of an action perfectly creates the ability to do more;* the faculties concerned by their more perfect functioning place all their elements in a position which will admit more force, make them more capable of carrying out their natural functions, and energize the cells of these *mental atoms,* if the term may be permitted, so that there is an inrush of the great life wave which pulses throughout Nature and ever seeks to ensoul whatever receptacles or channels may be provided for the purpose.

It cannot be too widely known that Nature has an inexhaustible amount of what for a better expression we might designate *"raw material,"* which she wants to be "worked up," and that man is one of the channels by which this can best be accomplished. The universal "urge," called by other writers the "surge," which is incessant, which is ever seeking expression, because *"to become" is the keyword of all manifestation,* prowls about, seeking admission through the doors man can open if he likes, and by obtaining that admission its purpose is achieved, for the forces and faculties it will then meet raise or transmute the original impulse.

The Master Key

CHAPTER X.

LESSON NINE.

METAPHYSICAL ALCHEMY.

By *metaphysical alchemy the *"raw material or mind-stuff"* is raised to another state, just as water is raised to the state of ice by one operation and steam to another. There is, in fact, a mental chemistry akin to physical, and the science of applied metaphysics deals with it. Any one familiar with philosophy knows that there is a general consensus of opinion that man's will is free to choose in the highest aspect, though having chosen the result is beyond his power of recall, or to modify; man has his sacred centre into which nothing may enter without his bidding, and were it otherwise he would be reduced to the level of a mere puppet, an automaton.

Thus the life-wave which seeks further expression by the coming into contact with the mental attributes of man is compelled to wait till invited to enter. That is why evolution seems so slow in the cases of some people; they do not recognize that outside themselves is this mighty world-wave, a veritable realm of massive vibrations, which can only be tapped by a coming into harmony with them. By opening oneself to their entrance one takes on new vibrations and new ranges begin to come within the sphere of one's mentality. The *dynamics* of thought show that the accession of new vibrations always means a fuller use of all the forces of the mind. It is by this accession that the absorption of knowledge becomes possible; the general way is to memorize certain ideas and to fall back on those ideas and

---

*Metaphysics, Met-a-fiz-iks, *s*, the science which seeks to probe the inner secret, or logic, of thought or being as the basis of and prior to that which is merely phenomenal and cognizable by the senses. (Gr. *meta.* and *physics.)*

*Metaphysical, met-a-fiz'-e-kal, *a*. pertaining or relating to metaphysics; analytic of pure being or thought; ontological.

60

apply them to anything which seems germane to them. If we brought a mind alert to the fullest extent, intent on the question in hand, senses one-pointed, five merged into one, with the massed forces of the mind the consciousness would absorb the facts like a sponge taking up water. The tentacles of the mind would fasten themselves upon the information to be assimilated and make it its own in a tithe the amount of time and a tithe the energy and difficulty. So, too, with memorizing* facts or committing long passages of poetry or prose to memory the task would become light and a real pleasure. Study ceases to be distasteful and laborious. The student settles to his work, knowing that he will be able to master whatever problems arise in his studies. Sleepless nights fade into the past and examinations are entered with confidence as to the outcome. An awakened intelligence brought to bear on whatever engages the attention of the mind is enabled to grapple with and solve problems which have hitherto eluded the grasp. It is in this way that men like *Edison,* who have shut themselves in from intrusion, have successfully thought out perplexities, and made the world the richer for their labors. Gathering up the forces of the mind to a focus, in the silence, few questions remain shrouded in impenetrable mystery to the student.

And in connection with study the student who wishes to obtain the best results along the line of acquiring knowledge should bring the physical into line with the mental to secure the best results. The mental powers are quickened a hundredfold by the observance of the lines laid down, but by obeying physical laws Concentration is rendered still more effective. It is well known that whatever part of the body is employed in any particular work is supplied with extra blood to enable it to deal with it more efficiently. So the process of digesting demands more blood being sent to the stomach to accomplish it under the most ideal conditions. If, therefore, a man eats a heavy meal and attempts to apply the instructions for concentrating for any length of time the forces of the system become divided, and only half the power is given in each case. In *China* for thousands of years students preparing for examinations, which impose a severe tax upon the retentive faculties of the mind on account of having to be learnt by heart, lengthy and tedious passages from the writings of *Confucius, Lao-Tze* and other *Chinese philosophers,* are kept without food for long periods,

*See part Four in regard to Memory.

and shut up in little cubicles until they are proficient. Many great men often fast when engaged in abstruse calculations and scientific problems. Nearly all thinkers and many musicians in unraveling complex theories and puzzles have become lost in meditation and altogether have forgotten the demand of Nature for food.

When, therefore, one has a more than usually difficult task let little food be taken prior to attempting its achievement. The writer will have occasion to revert to this question later, so will not seek to elaborate it more fully now.

Concentration is many times used in a destructive manner. Specialists and medical men in asylums are among the classes who have fallen victims to adverse Concentration. Throat and cancer specialists have succumbed to the diseases they have so closely studied. The pathology of the complaints has been as familiar to them as measles would be to the mother of a large family. They knew every phase, every indication, knew what to expect and when. They worked out in their minds the whole history of the disease, and slowly constructed it externally in their own bodies. The writer has a collection of newspaper cuttings giving these sad instances of the fatal power of a morbid, faulty *Concentration* for, like everything else in connection with the powers of the mind, Concentration is *non-moral;* it is power or force which may be used to promote health or generate disease; it is quite immaterial to it what the outcome is. *And so the mind of a morose and morbid tendency gloats and fastens upon some form of self-destruction till, following the logical sequence, action succeeds thought.* Many a victim of the *drink or drug habit is really under the sway* of *Concentration* and *Auto-Suggestion* put to the wrong use. Read the weird and gruesome stories of *Edgar Allen Poe* and you are almost forced to the conclusion that the end of such a genius could only be what it was.

Fortunately, as just remarked, the number of those able to concentrate is comparatively few, but they emphasize the danger and reality of this great power of the mind. The student need not hesitate to practice Concentration for fear he may develop into a monomaniac or some other monstrosity. Concentration is like a good horse: it is under complete control and can be relied upon to do only what is expected of it. *All mental forces are edged tools, but the possession of them requires ex-*

pert knowledge of them as he envolves them, and so does not injure himself.

Many diseases *are caused,* and, are the direct result of some form of *Concentration, conscious or otherwise,* weak or strong; it is giving attention to a thing for a shorter or longer period from time to time. When the religious devotee kneeling at the feet of a crucifix, her whole soul going out to the object of adoration and veneration, filled with intense pity and sympathy, dwells upon the wounds of nail-prints in the body of Jesus on the cross, she reproduces the *stigmata* on her own body in the corresponding part by her concentrated attention, and blood will actively flow.

The reason we have so many cases of chronic diseases is because attention passes from the *conscious* to the *subconscious,* which, in turn, reacts upon the ordinary mind, for whatever enters the inner regions of the consciousness must come forth as action and further thought, or tendencies which promote both thought and action.

Whatever is given attention to in the mental world is thereby intensified, and whatever is intensified demands and is supplied with increased force. Thus *Concentration* for even a short time on disease increases its hold upon us. The aim of *Constructive Concentration and Will Culture* is to fasten upon those states which promote healthy thinking, and by healthy thinking we secure a healthy body. Just as a sunbeam falling aslant a darksome corner transforms it to something quite different, so *Concentration* turning upon a symptom imparts new life to it, quickens it. Thus no one should allow their mind to dwell for a moment upon any weakness or imperfection of any part of their body; instead of this, those physical states of harmony and equilibrium should be dwelt on to which reference has been made.

Whenever the body feels buoyant, full of vim and energy, "fit," turn the feeling to good account. Divert the attention from ordinary, commonplace channels, from the channels in which the mind spends most of its time. The idle, profitless thoughts that come and go through the chambers of the mind in an irresponsible manner will receive no encouragement, no impetus, no supporting force from the real mind, but instead of this, while the idea of being fully alive, in good form, is present the student should take the opportunity of gathering up a feeling of exhilaration, concentrate all the powers of the mind upon it for a few seconds. Thus centered, he should try to exclude any conceptions of weakness, shortcoming, disease, of any kind. He must shut out utterly from his consciousness all ideas of the existence of illness. Try to imagine, if you can, that the world in which you live is one vast garden, bathed in perpetual sunshine, cooled by frequent showers of dew and tempered by soft zephyrs, the atmosphere laden with the most exquisite perfume, the music of birds filling the air and the joyous laughter of children and men, happy and contented in a world when poverty and sorrow were unknown. Have you not to confess such a conception of existence could not occupy the mind for more than a fraction of time, to be replaced by the usual view of life in which such an idealized and ethereal picture is only indulged in, if at all, as a contrast to the grim type of living which is today termed "reality"? Now, just as it would be almost impossible to the average man to keep his conception of existence on so high a plane, so the student will easily understand that there is quite as much difficulty in conceiving a world in which disease or ill-health has no place. We have to take cognizance of this fact, and it is because of this that we begin to understand something of the task we set for ourselves when we talk about concentrating on an ideal state in which illness is utterly unknown and foreign to one's ideas. It would be just as easy to imagine an ideal condition as that depicted above as mankind free from disease.

Yet this is the view which must be aimed at if one wishes to reach the point where the word "disease" conveys scarcely any meaning to the ears on which it falls. If the term "disease" is familiar to you, then it means that that familiarity is a link between you and it, and that you are very likely to attract it. There is a relationship between you and it, however remote it may be. You may not associate yourself with it, because you may have a constitution of iron, and have come off good old stock. The fact remains that you are conversant with the term, therefore disease does not strike you as being unnatural or strange, though it may be unpalatable, or even indifferent to you. You have heard it said that you can't play with pitch without getting tarred, and so the contact with the word disease, whether striking upon the ear by means of the spoken word or the eye by means of the printed symbols makes a link between you and it, and circumstances strengthen this link from time to time.

If you have read even a few *New Psychology* books you know the baleful effect the word *"fear"* has upon the consciousness, and how through the word alone a character may be undermined or weakened, or rendered negative and therefore not at its best to bring forth the highest possibilities in one. The rapidity or quality of instantaneousness connected with thought (which is so aptly expressed in the phrase "a flash of thought," applied similarly in the case of "a flash of lightning") shows us how quickly a connecting link is made in the mind, which leaps from point to point with even greater velocity than lightning is possible. So "disease" arouses in the mind the idea of some one who has been or is now ill, and the possibilities arising from this condition. If a friend is ill, a friend you have been brought up with since a boy, as hale and hearty as you, why should not you be affected in the same way? You laugh at the idea, but the mind has made its connecting link the instant the conception arose, and it is strengthened from time to time by various means until it penetrates the deeper precincts of the mind, and the carroding canker begins its malignant work.

Many in England are aware of how Lord Nelson when a boy did not know the meaning of the word fear, and the effect it had on his career in life. Suppose all men could all get the same notion of the word disease; that is, make themselves positive against it. Suppose one did not know what it meant; then if it meant nothing to us when you heard it, it could form no link with your consciousness. This is not only good psychology, but it is good sense. *If a thing is foreign to the mind it is practically non-existent.*

The old story of the Plague setting out to *Bagdad* to kill a specified number of people will occur to many. On its return it was accused of having exceeded the number of its victims, "Nay," replied the Plague, *"it was not I who slew the extra thousands, it was Fear."* This story is always worth bearing in mind, because it happens to be very ancient, and therefore shows that many thousands of years ago the effect of mental stabs upon the body was well known; further, it illustrates in a graphic manner the point the writer is contending for, viz., that keep a thing out of your consciousness; be fearless and positive, by training your mental and life forces to combat it, and it cannot affect you in the slightest.

It is no use trying to delude ourselves that we could absolutely obliterate the word from our mind so that we be ignorant of what it meant when we chanced to come across it, though a Hindu who had made a life study of *Oriental Psychology* and *Soul Culture* would have no difficulty in doing so. What I mean is that you should *expunge* it from your dictionary, in the same way that Napoleon abolished the word *"impossible." In a word, ignore it;* encourage the idea, however, that you can annihilate it in time. Every time it is forced upon your attention turn resolutely from it and substitute for it that magic word HEALTH. Believe in yourself for health. Concentrate on it, absorb it, drink it up, and think it up into the inner recesses of the mind. Fill the mind with it to the exclusion of all else for the time being. *Thus the intrusion of the word disease would be brief, it would be isolated instantly, cut off in a watertight apartment; an impassable gulf would be created, and in this way it is quite innocuous.* A close study of this work will show the power of Concentration in cases of disease.* Many have seen cases of metaphysical healing where the healer has battled with it for hours with a consciousness literally steeped in disease, chronic cases of many years' standing. Many have marked the improvement as Concentration upon perfect health has been persisted in, how when the mind of the healer has been withdrawn the old conditions have returned. This may possibly have happened in the case of the reader, and if so I would counsel him by all means to retain his belief in constructive thought coupled with Concentration and truth Faith, despite a thousand lapses or more. The inability to "demonstrate" the truths of the *New Psychology, Concentration* and *Mental Discipline* is no proof of the falsity of the teaching laid down here. *If one man out of a million proves it then it is the truth, and the others may do the same in due course.* We all know of instances where truth has triumphed over error which expressed itself in the physical body in one form or another extending over some years. If the reader belongs to the invalid class, if he has contracted the illness habit let him daily picture himself in absolute physical perfection, concentrating believingly on what he desires. *Have True, Intense, Deep and Sincere Faith.*

And here is a law which will be found serviceable to the

---

*I have treated this subject more fully in *Chapter XXXIII., Lesson Thirty-one*, "Concentration Applied To Health and Disease," "The Psychology of Faith and Doubt." See also, *Chapter XXXIV., Lesson Thirty-two*, "Concentration Applied To Fear And Disease."

sickly and victims of negative thought: Every impression is a focussed energy. This means that by concentrating on a definite point we immediately create an impression, and this impression becomes a center of energy for the time being. If during that moment of Concentration we will that vitality or health shall enter that center of energy, that will actually take place, and in this way a diseased organ can be built up. Although one possess no knowledge of physiology or anatomy, one can always strengthen a weak organ or part of the body by merely bringing more energy to it, for wherever there is energy there is an extra blood supply, and this means the addition of new life to the part.

The Master Key

CHAPTER XI.

LESSON TEN.

THE CLAIMING OF YOUR OWN.

Whatever *you* create by *your* thoughts is *your* own. If there is one aspect in which *Concentration, Will Culture* and *Mental Discipline* can be of help to *you* it is in the claiming of your own. *First, as to your "own." What is it? Whatever you create by your thoughts is your own.* This is not coveting what some one else possesses, or begrudging the position of those who are more fortunately circumstanced than yourself. That is a species of imitation, and the work of the imitator is always more or less a failure.

You create relationships with things when they are the children of our own imagination. An architect plans in his own mind a beautiful building and he transfers his ideas to paper, explains what he wants, and his wishes are carried out to the letter. The artist draws his picture first mentally in his mind, and his hand is only the transferring medium. The writer has not the space to explain all that *Emerson* implied when he wrote:

> "Whate'er in nature is thine own,
> Floating in air or pent in stone,
> Shall rive the hills and swim the sea,
> And like thy shadow follow thee."

The strange affinity between objects and human beings has long been a source of mystery. Many instances could be cited of people wishing they had certain things which they scarcely expected they would ever see, and how their desires have been gratified. You will be shown in this work that there is no legitimate way of getting anything without giving an equivalent, so if you wish to attract certain circumstances to yourself or yours you must first make the link between them

68

and yourself after the principals enunciated and laid down here. If a man does not properly relate himself to his circumstances, by having faith and the development of mental discipline, then there is inharmony, and the two have to part company. It is like the square man in the round hole, and your business in the Great School of Life and Business *is to know just what you want*, then make up your mind to secure it. Concentration here is of immense value. Having decided upon what the goal is, you must take the first problem which presents itself, go carefully over the various aspects it presents, closing the mind as taught herein, to all that is irrelevant to the matter. It is surprising how a little practice along the lines of *Mental Discipline* enables one to almost instinctively select those avenues of thought which will give us what we seek. Do not worry about ways and means, your part is to decide on the principle and the immutable law of life will do the rest.

A case in point may help to make this clear. Whilst writing this book an employee of a business firm related to the author how he got his first start. He had been "stopped"—discharged —at his work without any notice, and told there would be nothing for him for several months. It was a quiet time of the year and the corresponding period of the previous year he had been dismissed for a month. The firm had been in the habit of employing in the busy season men with scarcely any experience, and to these they gave the usual notice. This was resented, as was the employment of these casual workers, which meant rushing work out in a brief spell, and then nothing to do for the regular employees later. This man had foreseen this and the customary stoppage, and wished to go into business for himself, so as to be independent of the firm, which only followed the tactics of similar employers in his city. He had no capital and no friends or influence; *he had Concentration, faith and belief in himself*, however, and while fully making up his mind to be his own employer he saw no means of accomplishing it. As he left the workshop on the Saturday noon, having received his dismissal, he was met by a man he knew who was a contractor doing a fair business. Exchanging greetings the workman mentioned he had just been laid off, and that all similar trades would be quiet for a time. "Have you never thought of starting for yourself?" asked the contractor. The man admitted that he had, but that he lacked capital. The contractor there and then offered him a contract which would amount to $500, the money to be paid as the work was finished, though he pointed out that his usual custom was when a contract was given in that month (October) he did not settle for it till the following April. The offer was taken and the man never regretted it, building up a nice little business, which shows every prospect of healthy growth.

THE LAW OF ATTRACTION.

The fact of often thinking how the end in view might be attained had telapathically struck the contractor at an odd moment when the mind was not particularly employed, and only a few moments before meeting with the workman. The workman certainly thought it odd from the way he told the story. It seemed a strange coincidence to him, and a lot of similar *"coincidences"* would, if inquired into, be found to be instances of the *Law of Attraction* operating through its appointed channels.

Let a clean-cut mental image be made in the mind of what is desired, concentrate quietly for a few moments over it, and day by day repeat the process, adding details as required, but not materially altering the original. If it is an object you want do not see some one else's and wish it yours, but see the thing quite apart from its setting and in your own house. Means will be forthcoming which will materialize the object, if mental discipline is gained and the principles laid down in this work are adhered to.

If, on the other hand, one wishes to change their circumstances they should not mentally picture themselves in surroundings utterly removed from their present position; that is to say, a man always accustomed to earn five dollars a week would scarcely be likely to see himself earning five hundred dollars in the same period, because, speaking generally, a man content with such a small amount as five dollars a week would scarcely be an ambitious, pushing fellow, and any other type would not be likely to make a mental leap to a sum a hundredfold more than he had been in the habit of receiving. A man in such a position would be more likely to wish to see his income doubled or trebled, and in these circumstances he would the more easily bring himself into line with his surroundings. Try to imagine a clerk offered an appointment as an ambassador to a big European court. Would the man be at home with a diplomatic corps, or likely to shine in a piece of state-craft? No, the idea would never occur to the clerk himself, and if an enthusiastic but misguided friend got him pitchforked into the appointment we may easily conjecture the outcome of the action. Yet such a supposition would be on a par with the views one sometimes hears put forward by readers and beginners of the *New Psychology* who expect miracles instead of legitimate results compatible with the nature of the mental and psychological efforts put forth. It is the question of proper adjustment between man and his surroundings, of a man relating himself, or coming into harmony with the surroundings he seeks to enter.

Be perfectly sure that no one or no thing can keep your own from you, if you have confidence and faith enough in yourself to claim it. All is law, and skipping across wide gulfs is unknown. Get a clear-cut idea of the surroundings you believe you are cut out for, and step by step you will mount nearer to your ideal if you faithfully carry out the lessons laid down in this book.

Reverting to the question of increasing one's mental capacity, which was left for further consideration, the student throughout this work will be shown that he must gain *Discipline* over his mental forces and then use *Scientific Concentration* to energize his brain, because with the calling into activity of more brain cells the mentality is made the richer, and in the meaning of life; this is progress. If the brain area is not increased a man stands still, or merely marks time, and this is what too many are doing. It used to be laid down as a scientific fact that the number of brain cells was limited, also that the whole of the brain was used. Recent researches of *experimental psychology* shows both conclusions to be erroneous, and with regard to the latter the percentage of brain used in daily life is only *five*. What becomes of the other 95 per cent? And why should there be such a surplusage of brain? Respecting the former this proportion lies fallow, awaiting cultivation, and reflecting upon the second question we come face to face with one of the most profound facts of the twentieth century, though no writer, so far as the author is aware, seems to have remarked upon it. It is this: Nature rarely supplies that for which there is not a use. Why should man have mental material many times greater than he wants? It is because man has unfolded his powers to so small an extent. Evolution is moving forward very rapidly at present, and man will do the same, and require much more brain area than he has hitherto found necessary. *Man's magnificent brain area and mental forces are waiting for cultivation.*

Faith, Belief and *Scientific Concentration* on the idea of expansion will awaken into vibration unused folds of the brain. As you concentrate on these dormant tracts affirm: *"I desire that more and more of my brains shall be used." "That my mental forces will increase, and that I will have complete control and mental discipline over them."* Repeat this time after time, but not in a mechanical way, but full of the deepest feeling and faith in the expansion of consciousness. This thought should be given to the higher mind to store away on rising, a few minutes at noon, and again before retiring. After keeping consciousness for a moment or so on this unawakened center concentrate on it and see with the mind's eye movements taking place in this new mass of grey matter. Several writers have stated that they have felt their brains move when they were full of ideas, or felt particularly full of vim and buoyancy and often after certain foods.

Sometimes new ideas have produced excessive brain activity, but this can only occur in those cases where the training laid down for stilling the brain has not been followed. *Poise and power rightly go together.* They are really complimentary, and until the student has had some measure of success with the former he is not likely to be remarkable in the latter.

The uprising of new forces in the brain must be watched and trained in accordance with the instructions laid down further on in this work, and the faithful student will often be pleased to detect a feeling of exhilaration pulse through his mind, and he will know that mental virility and discipline is beginning to make itself felt. Originality and brilliancy are both possible where the conditions dealt with here are observed. When one mind follows another its thinking is commonplace and normal. *Thinking along the same lines as other people never permits your mentality to expand far.*

Originality can only take place where the consciousness seeks the upper regions of the mind. In the lower are all the commonplace, ordinary types of thought. Just as the atmosphere becomes rarefied at high levels, so the thoughts at high mental levels look at things from new standpoints. The imagination dwells on these higher levels, and if one wishes to soar above the well-named *common* sense, in the realms of the *finer* senses he has only to train his imagination, which is always done when the mind tacitly admits that there are higher thought currents and wills that his mind may reach them.

If a man expects to be always commonplace he will not put the mind in that position in which it can avail itself of the higher currents. The writer is always suggesting that the best books of all ages should be cultivated, as one will be weaned from the usual views of life and things, and see things through the eyes of great men. Indeed, to study the biographies of great men will not only prove an incentive to tread a similar path, but one will occasionally come across ideas which will illuminate *Lord Roseberry's* phrase respecting *Oliver Cromwell* as a "practical mystic." Hitherto many people have considered the practical psychologist as a neurotic, unpractical day-dreamer, but the idea is gaining force that one can enter the highest realms of being of which the mind can conceive and bring therefrom material that can be fashioned or adapted to the daily life.

The views of later thinkers concerning genius have undergone very great changes, and the most illumed minds now admit that the genius is no different in kind from his fellow-man, but only in degree. The man or woman that wishes to grow to the height of a genius can enlarge their mental capacity daily until they come in contact with the upper reaches of the sea of mentality, which is filled with the higher vibrations. Genius does not seem so far removed from us when we see how it is possible to mould character, master one's weaknesses, and enlarge one's consciousness and the more originality is adduced the more one tends to genius, as it is only a large measure of originality. The greater worlds around us, which we fail to cognize with our present limited senses, lie open to the inspection of those using what really is the super-conscious mind, the mind employed by all great men. This mind is only an extension of the everyday mind, the normal consciousness, much in the same way that the subconscious is. All who would attain beyond the present confines will find in *Scientific Concentration, True Faith* and *Belief* in one's self for success, the *Master Key* to the *Great* Powers within the human soul and mind.

The Master Key

Part Two

CHAPTER XII.

SCIENTIFIC CONCENTRATION.

ATTENTION AND MENTAL DISCIPLINE.

INTRODUCTORY TO PART TWO.

Attention is the great puzzle of *Psychology* and *Mental Science,* and very few of so-called authorities can say what it really is. Like the term "Consciousness,"* it cannot be defined by some, while with others its meaning can only be indicated.

Psychologists usually distinguish two kinds of Attention. First—Spontaneous, or Non-Voluntary Attention (as when something forces itself upon our notice), and, Second—Voluntary, or Conative Attention. Now it is this Conative Attention —the striving after a definite end—*which demands Concentration.*

Concentration is therefore attention with a definite aim. It

---

*Conscience is a collective of moral conceptions developed into self-realization, which, at a given moment, exists in the understanding to serve as a guide for the proper actions and conduct of life.

Some people have no conscience, while another has a tender conscience. Conscience in some often becomes atrophied, while in others it is cultivated and refined by individual and collective education and experience.

Conscience, like character, varies in different individuals according to their religion, education and mentality.

Business conscience is not always the same everywhere.

There are business men in the rural districts and certain communities who are uneducated; however, commercial honesty is often scrupulously practiced among them. They, while not as well educated as some of their fellow men, pride themselves on their individual honesty.

There is a class of city business men who, in spite of scientific, artistic, literary and commercial development, their moral conscience seems to have become atrophied. Again, among certain high class and successful business men, commercial honesty is proverbial.

involves, First—Volition (Will-Power) both before and during the attention-process; Second—Self-Control, that is, the power to keep the body still during the Attention-process; Third—Thought-Control, that is, the power to exclude all thoughts that have no bearing upon the phenomenon or subject-matter to which you are attending; Fourth—The power to feel or *create* interest in the object of attention.

Concentration may be said, therefore, to be *a particular attitude of mind,* popularly termed the attentive attitude, *directed towards some conscious end.*

The scientific treatment of any subject should be of such a nature that it teaches us to observe accurately, to analyze and classify its facts; it must also be explanatory. This standard, so far as it is possible in a system designed for popular use, is upheld in this work.

In one sense, this Course of Lessons may be said to be *normative;* that is, to define, or hold up a *norm,* standard or ideal of concentration; but primarily it is more on the lines of *a practical science*—it aims to teach the student *"to know how to do;"* that is, it lays down the rules for the attainment of *Concentration and Mental Discipline.*

The power of concentration can be trained to a high degree of perfection, and the author can assure students that if they will practice the exercises contained herein faithfully, in a spirit of thoroughness and earnestness, they will soon find their power of concentration growing—a power which they can extend to all the activities of life.

Students are admonished that there is no such thing as failure if they are earnest and sincere. *Success comes to the faithful.*

The student is reminded to study carefully the Lessons in Part Three on Attention, Observation and Interest; and also the Section on Fatigue in Lesson Seventeen.

DIRECTION FOR PRACTICING.

The student should practice each exercise in Lesson Eleven. When you begin studying Lesson Twelve omit practicing the exercises in Lesson Eleven (except Exercise No. 1), and confine your attention to the exercises in Lesson Twelve only.

Follow the same course when you begin studying Lesson Thirteen. Omit practicing the exercises in Lessons Eleven and

Twelve, and confine your attention to the exercises in Lesson Thirteen.

When you start studying Lesson Fourteen do as above, and confine your attention to the exercises in that Lesson.

After you have gone through all the Lessons pick out from each Lesson the most important exercises, say one exercise from each Lesson, and practice these diligently each day for a month.

When you find you have a grip of any one or two exercises, drop these and take up others, until at length you feel that you have a fair grip of all the exercises.

You will find that you cannot possibly practice all the exercises each day, for it would demand all your time, therefore make a selection of those exercises which you find benefiting you, and gradually take up others as directed.

As time goes on, endeavor to make exercises for yourself, as this will keep your interest fresh. Never let an exercise tire or exhaust you; let it alone for a time and take up one more congenial to you.

Remember, in all your exercising there must be no strain or tension of mind. Go about everything calmly and quietly; see that your breathing is natural, and never attempt to hurry results.

Concentration can only be acquired gradually by faithful practice. Like every other study, it must proceed step by step.

When you feel an exercise tiring you, drop it and take up another. Do not attempt too much at first; practice each exercise per day, for a few minutes only.

Do not practice when your mind is on other matters; no good concentrative work is done then. You will find that the better your health the better you will concentrate; therefore, guard well your health.

Do not let difficulties discourage you; if you are in earnest, you will overcome them in time.

The most difficult stage in concentration, just as in most studies, is the elementary; after it is passed and a measure of control obtained, you will find concentration one of the most natural things in the world to you.

Persevere then; conquer all difficulties, and you will say in the end, "It has been well worth the while."

The Master Key

CHAPTER XIII.

LESSON ELEVEN.

SCIENTIFIC CONCENTRATION.

ATTENTION AND MENTAL DISCIPLINE

SUMMARY OF LESSON ELEVEN.

The object of the Exercises in Lesson Eleven is to calm both mind and body (which forms the basis by which you gain control over both); to cultivate the Senses, and to acquire the habit of attention. You are thus introduced to Concentration in a simple and easy manner, asking nothing very difficult from you.

The student must endeavor to carry out faithfully the exercises in this Lesson, as all his or her building must be done upon it. Unless you obtain some measure of success over the exercises given in this Lesson, you cannot expect to succeed in the difficult exercises given in the following Lessons.

In practicing the exercises on the Senses students are reminded that the real object is not so much the *development* of the Senses, but rather the acquirement of the *habit* of attention; that is, a particular mental attitude. Concentration, *per se,* has nothing to do with better hearing or better vision— these are merely resultants.

ESSENTIALS OF LESSON ELEVEN.

In these "Essentials" your attention is drawn to the many things which you can concentrate upon in your daily life. Such practice will greatly aid you in acquiring the habit of attention and will tend to make easier the concentration demanded in study or in business.

You are to pay attention to your unimportant acts, so that you may break away from habits which make it impossible for you to concentrate upon important matters. Begin from now to pay attention to the following little things:

First—Pay attention while dressing, while you are putting your shoes on, while shaving (if a gentleman), while washing yourself, and while brushing your hair.

Second—Pay attention while eating your food. *Do not read while eating.* If conversation is going on around you, and you are obliged to enter into it, do so, but with the main thought on the act of eating.

Third—Pay attention while at your recreation. Drop all thought of business or study. You are out for enjoyment now, therefore take it easy—drop everything else and lay aside business affairs.

Fourth—The important point in doing any of these things is to attend to ONE thing only. Thus, when dressing, do not wonder what you are going to have for breakfast, or how you are going to spend the day. Think these out, if you like, before you rise. Say to yourself: "I am dressing" (this directs the attention of the mind to the fact); "I must dress quickly."

You will be surprised how much time you waste on dressing, or any other of the acts which I have enumerated. A good way to test this is to take your watch and time yourself how long each act takes you to perform. Note down the time in your note-book and then commence to concentrate on each act daily. You will soon find yourself beating your old records.

One student, a stenographer in the employ of a bank, found he spent twenty minutes in copying letters of a certain number of lines from his shorthand notes. He concentrated upon this work and to his great astonishment found it only occupied him fifteen minutes, and the work was better done.

Thus, over this one act he had been wasting five minutes. This is now a common experience with students; many report a great saving of time in performing certain work—time which they can, and do, use in other ways.

But now a word of warning—do not rush madly to beat your former times of doing any of these acts; always keep in mind that in concentration there must be no strain, no excitement, no worry, only confidence.

You must be cool, calm and collected in everything you do; and remember, before you undertake anything, to keep this attitude in mind. Say to yourself: "I am cool, calm and collected. I shall do my utmost to do this act well and quickly, but I shall not attempt to force myself or use strain; everything shall be done calmly and quietly."

You will find that everything you do will eventually be characterized by this spirit of calmness, coolness and collectedness—and everything will be much better done than formerly.

EXERCISE NO. 1.

RELAXING MIND AND BODY.

The first essential in concentration is to still the senses, to get quiet, to suspend confused mental activity. In the past, in common with the vast majority of mortals, you have obeyed the dictates of your mind. You have never realized its ceaseless activity and enormous power. It is, therefore, the object of this exercise to introduce you to the threshold of your mind world. You must learn the hidden powers of your mind, and then try to direct those powers.

For the purpose of this exercise you should select your bedroom, where you are assured privacy, for you must be by yourself, away from everyone. Lock your bedroom door and lie down on the bed. Lie in the middle of the bed, relax, and stretch your feet down as far as they will go. Next stretch your arms out, and be sure your head is on a level with your body; that is, not resting on a pillow. Raise your head and let it fall back on the bed as if (your head) did not belong to you. Do this three times and then let the head rest where it falls.

Now raise one arm and let it fall in the same manner, three times. Do the same with the other arm and then with each leg. Now lie perfectly still and try to think of no particular subject. Let the mind wander where it likes, but *do not let it pursue a train of thought*. The best plan is to think—"I am resting, just resting, that is all." After fifteen minutes, rise.

This is a most important though very simple exercise. Its object is to steady the nerves, to quiet the mind, to relax the muscles, and to give you tone. Once you come to realize the peace and the good this exercise will bring you, you will value it accordingly and practice it when wearied or worried. You will find, probably at first, that all your body will rebel at the inactivity, but this will prove to you the necessity for the exercise.

This exercise is the foundation of some very difficult exercises, and should be carried out every day, until it gives way to the exercises founded thereon.

EXERCISE NO. 2.

CONCENTRATING ON THE SENSE OF SIGHT.

This exercise is a great favorite with all students of concentration, partly on account of its simplicity and partly on account of the benefits to be derived from it.

Get a sheet of note-paper and in the center make an ink spot about half the size of a quarter dollar. Pin the sheet on the wall of your room and sit in your chair about eight to ten feet from the sheet, which should be on a level with your eyes. Then, without making a single movement, gaze at the spot steadily and count slowly and mentally up to one hundred. Do not mind if your eyes blink—the object of the exercise is to concentrate your mind on the counting. Try to think of the counting to the exclusion of everything else; that is, do not allow your mind to drift to any other subject.

This exercise, simple as it looks, requires considerable effort on the part of a beginner to keep the mind fixed on the counting. Do not count beyond one hundred till your mind gets used to the exercise, which will, perhaps, not be for a week or so. Afterwards you can extend, but do so gradually. Breathe naturally while counting (this is important). This exercise is one of the "Oh, I can do that easily" kind, *till you find that it is not quite so easy as it looks.*

The difficulty lies in the monotonous character of the counting, which does not prevent an active mind from carrying on a train of thought at the same time; and then other thoughts enter the mind, and finally you find you are not counting at all. Should, however, you be able to complete the counting, you will find when you review the mental process *that a few thoughts did cross your mind.* You will find it very difficult for a time to keep them out, but you should keep at the exercise till you *can keep them out—all of them.*

Do not at first practice this exercise more than twice a day. Only harm will come if you force matters. In time, the mind will be gradually got under control, and you will do the exercise easily.

A good time to test yourself at this exercise is after some one has annoyed you, or after you have heard or read some interesting piece of news. Then you will find the mind struggle to take your thoughts off the counting, and you will find that it will take you all your time to come off victor.

EXERCISE NO. 3.

EXERCISE IN ATTENTION.

You will find this exercise very valuable for the development of *Mental Discipline* and also in the training of your powers of observation. The regular practice of this exercise (and it is one that you can practice almost anywhere) will make you observe things that escape the eyes of most people. You will find, also, that you will observe when outside automatically, and moreover, you will be able to bring back to your memory what you have observed, should you ever require it.

Choose any little thing such as a lead pencil, a pen, a pen-knife, a key, a match-box, or a coin. Take it up in your hand and note the time at which you took it up. Commence now to examine the article. Let us say you have chosen a fountain pen. Examine it carefully all over as if you were bent on knowing everything concerning it. Do not hurry; no matter what the article is you choose, it should take you five minutes at least to go carefully over it.

Now to come back to our supposed choice—a pen. Note first the nib; what it is made of, its shape, the name of the pen, its maker, any scratches or inkstains upon it. Then examine the holder; note what it is made of, its shape, any name upon it. Then go over its surface carefully, noting each little scratch or dint. After you have finished your examination, see how long it has taken you and note down the time in your note-book. As your powers of concentration* develop you will find your examination of articles take you longer, and yet it will seem shorter. This is a good sign—watch for it.

Observe, you are not merely to stare at the pen. You must keep in mind that you are making a thorough overhaul of it. Do not allow your mind to stray from your task. At first, of course, you will find it do so, but bring it back again and again until you conquer. Trivial as this exercise may seem, you will find it a valuable one. It will train your powers of observation and you will extend these in other situations where they will stand you in good stead.

Choose a fresh article each day, for this will sustain interest—a very important feature for beginners in concentration, as indeed in every new study. As soon as you find the exercise tiring you, or making you feel drowsy, drop it for that day.

Sit perfectly still during this exercise. Use only such muscles (those of the hands and eye) as are absolutely essential to its performance. Keep also in mind the calm attitude.

This exercise is specially valuable for business men and women, as it cultivates observation, and that calm, cool, collectedness which tells so strongly in business.

EXERCISE NO. 4.

CONCENTRATING ON THE SENSE OF SMELL.

It is an established fact that concentration intensifies the powers of the senses to a remarkable degree. Very few people

---

*A watch-maker, and those who do watch repairing, knows, as the result of constant concentration, all parts of a watch, and can mentally picture its entire mechanism.

pay any attention to this in an ordinary way, therefore you should train your senses as you would train any other part of your organism.

In most people the sense of Smell is fairly keen and there is no desire on their part to cultivate it. It should be noted, however, that when you exercise your olfactory powers you generally adopt a peculiarly attentive attitude. Especially is this so when you are unable to locate a certain odor, or where you are uncertain of its nature.

Students should note this attitude when trying to detect, or to discriminate between odors. We seem for the time being to shut off every other thought from the mind but that of the odor.

As a means of acquiring the attentive habit of mind, students should analyze the different odors which assail their olfactory nerves. Concentrate upon odors when in the country, or when entering a house (as the smell of cooking, the quality of the air contrasted with that outside) when entering shops (a chemist's, for example).

Experiment also with perfumes or toilet waters sprinkled on a handkerchief, taking care that none gets on your hands or person. Note how the olfactory nerves are influenced by fatigue, i. e., how the intensity of the smell seems to grow less after a time.

Try to describe the different odors—their character, intensity; and also their effect upon you. Such practice, from time to time, will increase greatly your power of attention and it is practice that you can put into operation without interfering with your work, business or studies; for it can be done, mostly, as you go about from place to place.

EXERCISE NO. 5.

CONCENTRATING ON THE SENSE OF HEARING.

The following exercise is intended to develop the sense of hearing by concentrating upon it. If you practice it daily you will find your hearing become much more acute.

Get a small clock with a loud tick, such as an alarm clock, and put it on the mantel-piece in your bedroom. Then gradually walk backwards from the room, a step at a time (slowly is essential), listening intently the while to the tick of the clock.

As you find the tick growing fainter, walk more slowly, and when you reach the spot where you can no longer hear the tick, take a note of the place where you are standing, and see if you can reach a more distant spot a week or two later. Do not neglect to see that the clock always occupies the same position on the mantel-piece.

The great point to attend to in this exercise is the listening attitude. You must keep your ears on the stretch, as it were, for the sound of the tick, and (very important), never allow yourself to think of any other thing but the tick. Simple as these exercises of the senses seem, very few people can do them right away, for their minds *will* stray to other things.

You can, and should, extend this exercise of hearing to your walks outside. Go somewhere and listen to the great variety of sounds around you. Then pick out one sound and try to confine your attention to it for a few minutes. If you do this constantly in your walks, it will add a purpose to them, and you will find, unless there is organic disease, that your hearing will be greatly strengthened.

EXERCISE NO. 6.

EXERCISE IN ATTENTION.

The following is an exercise in attention. It is very, very simple, and yet you will find it makes a fair demand on your concentrative powers.

Take a column in a newspaper, and commencing at the top, cross out with a pen or pencil every letter O you come across. Go faithfully from the top of the column to the bottom. The simplicity of this exercise hides its real character. You will find that the attention *will* grow weary, that the letters will appear to run together, and your thoughts *will* wander away from what you are doing, unless you are able to concentrate. Now this you must try to prevent.

Say to yourself every time you find your thoughts straying —"All I am thinking about is to mark out each letter O. I am not thinking and must not think of anything else." When you have mastered this exercise, and by mastery I mean can keep your mind solely on blotting out the O's, you have made a big stride towards concentration.

The grand thing about this exercise is that you can practice it in so many places; at home, on your way to work or business, while sitting in train, automobile or car; in your lunch or dinner hour or at a theater between the acts, etc. Remember, however, to drop the exercise as soon as you find yourself growing really tired. Five minutes at it is sufficient for most students who have not had training in concentration.

It is a good plan to go over the same column on the following day, and count the number of O's omitted. If you will keep a record of these you will be able to note progress. Thus the fewer the O's omitted the better your attention will have been.

EXERCISE NO. 7.

CONCENTRATION WHILE COUNTING.

Select a clock with a loud thick, such as an alarm clock. Sit in your chair and listen to the ticks for a minute or two, and then begin to count silently; that is, inwardly, up to 200 ticks. You will notice that the tick in an alarm clock is fairly quick, so you must learn to count fast.

As soon as you have got accustomed to the quick tick, which you call one tick, commence to count, but do not look at the clock, or you will defeat the object of the exercise. As you count, gaze at the ceiling, then at the floor—anywhere, in fact, but at the clock. As you gaze about do not think of any of the objects you are looking at; that is, attempt to deny them entrance to your consciousness. Think only of the counting; nothing else.

This simple exercise is a splendid one for beginners, for the eye and ear fight for mastery. The eye sends message after message to your brain concerning the things it sees, and the ear also sends its messages of what it hears. One of these two senses will win the fight. You must make the ear the winner by refusing to attend to the messages of the eye. By proper attention and concentration you can master it.

EXERCISE No. 8.

CONCENTRATING ON THE SENSE OF TOUCH.

Blind people have developed the sense of touch to a remarkable degree, many being able to tell a piece of money simply by feeling the coin.

A very interesting touch experiment, and one which tends to cultivate the attentive attitude, is to try and detect the cold spots on the palm or back of the hand, or on the cheek or brow.

Take a lead pencil, with the point fairly blunt, and draw it gently over the palm of the hand. As you draw the pencil slowly over the palm surface, every here and there you will experience a sudden sensation of cold. These parts are the cold spots, and it is owing to these that the sensation of cold is carried by the nerves to the brain. If you mark these spots with colored ink you will get a chart of the cold spots on a given surface.

There are also warm spots, detected by dipping a steel knitting needle with a blunt end in warm water, then wiping it dry and drawing it over the palm-surface, in the same way as with the lead pencil. The warm spots, however, have not the same intensity as the cold spots.

Students can also cultivate the sense of touch by touching articles in the dark, or with the eyes closed. It is often *very* difficult to describe the nature of an article touched in a dark room, or when the eyes are blindfolded.

These exercises in concentrating on the senses will greatly benefit you, not only in concentration, but in making your senses keener, thus adding to your means of knowledge. For, remember, all knowledge is only gained by *synthesizing impressions* received through the different senses. Unless these impressions are clear and definite the work of thought is hindered and advancement in knowledge retarded.

EXERCISE NO. 9.

CONCENTRATING ON THE SENSE OF TASTE.

Students should cultivate the sense of taste by paying particular attention to the taste of the various kinds of food while at their meals. Very few people have a keen sense of taste, which is mainly due to their eating their food in a hurried manner.

To concentrate upon taste while eating anything tends to excite the salivary glands, thus aiding the process of digestion.

Students should note, too, that different parts of the tongue give different sensations of taste. Experiment and see which part gives the greatest intensity. Note, also, that the middle

• or center part of the tongue surface gives *no* sensation of taste. Try this. Put a grain of sugar or of salt in the center of your tongue and you will find that you can detect no sensation of sweetness or saltness.

Children have a much keener sense of taste than adults. The middle part of the tongue of a child, as also the mucous membrane, gives sensations of taste which are non-existent in the case of adults.

Expert tea-tasters have cultivated the sense of Taste to a high state of perfection. Some tea-travelers are so expert that they can pick out their own sample out of a dozen and more different sample cups of tea.

Always remember that the ultimate aim of all the exercises is to develop attention, i. e., concentration, without the strain which always accompanies it in the untrained man or woman.

EXERCISE NO. 10.

CONCENTRATING ON THE NERVES.

Lie upon your bed, thoroughly relaxed (see Exercise No. 1), and concentrate your mind upon your body.

Try to become conscious of the beating of your heart, the murmuring in your ears, the sound of your breathing. Do not pay the slightest attention to any other sound, say of an outside nature. Next concentrate upon the various parts of your body, such as the head, the feet, the arms, the legs; then the lungs, the heart, the bowels, the liver, the kidneys and other bodily functions.

Think that through these various parts and organs the blood is flowing and carrying life and health to every part; try to make your thinking so vigorous, so real, that you can actually feel the blood coursing through your system.

Say, now, to yourself: "I am alive; every cell in my organism thrills with life; every part of me is filled with vitality." Picture yourself standing up a perfect type of bodily strength, strong in mind and strong in body. Literally realize it with all the intensity of mind and soul.

This is a grand exercise to take just before going to sleep and before rising in the morning. Not only will it improve your concentrative powers, but you will find it will greatly improve your health, for you will find, as you advance, that the body is but a reflection of the mind—that as you habitually picture yourself in mind, so will you tend to become in body.

EXERCISE NO. 11.

EXERCISE IN VOLUNTARY ACTION.

Sit back in your chair and twirl your thumbs. Do it slowly and keep your gaze fixed on your thumbs. Do not think of anything but the twirling.

To fix your attention, if you find it difficult to prevent thoughts coming into your mind, count up to one hundred. After twirling the thumbs in one direction, twirl in the opposite direction.

This exercise is very simple, yet it makes demands upon you, for you will find it difficult to keep your thoughts solely on the twirling. Do not do this exercise in any public place; it is meant for your own room or anywhere where you are free from observation.

EXERCISE NO. 12.

CONCENTRATING ON SLEEP.

A very good exercise in concentration on sleep is the water method. The simplest is as follows:

Put a glass on a table in your room and fill the glass full of water. Now take up an easy position in a chair alongside the table and gaze into the depths of the water. Sit with your back to the light. At first, simply gaze into the water and think of its cool, calm depth.

Try to bring yourself to a quiet, firm realization that your whole physical body is taking on the calm, cool conditions of the crystal like water within the glass.

Many people sit by a stream of running water for hours. This has a quieting effect on the nerves and many times causes sleep.

Again, while gazing within the glass of pure, clear crystal like water, hold the thought of sleep and health and see if you can induce the on-coming of drowsiness and sleep.

Never mind if you cannot concentrate on sleep strong enough the first few exercises to become sleepy; this will come later if you continue the exercises faithfully. The object of this exercise is to simply keep the mind to a train of thought of sleep and quietness so as to greatly strengthen the entire nervous system. By being able to concentrate on sleep you will be able to calm the mind and render it passive and quiet at the dictates of your will.

THE INDUCTION OF SLEEP.

For the induction of sleep several concomitant conditions are necessary, chief among which are an exhaustion of potential interest, and the presence of monotony. The induction of sleep is the resultant of these joint conditions. Other conditions, of course, are more or less essential and conducive to sleep, such as a peaceful state of mind, a comfortable posture, absence of bodily pain, external excitement, etc. There are exceptions, however. Persons accustomed to sleeping in the midst of great noise and excitement find it extremely difficult to go to sleep where there is perfect silence. The faculty of imitation also helps to bring it about. When we see others dozing we are naturally inclined to follow their example, and at night the consciousness that all around us are asleep disposes us to seek the same condition. Talking about sleep is apt to induce somnolence, just as talking about food may provoke hunger. Monotonous sounds, such as raindrops falling upon the roof, or the breaking of wind tossed waves upon the seashore, tend to encourage slumber. Monotonous repetition of sleep Suggestions have a decided tendency to induce sleep. The unvarying accents of an unskilled lecturer is an instance of the effects of monotonous repetition. Muscular repose is also, as a rule, a necessary preliminary to sleep, though there are many instances of soldiers and others who under circumstances of exceptional fatigue and excitement have not been prevented from sleeping in the most strained and uncomfortable positions, amid the continuous roar of battle or the blustering of a fierce gale.

The transition from the walking to the sleeping state and *vice versa* is often sudden, but generally there is a noticeable gradation. To illustrate: a man sitting in an arm-chair *"dozes,"* but is brought back to a partial degree of consciousness by his head falling forward.

The Master Key

CHAPTER XIV.

LESSON TWELVE.

SCIENTIFIC CONCENTRATION.

ATTENTION AND MENTAL DISCIPLINE.

SUMMARY OF LESSON TWELVE.

To some students **Lesson Twelve** will prove more interesting than Lesson Eleven, since it gives more physical work and results are, perhaps, quicker seen.

Every student is advised to give some practice to Exercise

No. 15, as it is one that, like Exercise No. 23, has a marked effect upon character.

Students are requested to note the last paragraph in Exercise No. 19, and also the last paragraph in Exercise No. 20.

Again, the student should now begin to find his interest in Concentration and Mental Discipline growing, for he will begin to realize the important part it will play in his life if faithfully followed.

If ever you feel discouraged with the results of any exercise, please do not say to yourself: "I shall *never* master this." Say rather: "I *shall* do this better next time." *Believe* this as you say it, and you will find that you *will* do it better next time. This attitude is in accordance with the Law of Habit.

ESSENTIALS OF LESSON TWELVE.

There are certain little things which are fatal to Concentration and Mental Discipline in the highest sense, and these little things are things of which nearly every man and woman is, in some degree, guilty.

The *first class* comprises those people who cannot keep their hands still; who are always pulling at their watch chain or coat, or induling in little tricks of speech or gesture, or who move backwards or forwards in their chair when talking to you. This class also comprises people who delight in beating the floor with their foot, tattooing on desk or table with their fingers, biting their finger nails, twirling their mustache, etc.

The *second class* comprises all who worry over the merest trifle; who are irritable and nervous, so that they start at the least sound.

The *third class* comprises those who fire up at the slightest thing; who never, in the least degree, attempt to control their anger.

Now all the above are signs of a lack of self-control, and you, as a student of concentration, must stop any of the above acts of which you may be guilty.

An excellent plan which the student can adopt is to repeat the following affirmation every day. Even should you be, at present, absolutely guiltless of any of these signs, you will find the affirmation do you good, inasmuch as it will be a perpetual reminder to you to guard against them, and so preserve your self-control.

AFFIRMATION.

"From henceforth I shall guard against any defects of speech, or gestures which formerly characterized me. I shall not worry over trifles. I shall not be nervous or irritable. I shall not give way to passion. I shall be calm and self-controlled under all circumstances. From henceforth I am free from all these signs or acts *which show a lack* of self-control."

Repeat this affirmation with great earnestness every day, or several times in the day if you can, and try to *mean* and *carry out* what you say. Understand and realize thoroughly all it means and you will soon feel a difference in yourself—*a difference which others will quickly mark and cause them to have a greater sense of respect for you.*

EXERCISE NO. 13.

CONCENTRATION FOR CONTROL OF MUSCLES OF THE ARMS.

Get a sheet of note-paper and in the center make a black spot the size of a half dollar. Pin the paper on the wall of your room on a level (standing) with your eyes. Then stand away from the sheet a distance of from eight to ten feet, and extend your arm in the direction of the sheet. Keep the hand perfectly straight and point the second finger until it exactly covers the black spot.

Now if you run your eye along your arm to the fingers, just as in sighting when firing a rifle, you will notice if there is the slightest wavering of the second finger. Do not watch the hand; watch the tip of the second finger. If there is the faintest quivering of the arm the finger tip will show it.

What you must do is to try to keep the finger tip exactly in the center of the spot. At first you will find the arm very unsteady, but with practice you will soon find yourself gaining control over it.

You will find this exercise very tiring to the muscles of the arm, therefore, for the first week or so do not practice it longer than a minute at a time. You can practice several times a day if you feel inclined, but at each time do not extend its duration beyond a minute. When you are fairly successful at the minute stage, extend the time until you can hold the arm perfectly steady for five minutes. Practice first with one arm and then with the other.

This is an excellent exercise for any one, but it is especially good for all who wish to excel in shooting, penmanship or anything where steadiness of the hand and arm is required. Golfers will find benefit from this exercise. Remember to breathe naturally when doing this exercise. Take your mind off the arm now and again and see if your breathing is all right. This is absolutely essential. Retention of the breath means strain, and this you must avoid.

EXERCISE NO. 14.

EXERCISE FOR CONTROL OF MUSCLES OF THE LEG.

Put a coin down on the floor and stand away from it a distance of two feet. Stand upright with your hands by your side. Then raise and extend your leg until the toe of your shoe is immediately over the coin. Do not let the toe of your shoe go over the edge of the coin—try to keep it exactly on a line with the edge of the coin. Watch the toe, and see if you can detect any movement of the foot.

This exercise, also, is tiring, and should, like the arm exercise, be restricted to a minute or two at a time during the first week or so. When you have a fair amount of control at the two feet distance, gradually extend (i. e., move away from the coin) until your distance is nearing three feet. When you are successful at this distance you should try the Wall Exercise as follows:

Take the sheet of paper you use for your arm exercise and pin it to the wall about three feet from the floor. Stand away from the wall and raise your foot until the toe of your shoe covers the spot on the sheet. Gradually heighten the sheet until the spot approaches on a level with your eye. You will find the strain on the muscles become more severe as you heighten the sheet. You must try and avoid this strain by raising the height of the sheet gradually.

Practice with each leg alternately, and remember to watch your breathing, as in the arm exercise. Do not think of anything else when doing the exercise—keep the mind fixed on what you are doing.

EXERCISE NO. 15.

EXERCISE FOR CONTROL OF MUSCLES OF THE HEAD.

Sit back at ease in your chair (an arm-chair is the best), and gaze at the ink-spot on your sheet of note-paper which you have previously pinned on the wall on a level with your eyes.

Sit with your watch in your hand and gaze at the spot on the sheet for five minutes. Never mind if your eye blinks. Do not move your head in the least degree, not even when looking at your watch. You can easily do this by glancing downwards, as this does not involve any movement of the head.

Concentrate all your thoughts on keeping the head perfectly still. As thoughts come into your mind, try to reject them by saying: "I must keep my head perfectly still—I must think of nothing else."

Pay great attention to your breathing in this exercise; turn your attention to it now and again and see if it is full and rhythmic. This exercise is very important and not at all difficult. It gives a sense of power and dignity to one, and is valuable in many situations in life.

The man who has perfect control of all the muscles of the head and eyes always carries weight in conversation and in business interviews. It powerfully impresses those with whom you come into contact, and as you continue to practice it gives you a feeling of calmness and restraint that will soon be habitual to you and be manifested in all you do.

Do not practice this exercise for a longer time than five minutes the first week or so; afterwards, extend to fifteen minutes.

EXERCISE NO. 16.

EXERCISE FOR CONTROL OF MUSCLES OF THE ARMS.

Take a walking stick of a fair weight and point it at some object, and run your eye along the stick so that the end of the stick covers the object. Concentrate on keeping the stick firm and steady, directly over the object.

Try this exercise at different angles for the stick. For instance, point to a star overhead, then at a chimney-pot or object of a similar height; next to an object directly on a level with the arm when fully extended straight out, next pointing to some object on the ground. Try first with one arm and then with the other.

Practice this exercise in a place where you can do it without attracting attention. Keep your mind firmly fixed on what you are doing. Breathe naturally.

EXERCISE NO. 17.

CONCENTRATION APPLIED TO READING.

Take a page in any book, or an article in a newspaper, and read it carefully with a view to seeing if there are any mis-spellings. You must read very carefully, spelling each word silently. If you do this properly, that is, slowly and carefully, by the time you have finished the page or article you will find you have no idea of what you have been reading.

Test the accuracy of your work by going over the same ground on the following day. Test it further by going over it again two or three days later. A still better test is to commence with the last word of the page or article and read backwards, examining each word carefully as you come to it. Thus suppose you were testing *this* exercise you would examine first, the word "Day," then each—it—to—time, etc.

Do not confound this exercise with the work of a proof-reader, for it is entirely different. *He* must attend to the sense of what he is reading, as well as look out for mis-spellings—*you* must concentrate solely on the mis-spellings.

This is a simple, yet excellent exercise in concentration, for it makes great demands on your powers of attention. It is also one you can practice almost anywhere and at all times. You will find, if you stick to it, that good results will follow. Give five minutes of your time to it each day.

EXERCISE NO. 18.

CONCENTRATION APPLIED TO MEMORY.

Take a picture, in a magazine or newspaper, and look at it intently for ten minutes. Note the subject of the picture and its title, if it has one. Next note the various objects in the picture and their respective positions to each other. Next observe the details in the picture. If there are men and women in it note how they are dressed, etc. Never let your mind wander for an instant from the picture and its story.

Do not tie yourself to a ten minutes' examination if you find that it is not sufficient; take what time you like, so long as you take in every detail. When your examination is complete, put the picture away and banish it from your mind by reading a book, or going for a walk, etc.

Next day, at about the same time as that in which you made your examination on the previous day, bring the picture back to your memory. Take a piece of paper and try to make a rough sketch of the picture. Never mind if it is far from being an artistic production. Never mind even if you cannot draw at all; put on the paper *some* idea of the picture.

If there is a tree, and you cannot draw one, put down the word "tree" where you think it should stand in the picture. Employ the same methods if unable to sketch in the other details. Next compare your sketch with the picture and see what details you have omitted. See also if it agrees with the image of the picture in your mind.

This is an excellent memory* exercise and will greatly develop your powers of observation. It is also an excellent exercise in concentration, for unless your concentration is good you will stand a poor chance of remembering the picture in detail. Also see Lesson Seventeen in Part Three.

EXERCISE NO. 19.

CONCENTRATING ON SENSATIONS.

You are now to concentrate on certain sensations, such as Hunger, Thirst, Cold, Heat.

Lie down on your bed, or on a couch, and commence to think of Hunger. Try to think what it must feel like to be ravenously hungry with no means of satisfying your hunger. Picture the scene till you can almost feel the pangs of hunger. Turn, then, to its opposite; imagine yourself hungry and sitting down to a splendid repast. Picture the scene as each course is brought in until finally you retire from the table satisfied.

Next concentrate on Thirst until you feel your tongue dry

*Chapter XXV., Lesson Twenty-three, "Memory—Good And Bad Memories," and, Chapter XXVI., Lesson Twenty-four, "Cultivation of Memory" deals fully with the faculty of Memory.

and parched. Then concentrate on its opposite—a splendid drink of cool, clear water, held before you. Imagine it, as Charles Lamb says, "purling over your tongue." Next concentrate on Cold until you feel shivering all over; then on its opposite—Heat, until you are all in a glow.

You will find that the sensations make splendid exercises in concentration. You will find them, too, very valuable, for you gain by them great control, and great imaginative power.

There is a further aspect from which this exercise may be viewed. Every one knows that if we turn our attention when in pain to the part affected the pain seems to increase. On the other hand, if we can succeed in turning our attention to something else than the pain its intensity tends to grow less. With practice one can gain wonderful control in this respect, and we advise every student to make the experiment and carefully note results.

EXERCISE NO. 20.

EXERCISE IN ATTENTION.

Take a sheet of note-paper, or any kind of paper, provided there is on it neither reading nor writing matter. Make a fold right round the sheet, of about half an inch, and press down the fold with your thumb nail.

Now tear off this fold right round, so that you leave a ragged edge. Next hold the sheet against a dark background so that the edge will stand out quite clear. Make a mark in one of the corners, and commencing from this mark, let the eye wander slowly round the edge of the paper until it comes back to the mark again.

Try as you go round to imagine the edge to be a series of mountains and valleys, and let the eye travel up and down these. Keep the mind on this act—do not let it stray in the . least.

The object of the exercise is to train you in attention, and you must bear in mind that to succeed you must simulate interest in what you are doing. That is why you are told to imagine the eye traveling up and down the mountains and valleys.

This exercise should be done very slowly; it cannot be done effectively under five minute. To keep the attention on it, and the interest keen, for ten minutes, shows that your power of attention is growing. ·

To some students this exercise will prove very difficult, especially if they are more inclined to physical than to mental work. Like a cyclist they want to rush round the track, but they forget that even a cyclist must control this impulse if he is to win. The man who has control over his mind is the one who knows when to race ahead and when to restrain, and who acts accordingly.

EXERCISE NO. 21.

CONCENTRATING ON VERSE WRITING.

Writing verse makes an admirable exercise in concentration, besides adding to your vocabulary. Choose at first verses simple in construction.

Where the concentration comes in is in the endeavor to find words that will rhyme. Do not mind if you cannot write poetry—all you are to concern yourself with is the rhyme; the matter can be nonsensical or otherwise, as you please.

If you find that you cannot write even nonsense verses, try to form pairs of words that will rhyme, such as, to take the very simplest, cat, mat; doll, poll; ferry, merry, etc. Proceed in this way until you can form more difficult ones.

Students must be careful to keep the mind centered on the rhymes and not to stray away to the meanings of the words, for this will tend to set up trains of thought and then mind-wandering will almost inevitably follow. This, of course, applies only to nonsense verses, or forming pairs of words.

EXERCISE NO. 22.

CONCENTRATION APPLIED TO THE BREATHING.

The following exercise on breathing is one employed with great success by the Hindus. They use it extensively as a means of attaining what they term *"perfect concentration."*

Sit in an easy position in your chair—not a reclining position; one nearly upright is the best, and therefore a high, straight-backed chair is the best to sit in.

Take in your hand a lead pencil—if you cannot get one, shape a piece of stick the size—and press one end of the pencil against the right nostril, closing it. Now take a long breath, drawing in the breath gently. It should take you eight seconds to inhale.   Next hold the breath eight seconds, and then, placing the end of the pencil against the left nostril, expel the breath through the right nostril, taking eight seconds to do it in.

Next draw in through the right nostril eight seconds, hold the breath eight seconds and expel in eight seconds through the left nostril, shifting the pencil against the right nostril for this purpose.   Keep drawing in through one nostril, then holding the breath, then expelling through the other nostril, up to twenty times—each time you shift the pencil counting as one time.   As you get control over the breath, extend gradually the number of seconds for inspiration, holding, and expulsion, up to twenty seconds; but do not alter the number of times —keep to twenty.   Also avoid all movement other than that involved in moving the pencil.   Sit perfectly still during the act of inhalation and exhalation of the breath.

Every morning immediately on rising go to the open window of a room which has free ventilation.   Fold your arms across the chest and drew the upper arms close to the side.   Stand erect; expel all the air out of your lungs.   After a short time relax your arms and hang them at the sides.   Inhale deeply through the nostrils as much air as the lungs will hold.   The action must commence from the abdomen and then distend the chest.   The inhaled air must be held within for fifteen seconds and then exhale slowly through the mouth.   Practice this not less than five times a day.   In the beginning you may feel a little dizzy and this will wear off in time.

In this exercise you are to think of nothing but the act of breathing; concentrate your whole mind upon it.   You must try to avoid strain when inspiring, holding and expelling the breath.

This exercise has an excellent effect on the nerves and respiratory system.   It gives a cool, calm, dispassionate feeling.   It is, without doubt, one of the finest modes of concentrating that anyone can practice.   It should always be resorted to when you feel under the stress of a great emotion, and when about to face a severe mental task.   Students of the Mental Sciences (Logic, Psychology, Metaphysics, etc.) and the Higher Mathematics, will find this a valuable exercise.

EXERCISE NO. 23.

CONCENTRATION APPLIED TO SELF-RELIANCE.

The following exercise is one that is so simple that perhaps you will wonder why you are asked to concentrate on it. All that it consists of is summed up in the phrase: *"Keep your mouth shut."* This sounds ridiculously easy, does it not? Yet to carry it out is, with most people, a far from easy task.

Just notice for one day all the people you meet, and you will be surprised how few keep their mouth shut—*tight shut,* I mean. Now just notice, also, the men whom you know to be men of strong purpose, masterful men, self-reliant men—you will find they are all men who keep their mouth shut—*tight shut.* This indicates Self-Reliance and Firmness.

The fact is that if you practice this exercise constantly, only opening your mouth when speaking or when at your meals, you will find yourself developing a strong will. You will look at things differently; you will feel more manly, more reliant, more determined, and all this will tend to remake your character.

The writer is not asking you to practice this exercise for your health's sake—all recognize its importance in that respect —he simply asks you to carry it out for the benefit it will bring you from a mental development point of view.

This exercise is *not* easy to the man or woman who has not practiced it; you will find that you will have to check yourself *constantly,* and shut your mouth up tight. It requires *constant* concentration until the habit is acquired, and then you will do it naturally—automatically.

In practicing this exercise students should guard against giving their face an unnatural or unpleasant expression. Check this tendency by examining your face in a mirror occasionally.

The Master Key

CHAPTER XV.

LESSON THIRTEEN.

SCIENTIFIC CONCENTRATION.

ATTENTION AND MENTAL DISCIPLINE.

SUMMARY OF LESSON THIRTEEN.

This is a very interesting Lesson, but more difficult than Lesson Twelve, for it is largely mental, and must be very carefully practiced.

Be particularly careful to avoid strain, or fatigue, in doing any of the exercises herein. *Festina lente* (hasten slowly), must be your motto, *and ever before you.*

Remember the advice given in the last Lesson about being discouraged. Never admit the thought of failure.

Every student is also most earnestly admonished to give

some practice to Exercise No. 24; it is of special value to business men and women.

Exercises No. 31 and No. 32 are invaluable to you. If you practice them in the proper spirit you will never be numbered amongst life's failures.

ESSENTIALS OF LESSON THIRTEEN.

The force of desire is one of the greatest forces in the world, and it affords excellent exercises in Concentration. The desire to tell is, perhaps, one of its strongest manifestations. I commend the following exercises to you, which, if you duly observe, will greatly strengthen your powers of Concentration, and also your power of Self-Control. (It is not the author's purpose here to go into the moral benefits which will result from their practice.)

First—If you know, or learn anything against the character of any person, never tell it to another person. That is, speaking generally, of course; special cases may demand it. This desire, in the vast majority of people, is enormous—*if you can control it, the benefits are in proportion.*

Second—If you hear an important piece of news, restrain the desire to tell it to the first person you meet. By so doing you are concentrating. You concentrate all your powers of resistance not to tell. When you feel you have command over yourself, that is, when you feel the force of the desire to tell diminish, you can then tell your news without any loss of control. It is the *impatience* of the desire to tell that you are to guard against.

Third—If a person tells you an important piece of news, which formerly would have caused you to start, jump up, or to utter some exclamation of surprise—receive the news quietly. Do not let your friend make you lose control. You will find he will be taken aback, and perhaps he will wonder if his news was really as important as he thought it was. You will find that if you practice this that it will be of enormous benefit to you, especially if you are in business. People will respect you, and you will gain a name for coolness, nerve and imperturbability—*you will gain the name of a strong man.*

NOTE:—Do not receive the news in a wooden manner; use tact, in accordance with the circumstances.

You may, perhaps, think that, strictly speaking, the above

exercises are not concentrative, but a little reflection will show you that they are highly so. *The desire to tell says*: "You must do as I tell you." Concentration replies: *"No; by giving way to desire I am losing control over a part of myself.* I shall not do this; I shall concentrate all my powers of resistance against this desire, and so preserve my self-control."

Welcome occurrences to practice these exercises and you will reap great benefit.

EXERCISE NO. 24.

CONCENTRATING ON THE FACIAL MUSCLES.

1st. Position.   Sit upright in front of your looking-glass and gaze at the root of your nose; that is, just where the nose juts out from the brow. Breathe naturally.

Concentrate your attention on the facial muscles and try to avoid the slightest movement. Keep all thoughts at bay; think only of keeping the facial muscles perfectly still.

2nd Position.   Stand upright in front of your looking-glass and fix your gaze as above. Follow the same instructions as in the first position.

3rd Position.   Stand upright in front of a high mirror with your hands down by your side. Stand perfectly motionless.

Do not practice any of these positions, at first, for longer than five minutes; gradually increase up to fifteen minutes. Watch your breathing carefully in each position.

The ability to control the facial muscles will stand you in good stead on many occasions. Its value cannot be estimated, for these muscles are always trying to betray your thoughts to others. Bad News, Good News, Surprise, Fear, Joy, all employ the facial muscles to express themselves, therefore be on your guard and exact complete obedience from your facial muscles. Remember, people judge you by these muscles as much as by what you say—therefore gain complete control over them.

EXERCISE NO. 25.

CONCENTRATION APPLIED TO READING.

Read carefully a short story, and then write a precis* of it. Or take a speech reported in the newspaper and condense it into half-a-dozen lines or so. Remember, you are to read both the story and the speech once only, noting as you go along the essentials of each.

You will find that this exercise will make great demands on your concentrative powers, for it demands keen attention, and memory to a great extent, and with these the power of abstraction so that essentials may be clearly marked out as you proceed. Remember, you cannot say that you really know a thing unless you can tell it or write it out. If you fail in the telling or in the writing, it shows weakness of concentration, and the retentive powers of your memory; therefore, your time has been wasted.

If you are a student and wish to advance rapidly, tell what you know to a congenial mind. In this way you will discover defects in your knowledge—you will find that in many points you lack clearness and definiteness. Even if you haven't anyone to whom you feel you can talk about what you have read or are interested in, do not be discouraged.

Go into your room and imagine a friend sitting opposite to you, and try to tell him what you have read or are studying. This plan will reveal many a weak point in your knowledge and speech. Especially will it try your powers of continuity, that is, the power to finish as well as you began; to round up, as it were, your subject.

You will find this imaginary conversation or exposition a magnificent concentration exercise. In the same way, if you imagine an audience in front of you, you will soon develop into a good speaker. If you wish to become a *ready* speaker,† adopt the following plan:

Write out on several slips of paper the name of subjects to speak upon. Your newspaper will supply you with plenty of topics. You should have *some* familiarity with the subjects chosen.

---

*Precis, *pra-sēē*, *S.* an abridged statement; a summary (Fr).
†If interested in Public Speaking, See *Chapter XXVIII, Chapter XXIX and Chapter XXX.*

Put your slips to one side and take one at random each day. Have your watch in front of you and as soon as the seconds pointer is at 60, commence to speak upon the subject noted on your paper. You are to speak for one minute only; as soon as the time is up you must stop.

You must not make excuses as to inability or unfamiliarity with the topic—you must strike into your subject right away. Aim at speaking without breaks—force yourself to say something. In time you will learn to think quickly, *which is the chief requisite in readiness of speech.*

EXERCISE NO. 26.

CONCENTRATION APPLIED TO THINKING.

No man can be a thinker unless he can concentrate his thoughts on the subject matter before him. The ability to think clearly should be the endeavor of every man and every woman. A good way to develop this power is to take a verse out of the Bible, or a verse of a poem, or a proverb, and try to exhaust, or at least get a rough idea of its meaning.

To give an example. Suppose we take the verse: *"To him that hath shall be given, and from him that hath not, shall be taken away even that which he hath."* At first sight this appears ridiculous. How can anything be taken away from a person who has nothing?

Now on reflection you are met with a counter argument— It is impossible for a man to possess nothing, for no-thing does not exist. Let us examine the first argument—How can anything be taken from a man who has nothing?

Every man, by faith and belief in health, possesses a measure of health, sometimes indeed so little that we may say he has no health at all; yet if this person loses faith in the little he has, it means that even that little will be taken away from him.

The principle underlying this verse is a psychological one. It means that unless a man, by having faith and belief, follows the laws that make for health, wealth, or any other desirable thing, eventually his power to obey the law will be taken away from him. Take success, for instance; every man of whom we speak as a failure possesses, potentially, the powers that would lead him to success, but if he does not, or will not exert those powers by true faith, then in time they are taken away from him.

Try this exercise on a different verse or proverb every day and you will find your thinking powers develop to a wonderful extent. You will gradually acquire the valuable power of thinking for yourself—a power which very few people seem to possess.

In concentrating on "thinking exercises," as above, remember to sit perfectly still, to breathe naturally, and to avoid all strain. If thoughts do not seem to come to you, do not worry; leave the exercise till another day. Do not sit at this exercise, at first, for longer than ten or twenty minutes. Gradually extend as your power of thinking grows.

Students should understand that the author is speaking here of "thinking," in a popular sense. There must always be a wide difference between such thinking and that of the *trained* thinker—one with a philosophical training in the niceties and exactness of language and literary subjects.

EXERCISE NO. 27.

CONCENTRATION APPLIED TO THINKING.

The following exercise will make greater demands upon you than *Exercise No. 26*. It calls into play the retentive power of memory, and requires keen concentration throughout.

Take any book which for you is fairly difficult to understand, and read it carefully for ten minutes; then put the book to one side, and for twenty minutes think over what you have read. At the expiration of the twenty minutes, try to write down, *in your own words,* an account of what you have read.

At first, if the exercise is absolutely new to you, you will find the thinking exceedingly difficult. First there will come a feeling of heat, next one of strain and fatigue consequent on your endeavor to reconstruct the subject, in your own words. Following this will come mind-wandering, and you will have to pull your thoughts back constantly, as it were, to the process of reconstruction.

The exercise is very similar, in its physical aspect, to that of lifting a heavy weight. You experience heat, muscle fatigue, and a feeling of letting go the weight—all of which proves that both exercises, the mental and the physical, can only be mastered by degrees.

This exercise in thinking is one that makes very great demands on your concentrative powers, but you will find, that if you persevere with it the constant practice will soon develop your thinking powers—in other words, your thought power and memory will grow, just as your muscle power will grow— by steady and careful practice.

EXERCISE NO. 28.

CONCENTRATION APPLIED TO MEMORY.

Here is another excellent memory exercise which demands high concentrative effort. As the concentration, so will the memory tend to be.

Read carefully a short sentence once only; *read it aloud,* for this will, in most cases, help the memory. Now see if you can write it down. Next try a longer sentence and see if you can write *it* down. Try now to write both sentences. Gradually extend as you find your memory grow—you will get good results if you keep on.

As a variation, read a sentence and mark it No. One. Then read a sentence in a totally different book, and mark it No. Two. Try now to write down sentence No. One. Other variations will suggest themselves to you.

To succeed in this exercise will mean succeeding in concentration, for you cannot obtain results without great concentration. You must keep out of mind every thought, but that on which you are engaged; never give way in the least, even though some good idea comes into your mind. To give way is fatal to concentration.

Do not be in despair if you make slow progress. Remember, you are fighting all your past inattention, and that is not overcome in a week or so. Always make a point of reading each sentence aloud—your ear is a valuable ally in the fight. This will not apply if you are deficient in auditory memory— see under "Mental Imagery" in Part Four. Also study Lessons 23 and 24, in Part Four.

EXERCISE NO. 29.

CONCENTRATION APPLIED TO BAD HABITS.

If you are a victim or slave to any bad habit, you can obtain great power over it by the following exercise in concentration:

Lie down on your bed or couch and shut your eyes, and imagine *yourself* standing in front of you.

Suppose, for example, you are a slave to drink. Imagine that you are talking to your imaginary self about the horridness of drunkenness. Then imagine you are giving advice as to how to control this awful habit. Picture to him (that is, yourself) the delights of sobriety, contrasted with the degradation of drunkenness.

Imagine you are trying to instill into him your own hatred and horror of drunkennes.. *Feel* this horror, this hatred, until your whole mind and body *thrills* with the feeling. Then, at length, dismiss him by telling him that the habit will have no power over him any more; that you will help him to overcome it, and he *will* overcome it.

If the concentration in this exercise is perfect, you will find growing up in you a hatred against the habit which enslaves you. Cases are on record where men addicted to drink have so talked to and admonished themselves in this manner that whisky made them ill whenever they took it, and they were forced to give it up.

EXERCISE NO. 30.

EXERCISE IN ATTENTION.

Hang your watch up on a nail on a level with your eye (in a sitting posture). Now sit away from the watch a distance of from three to four feet, according as your eyesight is good.

Now fix your gaze on the second hand and let your eye follow it in its travels round the minute center. Gaze for five minutes, and think only of the second hand and its journey.

This exercise will afford you an excellent test as to whether your concentrative powers are growing. When you first take up the exercise the pointer will seem to travel at a very slow rate, and sometimes you will imagine it has stopped or is going to stop. But as your concentration develops you will find that the pointer will seem to go round much quicker, until later it will seem almost to race round.

This is a capital exercise for any odd moments you do not know what to do with, such as when you are waiting for someone, or waiting for your meals to be placed on the table. In cases like this prop the watch up on the table, or hold it in your hand away from you.   Remember to keep perfectly still during this exercise—this is necessary.

EXERCISE NO. 31.

CONCENTRATION IN FAITH.

If you are a believer, you will find Faith an excellent means for developing concentration.   Even should you not be a strong believer, you may, as a student of concentration, imagine yourself as addressing your petitions to the invisible forces of life.   Many can assure you, from personal experience, that you will get results.   If you doubt, read the history of any creed, and you will find that every creed gets results by faith.

It is owing to this universality that some ascribe the answering of prayer, not to a spiritual agency, but as founded in unknown psychological laws.   You can be pragmatic, and choose according to your faith.

We will suppose, then, that you have a desire that you wish fulfilled, or that you want special guidance in a difficulty.   Concentrate your mind on this (in the privacy of your own room) and express your desire, making it perfectly clear and definite what you want.   Have absolute *Faith* shown in what way you can co-operate to have your desire fulfilled.   Everything depends upon your *Faith* definiteness; you *must* know what you want and Believe you will get it.

You will find that according to your ability to concentrate, believe and state clearly your wants, that things will come your way in connection with the thing you desire.   How they come cannot be told from a material standpoint, but thousands of people have found that they *do* come in answer to their petitions, or faith, and the author most earnestly advises you to follow in their steps.

Even should you *not* gain the thing you desire, you will greatly advance in concentration, and so, indirectly, you may gain the power to get, yourself, that which you have had faith in.

Give thirty minutes to this exercise, and remember to picture in your faith mind the thing you want, always finishing up by picturing yourself in mind, as really possessing the thing you have asked for.   Sit perfectly still during this exercise. Close your eyes if you find it more helpful.

EXERCISE NO. 32.

CONCENTRATION APPLIED TO AN OBJECT IN LIFE.

Every man and woman desires to succeed in life and the surest way to do this is to have an object in life, and to concentrate on that object daily with the faith and belief that you will gain it.

The method advised here is as follows: Sit at ease in your room, and think upon what you wish to be. Imagine you see your desired end, and then try to define, that is, make clear all the steps leading up to it. Then see your end achieved.

Try to picture yourself the successful man, or woman, you wish to be. Imagine how you would act; how you would speak. Now go over the steps again and use auto-suggestion on yourself by repeating the following:

Say: *"I can be this kind of a man. I will be this man. I am this man.* Nothing shall stop me from being a success. I know the steps I must take to reach my end, and I shall let *nothing* hinder my taking these steps. I believe I shall eventually reach my end in view. I SHALL. I SHALL." (Say this aloud.)

After you have concentrated in this manner, *try to follow and live out the character in your daily life.* Make every effort, and you will find that if you do not actually reach what you are aiming for you will certainly reach a much higher point, or position, than you would otherwise do.

By following the above plan, you will be doing consciously what many successful people have done unconsciously. These people have always had an end in view: they have concentrated upon it with faith day and night, and they have said to themselves when faced with difficulties: "I *shall* succeed. I believe I shall win. *I shall let nothing keep me back. I shall attain my desired end."*

Read biography and you will see that this is true of all really successful people. You will find, too, that Science, in the new developments in Psychology, *is in agreement with the principles here laid down.*

You will find this a grand exercise in concentration. Give one-half hour to it at each sitting. A word of warning—Do not let the exercise degenerate into mere day-dreaming; be in dead earnest all the time.

The Master Key

CHAPTER XVI.

LESSON FOURTEEN.

SCIENTIFIC CONCENTRATION.

ATTENTION AND MENTAL DISCIPLINE.

SUMMARY OF LESSON FOURTEEN.

This is a very difficult Lesson, so difficult that no student can hope to *master* all of it without sincere study, but the *attempt* to master will have valuable results; and as you begin to make a little headway it will have an important bearing on your future career.

Exercises No. 33 and No. 35 are particularly difficult and must be attacked very, very carefully. Follow instructions implicitly.

Pay particular attention to Exercise No. 39; it is one of the most important in this Volume.

Exercise No. 40 is very important, and will repay you splendidly if always acted on.

ESSENTIALS OF LESSON FOURTEEN.

The author wishes to speak to you here of several things which detract from attention and so hinder perfect concentration and mental discipline.

Nearly every man or woman who has a knotty problem to solve (be it one of study, business or connected with the ordinary affairs of life) is guilty of some mental weakness which accompanies the act of attending to the problem.

Some men sit smoking a pipe, and watching the smoke as it rises from their lips.   Some people cannot think the problem out without a drumming accompaniment of their hands on the table.   Some sit all bunched up, every muscle tense, and every nerve on the stretch.   Others are on the move all the time— some with every part of their body; others by walking rapidly to and fro across the floor.   All these people are thinking. They will tell you they cannot think otherwise than by following one or other of the above methods.

Now suppose that any of these people are so situated that they cannot employ any of these tricks of attention.   What happens?   They are practically helpless.   This should be *one* reason why *you*, as a student of concentration, should not employ any of these tricks.

Again, if you analyze any of these methods, you will find that none of these people attain anything approaching "perfect attention."   The attention of the smoker wanders to the wreaths of smoke, and to their manifestations of form.   The people who drum on the table, find their thoughts wandering to the table or the drumming, and so on with the other cases.

Now there is only *one* way in which perfect attention (relatively) can be gained, and that is by being perfectly still.   No matter what the problem may be you have to solve, sit down to it quietly.   Sit upright in your chair and never move a muscle.   Do not move foot, hand, finger, head, or in fact any part of your body, unless absolutely obliged to do so. BE QUIET.

At first you may not succeed so well as formerly, as your whole body will rebel; but you will find, as you keep on, that you will think better and quicker than formerly, for instead of wasting energy on the thinking you have saved it, and are now ready to act on your thinking.

If your thinking has to be long and keen, sit perfectly still with your eyes closed (if circumstances will permit), and see that your muscles are in their normal state.

Remember in all your thinking to observe the following rule: Sit (or stand, if the conditions must be such), perfectly still, every part of your body at rest, every muscle relaxed. By so doing you will think without strain, and the quality of your thinking will be higher, and the time spent much shorter.

EXERCISE NO. 33.

CONCENTRATION APPLIED TO READING.

Go into a room where a conversation is going on. Take up a book and try to read, making up your mind that you will not listen to a single word of the conversation. Say to yourself before commencing: "I WILL (i. e., determine) that I shall not hear a single word of this conversation."

Read for five minutes and then try to see how much of the conversation you can write down. Never mind if it seems disjointed. Write down what you can remember, even though it should be just a few words. Note—this is not a memory exercise, therefore, the more words you are able to write down the worse for your concentration, for it proves that the conversation has affected you, and hindered you concentrating on what you have been reading.

This is an extremely difficult exercise (not the writing down, but the ability to keep the mind closed, as it were, to the conversation that is going on around you). Especially will you find it difficult if the passage you have selected requires close attention, or where the subject is not particularly interesting.

This exercise makes great demands on your concentrative powers and is, therefore, very important. It is extremely valuable to students, or to business people, who have often to attend to intricate problems, or complicated detail, while the hum of conversation is going on around them.

To some people this type of concentration is natural, as is instanced by some authors who can write while surrounded by conversation and other distractions.

Always remember to preface the exercise by affirming that you will not hear a single word of the conversation around you. This will help you.

Seek occasions to practice this exercise. You will find them in your home, in a railway train, in a restaurant, while sitting in the park, etc. Do not be discouraged if you make slow progress; like all true progress it is a gradual process.

Some of the other exercises in this section will help you to attain this type of concentration.

EXERCISE NO. 34.

CONCENTRATION APPLIED TO MUSCLE CONTROL.

In some of the other exercises there has been directions given to control the muscles. The following exercise is to develop still further control of the muscles, but it is one that needs, at first, the co-operation of another person.

Whenever the ordinary man or woman contracts a muscle, sympathetic attraction is set up in various other muscles; this can be prevented by concentrating the mind solely on the muscles you wish contracted.

Suppose you clench your fist with the arm fully extended, and then draw your arm up to your shoulder, and suppose someone is holding your other arm—the instant you clench your fist and draw up arm No. 1 your friend will feel arm No. 2 contract sympathetically.

Now the way to overcome this is for your friend to keep lifting arm No. 2 and letting it fall, while you are contracting the other arm. By so doing the muscles become, in time, relaxed, and you can concentrate perfectly on one set of muscles in arm No. 1 without (comparatively) any sympathetic attraction being set up in arm No. 2.

Practice next with the legs, first with one and then with the other, until you have the same control over them as you have obtained over the arms. After a time you can dispense with the aid of a second party. You will find these exercises very difficult for a time, but as they are not impossible, you can look forward to conquering them.

You can easily avoid telling your friend what you are after. Tell him you have read about sympathetic attraction and are desirous of experimenting. Practice when convenient for your friend to attend.

EXERCISE NO. 35.

EXERCISE IN ATTENTION.

Lie down on your bed, stretch your feet down as far as they will go, then stretch your arms out to their full extent across the bed. Now relax. (See Exercise No. 1.)

After you have rested a minute or two, try to make your mind a blank. As each thought comes into your mind, by an effort of will, try to reject it, that is, do not follow it up and so allow a train of thought to be established. Resolutely put each thought to one side and try to think of nothing—make the mind a complete blank.

The first trial of this exercise will make you declare it impossible. It is *not* impossible, for many students of advanced concentration, especially in India, have accomplished it. Of course, it cannot be sustained for a long time, although some Indian Students declare it can. But whether long or short, it is a valuable exercise in concentration, because it develops great will-power, and thought-control.

As has been said, the first feeling is one of despair, but after a few weeks' trial you will not be so discouraged. You have much the same feeling when first you commence to learn a musical instrument. You think is impossible to make headway, but gradually the power comes, and you cease to wonder.

You must be exceedingly careful in your first attempts at this exercise. Do not practice it for longer than a minute at a time, and only once per day for the first week or so. Extend very gradually. When you can keep the mind blank for nearly three minutes you will have developed a wonderful control over your thoughts.

EXERCISE NO. 36.

EXERCISE IN ATTENTION.

Lie down as in the previous exercise, and make the mind a blank for a few seconds. Then instantly commence to think of a subject. (Decide on the subject before lying down.)

Suppose, for example, you choose health. (Never mind if at the time you are not in good health.) Try to think what it means to be in perfect health; what your appearance would be like, the pleasure it would bring, the freedom from illness.

Then, when you feel you have exhausted the subject, banish it by making the mind a blank again.   After a few seconds rise.

You should choose a fresh subject each day, such as Wealth, Power, Position, Influence, Love, Happiness, etc.   Think also of any particular ideal you should like to see realized, but never think negative thoughts, such as, Fear, Ill-health, Misery, Hate, Death, etc., for it is a law in concentration, for which there is a sound psychological basis, that what we concentrate upon, that we tend to become.

Many people take advantage of this law by concentrating daily upon their future, mapping it out clearly, and WILLING at the same time, that it SHALL come to pass.   (Exercise No. 32 exemplifies this.)

The difficulty in this exercise is to keep the mind to its subject, as, after the period of blankness, it tends to rush along at top speed.   Keep a firm control over it and never allow it to wander from the subject.   As soon as the exercise is over (15 minutes) banish from the mind the subject you have concentrated on.

EXERCISE NO. 37.

CONCENTRATION APPLIED TO DEFINING.

One of the most difficult things in the world of thought is the power to define.   Suppose you are asked to define the word chair; you will probably answer: "Something to sit on."   But you can sit on the ground, would you call it a chair?   Then you try again: "A chair is something we sit on to eat our food, or sit in to read."   But this does not tell us what the chair is, what it is made of, its appearance; you have only told us certain uses to which we put it.

You should read a book like *Davidson's—"The Logic of Definition"* and you will get an idea of the difficulty of the subject.   Or read under *"Definition"* in any good book on *Logic.*

To give a good definition makes great demands on most people's concentrative powers.   Ask yourself what a table is, or a book, desk, clock, piano, lamp, etc.   Then look up these words in a good dictionary and see how the dictionary definition agrees with *your* definition.   Of course, the dictionary definition is often far from accurate, yet for the purpose of this exercise it will, generally speaking, suffice.

In defining anything, be on your guard against merely describing it. For instance, if you were asked to define the word "Negro" and you replied: "A black man" that would not be definition, but description. A definition is the explicit statement of all the attributes of a term, and only such attributes as are implied by the name.

You will find that defining things will make your ideas distinct and adequate, and the effort will do you good, even though you fail to give a definition that will satisfy a professor of *Logic*. Practice this exercise in any spare moment.

EXERCISE NO. 38.

EXERCISE IN ATTENTION.

Take any simple word of three letters, such as, MAY, CAN, PEN, CAT, TOP, HAT, etc., and write it down in bold, black letters.

Write it in the center of a piece of clean writing paper (i. e., free from any other writing matter), and gaze steadily at the middle letter. You must try now to obliterate out of your mind the idea of the word. Concentrate solely on the middle letter.

Suppose the word you have written is MAY. Do not let the thought of "MAY" cross your mind, think only of the letter "A." You will find that the mind *will* struggle, it *will* want to take in the word as a whole, and *will* try to spell or pronounce the name mentally. This you must try to prevent.

This exercise looks very simple, perhaps, but in reality it is very difficult, and that is the reason the author has kept it back till now. It cannot be done until the mind has had a fair amount of training, such as has been given you in previous lessons. Try it on a series of words, two minutes at each, at different intervals during the day, and you will find that it is not so simple as it looks. This is an excellent exercise for anyone troubled with mind-wandering.

EXERCISE NO. 39.

CONCENTRATION APPLIED TO SPEECH.

The best way to obtain extraordinary accuracy and flow of language is to lay it down as a fixed rule to do your best on every occasion, and in every company, to impart whatever you know in the most forcible language you can put it in; and that by constant practice, and never suffering any careless expressions to escape you, or attempting to deliver your thoughts without arranging them in the clearest manner, it will, in time, become habitual to you.

This plan makes an excellent exercise in concentration, for it requires constant watchfulness, constant concentration to achieve success. The majority of people never try to express themselves well. They would be ashamed, probably, if someone were to present them with a verbatim report of any conversation they had taken part in, where they were unconscious that they were being reported, or even watched.

You should commence from today, and instead of using sentences with no character or swing about them, try to express yourself in the best language you can find in which to clothe your thoughts. But remember, do not go to the other extreme and use long words where short ones would do, or stilted, or pedantic language.

Let your sentences be simple, with no long involved phrases or subordinate sentences to try the patience of your hearers. Speak naturally (i. e., with no suggestion of artificiality), yet with strict regard to grammatical principles, and you will find that your conversation will be sought after.

Read *Boswell's "Life of Johnson,"* and you will get an excellent idea of what good conversation is, but remember to avoid some of the Doctor's errors due to his fondness of hearing himself speak.

I cannot too strongly urge upon you to pay attention to this exercise. To business men, and to professional men, it is simply invaluable, as it will mark them out from the ordinary man wherever they go, and will command the attention and respect of all with whom they come into contact.

EXERCISE NO. 40.

ERRORS IN CONCENTRATION.

The author, in this exercise, wishes to draw your attention to some kinds of concentration that are wrong, so that in future you may guard against them.

Emerson has a saying: *"If you are interested in a book, put it away."* Do you know what he meant? *He meant to guard you against concentrating wrongly.* Anything you are interested in you concentrate on naturally. The danger is that you get so interested that you do not notice the effect upon your nervous system, or the effect upon your muscles, or upon your eyes.

Always be on your guard then in reading an interesting book. Stop every now and then and note if there is any strain anywhere—especially watch your breathing, for it is the first to suffer from this wrong concentration. It is a good practice to put the book to one side in its most interesting part and concentrate upon something else. This will show you if the book is having too strong an effect upon you, for if it has, it will be impossible for you to concentrate upon anything else. Never let a book make you say: "I could not put it down till I finished it." If you do so, you have paid for the book in more than cash.

Watch your concentration in games. If you win, never let it lead you to excess; if you lose, never let it make you angry. In other words, you have concentrated wrongly on the game if it makes you too pleased, or if it annoys you. The havoc worked by wrong concentration in games, especially on the nerves, is strongly shown in chess contests. The strain on the players is something terrible, and many chess players have had to give up the game altogether, simply on account of the strain. A training in concentration would have avoided all this, and given them an enormous advantage over their opponent.

Note carefully your concentration when you are at the theater watching a play. Prepare yourself beforehand by determining that you will take special care to control your emotions. Take your mind off the play now and again and examine yourself critically. If you are all -strung up, you have concentrated wrongly. Instead of concentrating on the play, you have simply let yourself be hypnotized, and the actors have done what they liked with your emotions. Follow the same method or plan when listening to a speaker, or to a musical performance.

Watch your concentration in an argument. If it makes you lose your temper, you have concentrated wrongly. Instead of aiming at the validity of the argument and trying to confine your opponent to the same *you have handed over to him your strongest weapon, viz., your self-control.* You should concentrate upon the determination of the argument, and your desire should be that the right or truth will prevail. Whichever way the argument goes then, that is, whether you win or lose, will not matter to you—you have done what you set out to do—you have concentrated rightly.

If you follow out the principles given in this work, that is, here, make exercises of them, you will benefit in health; you will gain a reputation for calmness and coolness; you will develop your powers of concentration and mental discipline to an extent unknown to the vast majority of mankind.

HEALTH AND MENTAL FORCE.

Whatever contributes to the health, vitality, goodness of heart and soundness of mental force contributes to success in life.   Health and vitality being the leading requisites, the health habits of the student should be good, his *will* strong, while patience, endurance, perseverance and sympathies should be marked features in his character. He should have a good, full, clear eye. His gaze should be *honest*, steady and *penetrating*.

Health is largely a question of constitution—it is in-bred— "Comes by Nature." Its maintenance is requisite, but the *how* of its preservation and maintenance need not be entered upon here.* Every student's life should be governed by "temperance in all things;" he should abstain from gross foods, impure drinks and associations, cultivate the good and true within himself. I might say that early and regular habits—morning bath, simple diet, adequate physical exercise, calmness and evenness of mind, will largely contribute to successful results. As for the rest, the student must study and practice.

VITALITY.—To add and store up vitality and to make your physique appear attractive, think and practice the following:

(1)   At meal times make it a point to masticate every morsel as thoroughly as possible, and think and picture within yourself that you are extracting a good deal of strength from the food.

(2)   When practicing the breathing implant the idea in your mind that you are absorbing within you Nature's life forces in abundance.

(3)   While taking a bath concentrate and believe that you

*Those interested in the Psychology of Faith, Health and Disease should study *Lesson Thirty-two, Thirty-three and Thirty-four.*

are drawing health and strength from the water you bathe in to vivify your system and to make your physique strong.

THE WILL.—Next to health comes self-government, the development of *will* and the power to concentrate your energies. *Will* can be cultivated by the exercises given in Part Four, but the initial power of *will* will depend upon your *Concentration and Mental Discipline*. A person deficient in Firmness, Self-esteem, Conscientiousness and Continuity is not likely to have a strong will. But if, in addition to the foregoing, they have those faculties which tend to timidity, lack of concentration, want of courage, as far as *will* is concerned, they would not develop concentration.

If you grasp the elementary principles of Concentration and Mental Discipline you will be the master of the laws through which the human mind is moulded and swayed and of that intangible and subtle power which controls where even daggers fail.

"How poor are they that have not Patience!
What wound did ever heal but by degrees?"
—*Shakespeare.*

Patience and perseverance is the price of success. It matters not how unimportant these instructions may seem to you, or how simple they may appear; make up your mind to follow them in every detail; do not pass judgment upon a thing until you have given it a fair trial; remember the greatest things in life are often the simplest things. It may seem to you that the exercises are too simple to produce the astounding results which the writer claims, but if you will only give the Lessons a thorough trial you will be more than enthusiastic in your praises of them.

When you finish Part Two you will feel astounded at your success and the degree of your advancement. The salient and all-important advice is *"Learn each lesson before taking up the next."* Unless you succeed in the first and until you succeed in that, you should not take up the next lesson. If you proceed contrary to directions, the author is not responsible for your success. Remember, the instructions now laid before you are the foundation over which you will have to build the structure of success. They are THE MASTER KEY, and without it the doors of Concentration will not be opened to you. Master it well and your complete success is certain.

Self-Control is that quality in man which attracts interest, confidence, friendship and love of mankind. This is the secret of success.

"In character, in manners, in style, in all things the supreme excellence is simplicity."—*Longfellow.*

In conversation observe the following rules: Never interrupt a person while speaking; appear to pay attention and to be interested in the conversation, but do not let his thoughts produce any real impression upon you. Avoid arguments on any and all subjects, for every one has got his own opinions. Do not attract attention by either your loud talk or laughter, or show your egotism by trying to absorb in conversation. Avoid whispering or conversing in a language that all the parties may not be acquainted with. If you are gifted with wit, do not make a display of it. Do not use slangwords and never indulge in idle or ill natured gossip. Do not boast of your achievements. Never make fun of the peculiarities or idiosyncracies of people with whom you come in contact.

"Costly thy habit as thy purse can buy
But not expressed in fancy; rich, not gaudy;
For the apparel oft proclaims the man."
—*Shakespeare.*

Always be simple, neat and clean. Keep your body clean and void of any bad odor, and let your clothes be brushed and neat.

Be always polite, for politeness is the oil that lubricates society. Avoid arrogance and sycophancy. Be plain and unassuming. Study the characteristics of each and every man whom you wish to influence. Never get excited in conversation. Always be obliging and ready to assist others out of misfortunes and dilemmas. Be as agreeable to your social inferiors as to your equals and superiors.

If you are quick tempered and apt to give way to a fear of misfortune or worry, you should pay particular attention to the lessons given in Part Four, under "Will Culture."

Cultivate a frank and open manner. Always be earnest when you talk. It not only holds the attention of the people to whom you are talking, but it is also a valuable aid to you.

Cultivate an agreeable tone of voice, avoiding a mumbling utterance on the one hand and a loud, boisterous tone on the other. An excellent rule is to pitch the voice to the tone of the party with whom you are conversing, providing always that you do not shout, in order to keep pace with the other person. If the other man shouts, keep your own voice even and subdued and he will soon drop to your pitch.

The eye is the all-potent factor in influencing people. It not only seems to hold the attention of the person to whom you are talking, but it is also a power in impressing your will upon another. The eye of the man who has mastered the laws of mental control is a powerful weapon.

NOTICE TO STUDENTS.

After you have finished this Lesson, you are advised to read over again the "Hints on Practicing" given in Lesson Eleven, and follow the advice there given as to future practice.

Students whose time is limited are advised to give special practice to the "Essentials of Concentration" in each Lesson. Try to carry these out in your daily life, i. e., LIVE the exercises.

Busy students should give prominence to the following exercises: Exercises Nos. 1, 3, 15, 22, 23, 24, 32, 33, 35, 37, 39, 40. If these are practiced whenever possible students will not fail to make considerable headway in *Concentration* and *Mental Discipline*.

The Master Key

Part Three

CHAPTER XVII.

LESSON FIFTEEN.

ATTENTION.

VOLUNTARY ATTENTION—NON-VOLUNTARY ATTENTION.

WHAT IS ATTENTION?

The mind is always busy—the stream of consciousness is ever flowing; even in our sleep we are never wholly unconscious, for the mind has its sentinels ever on the watch, and our dreams are but an echo of these.

Thousands of messages are being sent to and from the brain every hour of our lives; some of these are rushed into consciousness, and as we become aware of them we are said to attend to them. *Attention of this character is termed *Non-Voluntary*. We are compelled to attend even though our attention is but momentary.

But when we deliberately turn the stream of consciousness into a definite channel and attend to one object, such attention is termed *Voluntary Attention*, and it is this kind of attention which chiefly concerns us in Concentration.

Voluntary Attention, therefore, is simply nothing else than the mind's directive power—the power to turn the stream of consciousness aside from its mad rush into a definite channel or train of thought.

Students should distinguish between the terms *"Consciousness"* and *"Attention."* *"Consciousness"* may be said to be that state of mind which results whenever sensory impressions

*See example under section *Forced Attention*.

124

produce a mental experience. *"Attention,"* on the other hand, emphasizes the selective character of the organized process of mental life.

FORCED ATTENTION.

By *forced attention* is what might be termed Non-Voluntary Attention. There are many ways in which we are forced or compelled to pay attention, as shown in this chapter.

Business of any kind tends to attract our attention. We feel compelled to notice a very tall man or woman, or anything of abnormal size. Loudness comes under this category; a loud sound commands more attention than a weak sound—it arouses attention in half the time that a weak sound will take. Shocks, or anything of a startling nature, instantly command attention. We may say, therefore, that intensity of any kind is a facilitating influence in gaining attention.

Neatness, cleanliness and orderly arrangement command more attention than their opposites; the latter fill us with disgust and our attention soon dies away. In some schools and laboratories it has been found that students pay much greater attention and do better work where all the appointments are well ordered than where these are of an indifferent character.

Expectation forces us to attend. If we are expecting a friend calling at our house, we hear and attend to every ring at the bell. The same applies when we are expecting a letter by the morning's post.

Curiosity also compels attention. If we see a crowd around a shop window we feel compelled to go and see the cause. This feeling is strong in children, and should be taken advantage of by all who are entrusted with their training.

The unusual also commands attention. Public speakers, clergymen, writers and many others take advantage of this fact to arouse attention. A certain divine, preaching once on the subject of "Sin," illustrated the rapidity of the "downward path" by sliding down (hobby-horse style) the pulpit rails. He did not have to complain of inattention afterwards.

Movement. We are more inclined to pay attention to a moving object than to a still object. Scouts are aware of this. Where it is necessary for them to raise their heads to the horizon line or sky-line (as in looking over a hill top) they are careful to raise the head very gradually and as gradually let it descend.

Pleasure. Once an object gives us pleasure it tends to draw our attention to it on another occasion. Bad habits and vices, viewed genetically, illustrate this fact.

Experience. Our past experience plays a great part in commanding our attention. A retired army officer, or a detective, for instance, will feel compelled to attend to anything which recalls his past experience. This applies to any walk of life; anything connected with an individual's experience will force him to attend to it, through the law of habit.   ·

Interest. A man who is anxious about his weight will notice any appearance of stoutness in his friends. The same applies to a man anxious about his hair; that is, turning grey, or showing signs of baldness. People who are about to furnish will notice furniture shops and the furniture in the houses of their friends. People who are about to take their holidays will notice anything relative to holiday resorts, especially where reference is made to the place to which they think of going. Students of all kinds will notice at once anything in books or newspapers bearing on their studies. And business men, also, will feel compelled to attend to anything in newspapers, etc., referring to their line of business.

NOTE.—The author particularly requests students who wish to gain control or influence over their fellows to ponder over the above points, and also make a close study of *Personal Magnetism, Chapter XXVII.; Lesson Twenty-five.* They can be—and are—made use of by business men, schoolmasters and teachers, clergymen, writers, etc., to their great advantage.

HOW INATTENTION MAY BE TURNED INTO ATTENTION.

The simplest way to turn *Inattention* into *Attention* is to see a practical gain as the resultant. Suppose a schoolmaster tells his pupils, on a day when they will all seem stupid and listless, that as soon as they finish the problems on which they are engaged they may go home; you will soon see a difference in their attitude. A stranger coming in now would pronounce them a fine lot of little fellows—*so attentive, eager, etc.* The reason, of course, is that they see personal advantage as a result of their labors.

Note.—Students who can see a practical gain—not necessarily a monetary gain—as likely to result from their work, will more than double their capacity for that work.

Notice how a new set of conditions turns *Inattention* into *Attention*. Let us suppose you are on a first visit to a certain town. You will notice that every street, building, tree, garden, the passers by—their speech, gait, dress, gestures, etc.—makes a bid for your attention; you feel you *must* attend to what is going on around you. Should you stay in the town for any length of time, your attention in this respect will weaken. Hence, familiarity tends to weaken attention, and inversely the novel or unusual stimulates it and calls forth its powers. Thus it is that when first you enter a town you will probably notice and comment upon things of which the inhabitants of the town are ignorant. After a lengthy stay you will be in much the same position; strangers may be able to point out things which *you* have never noticed.

Test the above by observation in your own city. Look at buildings of any kind and see if there is anything about them which you have never noticed before. Look at your friends and apply the same test.

Repetition tends to turn Inattention into Attention. For instance, have you ever noticed how a drumming on the table by some one when you are reading is at first almost unheard, and then it seems to steal further into consciousness, until finally it creates intense irritation? This phenomenon is termed the *"summation of stimuli,"* i. e., the power of a weak stimulus to gain attention by repetition. Advertisers make use of this fact; they know that repetition tends to turn *Inattention* into *Attention,* and so they keep their advertisements constantly before the public. Many students know the power of repetition; a text-book, which at first seemed powerless to gain their attention, by constant going over it gradually develops more and more attention, until finally interest is created.

The following, also, illustrates the power of repetition: Get a puzzle-picture and examine it carefully. Note how the hidden face, for instance, gradually unfolds itself, as it were, until finally it dominates the picture. You cannot think now that it is possible for anyone to glance even casually at the picture without discovering the face. Continued or repeated repetition therefore clarifies the vision.

The *camera* illustrates how *Inattention* is turned into *Attention.* If you examine a photograph of a landscape, you can tell at a glance what portions of the scene the photographer wished to make prominent, for that portion will stand out distinct; the other portions of the scene will be indistinct. Similarly, if you were to look at the actual landscape which the photograph illustrates, you will see clearly only those portions on which you focus your attention; the portions outside the focus will be indistinct, or not seen at all.

If you find it difficult to pay attention to anything, you can facilitate the process by preparing the sensory and motor centers.* For instance, if a friend tells you he is going to strike a note on the piano, your ears will be prepared to hear the note, and you will hear it quicker than without this preparation. Now apply this to study. Before commencing your studies, prepare the brain by a rough idea, or review, of what you are about to study. Say to yourself: "I am going to study —— text-book" (name the book). "I shall pay strict attention to it; I shall not waste time; I shall read quickly and try to apprehend as quickly as possible what I read; I am going to give *all* my attention to my work; I shall shut out everything irrelevant."

Preparation of this kind acts as a stimulus; the thinking centers—if I may so term them—and the memory centers are ready for action, and you will work with much greater rapidity and exactness.

If you find it difficult to keep your mind on what you are reading, you can make the process easier by silently articulating each word. Many people adopt the same plan in listening to a speech, a sermon, or a lecture, when they find it difficult to keep the mind in the track of the thought.

ATTENTION TO DIFFERENT OBJECTS.

There is a difference of opinion among psychologists as to the number of objects we can attend to in the same attention-process, but the majority seem to lean to the view that under such conditions we cannot attend to more than one or two objects. The power, however, varies in different individuals, depending on the natural powers of perception, and also on the amount of practice they have had, for practice greatly quickens our perceptive powers.

When objects are grouped in threes or fours, where the objects are related somewhat, we can attend to a greater number of objects. Where the objects are unrelated, the number

---

*For an explanation of these terms see under *"Interest" Chapter XIX*, Lesson Seventeen, in Part Three.

is not so large. Familiarity with the objects likewise helps
us as to the number to which we can attend; anything which
we have seen only a few times takes us longer to grasp than
that with which we have long been familiar. The student
should remember that the mind takes in each group as a unit
—the number of individuals comprising each group is the resultant of practice.

STRAIN IN ATTENTION.

Strain in attention is chiefly due to—
First—Wrong posture.
Second—Faulty respiration.
Third—Worry; the latter is the chief offender.
It is the person who worries who finds the greatest strain
in attention. Students who puzzle their brains over a problem
know the harmful effect of this kind of attention. Business
men, too, know how worry saps their energy when it enters
into the attention-processes of business.

The attitude to adopt in such conditions is to attend quietly
and calmly, and if no result can be obtained (as in trying to
solve a problem) it is well to leave the matter over if possible,
and come back to it again later on.

Students often waste precious time trying to grasp the
meaning of a statement (for which they are not prepared)
in a text-book; they refuse to leave the page and they will
worry an hour or more in a vain attempt to master the statement. The best *method* is to mark such passages and *read on.*
Often a few pages further on in the book one will come across
something which illuminates the difficult passage and you realize its meaning in a flash.

Similarly, a business man who adopts this method will
refuse to worry over business difficulties relating to details
which he cannot fit into their place. Later on in the day or
week he will often find the solution in something else which
seems totally unrelated.

Wrong Posture and *Faulty Respiration* have a great deal
to do with the feeling of strain in attention. Notice people
listening to a speaker, or watching an enthralling play, or reading an interesting book. Notice the tensity of the muscles,
the shallow breathing, the huddled up position of the body. Is
it any wonder that such people find attention a strain?

Students of this work should guard against wrong posture and faulty respiration in attention. The student who cultivates control of mind and body when listening, watching, or reading, and sees that his muscles are properly relaxed, will find the feeling of strain reduced to a minimum.

THE HABIT OF ATTENTION—HOW TO CULTIVATE IT.

To cultivate the habit of attention demands as its prime requisite an inclination to attend. Given the inclination, you must next learn to direct it and control it.

The easiest way to cultivate attention *is found in repetition;* that is to say, that which has gained the attention in the past makes further attention an easier matter. To extend the field of attention the student must always go back to the old; that is, he must always show the old in the new—he must correlate his experience.

The great difficulty in attention is to *keep* the attention riveted to its object, and the simplest way to do this is *"to make it show new aspects of itself."* Suppose you determine to keep your attention riveted on a hat for five minutes. The simplest way to do this is to ask yourself questions about the hat. What kind of a hat is it? What shape? What condition is it in, *i. e.,* does it show any marks of wear? if so, examine these; who is its maker? examine it and see if there is any name on it; what size is it? etc., etc.

Apply the same principle to business, study, or sport. Ask questions about them; ask their relation to yourself; ask what difficulties they represent and how they can be overcome. Ask other people how any of these things appeal to them—get their point of view. If you go about your questioning in a definite manner interest will be created and difficulties will vanish.

Another way to cultivate continuous attention is to *practice the dismissal of irrelevancies.* As ideas and thoughts arise unrelative to the object of attention, practice putting them to one side. *Refuse to entertain them.* Say to yourself: "I am attending to ——" (name subject or object). "I refuse to think of anything else." This habit can be acquired by constant practice, and as soon as interest is created in the subject you are attending to the necessity for thought-dismissal will not exist.

The habit of attention is facilitated by practicing control over respiration. "The French designate a clever but superficial thinker as one incapable of any work *'de longue haleine'* (of long breath)." Students should pay great attention to the exercise on breathing in Lesson Twelve of this work.

Students who wish to attain the highest powers of attention must cultivate repose. *Prof. Bain* puts it concisely: *"To think is to refrain from speaking or acting."* Movement and the Attention-Process are opposed—the one negatives the other. The brain needs all its energy for the Attention-Process, for attention involves expenditure of energy. Hence to walk about, to drum on the table, or to indulge in other forms of movement, is to waste the energy the brain requires for its task.

The Master Key

CHAPTER XVIII.

LESSON SIXTEEN.

OBSERVATION.

DO ALL PERCEIVE THE SAME THING?

It is a common fallacy that an object sends the same retinal message to every eye, and that therefore every eye must see alike. Psychologists are able to prove that this is erroneous. Apart from the part that experience plays in observation, pathological conditions must be taken into account.

As a general rule, it may be said that we merely see what we have seen before; that is, in some way or other a new object is generally related to something we have seen in the past.

WHAT IS INVOLVED IN OBSERVATION?

To observe does not mean simply to stare at an object; what we see in any field or view (*i. e.*, as spread before us) depends on what we bring with us to that field. The difference, therefore, between a *trained* observer and an *untrained* is the difference between their experience.

An object *may* send the same retinal message to two observers, but the interpretation of the message depends, not on the physical eye, but the mental eye, *i. e.*, the mind behind the eye. A botanist will see more in a flower, or a geologist in a stone, because they know more about flowers and stones. It is this that makes *Professor James* say: *"A blind man like Huber,* with his passion for bees and ants, can observe them through other people's eyes better than these can through their own."*—(Talks to Teachers.)*

Let a farmer, a naturalist, a geologist, a surveyor, or an artist, look at the same view, and each will see something that the other does not see, for each interprets the view according to the stock of knowledge representing his past experience.

No one observer can see all that takes place in front of him, for, experience apart, what you see depends on what you attend to, and you cannot attend to everything. Even a camera cannot register all of a view, for the photograph only represents those parts to which the photographer wishes to give prominence.

To a very great extent observation is subjective; that is, it is the work of the mental eye, which sees a very different object to the physical eye. Conjuring tricks, illusions, the mistakes we overlook when reading, all illustrate the subjective element in observation.

Again, the eye does not always see the same picture when looking at an object. To demonstrate this, by personal observation, look closely at the *cubes* shown in the accompanying illustration.

First, look at them and see whether there appears to be *six cubes,* or *seven cubes.*

Second, turn the illustration upside down and you will find there appears to be *only six cubes.* By looking at the *cubes,* from different angles, you will see sometimes only *six* and sometimes *seven cubes.*

You will also see the *cubes* change, right before your eyes, from *six* to *seven,* and from *seven* to *six cubes.* This well illustrates what I mean by "affected perception" and an *optical illusion.*

Our eyes are constantly deceiving us, and they require constant watching and checking, for what they seem to register may be very far from what they do register. It is owing to this that the reports of different observers show such variation, even when the observers are beyond reproach.

HOW PERCEPTION IS AFFECTED.

Perception is affected in many ways, and students should know the most important of these, so as to be on their guard as occasion arises.

First—Expectation is perhaps the commonest, and, thereby one of the principal means whereby perception is affected. You see what you expect to see.

You go to a conjuring entertainment. The conjurer tells you first of all what he is going to do; you expect him to do it, and therefore you see him do it. Were he not to make his directive statements you would see in many instances something quite different from what you think you see. If you were not so careful to watch his right hand (*at his bidding*) you would see him doing the trick with his left hand.

Experiment when next you go to a conjuring entertainment. Disobey the conjurer's directions and glances, and you will see something the conjurer does not wish you to see, unless he is even then too quick for you. Conjurers themselves employ this method when they wish to *discover the secret* of a brother conjurer's tricks. If they do not discover the secret on a first visit they will pay a second or third.

Faulty inference is really the rock on which we split in expectation. When we know that a certain effect always follows from a certain cause, if we think we detect the cause we expect the result to follow, just as 2+2=4. Therefore, when you see a violinist's bow, in a *diminuendo* at the end of his solo, still slowly travelling over a string, you think it is touching the string when it may not. You have always associated the travelling bow as in contact with a string, hence when the violinist tricks you with the moving bow you think the sound is still dying away beyond reach of your ears.

It is therefore an easy matter to deceive a person. If you lead him to believe you are making certain movements which he has always associated with certain acts. If he thinks he sees the cause, he is certain he sees the effect.

Note, too, how a ventriloquist works on your expectation. He tells you that the voice you hear proceeds from a man on the roof; without this direction from him you could just as easily imagine the voice as that of a man in the cellar. You hear what you expect to hear.

Second—Interest affects perception. If you receive a letter which you have been expecting and in which you are greatly interested, grammatical slips in the letter will probably be overlooked by you and important details may be only half grasped. Likewise when your interest in a book is keen, you will probably never notice a single mis-spelling or typographical error. An author often passes error after error in his proofs; his interest in the subject-matter is too keen. Months after, when to a great extent his interest has died out, he will notice these errors.

The faults of interest are due to the mental eye which sees *what it expects to see.* Put this to experiment. Tell a friend you are going to expose to him a word on a card for just one-fifth of a second. Tell him the word represents something he wears on his head and show him on a card **IIAT**. Write it fairly large and distinct. He will expect to see some such word as *"hat,"* and he will therefore read it as **HAT**

If you wish to guard against the mental eye, in reading, you must train yourself to see the individual letters of a word, for, as a rule, we only see words as wholes, hence the mistakes we make in passing mis-spellings, transposed letters, etc.

Interest can inhibit a retinal message entirely. A student examining an object through his microscope rarely sees anything with the disengaged eye. His interest and intentness act as an arresting influence on the stimuli sent to the eye that is disengaged.

Third—The customary or familiar greatly affects perception. We are so accustomed to see our friends day after day that we do not notice signs of ill-health in them, unless very pronounced. We saw, also, how our familiarity with words as wholes prevents our seeing mis-spellings, etc.; but often familiarity plays us another trick in reading—we fail to note the omission of words like "the," "and," "but," "in," "with," etc. —*our mental eye supplies these.*

This fault is often responsible for serious mistakes in business. A business man often thinks he has read in a letter or order what he has not read. It is only when his correspondent asks him to re-read the letter that he sees the error. Some business men actually trade on this weakness; in their advertisements, or on their tickets, words which totally alter the meaning of their statements are put in small print, or in a place not likely to be noticed. **as** HAND-SEWN in a boot or shoe advertisement will illustrate this.

NOTE.—The ear, too, is deceived by this subjective element. An old conundrum will illustrate this. *"A farmer had twenty sick sheep; five of them died; how many had he left?"* If you ask a person to solve this, taking care to speak the conundrum quickly and naturally, you will find that hardly anyone will notice the word *"sick";* their ears will interpret it as *"six,"* and they will answer 21 (26—5), or they will reply *"21 alive and 5 dead,"* and so on. It is only a student of phonetics, or one familiar with such conundrums, who will be likely to detect where the key to the conundrum lies.

Students should concentrate their attention on a person's conversation and see if they can detect any omitted words, or words wrongly or carelessly pronounced. Quick speakers supply the best tests.

Try, also, the following experiments on your friends: *First,* ask them if they have ever seen "a black *pland* with yellow leaves." In the majority of cases they will think you are asking about a black *plant.*

Second—Repeat the lines: "There is a green *ill* far away, without a city wall." Ask your friends if they detect any error. Very, very few of them will notice the omission of the *"h" in "hill."*

Familiarity with a town (as you saw under "How Inattention may be turned into Attention") tends to lessen attention with respect to details in the town. Similarly a shopkeeper will not notice the disorderliness of his shop, or the service given by his assistants, through long familiarity with the same, while a stranger will notice these at once. Shopkeepers should, therefore, get away from their business occasionally and visit shops in other towns. This will often open their eyes to many faults in their own shops on their return home.

In crossing out letters (as, for instance, in crossing out O's) we make fewer errors (*i. e.,* pass the O's) where the subject-matter has no interest for us (as in an unfamiliar foreign language). Familiarity and interest act as an arresting influence —they hurry us along and we omit to cross out many of the O's.

A quick, intelligent reader is apt to pass errors that a slow reader of lesser intelligence will probably notice—where both are ignorant of concentrative methods. Teachers of the first class are liable to pass errors in the exercises of their pupils (especially errors in spelling) which teachers of the second class will notice, the reason being that the former's grasp of the words as totals is too rapid.

NOTE.—The ear is likewise affected by familiarity; the character of sounds may be entirely altered in this way. Thus, if a violinist plays for any length of time on a violin which at first appeared to him to be harsh in tone, in time he will not notice this harshness so much. The illusion will vanish, however, as soon as he plays on a better instrument.

Fourth—Emotion is answerable for defective perception. A person under the stress of emotion is never a reliable witness. The following will illustrate this:

Dramatic psychological experiments are very popular with many professors of psychology. The professor will be lecturing to his students when suddenly the door will open with a loud bang, and in will rush two men, followed perhaps by a policeman. There will be a scuffle, words will be spoken by the parties, a revolver will be fired, and the professor will, perhaps, take a part in the scene by ordering the intruders out; and then, as suddenly as they appeared, the actors in the scene will rush out of the door.

The professor will then appear greatly moved by the unpleasant incident, and will ask a certain number of the students to write a report of what has taken place. The whole scene will have taken only half a minute, and yet these students who have been trained to observe will vary in their statements as to the time from a second or two to several minutes; while their reports as to the dress of the actors, their speech, actions, etc., will likewise show considerable variations. Some of their statements will be false, others inaccurate, others pure invention, while many will perhaps fail to observe at all the leading features of the scene.

Even where the audience has comprised men of the greatest attainments in Science the results have been very similar, proving that the best of us are very fallible and our observations not to be trusted when under the influence of emotion. Students should therefore guard against giving way to emotion if they wish to have perfect control of themselves and their faculties.

Fifth—Breathing. Any obstruction of breathing, not only affects perception, but also our general efficiency. Children suffering from adenoids are never so good at their studies as children whose nasal passages are normal. Many know, when suffering from a cold in the head, when the nose is stuffed up, how it affects their efficiency; they feel it impossible to give things the same attention as usual.

Sixth—Fatigue, or any exertion affects perception. Most all readers know how a book seems to be blurred and the print run together when they attempt to read when thoroughly tired.

But even when we are only slightly fatigued our perceptive powers are affected. Experiment as follows: Go through some form of physical exercise of a slightly tiring nature, or run up and down stairs for a few times, or run a hundred yards at top speed. Now attempt to read small print; you will not see it so clearly as before exerting yourself.

Seventh—Habit greatly affects perception. When we are accustomed to do things in an automatic way we are liable to overlook the necessity of varying the same to meet changed conditions. The following will serve to illustrate this: An old cocoa mat at an office door was replaced one day by a new one. The new mat was, of course, slightly higher than the old one, which usage had worn down. It was noticed that as each clerk entered or left the office the first day or so after the new mat had been put down that he stumbled. At each stumble they *noticed* the new mat, and in a day or so the stumbling ceased. Unconsciously each clerk had adjusted his leg movement to meet the new conditions.

Eighth—Mist interferes with perception. Objects near at hand seen through mist appear to us to be distant. Artists make use of this fact in their pictures when they wish to convey the idea of distance.

Ninth—*Time-exposure* greatly affects perception. Laboratory experiments have shown that where the time-exposure (as in showing words, letters, or figures on a board) is reduced from one second to a tenth of a second, the number of words, letters, or figures seen is reduced considerably. The results are more marked in the case of children than in adults.

HOW PRACTICE QUICKENS PERCEPTION.

The stock illustration of how practice quickens perception is that of *Houdin* the conjurer and his son. They began with one or two dominoes, merely glancing at them and then giving the sum of their points. Through long practice they attained such skill as to be able to give at a glance the sum of the points on twelve dominoes. Next they extended their glancing to shop windows, to the contents of rooms as they passed through, until they attained such proficiency as to appear miraculous to anyone unacquainted with their methods and the long training they had undergone.

Agassiz, the great geologist and zoologist, is another example of wonderful proficiency in observation. A student who passed through his hands has related the teaching methods of *Agassiz.* This student, on his arrival in the class, was handed by *Agassiz* a specimen of a fish and told to examine it carefully, so as to be able to give a full report of all he had seen. He was told not to cut the fish, nor to measure it with any instrument—he was simply to give the results of his observation. In ten minutes he was ready with his report, but *Agassiz* refused to take it. He kept the student examining the fish for three days before he expressed himself as in any degree satisfied. The student never forgot this lesson in observation, which he regarded as laying the foundation of his future attainments in zoology.

Practice simply means repetition, and laboratory experiments prove that repetition quickens perception. This must not be confounded with the work of memory as due to residual traces; the eye gradually acquires the power of seeing a greater number of objects, also details which escape us at a first glance, although these details may have been in the focus of vision. Experiment as follows:

Look at some cheese dust with the naked eye; look at it closely for a minute—you can detect no movement; it appears dead. Now look at it through a strong magnifying glass and it is a world of moving objects. (Note this does not apply to *all* cheese dust.) Next put the glass down and look closely again at the dust; after a time you will see a slight movement here and there—your perception has been quickened.

Try similar experiments with various things, such as a leaf, a flower, a piece of paper or cloth; you will find you will be able to detect things which at first you were unable to see.

Next take any little object in your home and write a full description of it. Go over the description next day and see if you can add to it. Continue for a week. Now get a friend to examine the object and ask him to write, or give you a description of it. Point out little things he has omitted and see if he can bring to your notice anything *you* have omitted.

The effect of repeated practice, as above, is to make that which is like come to the front; thereby the fatigue of attention is lessened and we are able to attend to the unlike—*i. e.,* new aspects of the object of our attention. You will notice this in reading a new author. You will gradually find the peculiarities of his style (that is, that which he is fond of repeating) forced into notice. Pet phrases, unusual words, the set of his sentences, will grow familiar, and your attention is then set free to notice other details. Experiment with *Macaulay* or *Carlyle*.

When attention is turned on the unfamiliar it gradually becomes familiar. When first you hear a foreign language it sounds a jingle or babel of sounds, but when your ear gets accustomed, through increased attention, to the sounds you are able to distinguish detached words in a sentence, and finally all the sentence.

Who are the best boxers, the best fencers, the best athletes? —*those whose movements are the quickest*. Their quickness of movement liberates their attention, and they are (especially in the case of boxers and fencers) freer to attend to the tactics of their opponents.

NOTE.—The ear shows the same results in efficiency from practice.

Experiment as follows: Strike the note C (*middle C*) on the piano. Listen to it carefully. Can you detect the overtone? If not, strike it again, and then, holding the note down, strike softly the octave higher. You will note how the two C's seem to sound as one, only fuller and richer than before. If you continue striking the lower C, listening carefully, you will note how the overtone (which is similar in pitch to the upper C— the octave) seems to rise up out of the lower C. Practice until you can hear the overtone distinctly and easily.

Reaction time (the interval between a stimulus and the response to it) in perception is greatly increased by practice. This also applies to reaction time in hearing. Students should note the following:

Clever people, sharp business men, etc., often feel annoyed because men or women (especially of the country or lower laboring type) do not let them pass quickly when asked to do so. The reason is, that in many cases they *cannot* do so—their reaction time is too slow. The time between your asking them to allow you to pass and their standing aside does not seem slow to them, for it is their natural response; but it seems painfully slow to you, for *your* reaction time is much quicker. Teachers should note this, and make allowance for dull pupils who fail to attend as quickly as clever pupils.

SIGHT ILLUSIONS.

The subject of *Observation* would not be complete without some reference to *Sight Illusions*. I shall treat in this section some of the most noted of these.

According to the attention you give an object will be the estimate you form of it. Thus it will be large or small, long or short, heavy or light, according to your attentive powers. What is called the interrupted distance illustrates this.

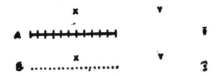

The space marked X in A and B appears greater than the space Y, for the simple reason that the intersecting lines in A and each dot in B catches your attention. Similarly if you take two right angles, as in Figs. 1 and 2, shown below, and

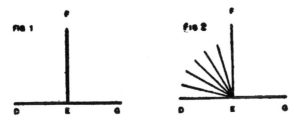

shoot out lines from E, as in Fig. 2, the angle D. E. F. will look larger than either of the angles in Fig. 1 or the angle G. E. F. in Fig. 2.

Note, also, in the Figures 3, 4 and 5 (shown on next page) how the perpendicular line in each figure appears dissimilar; the line in Figure 5 appears longer (owing to the offshoots) than the line in Figures 3 and 4.

Vertical distance is easier to grasp than horizontal distance. Look at the lines in Figure 6; which appears the longer? (Do not measure.) You will say the vertical. Now turn the page so that the horizontal line is vertical; which appears longer now? Draw a vertical line upon a horizontal line, without measuring, so that both appear to be of the same length. You will find you have made the vertical line too short. This is best seen where the two lines are two or three inches long.

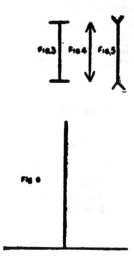

Examine carefully the lower and upper halves of the figures and letters below.

88888   XXXXX   SSSSS   EEEEE

Now turn them upside down and you will see how marked is the difference between the upper and lower halves. Write down these figures and letters and you will see how the eye persists in the illusion. This is particularly noticeable in the 8's and the S's; you think you are making the two halves equal.

Your judgment of the size of an object is determined by your acquaintance with it in everyday life. Thus, when you see a clock on a public building you judge its size by the clocks with which you are familiar; similarly the figures of men and women which you see high up on public buildings, or on churches, are interpreted as being of similar size to the men and women you meet every day.

Shadows are responsible for many sight illusions. You know that a tall person casts a longer shadow than a short person, and you judge all shadows accordingly. Now, when the sun is nearly or exactly overhead, it casts quite a.different shadow to what it does in the early morning or in the evening. At these times the shadows will be much greater than during the day. Hence if you were to estimate the height of a building in the early morning or in the evening your estimate would be probably much greater than if made during the day.

There are many more illusions of sight, but I think the above will be sufficient for the student's purposes. Students should keep a note of any illusion which they notice themselves.

HOW TO CULTIVATE OBSERVATION.

The preceding sections will have supplied the student with means as to the cultivation of Observation. I shall repeat one or two of these and add others for additional practice.

The first requisite in cultivating observation is to go about *with your eyes open;* most people certainly do not do so. Begin from today to look at your fellow men and the world around you with seeing eyes. Look at things with the definite aim of seeing them. Start in your own home and look with the eyes of a stranger at the objects which are so familiar to you.

Begin simply—do not try to be a *Sherlock Holmes* right away. After you have practiced looking at home objects extend to objects outside. Look at public buildings, vehicles on the street or road, and any names or number on them, railway trains, engines, cars, trucks, ships, animals, etc.

Make a special study of men and women you meet in the street, and also when traveling. Note their general appearance, features, dress, gait, gestures. Try to form an estimate as to their occupation or station in life, their habits, moods, etc.

Try *Houdin's* methods. Glance at shop-windows in passing and see how many articles you can remember. Glance at men and women and see what details you can take in at a glance. Check results by comparing with the person, if still in sight. Glance at boardings where a number of advertisements are displayed. Describe to yourself what you have seen and then look back and verify results. Glance at anything in passing and describe what you have seen.

NOTE.—In glancing exercises, as above, it is essential to get the habit of describing quickly. If you are uncertain about anything, such as whether a lady's dress was pink or blue, do not puzzle yourself trying to remember. Leave it and *hurry on* —to stop is fatal. If you delay even a second or so, you will have forgotten most of what you have seen. The golden rule in glancing is to describe first the things you remember with ease and then recall the things of which you are uncertain.

It is also a good plan before commencing glancing exercises to look at objects and describe them while looking at them. This gives what may be termed preliminary definiteness. When you have made a habit of this, you teach the eyes to function quickly, hence glancing exercises are facilitated.

Walk along the street with the definite aim of seeing how many different kinds of articles you can see.

Read a report of any incident (such as a fire) in two different newspapers, *i. e.*, controlled by different firms. Note the points where the two reports agree and where they disagree. It is essential that the reports should not have been supplied by a news agency, otherwise they will be alike in every detail.

Co-operation of Friends. If you can get a friend to co-operate with you, you can try the following exercises in observation. These exercises will cultivate quickness in perception, and also memory for details, location, form, etc. Failing a friend, an intelligent child will make a good co-operator:

First—Take a small article, such as a key, a coin, or a brooch, and get your friend in your absence to put this article somewhere in the room where it can be seen easily. The article must not be hidden or covered in any way—it must be plainly visible. As soon as you enter the room your friend begins to count in a measured tone, 1, 2, 3, and so on. Keep a record of the number your friend counts up to before your discover the article.

Second—Spread a number of small articles on a table. Begin with six to ten articles. Each article must be different and easily named; for instance, spoon, knife, watch, ring, match-box, thimble, book, pen, pencil, key. While you are out of the room your friend removes one of the articles; you must name this article when you come in the room again.

Third—After you get fairly expert at the above, get your friend to arrange all the articles in a straight line, *i. e.*, in a definite order. While you are out of the room he must change the order; for instance, where the spoon was when you left the room, let him put the pen, and so on. At first he should not change more than two of the articles. You are required to mention the articles which have been moved and put them back in their original order.

Fourth—Get some one in your home to remove some article from your bedroom while you are at business. On your return home see if you can tell what article has been removed. Let your friend commence with fairly prominent articles, until you have advanced in the exercise.

Fifth—Get your friend to make from six to ten definite movements, a list of which he has prepared beforehand. He is to make these movements in the order of his list. You must write down all you see him do. For instance, (1) with the right hand he touches his head, (2) then his watch-chain, and so on. Tell him he must try to deceive you by making two movements at once, such as touching his ear with one hand and a button on his coat with the other. If your friend is smart, your powers of observation will be tested considerably. (This exercise cannot be done by a child co-operator.)

Every student of this work should make Observation a daily study. Every time you go out look about you with the definite aim of seeing something. This definiteness of aim will itself help you to see better, for it will prepare your eyes to see things, just as when you are expecting the clock to strike your ears are prepared to hear it strike.

The Master Key

CHAPTER XIX.

LESSON SEVENTEEN.

INTEREST.

INTEREST AND ITS MEANING.

To define *"Interest"* is not easy; like love or hate it must be experienced before it can be understood. *Kant* defines it as *"a cause determining the will,"* but perhaps it will be better understood as *"a feeling which binds our attention to an object* (the writer uses "object" in a wide sense) with the expectation that such feeling will bring pleasure in some form, or advantage in some form." The ultimate aim of Interest, as affecting the individual, *is therefore satisfaction.* When satisfaction is attained Interest tends to fade or die away; to stimulate it further, we must see ahead new forms of satisfaction.

Interest may be said to manifest itself in two forms: *First, Sensory Interest; Second, Motor Interest.* The following will simplify these terms:

Suppose you see some delicious fruit in a store window. As you look at it you are pleased with its appearance, and you think how good it will taste, and thus gradually your interest in the fruit grows. This is Sensory Interest, *i. e.,* the appeal the fruit makes to the senses. At a further stage you feel you *must* have some of the fruit, and you act on this feeling and go into the store and make a purchase. The feeling which prompts you to go into the store is Motor Interest.

In *Sensory Interest* the object makes a visual, auditory, gustatory, olfactory, or tactile appeal. In *Motor Interest* we feel a conation—a striving, or tendency towards the object. *Motor Interest,* therefore, tends to manifest itself in action.

146

HOW TO CREATE OR "GROW" INTEREST.

If an object is uninteresting to you, you can *"grow"* interest in it by associating it with some interesting fact in your experience.

A man past fifty, who could not read, was interested in electricity. He used to get his grandson to read to him anything relating to electricity. One day the boy read something which greatly interested the old man. At first he could not believe what the boy had read. "Does it *really* say that in the paper?" he asked. The boy assured him and read the passage once more. "Well," said the old man, "if it says that about electricity, *I'm going to learn to read."* And he *did learn to read;* his interest was so keen that he persevered with all the difficulties of his task, until he could read the papers himself.

Interest does not usually grow so quickly as in the old man's case; the growth, at first, is often imperceptible. Take the case of a young man in a large business house. His work is uninteresting—how can he grow interest in it? The best way is to see an end to aim at, but even this is not always easy. The safest and simplest way is to look at his work from a development point of view.

Thus, suppose a certain section of his work has always taken an hour to do, he can set himself to try to reduce this time to three-quarters and then to half an hour. As he applies the same method to other sections of his work he attracts the attention of those above him. He has been careful also to see to the character of his work, that not only has it been done quickly, but neater and better in every way. The attention of his superiors turns to interest—he is promoted, and as more responsibility is put upon him his work gradually increases in interest, and as promotion after promotion follows his interest strengthens, until in many instances it becomes an absorbing passion.

Another way to create interest in that which lacks interest for us is *"to make it show new aspects of itself, to prompt new questions, in a word to change."* "Try to attend steadfastly to a dot on the paper, or on the wall. Either your vision becomes blurred or your eye wanders away to something else. But if you ask yourself questions about the dot—how big it is, how far, of what shape, what shade or color, etc., you can keep your mind on it for a comparatively long time." The rule, therefore, for creating interest in an uninteresting thing is to associate it with something in which you already have an interest.

Students who wish to create interest in any special study, as in a science, for instance, should be on the lookout in books, magazines and newspapers for anything referring to this science. Students who adopt this plan will find their interest grow steadily; new points of view will gradually widen the field of knowledge; possibilities will be seen hitherto undreamt of; that which seemed a useless study will show utility in many forms.

A psychologist was once trying an experiment in observation with two children whom I will call A and B, and one of the objects on the table was a locket belonging to the child B. It was noticed that whenever this object was removed the child instantly detected its absence. Her interest in its ownership was of course the reason.

Students of this work should have no difficulty in growing interest in *anything*, for they can always look upon it as an exercise tending to increase their powers of concentration.

Note, that the fundamental rule for creating interest in anything is to give it repeated attention. According to your attention will be your interest and conversely, it may be said, according to your interest will be your attention.

FATIGUE.

Every psychological student should know something about Fatigue and its manifestations, for ignorance of the subject is responsible for many foolish and hurtful actions.

When the body is fatigued the supply of blood to the brain is very small, hence attention is almost an impossibility. Even the slightest act of attention is wearisome and one is inclined to be cross and irritable.

When the brain is fatigued it is an act of folly to indulge in violent bodily exercise, for this is to still further fatigue the brain. Walking is the best exercise, for it is automatic, and makes very little demand on the brain.

Students should never attempt to study after violent exercise; slight exercise before studying is often beneficial, but violent exercise is harmful.

The student is cautioned as to how he regards the theory that the body has reserves of energy. It has been proved experimentally that when the normal energy of a muscle is exhausted it is injurious to stimulate it to further action. And not only does the further stimulus prove injurious, but the character of the extra work resulting from the stimulus is of little account. Again, when a muscle is fatigued, the effect of the extra stimulation is much more severe than if the muscle were engaged on a heavier task when in its normal state. It pays, therefore, to rest the muscle, and take up the task again later.

It is a common fallacy that change of intellectual work rests us; this is true only when our health is good and where there is felt a sense of relief and pleasure in the change. If the brain as a whole is fatigued, total rest is essential.

Fatigue is lessened in any sphere by the working of the law of habit; that which at first was felt as a strain is lessened as systematic exercise is brought to bear upon it.

Students on the eve of an examination often fatigue themselves by thinking too much of the ordeal they have to undergo; psychologists term this "excitability in a motor sphere." One sees it also in anyone who has to speak, sing, or play on an instrument, before an audience. Such perfunctioning, or feelings, should be dismissed at once, and the mind turned into other channels. The student, speaker or singer who cultivates the "I *know* I shall do well" attitude will find his task much easier to accomplish.

The best schoolmasters and teachers are those who know how to regulate and lessen fatigue of their pupils, by turning their attention into new and less exhausting channels. Public speakers are adepts at this lessening of fatigue. As soon as they see the attention of their audience difficult to hold, they introduce a humorous story, or a personal touch, which relieves the strained attention of their hearers.

Students should experiment and take note of the best intervals of repose between their studies, and stick to these intervals. The intervals of effective rest vary with different individuals, but as a general rule the interval between each subject studied should be greater when one is tired, for then it takes longer to recuperate our energy. In normal situations long intervals of repose are fatal to good and effective work; the brain seems to take longer to function after prolonged rests.

Fatigue and fasting make the senses more acute and the

nervous system more excitable. Sometimes people who fast hail this acuteness as a sign of well-being, but in reality it is a warning that the organism is, for the time being, not in proper order for the prolongation of existence.

Students should note the effect of fatigue on the memory; sometimes the effect is so great that we cannot remember even the most familiar things—things which belong to our daily activities. Schoolmasters and teachers will have noticed that when children are tired they make the most absurd mistakes in Composition and in Reading. It seems clear, then, that study of any kind should be put aside as soon as we feel tired or exhausted. If we persist, it will be found that our time has been practically wasted.

Author's Note—Students will find a further section on "The Effect of Fatigue on Thought-Control" in *Chapter XX, Lesson Eighteen.*

The Master Key

LESSON EIGHTEEN.

THOUGHT CONTROL.

WHAT THOUGHT CONTROL CAN DO FOR YOU.

Control your thoughts and you control your world.

Mr. Dickson has just finished his breakfast, which he has thoroughly enjoyed. He takes up his newspaper for a quiet fifteen minutes' perusal. Suddenly he notes that a client has "gone smash." In consequence the satisfaction brought by his good breakfast vanishes, and he goes to business in an unhappy frame of mind.

Robinson has not enjoyed his breakfast; it has not been cooked to his satisfaction. He opens his newspaper morosely, and suddenly notes that wheat has gone up two points. In consequence he forgets his badly prepared breakfast, and goes to business in a happy frame of mind.

A tourist on a long walking tour is delighted with the fine weather he is having. The farmers in the districts through which he is touring are in despair because of the long drought and its effect upon their crops.

What can we learn from the above cases? We can learn this: The world for each of us is what we *think* it. There is a correspondence between the things we see, hear, touch, taste, and smell, but we look at them from different standpoints— from *our* standpoint. The world for each of us is *our* world; it is what we *think* it is.

Every day millions of men, women and children look out each morning on their world. To some it is a glad world, a beautiful world, a happy world; to others it is a sorrowful world, an ugly world, a miserable world. It is such a world because they *think* it so.

Now can you alter the character of your world, or must

you always accept and interpret it in the same way? You need not, you *ought* not unless it is the right way; for just as your thought makes the world a miserable world to you, so can your thought transform it into a happy world for you.

How is this to be done? you ask. The reply is, by learning to control your thoughts. The fear-thought need not always make you afraid; the anger-thought need not always make you angry. *Control your thoughts, and you control your world.* It is the object of this work to teach you the secret of *Thought-Control and Mental Discipline.*

Thought can turn a brave man into a timid man; a strong man into a weak man; a cheerful man into a sad man; a proud, domineering man into a humble, abject, cringing man.

Thought can change the character of respiration, can impede or assist digestion, can alter the quantity of the secretions of the body, can induce many diseases, and banish many diseases. It can induce nausea, and even death itself.

Thought can fill us with hope, or plunge us into despair; can fill us with inspiration or crush all initiative; can make us persevere against any odds, or raise up difficulties to bar our every step.

Your thoughts can make you or unmake you. *Your* thoughts can do this, nay, *are* doing this. Will you not have a say in the matter? Will you not see to it that only good thoughts, brave thoughts, inspiring thoughts, hopeful thoughts, cheerful thoughts, shall form *your* world?

You *can* do this. Begin from today to encourage such thoughts to dwell with you. Cast out of your world every thought that tends to rob you of your peace of mind and your hope of success. You *can* do this, for it is mainly a matter of trying.

YOUR THOUGHT ATMOSPHERE.

You would not consider a consumptive a wise man if he went to live where it was always damp and cold. You would feel constrained to tell him to seek a climate where it was always warm and sunny.

You must take the same medicine. If you are to make any advancement in life you must live in a congenial atmosphere. It must be in an atmosphere of thought, faith and belief, that will help you to develop, by stimulating all your energies, all your faculties.

It may be that you are in a business or line of life for which you feel unsuited. Is this a congenial atmosphere? you ask. It is not if you *feel* it, *think* it unsuited for you; it *can* be if you will alter the character of your thought-world.

Many people live an unreal life in such circumstances. Whilst at their business they seem bright, cheerful, industrious. It is only when the day's work is over, when the glamor of excitement and hurry has passed, that they catch a glimpse of their real world. Then the regrets, cares, disappointments, come forth from the slumbering background—these people are now surrounded by their real atmosphere.

It is usual in such cases to offer the advice—"Get out of your present business; change into a new line of life." Now this is, in the majority of cases, well-nigh impossible if it has to be done in a sudden leap. No! the best advice to such a man is to get rid of his inner Thought-World, the world of regrets, cares and disappointments. Consider—what good do such thoughts bring you? None. Then why cherish them; why hug them to your breast as a miser hugs his gold? The author shall not offer you the cheap advice: "Be brave; persevere." No, he shall put the matter fair and square to you.

The message of *Thought-Control* to you is this: By living in this inner atmosphere of regrets, cares and disappointments you are not advancing one iota towards the life you seek; you are tending to put that life beyond your reach. By changing your thought-world you tend to make the life you seek possible.

You must cultivate the attitude, "Well, I'm in this business, and I'm going to make it the stepping stone to my real career; I'm not going to allow it to fill me with despair; I'm going to master its secrets, and I'm going to live in hopes of the real thing turning up. I'm going to be cheerful, hopeful, persevering. I'm going to *win* in spite of all odds."

When a man gets into an atmosphere like this he feels it to be congenial. Very often, too, such an attitude results in the man feeling his interest in his present business grow to such an extent that it ceases to be distasteful. New points of view reveal possibilities in the business he never thought to exist. He sees vistas of further possibilities until the life he hankered for sinks further and further into the background. He is at home; he has found himself—his thought-world is congenial.

MENTAL ATTITUDE.

If you were to ask a friend: "What do twice two and a half make?" he would probably hesitate before replying. If you were to add to your query: "Now be careful how you reply," his hesitancy would be still more pronounced.

Queries stated in the above manner, and all kinds of conundrums and catches, illustrate that we approach a subject with a certain mental attitude. Tell a man a thing is difficult and you make it difficult for him; tell him it is easy and you make it easier for him. Much, of course, depends upon your manner, as shown above, in making your statements.

In approaching any new study, or on undertaking any new task, it is well to understand your mental attitude beforehand. If you think the study or undertaking difficult you will certainly make it more difficult of attainment; for when we think anything difficult we put a bar on our power that greatly hinders progress.

Cases are on record where new systems of working have been introduced into offices, systems with a certain amount of complexity, and the clerks have made slow progress with them, simply because they offered something strange, something difficult. Weeks have elapsed before the staff thoroughly grasped the system; and instances are related where members of the staff have become ill from worry in their efforts to grapple with the new conditions.

Now note this. Where it has been necessary to engage temporary clerks, it has been noticed that they have mastered the system in a much shorter time than the permanent clerks. Why is this? *Simply because the temporary clerks approached the work with a different mental attitude.* They knew nothing of the relational difficulty between the old and the new system; they saw the work had to be done in a certain way and they quickly mastered this way.

A friend of the author, a professor of music, was very strict with regard to his pupils' mental attitude. He would never allow a pupil to say a solo or study was difficult. He would make the pupil point out the difficult passage and he would carefully analyze it, note by note, until he made the pupil play it. He would tell the pupil not to worry because he could not play the passage up to time—"that will come with practice," he would say; and he said it in such a confident tone that his pupil believed him and was inspired to practice, until success crowned his efforts.

Teachers have often noticed that when a number of their pupils have failed to answer a question (verbal) the power of the other scholars to reply has been slight. They look on the question as a sort of conundrum which it is hopeless to answer, and they therefore give up the attempt.

Two students will enter an examination room. The one will rapidly glance at his paper and put it down disgusted—it is difficult. The other will read each question carefully and calmly, and will finally conclude the paper possible. *Which student is likely to pass?*

Every student of *Thought-Control* and *Mental Discipline* will realize that it is important while recognizing the difficulty of a subject to put this thought out of the mind at once. Refuse to acknowledge its difficulty and you will make the subject easier for you to grasp.

The fact is very few exert anything like the power or ability they possess. They are like the traveler who suddenly finds a high wall closing his path. "I can never get over that; I shall have to go back," he says. As he turns to retrace his steps he sees a bull or a wild animal coming tearing along towards him. He alters his tone now. "I *must* get over that wall," he says. He makes a desperate attempt and succeeds in getting over the wall.

If you wish to succeed in anything remember that no effort is ever lost. Every act, every attempt, is registered in the neural paths of the brain, and each successive act or attempt will deepen and broaden these paths, giving greater facility each time. You may not be able to see this for a time any more than a musician can tell the finer gradations of tone which no human ear can detect, but if you persevere you will find that facility *will* come.

THE PART PLAYED BY IMAGINATION.

A butcher, while hanging up a heavy piece of meat, slipped, and the hook pierced his arm. He was in terrible agony and could barely suffer himself to be touched. Yet when the arm was examined it was found uninjured, the hook having only pierced his coat sleeve. Such is the power of Imagination—such is the power of Thought.

Every student of Thought-Control should understand the part played by Imagination.* Once he recognizes this he will be on his guard, and will test his experiences in the light of this knowledge.

Cases are on record where men present at the exhumation of a body have become seriously ill as soon as the coffin was exposed—they had felt the odor of decomposition. Yet when the coffin has been opened it has been found empty, or perhaps filled with stones, soil, etc.

Men have been bitten by dogs, which everyone declared to be mad, and have afterwards died, with all the symptoms of hydrophobia. Yet afterwards when the dogs have been examined they have been found free from any trace of rabies.

The writer need not multiply examples; you will doubtless bring to memory many such cases yourself. You will remember how you have awakened in the middle of the night; your bedroom door has been left ajar, and now you see it open gradually until your hair stands on end with fright.

Now in such cases, if you will only remember that imagination tricks all of us, you will at once assume a critical attitude. Has the door *really* opened further? You watch closely, and as the critical attitude grows your fears grow less, and finally you get up and examine the door, to find that it has not altered its position one inch.

The following illustrates the critical attitude. One night a young lady was awakened by a mysterious tapping at her bedroom window. She looked in the dim light towards the window and distinctly saw outlined a ladder placed against. the stonework at the top of the window. Instantly she thought of burglars; she could hear them with their instruments attempting to raise the window. A minute or two elapsed; no burglar appeared, and then she adopted the critical attitude.

The result was this. The ladder was the tapes of the venetian blind which had been left partly open. The tapping was a creeper growing on the outside of the house, which the wind every now and again dashed against the window.

Now if you will remember in all such cases to adopt a critical attitude, you will find that your fears will grow less,

*Students should also give close attention to *Lesson Thirty-one*, "Concentration Applied To Health And Disease," "The Psychology of Faith and Fear," also *Lesson Thirty-two*, "Concentration Applied To Fear And Disease.'

and then you will control your thoughts instead of being controlled by them.

CONFUSION OF THOUGHT.

A young man bought two eggs with the intention of giving them to his landlady to boil for his supper. Arrived at his lodgings he threw the bag containing the eggs on the table, with disastrous results to the eggs.

You have here an illustration of thought-confusion through two thoughts being uppermost in consciousness. The young man intended to take the eggs out of the bag, and then throw the bag away. The throwing was the stronger idea (or impulse) and the eggs suffered in consequence.

Common illustrations of the same confusion of thought are: *First,* that of looking at your watch and yet not being able to give the time; *Second,* the man who puts his watch in the pan and holds the egg in his hand; *Third,* asking a question and not knowing what you have asked; *Fourth,* locking a door and not knowing afterwards whether you have really locked it.

Studious people, business people—anyone who thinks deeply, is liable to make mistakes like the above. This tendency can be cured, to a great extent, by cultivating awareness when doing anything. To this end you must pay attention to all your acts; you must have a definite aim and carry it out quickly and quietly. You must have orderly habits, and, as far as possible, set times for doing things.

Nothing is so beneficial, however, for avoiding confusion of thought of the above type as learning to do all your actions quickly and quietly. Dress quickly, walk quickly, read quickly, think quickly; get through your business quickly. You will find such practice lead to great clearness of thinking and precision in all you do.

THE EFFECT OF FATIGUE ON THOUGHT-CONTROL.

When you are tired, either by mental or by physical work, you will find it difficult to control your thoughts. It is when you are tired that you often *"speak without thinking."* Note, for instance, how cross a child becomes after a tiring walk, and how it will speak to you in a manner bordering on rudeness and impertinence.

Just as you should never work a muscle to the point of

exhaustion, so should you never study to the point of exhaustion. If you do you will note how your thoughts will all be poisoned by the toxic element in your blood induced by the fatigue. You will be inclined to vote the study a bore; you will wonder why you took it up; you will think a mastery of it impossible.

All mental and physical work pursued to the point of fatigue interferes with your thought-control. You must see to it that you never study for long periods unless you have trained yourself to study by carefully graduated periods, for here the law of habit tells with good effect. When you form habits of study within your strength you diminish the tendency to fatigue, and consequently you can have perfect control over your thoughts. Where your interest in a study is keen, and the habit of study is a gradual growth, you can study for a long time without any symptoms of fatigue.

Students are warned, when doing mental work which is strange to them (for instance, a new study), to approach it very gradually. If you can spare an hour to the study, divide it or quarter it rather than give the whole hour to it right away, for nothing is more exhausting than mental work to which we are unaccustomed. The brain is rapidly tired and thought-control is well-nigh impossible.

EMOTIONAL AND SENSATIONAL FACTORS THAT HINDER THOUGHT-CONTROL.

It is characteristic of *Emotions* and *Sensations* to extend beyond the particular part of the brain affected by them, to other parts. It is owing to this fact that the *Emotional* and *Sensational Worlds* have such an important bearing on Thought-Control. In this part I shall, therefore, touch on several factors related to the Emotional and Sensational Worlds that hinder Thought-Control.

I shall first deal with *Fear*, for it is by far the most important. I shall then deal with *Worry, Excitement, Expectation, Self-Consciousness, Accidents—Mistakes—Errors and Adverse Criticism.*

FEAR.

Fear tends to suppress all mental activity other than that which the exciting object calls forth. In every emotion the

blood rushes to the head; this is very pronounced when Fear is aroused. The heart works at treble pressure, the breathing becomes labored, the throat becomes dry. The voice sometimes finds utterance in cries, shrieks, or screams; at other times speech or utterance of any kind is impossible. The body under the influence of Fear trembles, shudders and sometimes is incapable of movement. The eyes see strange sights—they see what the imagination bids them see.

It will be apparent to you from the above that Fear must color our thoughts enormously. How, then, can we control Fear, and so control the thoughts which it arouses?

The first thing to be done is to control the feelings to which Fear gives rise. Now all feelings, whether pleasurable or painful, tend to increase in intensity when we attend to them. Doctors know this—many of the medicines they give us are simply means to withdraw our attention from the affected part to some other part, so that nature may be left undisturbed to deal with the seat of the disease.

To control your feelings, then, you must neglect them, that is, give them little attention. You must think of anything but fear-thoughts. In other words, you must cultivate *"inhibition by substitution."* This is the name given by the author to what he understands when we control one thought by its opposite or contrary thought.*

But how must we proceed to control Fear† when the exciting object is not a mere idea, but is actually present before us? It is evident that something else is necessary beyond merely controlling our feelings.

The first thing to do is to arouse the instinct of Self-Assertion. When this instinct is aroused it induces you to act. You must also think of brave deeds or bravery in any form; you must refuse to listen to fear-thoughts.

Every student of Thought-Control should recognize that Fear is useless; it is simply a drag upon energy, and if it is encouraged it is bound to make us weaklings.

In my youthful days I used to wonder how I should get through, on the morrow, the work of a busy day. On one memorable day the thought came to me—*"You have always*

*See *Chapter XXII. Lesson Twenty*, Habit, also *Chapter XXIII. Lesson Twenty-one*, Will Culture—Mind Training.
†Students should also give close attention to *Lesson Thirty-one*, "The Psychology of Faith and Doubt," also *Lesson Thirty-two*, "Concentration Applied To Fear And Disease."

got through so far; the chances are that you will get through again." Since that memorable day the morrow lost its terrors for me.

I ask *you* to put on paper the things that have worried you and are, perhaps, still worrying you; and then put alongside of the items the number of times the worrying thing has come to pass. Said an old man, who was dying, to his son: "My son, I have worried all my life, and nine-tenths of the things I worried about never came to pass." It is the same with most people; the mass of the things they worry about never come to anything.

Next time you are inclined to worry about anything look at it in this light. It is long odds against the thing you worry about coming to pass; take a sporting chance and *do not* worry. If the worrying thing were a racehorse you would get tired of betting upon its chance for you would lose too much money. It wins a very small proportion of the millions of races it enters, therefore, once more remember, the odds are long against the worrying thing coming to pass, so *do not* worry.

You will say, perhaps: Oh! yes, the above is all right in minor cases, but what about the crises of life? Well, even then, what good does worry do for you? Remember worry is a species of mental inflammation; it spreads over all the brain until it paralyzes initiative and effort. Now if a crisis is in front of you, is this the state of mind that will help you to grapple with it?

If you are to deal successfully with a crisis you *must* control the worry mood. Now there is only one way in which to do this, and that is to seek a change of thought. Refuse to brood over the worrying thing. You will not be able to prevent it coming into consciousness, but you *can* prevent it forming trains of thought. If you have practiced faithfully the exercises given in this work you will know that this *is* possible. I strongly advise anyone who is troubled by worry to practice daily the three rules given under "How to *Cultivate Self-Reliance,*" in Chapter XXIV, Lesson Twenty-two, and Chapter XXIII, Lesson Twenty-one, *"Will Culture—Mind Training.* Such practice will give you the fighting spirit—the frame of mind to which worry must succumb.

EXCITEMENT.

Excitement is a valuable stimulus; it is also a great deterrent. A speaker who feels the stimulus of excitement arouses the emotions and passions of his audience. Let him lose control over his excitement and he becomes incoherent and extravagant, and his audience has nothing but contempt for him.

A pugilist, under the spell of excitement, hits his hardest blows; so does a cricketer, etc. But let the pugilist or cricketer lose control over his excitement and forthwith he strikes at random and is speedily routed.

Every student of *Thought-Control* and *Mental Discipline* should recognize the good points of excitement, and should guard against the bad points. He should learn how to control his excitement, and so make it serve his interests instead of destroying them.

To cultivate control over excitement you must resolutely cultivate the habit of keeping the mouth tight-shut as given in Lesson Twelve, Exercise No. 23.

The muscles which close the teeth are considered the most excitable in the body. In fevers, chills and shivering epileptic fits these muscles are the first to be affected; and when death occurs these muscles are the first to show rigidity.

Just notice the next time you are under the spell of excitement, or note it in another person, and you will see how these muscles, if they do not set the teeth chattering, at least cause the lips to tremble and the cheeks to quiver. This is very marked where the excitement turns to, or is mixed with, fear.

Note, too, how your speech is affected in strong excitement. You stammer and stumble along; your sentences are broken, and there is no continuity of thought. Cultivate the habit of shutting your mouth tight and you will find it will help you control your excitement; and as you control your excitement, so are you enabled to control your thoughts.

A further aid to control over excitement is attention to your breathing. When you are excited your breathing is rapid and consequently short. This affects thought; therefore, when you feel excited practice taking deep breaths until you feel the excitement under control. You can, of course, practice the tight-shut mouth at the same time, thus making the cure more rapid.

EXPECTATION.

You are expecting someone to call in ten minutes' time; it is an important call, and you take up a book or a newspaper to put in the time until your visitor appears. But you cannot read; you feel strung up—you are not yourself. This will show you the important bearing Expectation has on Thought-Control. If you can control your thoughts you greatly lessen the strain which always attends on Expectation.

The reason you feel strain in Expectation is because the expectation of something coming, something happening, sets the muscles in a certain direction; in psychological language, they are prepared for the stimulus.

It is owing to this fact that expectation* of pain always increases the pain. Every medical man knows that the patient who gives him most trouble *after* an operation is the one who *prepares* himself for the operation by casting his muscles in a rigid mould. The reaction is in proportion to the rigidity— the "bearing up." Likewise when we expect a fall and prepare for it (if time permits) by contracting our muscles, we make our injuries, and the shock to the system, more severe. A drunken man taking the same fall will not hurt himself nearly so much, since his muscles are relaxed.

Now remember, Expectation is the *thought* of something about to happen, or something coming. To control your thoughts is to control the strain of Expectation; and to control your thoughts you must turn them aside from the thought of what is coming, or about to happen. You will find you can get wonderful results by a little practice. Next time you are waiting for a friend, practice turning your mind off the thought. *Exercise No. 1* will greatly help you to control Expectation.

SELF-CONSCIOUSNESS.

A young man had to perform a violin solo at an important local concert. The thought of the audience he had to face made him terribly nervous and as he went on the platform he felt like a criminal about to be hung. While the accompanist was playing the introduction to his solo, the young man,

---

*See Chapter XXXIV., Lesson Thirty-two, "Concentration Applied To Fear And Disease—Expectancy And Attention."

who held a position of trust in a business house, suddenly remembered an important letter to which he should have attended before leaving business. As he thought in a flash of the consequences of his neglect, all his nervousness vanished, and he played with a reckless abandon which brought down the house.

This incident illustrates the marvelous power of a change of thought. It shows one that the ability to turn one's thought into another channel must be a valuable acquirement. It is pre-eminently the acquirement to aim at, for everyone who is self-conscious. It is simply a matter of training and practice in putting resolutely to one side thoughts we do not wish to dwell upon. *Exercise No. 1* shows you how to proceed, but with this variation: you must put thought after thought to one side until you come to one on which you can build a pleasant and interesting train of thought.

If you are self-conscious in the presence of strangers, or in fact anyone, adopt the following plan. Immediately the person is before you, greet him in a frank, genial manner, as far as the nature of the occasion permits. While he is talking take note of his language; that is, how he expresses himself —the nature of his vocabulary, his intonation, pronunciation, etc. Note, too, his gestures, mannerisms, dress, etc. All this will tend to take your mind off yourself.

Next, as you find you are succeeding in gaining command over your feelings, determine that you will influence him. Control your facial muscles; see that your body is in perfect poise. Listen carefully to all he says and let him *see* that you are attentive. While he is speaking, be sure that your mouth is shut close, yet not so as to interfere with a pleasing facial expression. When *you* have to speak, look him steadily in the face, fixing your gaze upon an imaginary dot on his nose, in a direct line with his eyes. This gives the effect of a steady gaze and yet you avoid looking at his eyes.

Blushing, that bug-bear of most of those who have not studied Mental Discipline, but especially of the self-conscious person, can be controlled to a great extent by following the advice given above. When you are inclined to blush on being introduced to a person, remember that the vital point is to *think of him* (or *her*) not of yourself, or what he may be thinking of you. If you will practice in this way you will soon find that you can greatly control the habit of blushing.

ACCIDENTS, MISTAKES, ERRORS.

You are invited to a dinner and during the meal you have the misfortune to upset a glass of wine or water over a spotless cloth. Instantly you are overwhelmed with confusion or shame, and in spite of your host's cheery "It does not matter," the unpleasant incident troubles you for many a day.

A business man, in sending out his accounts, sends, in error, a sharp letter to one of his best customers. No matter how he manages to smooth over the mistake it rankles in his mind for weeks and weeks, whenever he thinks of or meets this customer.

A clerk in a business house makes an error in a contract which costs his firm hundreds of dollars. The firm, knowing him to be a capable man, treats him with great leniency. In spite of this the memory of his error causes him annoyance for years afterwards.

How are we to control the thoughts which accidents, mistakes and errors like the above tend to raise? There is only one thing to do, and that is never to *brood* over them.* You cannot help these thoughts arising, but you can help dwelling upon them. If you will resolutely refuse to think of them the law of habit will give you the victory over them.

You must adopt the same plan in dealing with memories of the past. Thus you suddenly detect the odor of a fine cigar or a certain perfume when out walking. Instantly it recalls an unpleasant incident in your past life in which such odor or perfume played a part. Now you must not dwell on this memory, for if you do it will grow in intensity until it has you in its grip. You must follow the advice given above, viz., refuse to think of the incident by *instantly* turning your mind to some other subject.

ADVERSE CRITICISM.

There are few men who can control their thoughts under adverse criticism, yet it must be done if a man is to succeed. Some people take it so badly that they make themselves ill; they lose heart and abandon their work for a considerable

*See *Spontaneous Revival*, in Section on *The Nature of Recall, Chapter XXV., Lesson XXIII.*

period; indeed, in some cases, they abandon it altogether. Some commit suicide.

What course should be adopted towards adverse criticism? The best plan, undoubtedly, is to turn critic yourself. Take the adverse criticism and criticise it carefully and calmly, for it *may* have some good points; it *may* be able to teach you something.

It is not advisable, however, to undertake the critical work when you are smarting from the blow dealt by the adverse criticism. Get away from your work for a day or so; forget it by reading an interesting book, or watching a fine play, or going off for a trip somewhere. When you feel the pain lessened after this interval (which you are almost bound to do) go carefully over the criticism and note where it is just and where it is unjust.

Ole Bull, the great violinist, in his early career, saw a severe criticism of his playing. After careful consideration, he went to the publisher of the paper, and asked who had written the criticism. "If you want the responsible person," said the publisher, "I am he." "No!" replied *Ole Bull*, "I have not come to call the writer to account, but to thank him. He has shown me my faults, and he must now show me how to rid myself of them."

Here we have the spirit of the true artist, the spirit that should animate all under the fire of criticism. *If the criticism is just, we are foolish to ignore its lesson; if it be unjust, we are foolish to let it disturb us.* .

The Master Key

CHAPTER XXI.

LESSON NINETEEN.

THOUGHT CONTROL.

THOUGHT-CONTROL IN PUBLIC.

We shall look at *Thought-Control in Public* from two aspects. *First,* from the point of view of the audience; *Second,* from the performer's point of view. Under the *First,* we shall deal with Thought-Control when a member of a crowd—a crowd in this sense means a collective body of men or women, engaged in something in common. Under *Second,* we shall deal with Thought-Control in Speaking in Public; and Thought-Control in Playing or Singing in Public, i. e., Public Performances.

THOUGHT-CONTROL IN A CROWD.

It is essential that you should recognize the following fact. A crowd is a collective mind, and when you are a member of a crowd you are a different man. It matters not whether you be of good birth or well educated; you many times *sink your individuality* for the time being, and act like a different person.

The intelligence of a crowd is never great—dramatic psychological experiments go to prove this—for crowds are largely dominated by the instincts and emotions. Attend a congress of any body of men or women and you will note this fact at once. One can often note this in a careful reading of the newspaper reports of such gatherings. You will find intelligent men and women acting and speaking quite different from your conception of them. The reason of this is that crowds are contagious and their speech and acts are contagious; for the time being every man and woman is a different individual.

166

To guard against the influence of a crowd it is only necessary to be *aware* of its influence.   Never lose sight of the fact of this influence; remind yourself of it during the meeting, and *determine* that the meeting shall *not* influence you.   Much can be done in this way, as a few trials will convince you.

THOUGHT-CONTROL IN PUBLIC SPEAKING.

Success in speaking in public* demands more than a thorough grasp of the subject on which you are to speak. You must understand the art of controlling an audience, and this involves an understanding of the nature of Fatigue, both in its application to yourself and to your audience.

The first thing you should note is this.   An audience, generally speaking, is sympathetic towards you; it would much rather you did well than badly.   The second point to note is, an audience wants to be interested—secure its interest and you have its attention.   Note, too, that the commencement of your speech is where you must lay the foundation stone of interest; an interesting start and your audience is sympathetically aroused, and then the deadly fear which at first possessed you will gradually vanish as you feel you have your audience in your grip.

Now if your speech or lecture is to be conducted with the minimum of fatigue to you and your audience, you must note the following:

It should be understood that where a speaker or lecturer is concerned with elegance of language, the flow of his sentences, etc.; or where he goes greatly into detail and quotes numerous authorities and dates, he (and his audience likewise) is sure to suffer from fatigue.   If, on the other hand, he adopts an easy style of delivery, approaching a conversational style, neither he nor his audience is nearly so liable to suffer from fatigue.

Much, too, depends on manner; a genial, happy, smiling speaker, generally gains the good-will of his audience at once. Further, the genial, happy attitude of the audience reacts upon the speaker—he gains confidence in himself and his sense of strain vanishes.

---

*See *Lessons Twenty-six, Twenty-seven, and Twenty-eight*—as these Lessons deal exclusively with *"The Art of Public Speaking."*

THOUGHT-CONTROL IN PUBLIC PERFORMANCES.

Everyone who has played, or sung a solo in public, knows that the most trying part is not while you are playing or singing, but the thinking beforehand of the ordeal you will have to undergo. It is this prefunctioning that causes all your trouble. To gain control over this you should follow the advice given throughout this work, and you will find it greatly minimizes your discomfort.

When you are actually before your audience you can greatly control your nervousness by concentrating upon the accompaniment. And in this connection I strongly advise you, whenever possible, to have your own accompanist. Get the idea in your mind that you and your accompanist are engaged in interpreting the composer's ideas. *Feel* that you are both doing all you can to express the composer's ideas. Once you thoroughly *feel* this you will soon forget your nervousness, and your audience will enjoy your performance.

When you have no accompanist, feel that you are responsible to your audience for the view they shall take away with them of the composer's intention. To this end you must not be hampered by technical difficulties; you must be able to give your whole mind to expressing what the composer felt when he wrote the piece you are playing. As you gain, by practice, the power to concentrate upon your playing, you will soon find your nervousness disappear.

THOUGHT-CONTROL IN STUDY.

When you feel confused and distressed in grappling with a problem you should leave it for a few minutes and take your mind off it entirely. Sit still, or lie down, and concentrate upon the words *"Rest"* and *"Peace."*

Say to yourself: "I am at rest and filled with a sense of peace, I have left the world of problems behind in the sure hope that when I am thoroughly rested I shall have no trouble with them."

Cultivate daily this spirit of confidence that rest will restore your powers and enable you to deal successfully with any difficulty you may meet with in your studies. This confidence will grow if you practice it consistently.

In this country people do not sufficiently recognize the value of intervals of rest; they go on until they are thoroughly tired, and perhaps disgusted, with what they have done as regards their studies.

Among intelligent Hindoos great stress is laid on the value of rest. They know that it restores the excitability of nerve and muscle which fatigue has diminished. They devote a part of every day to gaining control over the breath, relaxing their muscles, and quiet meditation. They claim that such practice gives them "physical repose, a calm facial expression and imperturbability of manner."

The great point to guard against in study is to refuse to let it induce the worry-mood. Look at it calmly and quietly and cultivate the attitude—"I know I shall master this problem, or this difficulty."

Remember that emotional states, of which intellectual worry is a type, spread beyond their own area, hence if you can prevent this spreading, by controlling the mental distress, you limit the disturbing elements which are interfering with your progress towards a solution of your difficulties.

Remember, also, that worry in intellectual matters inhibits the ideas of which you are in search. You will have noted this when worrying over a name which you are unable to recall. A few hours afterwards, when you are sitting quietly or perhaps out for a quiet walk, the name will suddenly flash into consciousness. Your brain has rested in the interval, and the nerve-paths which worry had inhibited have now free play and they send up the name you wanted into consciousness.

THOUGHT-CONTROL IN BUSINESS.

There are two points in relation to Thought-Control to which the writer wishes to direct the attention of business men and women. *First, annoyance from correspondence; Second, annoyance from employes.* No business man or woman, especially one at the head of a large business, can afford to suffer daily vexation from these two sources. You *must* obtain control over them if you are to have that calm, cool outlook which modern business conditions demand.

When a business man receives a letter which annoys him greatly he usually gets into a rage, and perhaps vents it upon his employes. He reads and re-reads the letter until he loses all control over himself and very often he sends a stinging or sharp reply to the letter—*a reply which maturer and later judgment will see to be injudicious, and prejudicial to his interests.*

What is the best and wisest course in dealing with such a letter? It is certainly this—put it to one side *instantly* as soon as you have read it. It is the mental *shock* which such a letter gives that one has to control, and this is best controlled by attending to other matters. Get away from the letter and come back to it later according to the time you are limited in which to send a reply. You may not need to reply until the evening post, or it may have to go by the midday post—in either event, observe an interval before reading the letter again.

If you will follow the above plan you will find that the letter will not affect you nearly so much on a second and later reading. It is probable, too, that you will see quite a different meaning in the letter on a second reading than you did in the first reading. Remember, you cannot deal critically with any matter requiring thought and cool judgment when laboring under the stress of emotion.

You must adopt the same attitude when dealing with annoyances caused by your employes. Some employers are foolish enough to storm at their employes right away. Such treatment is often most unjust; it is *always* foolish, for it robs you of a great part of your employes' working power for the remainder of that day, and possibly for days afterwards.

With regard to annoyances of this kind you must not attempt to deal with them right away unless you are sure of yourself. It is better to leave the matter for a time until your anger has subsided; you can then deal with the annoyance calmly and critically without loss of self-respect or loss of the respect of your employes.

Business men and women are advised to read carefully the following section—*Thought-Control in General*—for many of the annoyances of business can be greatly controlled by following the advice given therein.

THOUGHT-CONTROL IN GENERAL.

You run to catch a train, only to find that when you reach the railway station your train has gone. You set off for the theater and on arrival find a notice up—*"House Full."* You have overslept, have to rush your breakfast, and arrive at busi-

ness five to ten minutes late, to receive a severe reprimand from your superiors. You arrange to meet a friend; he fails to keep the appointment.

I need not extend the list; you can supply any number yourself, for these are the little annoyances of life to which all are subject. In all such cases you suffer disappointment or are angry; you blame yourself or some other person for causing you annoyance.

How shall you control your feelings in cases like the above? You should understand the matter thoroughly and this will give you the key. In all such cases your trouble is caused by continuing to think of the annoying thing. You turn it over and over in your mind until your mind is thoroughly inflamed.

Now look back on any of the occasions a week or so after. How do you feel with regard to them; do they cause you the same pain? When you think of them is their sting as sharp as at first? No; you feel you can look at them quietly, without practically any discomfort. This proves to you that in all the above cases you have been in the grip of an emotion which you were unable to control.

Now an emotional state cannot be checked if it gets beyond a certain point. It must be dealt with the instant it makes its appearance or it spreads with alarming rapidity until it embraces the whole of the brain area. Once this happens you cannot check the emotion, for all emotional states, as I have said before, tend to persist long after their birth.

Under all cases of annoyance, therefore, you must practice turning your mind *instantly* off the annoyance. The thing is done—you cannot recall it. If you recall cases that have annoyed you, you will probably say: *"How foolish I was to let that annoy me."* Very well, then, recognize that folly now, and apply it to future cases of annoyance. Much, very much, can be done in this way. Look upon annoyances as training ground in control and you will find half of their power to annoy you gone. *Practice will reveal to you that you can gain enormous control over emotional states.*

The author advises every student to be like a certain commercial traveler he knows. When he loses an order he does not brood or worry over it. He will say to himself: *"Worry is no good;* I'm off after *new* business." You see the point? You have been disappointed—*forget it; go forth to new activities.*

THOUGHT-CONTROL IN ILL-HEALTH.

Thought-Control in Ill-Health is one of the most difficult forms of control. The reason for this is apparent.

When you are ill, mental exertion is extremely difficult. A book which is easy to you when in good health is intolerable when you are ill. Your thinking lacks continuity; you cannot follow the line of argument.

Your brain soon gets tired when you are ill; if you make demands upon it you cause it to send stronger *stimuli* than you ordinarily need to send, in order to contract the muscles; the nervous system is then called upon to lend its aid, and to do this involves a greater intensity of nervous action.

Further, when the brain is tired, as it always is when you are ill or your health below par, it feels everything to be a trouble. It can only think gloomy, sad, dispiriting thoughts. How, then, can any system of control deal with such thoughts.

Now I know for a fact, and you know for a fact, that there *are* people who can do this. How *do* they do it? You will invariably find in all such cases that these people have practiced control over their thoughts when *well*—their control in ill-health then is simply the work of the law of habit.

If you wish to have a measure of control over your thoughts when you are ill, you must lay the foundation by practicing control over your thoughts when you are *well*. *Begin today.* Encourage brave thinking, cheerful thinking, sunny thinking, and you will find the benefit of such practice when you are ill. You will find these thoughts breaking in like sunshine through a cloud, when the gloom of ill-health surrounds you. You will find them cheer you, inspire you, encourage you, to bear with the ill-health until they can rouse your powers to overcome it.

The above is not mere talk, for it is given to you from the personal experience of many. I *know* the benefit such practice has been to me, and I can assure you that if you will follow my advice *you* will know it to be true, should you ever be under the gloom of ill-health.

There is another point to which I would draw your attention under this section, and that is the subject of *Moods;* this has an intimate connection with ill—or indifferent—health.

You get up in the morning feeling out of sorts—you feel inclined to be angry, or quarrel with everyone. If you allow such moods to go unchecked they will cause you a great deal of annoyance. *Control them as follows*:

As soon as you find yourself as above any morning, refuse to acknowledge the mood. Go down stairs resolved to be bright and cheerful. Greet your people with a cheery "Good Morning" and a smile. Carry this attitude with you to business. I can assure you that if you will adopt this plan you will find it effectual in ridding you of your unpleasant moods.

SUMMARY OF LESSON NINETEEN.

Students will note that this Lesson deals mainly with the character of Thought and its influence on your lives. It is also devoted to Emotional and Sensational states and their effect upon one's thoughts. Again, it deals with Thought-Control in specific situations.

Your World. The world is *your* world—it is what you *think* it is.

What Thought can do for you. Your thoughts make or unmake you. You should cherish only such thoughts as will be of service to you.

Thought Atmosphere. Study this Lesson carefully. Get rid of the inner thought-world of regrets, etc. Such thoughts are useless. Change your thought-world and you change your life.

Mental Attitude. Train yourself to approach everything with a certain mental attitude. It is difficult or easy as you think it so. *Do not dwell on difficulty;* recognize it and then dismiss it. Recognize that no effort is lost; facility will come according to the Law of Habit.

Imagination. Understand thoroughly the part played by imagination in *Thought-Control.* Adopt a critical attitude and your fears will vanish.

Confusion of Thought. This is caused by two ideas being present in consciousness at the same moment of time. Its victims are usually all who think deeply. Cultive quickness and definiteness in all you do, to control this.

Fatigue. Mental or physical fatigue makes Thought-Control difficult. Never work or study to the point of exhaustion. Note that training greatly reduces the tendency to fatigue. Be careful how you approach a new study.

Emotions and Sensations.   Note that it is characteristic of
Emotions and Sensations to extend beyond the immediate
brain area affected by them.

Fear.   Fear tends to suppress all mental activity other than
that which the exciting object calls forth.   To control
fear caused by the idea of something, we must ignore the
feelings aroused, by concentrating on other feelings, i. e.,
their opposites.   To control fear of an exciting object arouse
the instinct of Self-Assertion.

Worry.   The things you worry about rarely come to pass;
encourage this thought; it will make you think lightly of
worry.   Control worry by seeking *First*, a change of
thought; *Second*, practicing *Exercise No. 1 and No. 2*.   Remember that worry is always useless, for it paralyzes initiative and effort.

Excitement.   To control excitement pay attention to your
breathing.   Take deep breaths and practice the tight-shut
mouth.   Remember that excitement is a stimulant as well
as a deterrent.

Expectation.   Expectation is the thought of something about
to come, or happen; it is generally attended by strain.   To
control it practice turning the thoughts aside.

Self-Consciousness.   If self-conscious in the presence of
strangers you must think of *them* never of yourself.   Turn
your mind aside by noting their speech, dress, etc.   Blushing yields to the same treatment.

Accidents, etc.   To control the thoughts which these tend to
raise you must not brood over them.   *Instantly* turn your
mind to some other subject.

Adverse Criticism.   As soon as you have read the adverse
criticism leave it; when the mental pain is lessened, criticise
carefully the adverse criticism.   If it is just, recognize it;
if unjust, disregard it.

Thought-Control—In a Crowd.   A crowd is a collective mind;
its acts and words are contagious; its intelligence is never
great.   To guard against its influence be aware of it.
Remember the individuals of a crowd are, for the time
being, different persons.

In Public Speaking.   Success in Public Speaking demands a
knowledge of *First*, your subject; *Second*, crowds and how
to influence them; *Third*, fatigue.   An audience wishes
you, *First*, to do well; *Second*, to be interested—you must

do this right away. Cultivate an easy style of address; be genial and your audience will be genial—this reacts on you and gives you confidence.

In Public Performances. The *thinking* of the ordeal is the trying part. Control your nervousness by concentrating on your accompaniment. *Feel* that you and your accompanist are interpreting the composer's ideas.

In Study. When beset by intellectual difficulties, leave them, and concentrate on *"Rest"* and *Peace."* Cultivate the spirit of confidence that Rest will enable you to conquer the difficulties. Note how the Hindoos value Rest. Guard against the worry mood in study; it spreads over the brain and inhibits the ideas you are in search of. Rest removes the inhibition.

In Business. Business men and women should control annoyances from, *First,* Correspondence; *Second,* Employes. An annoying letter should be put aside *instantly*—this controls the mental shock; it should be replied to after an interval. Adopt the same method re annoyance from Employes— observe an interval and deal with the matter later.

In General. To control the little annoyances of life, check *instantly* the feelings to which they give rise. It is the brooding over them which causes you trouble.

In Ill-Health. All mental exertion is difficult in ill-health; gloomy, dispiriting thoughts rule; the demands on the nervous system are greater. To control, you must begin when you are well; the law of habit will tell; the cheerful, hopeful thoughts formed when you are well tend to rise when you are ill. Note how to control your moods—it is simply a matter of determining to act different to what they suggest.

The Master Key

CHAPTER XXII.

LESSON TWENTY.

HABIT.

FIXED HABITS, GOOD HABITS, BAD HABITS.

It is the first week in the New Year. You write out a cheque and present it to your bankers for payment. If you watch the cashier closely, you will notice that almost the first glance he gives at your cheque is in the direction of the date. Why does he do this? Simply because experience has taught him that the probability is that you will have put the date of the past, instead of the present year.

Here you have the nature of *habit exemplified*, viz.—that tendency of the mind to repeat its processes with their characteristic movements. According to the frequency with which you have performed an act, or thought along certain lines, so will you tend to repeat these acts or processes more readily; likewise you will give preference to that which you have done before, or thought before, rather than to new ways of doing or thinking. Many are creatures of habit—once they get into a rut they tend to keep to it.

The effect of habit on the plasticity of the brain is like the effect made upon a piece of paper when you bend it or crease it. The crease remains in the paper no matter how you attempt to straighten it out again. In like manner every thought we think forms a pathway through the brain, and once made we cannot destroy its traces, although we can modify its influence by other thoughts.

OUTSTANDING FEATURES OF FIXED HABITS.

A fixed, or "set" habit, is marked by the following outstanding features: *Automatism* and *Facility.*

If you analyze Automatism you find the following peculi-

176

arities: *First*, it always acts in the same way; *Second*, it is antagonistic to interference or adjustment; *Third*, it seems to be, independent of attention.

First—Illustrates why you act in a routine way; why you tend to go to business always along the same streets; why you perform your work in a certain order or arrangement; why you prefer one restaurant or hotel than others—it is all a matter of custom with you.

Second—Illustrates why you hate innovation or new methods. Business men are very familiar with this attitude: commercials introducing a novelty, or a time saving device, know how difficult it is to get their first order if the new *"line"* interferes with their customer's fixed business methods.

Third—A familiar example of this peculiarity is seen when you watch an expert musician. He will, perhaps, be talking to you while his fingers are making the most complicated movements.

I will now take the other outstanding feature of habit—*Facility*. If you watch a clever juggler, or a *virtuoso*, you are struck by the ease with which they seem to go through their complicated movements. If you go home and attempt to imitate their movements you are at once aware of the enormous difficulties they have overcome. How is it that these people can perform with ease that which is an impossibility to you? Leaving genius or talent out of account, the reason is simply this: their muscles, by long and arduous training, have become accustomed to these complex movements, hence they can go through their performance *with a minimum of attention, and fatigue.*

The acquisition of skill proceeds on the following lines. At first you use more muscles than are required for the work in hand. If you are working intelligently you will note this, and your constant effort will be to use only such muscles as are absolutely necessary; gradually the interfering muscles are got under control, at each renewal of effort, until finally you can perform with ease. Once you reach this stage there is no need for attentive effort (conation) ; hence future performances become more and more automatic. In the case of a musician, when he reaches the above stage, he is not hampered by *technique,* hence he can put *his soul* into his playing.

THE FORMATION OF GOOD HABITS.

In forming a new habit your success will depend greatly upon the strength of its start.   A powerful, determined set off is of prime importance and the best set off is when you act upon your impulse of the moment, for at such times the better part of your nature is uppermost.   (The writer is dealing with good impulses, of course.)   "Habits are formed only in the service of the instincts," therefore, when you decide, under emotional stress, to form a new habit, it is essential to act *at once* while the impulse is with you.

Again, you should embrace every opportunity, when the impulse returns, to strengthen your original resolution, for this will make a strong impression on the *neural* brain paths.   It is important also, once you have "turned over a new leaf" to give the new habit constant attention and encouragement.   *Never say*: "I will make an exception just this once"—such treatment tends to kill a new habit, for the "just once" is apt to be repeated on another occasion.

The old theological writers used to say: *"Satan likes a man who will argue with him."*   Once you have made a good resolution, never look behind; do not begin to wonder if you have done right, or if it will turn out all right—*go ahead with it.*

In forming habits that involve the acquisition of skill, it is of vital importance that the first steps be strictly accurate. Thousands of pupils, who have learned the piano or violin from an indifferent teacher, are doomed to remain poor players all their lives, no matter how they practice.   Their only salvation is to commence again under a good teacher, and this will entail much trouble, even where the desire to learn is keen. Students will understand the reason of this by a careful consideration of the next section.

THE PERMANENCY OF HABIT.

Dr. Schofield relates in "The Unconscious Mind" how *Houdin* the conjurer trained himself in the difficult habit of reading aloud while keeping four balls going in the air.   He did not practice this for many years, and yet, after thirty years found he could still read and keep three balls going.

It is owing to this permanency of habit that musicians who

have been *thoroughly* trained in their youth, and have, perhaps, drifted into other professions, are able to resume their practice years after, with but a slight falling off in skill; a little practice, and they soon find themselves able to perform the works of their youth.

If you are conscious that you are forming bad habits you should remember the permanency of habit.

We may forget and forgive, but the neurines* never forget or forgive.

HOW TO CURE BAD HABITS.

In Chapter XXV, Lesson Twenty-three, on *Memory,* under section "The Art of Forgetting," you are told, in attempting to forget ideas which you do not wish to remember, that you cannot oppose such ideas directly.

It is the same with bad habits; it is useless to fight them—you must get away from them by banishing them to the sea of forgetfulness as advised elsewhere in this work.

It is the error of many to fight useless battles—useless either because being weak they are sure to be beaten, or because though strong they gain victory at too great a cost.

How then should you deal with bad habits? An example will, perhaps, be the best way to illustrate this. Take the case of a man who has given way to vice. After every transgression he is overwhelmed with shame; he hates himself; he will never give way again. If he has been brought up in a Christian home he prays to be delivered from the evil which is sapping away his life, but in many cases his prayers are of no avail. Why? Because the *man* has not really altered. His desires are as strong as ever and are, for the moment, merely in the background. The *neurines** are quietly waiting, ready to respond to the slightest *stimulus.* On the other hand, *should* the man succeed by fighting, it will be at the cost of *terrible mental anguish.*

Is there an easier way than fighting? There is, and it is as I said above, by running away. *What this man should do is to cultivate friendship with Virtue.* He must *think virtue, love virtue, live virtue.* He must surround himself with virtuous friends, virtuous books, virtuous influences. He must *meditate upon virtue* and constantly encourage himself to walk in

---

*Nerve-cells.

her paths.   By following this plan he will give vice nothing to feed on, and, like everything else that must have sustenance, vice will soon starve and die when food is withheld it.

Further—our man must not dwell on his lapses; he must not call down the wrath of God to destroy him—he must *forget* his lapses, and march steadily onward.   The greatest stumbling hlock in the overcoming of bad habits is this tendency to dwell on your lapses; you must get away from these by using every influence to forget them.   *To conquer bad habits forget them by concentrating upon their opposites.*

Minor bad habits, such as biting the finger nails, indulging in gestures, and the loss of control, as told elsewhere in this work, are best overcome by becoming conscious of the habit. Nearly all these habits are purely automatic, and if you concentrate your attention upon them and fully determine to be rid of them, you can be sure of victory.

For Summary of Lesson Twenty, see page 206.

The Master Key

Part Four

CHAPTER XXIII.

LESSON TWENTY-ONE.

WILL CULTURE—MIND TRAINING.

THE NATURE OF VOLITION.

"A volition is the self-realization of an idea with which the self is identified."

It has been said that *"Volition** is nothing but Attention," and "Attention with effort is all that any case of Volition implies." *Volition, however, cannot be dismissed so easily—what do you mean by effort?*

Before you can attend to an act of Volition you must have an idea upon which to focus attention. This idea must be one with which you can identify yourself; it must have a definiteness of aim, so that the end to be achieved can be foreseen.

Suppose you resolve to master a problem in mathematics. The problem forms your idea and upon it you focus all your attention. You know the problem to be difficult, yet you feel its difficulties are not beyond your powers. The end in view is the solution of the problem, and you know when you reach this end that you will experience pleasure—satisfaction.

When you *"will"* to solve the problem you know it will require close attention; do you feel that your attention is the *"MASTER KEY"* in the situation? No—you feel that the *"MASTER KEY"* is the spirit within you—the *"Self"*—which

---

*Volition is to be preferred to the term *"Will"* since *Will* is used in a dual sense. (1) As the faculty (so-called) of willing. (2) As the act of willing. Volition is always used in the sense of the act of willing.

181

will not be satisfied until the problem is solved. *Attention* is of vital importance, but *Volition* is something more than this; it is the conative spirit within you—the striving, urging, driving, *won't-be-beaten* element, which will not rest until it is satisfied, and then, like all conation, ceases, *leaving Will triumphant.*

But suppose while you are attending to the problem some idea, other than the problem, enters consciousness—an idea rooted in your instincts or impulses; and suppose this idea is strong enough to make you abandon the problem—*this alien idea will not be a Volition, for it is not identified with the "Self"; it was not willed by you.*

You will now see that for an idea to constitute a Volition it must be one that is identified with you; you must be able to keep it at the focus of consciousness; you must be able to inhibit all other ideas, and the power that is going to enable you to do this is the thought of what you are going to do coupled with the conative spirit within you, urging you to satisfy it—this forms your impulse to action, and according to its strength will be the probability of your succeeding in solving the problem.   So recognized is this that when you speak of a certain type of man as about to do something we say: *"Oh! he is sure to succeed; he has got it in him."*

This initial impulse calls upon the whole organism to support its efforts—common speech recognizes this when it says: "Smith has succeeded, but it took it out of him."   Just as the thought of strength adds to our strength, this initial impulse with its mental and physical helpers, forms the motor force which lies behind Attention, and as it gathers strength, *forces* you to attend.   The conative element—the striving, struggling, driving element, is, therefore, *the prime essential in Volition,* and Attention may, therefore, be said to be merely its attendant.

FACTORS THAT INFLUENCE VOLITION.

Every time you will to do something, that is, every time you focus attention on an idea with the object of carrying it out in fact, there are certain things which help you and certain things that hinder you in the *Volitional* process. These things or factors have a dual nature—sometimes they are friendly to your cause and help you enormously; at other times they wreck your resolutions and plunge you into despair.

That you may consider these factors, I will group them as follows:

> *First, Emotions and Instincts; Second, Desires and Motives; Third, Suggestion. The student should examine each of these three groups carefully, for their analysis will help greatly when he comes to the question of "How to educate the Will." Students are, therefore, requested to give particular attention to the remarks under each group.*

THE EMOTIONS AND INSTINCTS.

In treating the *Emotions* and *Instincts* I shall deal first with *"The Nature of Emotion"*; next *"The Nature of Instinct,"* and lastly, *"The Emotions* and their correlate *Instincts."*

THE NATURE OF EMOTION.

That the student may understand better what is meant by Emotion, I will here give the order of the events in an emotional state. *First,* perception of an exciting object; *Second,* mental shock; *Third,* correlation of bodily disturbance or commotion with the shock.

If you are walking through a field and you suddenly see a bull coming tearing after you, the perception of this exciting object causes you a mental shock—the mental distress is immediately followed by bodily distress. The emotion of Fear now arouses its correlate instinct, Flight, and you take to your heels as best as your mental and bodily distress will allow you.

The above illustrates the *perceptual class* of emotional states; the other classes are the *ideational class* and the *organic class.* Thus, sometimes, the thought of something, the mere "idea" is sufficient to commence the emotional process; at other times, organic changes; that is, a disturbance in the *viscera,* or any bodily organ, is sufficient to arouse an emotion. Drugs and alcohol have a like effect. Thus, *"Bromides* will render a brave man—one quick to anger—timid and dull, while tonics —*cafeine, kola* or *alcohol*—taken in excess, can make one who is generally low spirited and not particularly heroic, merry, adventurous or even cruel."

Emotions are marked by two characteristic outstanding

features—*First*, their tendency to persist when once aroused; *Second*, to attack any object which presents itself.   This latter feature is very marked in animals.   Thus, a number of dogs attracted by, and failing to understand, the cause of another dog's howling, commence to fight with each other.   Their emotions having been aroused, the dogs seize on the first thing that presents itself—another dog.   Men are like animals in this respect.   Let the emotion of anger be aroused and they are ready to fight with their dearest and closest friends.

THE NATURE OF INSTINCT.

Primitive man was dominated by his instincts.   If he was angry he "let go" without considering the result; if he was afraid he took to his heels at once; if he wanted a wife, he did not wait to get her parents' consent; he took her by force, if need be.*   With primitive man his instincts were impulses to act immediately, and this features is still prominent today.

Instincts may be regarded as innate tendencies of the mind to act in a specific way—ways which you usually say are independent of education, previous experience, or a knowledge of ends.   They are distinguished from a reflex action since they involve perception as well as sensational factors.   They cannot be acquired nor entirely eradicated, but suffer modification to a certain extent through environment.   Many instincts are not constant, they ripen at a certain age and then die away.

It is owing to the power of instincts that education has such feeble results in moulding character.   *To understand a child you must understand its dominant instincts*—all your fault finding, your admonition, your punishments, will be of little avail unless you understand the part a child's instincts plays in its life.   And this applies to yourself also; if *you* wish to understand yourself you must study your instincts and the part they play, and have played in your life.   *Your instincts are the hidden forces that are constantly spurring you on to good or evil;* they inspire you to, or deter you from, actions that lead to success in any pursuit; they color all your thoughts; they can plunge you into the depths of despair, or raise you to the heights of bliss—you *cannot* ignore them.

---

*See the interesting account of Marriage by Capture in "A History of Politics" by Edward Jenks, M.A. (pp. 26-27).

THE EMOTIONS AND THEIR CORRELATE INSTINCTS.

Every emotion has its corresponding instinct, and every instinct its corresponding emotion.

Fear is, perhaps, the strongest of the emotions; once it is aroused it raises the instinct of *Flight*. Where the fear is overpowering, the instinct of flight gives way to that of *concealment*. In both cases the respiration suffers, but in the paralyzing fear which leads to concealment, the heart beat grows less and almost stops, just as if the organism were trying to stifle all noise.

The emotion of *Anger* is correlated with the instinct of *Pugnacity*. Closely allied with *Anger* is the emotion of *Disgust* leading to the instinct of *Repulsion*—you seek to push the offending object out of sight. The emotion of *Wonder* rouses the instinct of *Curiosity*. If Wonder attains a certain stage it passes into the emotion of Fear. The emotion of *Exhilaration*—the joyous, full of life feeling, rouses the instinct of *Assertiveness*—the *"I'm the man," "I can do it," "I'm master," "Get out of the way"* feeling. The negative of the emotion of Exhilaration is the emotion of *Depression* or *Despondency*—the "Life is not worth living," "Everything is going to the dogs" feeling, with its correlate instinct of *Self-Repression*—the humble, slinking, crouching, "lick the dust" feeling. What are called the *Tender Emotions*—Pity, Sympathy, Gratitude, etc., are connected with the *Parental Instincts.*

All the other emotions and instincts are either derived from the above primary emotions and instincts, or are composite forms of them. Thus Joy and Sorrow, Love and Hate, are commonly regarded as complex emotions, since several factors combine to produce these states.

Emotion* is the *feeling* that results from the bodily changes following the mental shock aroused by the perception of the exciting object.

---

*Students who are interested in the subject of the Emotions and Instincts should read under their respective chapters in Dr. McDougall's admirable work—"Social Psychology." See also Prof. Stout's "Groundwork of Psychology" (which contains a chapter on "The Tender Emotions" by Alexander F. Shand); Prof. James's "Text Book of Psychology"; Ribot's "The Psychology of the Emotions.' All these works are easily procured through a good bookseller.

DESIRE AND MOTIVE.

Desires and motives play an important part in Volition; therefore, you should attempt to get a rough idea of what is meant by these terms.

A Desire is commonly regarded as an uneasy sense of want, a longing for something which craves for satisfaction. But a desire is more than this; it is also more than an impulse, for in real desire we are always conscious of the end we seek. The origin of a desire may be either physical or mental, but it is always a mental (psychical) process.

It is important to note that the strength of a desire lies not in itself, but in the totality of desires which go to make up a person's character. Thus if you have a sudden desire to steal, this single desire will have no force unless it is associated with other desires in your being which tend to support it. Again, you may have a desire for learning, to be a learned man; but if the dominant desires of your nature are for ease or enjoyment, your desire for learning will have little chance in a conflict with these stronger desires.

A Motive is more than a desire. A desire may be a *quasi-impulse* to act, but a motive is that which induces you to act. You may desire wealth and get no further, but if wealth becomes a motive it leads you to act in such ways as will result in the attainment of wealth.

Motives may be either good or bad, but in either case their objective is something you hope to achieve—you conceive an end and you work for this end. It is not always easy to know or distinguish your real motives for acting in a certain way, and in nothing do you deceive yourselves so much as when you say your motive for doing a certain thing was so and so; it is only when you come to analyze your motive that you find it something totally different from what you thought it was.

SUGGESTION.

Suggestion is of vital importance in understanding the *Volitional Process.* Consider for a moment the part it plays in your life.

A great scientist announces that apples contain an element which is the true elixir of life and forthwith thousands of people, on the strength of this statement, commence eating apples. A fashion paper announces that a certain color will be the vogue in the coming season, and thousands of ladies order their dresses accordingly. A music teacher has certain little mannerisms in playing—all his pupils tend to copy these as part of his system. A medical student conceives that his professor in going through the wards has a perfect bedside manner—he adopts this unhesitatingly when he gains a practice of his own. The writer need not extend the list. If you reflect a little, you will be convinced that everyone in some way is influenced by suggestion.

Suggestion seems to be rooted in the innate tendency of animals to imitate or copy the actions of other animals. Just as we can hardly think of a movement without some attempt to carry it out, so when we see other people doing a certain act that appeals to us we feel the impulse to follow their example.

Watch a football crowd and you will notice how the crowd breaks out into movement when the players get the ball away. Note in yourself the impulse to run when you see in a *Rugby* game a three-quarter back rush down the field with the ball. Similarly when seated in a cab, hurrying to catch a train, many people can hardly resist the impulse to be up and doing, and you will find them in continual motion all the way to the train.

Suggestion is a process of communication resulting in the acceptance with conviction of the communicated proposition in the absence of logically adequate grounds for its acceptance.

Liability to suggestion depends on the following factors: If the suggestion is made by a person its power over you will depend on,

First, the strength of the personality of the one making the suggestion.

Second, his relations to you.

Third, the degree of your knowledge involved in the suggestion.

Fourth, your receptiveness at the time when the suggestion is made.

Under (*First*) note that personality is a complex. Some people impress you by the *manner* in which they make the suggestion. It may be conveyed in an impressive manner, or by a hint, gesture, or command. Personality, again, passes into (*Second*) your relation to the person making the suggestion, whether as superior, (in position or intelligence) employer, teacher, friend. Clergymen and doctors may be taken as types of relational suggestion. If your doctor says you look better, you feel better. Note, too, the part the instinct of Assertiveness plays in relational suggestion. If you feel you are in the presence of your inferiors, (as regards position, influence, wealth, learning), the impulse to assert yourself becomes dominant; whereas in the presence of your superiors the instinct of Self-Repression—the *"keep in the back ground"* feeling—tends to manifest itself.

The degree of your knowledge (*Third*) or convictions, in any subject will be the measure of your suggestibility, in that subject. You will understand this better if you reflect how readily children accept a suggestion owing to the limitations of their knowledge. If a suggestion is in agreement with your convictions it has you in its power at once.

Your receptiveness (*Fourth*) in suggestion varies greatly according to time, place and circumstances. If you are tired, suggestions to *"give up"* what you are doing will have great weight with you. A suggestion to reform which in ordinary circumstances would have no weight, becomes well nigh irresistible when made by a popular preacher from his pulpit.

I will now consider briefly the circumstances under which suggestions come to you, not from a person, but from outside influences. Such are, books, newspapers, travel, advertisements, plays. The power of suggestion here will be your receptiveness at the time, and your degree of knowledge of the subject. These non-personal suggestions play an important part in one's life; it would hardly be too much to say that they exercise a greater power over us than personal suggestions, for often a suggestion from a person is marred by some mannerism on his part which arouses instincts antagonistic to it.

TYPES OF WILL.

The part played by Type is one of the most interesting sections in the study of the Will. I shall describe, briefly, ten main Types of Will.

The Impulsive type. This is the commonest of all the Types of Will. It acts on the spur of the moment without regard to consequences. It is dominated by the instincts, refuses to listen to reason, and in consequence often plunges its possessor into disaster.

The Imperative Type. The Imperative or Commanding Type
is dominated by the instinct of Assertiveness. It demands everything to give way to it, and seeks to bend everything to its purpose. It differs from the Impulsive Type in that its ends are
clearly marked out and the means necessary thereto generally
well conceived.

The Confident Type. This Type is closely allied to the Impulsive; it is distinguished therefrom by a belief in its ability to
execute anything it undertakes. It regards success as certain,
yet often fails through neglecting to take the means necessary
to success. It is apt to jump to conclusions, disregard data, and
rely on chance to carry it through. (It must not be confounded
with the confidence which is rooted in experience and knowledge.)

The Contrary Type. Many children display this Type in a
marked degree. They delight in acting contrary to instructions
and advice. It is prominent also in some men who seem to think
its possession a mark of superiority, or a higher degree of intelligence. Its possessor is not to be envied for it *"sets the back up"*
of everyone who comes into contact with it. Some people term
this Type the spirit of *"pure cussedness."* Every man who seeks
for success and recognizes that he belongs to the *Contrary Type,*
should recognize that he is running the race with needless weight.

The Automatic Type. Business men are familiar with this
Type—the routine type. It tends always to work in familiar
paths. If a thing has to be done, it must be done on old lines;
it never seeks novel or better ways of doing things, and indeed
distrusts any departure from custom. It is almost entirely the
creature of habit.

The Unconscious Type. It seems a contradiction to speak of
any Type of Will as the Unconscious Type, yet you will all understand what is meant by it if you consult the annals of genius.
The genius feels an innate power spurring him on, he knows not
where. You will readily recognize this element when you speak
of his work as the result of his genius. Many who are not
geniuses have felt a touch of this hidden, subliminal power; they
set out to do a thing not very confident of success, yet the result
may be a brilliant success. You speak of it afterwards by saying,
"I worked better than I knew."

The Fatalistic Type. This type works under peculiar conditions; if a thing *is* to be a success, it *will* be a sucess; if it is *not*
to be a success, it will *not* be a success. Often this type recognizes that reason is against its mode of working, but it shuts its
eyes to the fact and keeps to its course.

The Indecisive Type. Everyone will recognize this Type; we
have, perhaps, all belonged to it at some time or other. It conceives an end and the means to an end, but almost immediately

other ends are conceived which negative the former. The mind wavers between ideas and very often the project gets no further than the initial stage.

The Thoughtful Type. This Type makes everything subject to reason; nothing must be decided upon until it has been carefully worked out. It is often marked by indecision or *fatalism* if the thought is unduly prolonged.

The Ideal Type. "It is important that you should get rid of the habit of thinking of the Ideal as something too good to be true." You should regard it rather as the principle which determines your actions. The Ideal Type, then, is distinguished from the other Types in that it seeks to make use of everything that will help its purpose. It understands and makes use of its impulses; it knows when to assert itself; its confidence is based on its own powers correlated with its past experience and knowledge; it knows when to differ from an opponent, and is not above correction; it knows what part in action can be left with safety to automatism, and it knows also the value of a careful, thoughtful review before acting. This is the Type I commend to you, to take as your guide in the Volitional Process.

THE FREEDOM OF THE WILL.

You are suddenly faced with a temptation to steal. You have two alternatives—to obey the impulse or to dismiss it. Determinists, or *Necessitarians,* hold that whichever way you choose is determined by laws over which you have no control. Your present decision is the resultant of past decisions; it represents your present circumstances, your past history and your character as a whole. Libertarians, or Indeterminists, hold that in the moment of decision your power to choose the one or the other alternative is equal, no matter what your past has been, or the nature of the present conditions.

It is now generally recognized that these two schools of writers simply represent opposite sides of the same truth and that the idea of self-determination combines the two sides. *You* are free to act in as far as *yourself* will allow you—there is nothing outside of you forcing you to act contrary to your inclination—the resistance, if there be any, comes from within *you.*

The above will enable you to understand what is meant by circumstances; they are not mere external conditions; they are only circumstances in an ethical sense in so far as they affect your lives. In conditions or circumstances common to two

plays the leading role in your life; the type your intimate
friends mostly know you by.

If you were asked to name the type to which your friend
Baker belonged you would not judge him by occasional glimpses
of his character; you would sum up his character into a whole
and you would say: *"On the whole I think Baker belongs
to the Impulsive Type."* In seeking to understand *your* type,
therefore, you must ask yourself fairly: "Which of these
types is most characteristic of me?" When you can answer
this you will have found your type.

Once you have found your type you will have found also
your mental attitude towards life. Suppose you fix your type
as the *Confident Type;* your mental attitude is the *"it's all
right,"* "success is sure," "everything is rosy" attitude. The
confident man lives for a time under the emotion of Exhilaration; when his plans go wrong, he generally takes a deep
plunge into the emotion of Depression—he tries to get out of
your road when he sees you coming.

Once you have found your type you should do all you can
to get into the Ideal Type, for this is the type that gives the
greatest pleasure and the minimum of pain. It is the persevering type par excellence.

HOW MOTIVES DETERMINE SUCCESS.

An analysis of your motives for doing anything will be
a gauge as to your success. You recognize this when you reply
to anyone: "If that was your motive it is no wonder you did
not succeed."

I will illustrate. Suppose you wish to learn the Violin—
what is your motive? You may reply: "I would like to play
well, so that I may entertain my friends, or take part in a public
performance." Your real motive may be simply to excel a
friend who has just commenced to learn the instrument. You
would like to be a great preacher—*what is your motive?* "I
want to do good in the world, raise men out of the depths of
despair, and to put their feet on the right road." Your real
motive may be the applause of men. You would like to be
a great writer—*what is your motive?* "I want to instruct (or
amuse) mankind." *Your real motive may be simply to make
money.*

The above examples will show you the part *Motive* plays

in *Volition,* and how it interferes with your success. Your real
motive is always the dominant factor in *Volition;* it is, therefore, of the utmost importance to every student of the Will to
thoroughly understand his motives, and careful analysis is the
only means of securing this.

Your real motives may be right or wrong as judged by
worldly standards; their strength will lie in their power to urge
you onwards to your goal. When you *know* your real motive
you add to its impulsive, driving power; you have no conflict
between the false and the real motive constantly retarding your
progress.

HOW TO CONTROL YOUR EMOTIONS AND IMPULSES.

The phenomena of hypnotism has demonstrated that if you
place a subject in a characteristic attitude he instantly assumes
the character represented by the attitude. Thus, if you place
him in the attitude characteristic of boxing, his face assumes
the determined or angry look of a man about to fight. Put
him on his knees, and fold his hands in the attitude of prayer,
and his face *"takes on" a devotional look.*

What may you learn from the above? You may learn this
—you can simulate any emotion if you will imitate as far as
possible the bodily changes and facial expression which accompany it.

Suppose you simulate Anger. For this purpose you imagine some one standing in front of you who has done you an
injury. You look steadily at him and rise threateningly; your
muscles become tense, your breathing labored; you clench your
fists as you feel the pugnacious instinct aroused. If your sim-
ulation is perfect you *feel* angry. And yet there is something
lacking—it is the mental shock. Yet this can be made real if
you bring to memory a case where you had reason to be angry;
and then you note the tendency of the feeling to persist, which
is a characteristic of emotional states.

To control an emotional state, then, you can simulate its
opposite. If you are sad, you can simulate joy and gladness;
if you are afraid, you can simulate boldness; if you feel full
of hate, you can simulate love.

Another way to control an emotion is to analyze it. When
you are angry and are conscious of it, ask yourself why you

are angry. Go over the ground; reason it out with yourself if circumstances permit. Some people employ this method with marked success, but usually it does not give such good results as the former method.*

How shall you control an impulse? By learning to recognize its character instantly. Is it a good impulse? If so, follow it. Is it a bad impulse? Then check it instantly. Impulses by their very nature *demand* immediate action; you must gratify this—act quickly whether the impulse be good or bad. In the former case, follow it; in the latter, dismiss it.

You will say, perhaps, it is impossible to check a bad impulse. If this were so a thief would always be stealing, policeman or no policeman. The fact is no one obeys an impulse (abnormal cases excepted) without a brief interval of reflection. The thief looks round to see if the way is clear; the liar rapidly sums up the situation before replying. I am speaking here of what may be termed the initial impulse. It is characteristic of impulses that according as they are heeded so do they gather strength. You see this markedly in the case of an angry man who eventually comes to blows.

QUALITIES TO CULTIVATE.

The man who aims at success must cultivate good qualities. He must be industrious, hopeful, cheerful.

What is the great enemy we all have to fight when we seek to cultivate industry? It is *Indolence*. Fight, then, your indolent moods; be chary of saying, "I do not feel in form today." Do not act on this mood without first testing it. If you are *really* unwell you will be unable to go on with your task; if you are merely lazy, the fit will wear off if you keep to your task. The best way to fight indolence is to have set times for doing things and keep to these times. Make a time chart and stick to it. *Live by Rule.*

Hope is a quality that is possessed by every successful man, and it is a quality that *can* be acquired. The hope you must acquire must have its basis in *faith in yourself*. This hope is very different from the Micawber type—the hope that hopes that something will turn up. When you have faith in yourself you feel you *can* hope, *ought* to hope. Make milestones

---

all deal further with the control of an emotion in the section on 't-Control."

on the road of hope; that is, review your work occasionally and note the progress you are making.

> "A merry heart maketh a cheerful countenance;
> but by sorrow of the heart the spirit is broken."
>
> —(Prov. XV; 13.)
>
> "He that is of a merry heart
> hath a continual feast."
>
> —(Prov. XV; 15.)

Cheerfulness must be cultivated. Cheerfulness is largely a habit of mind, and like all habits, can be acquired. We all like to meet the cheerful man; we feel he is an inspiration to us. But the cheerful man is more than this—he is an inspiration to himself. He feels that his cheerfulness increases his energy; enables him to work easier. He feels, too, that it attracts people to him, and gains him an audience at doors where the despondent man knocks unheeded. But remember, true cheerfulness is not a veneer; it is solid, "all of a piece"; it is the *whole* man.

> "A merry heart doeth good
> like a medicine; but a broken
> spirit drieth the bones."
>
> —(Prov. XVII; 22.)

To cultivate cheerfulness you must adopt the attitude of the cheerful man. You must encourage cheerful, joyful thoughts, and be on the lookout for them. You must encourage such words as Happy, Joyful, Merry. Get amongst people and books of this type, but be sure they are the right type with no veneer, or lack of backbone about them.

Get up in the morning determined to be cheerful. Greet your friends and associates with a smile, a smile that is the essence of good nature. Cultivate the art of smiling by looking at yourself in a mirror. Note how the mind takes on a different attitude when you smile—if you can keep on smiling, despondency must say good-bye. Do not confuse a smile with the idiotic or silly grin which some people seem to think it; *remember smiling is an art, and must be used with art.*

Cultivate *Politeness* and *Courtesy*. If you wish to make the wheels of life run smoothly, you will be polite and courteous. Note that politeness is really a bending down, as it were, of a superior to an inferior; it therefore demands infinite tact. *A polite man is an educated, refined man; one who seeks opportunities to please; one who is full of delicate attentions and seeks to anticipate the wishes of others.*

A courteous man is one who pays particular regard to address and manners.

Courtesy is practiced between strangers; true politeness is practiced between strangers and friends alike.

To cultivate Politeness and Courtesy you must have models. Study the people with whom you come into contact. The best of us can learn in this way, for no man can claim to be an absolute model. Note specially what is pleasing to you; and note also its effect on others when you come to employ the methods and art of your model. You will learn much in this way if you are observant.

Cultivate *Charm.* Charm is an elusive and indefinable quality; I speak of the charms of person and of mind. It is an inherent quality; that is, its springs are within. Charm is always interesting, always potent. To cultivate it, as in the case of politeness and courtesy, you must have models. Note the persons who seem to you to possess charm, and try to discover by careful observation and analysis wherein lies their charm. Its elusiveness will probably defeat you in discovering *all its secret,* yet if you can take away something of it you will have done well.

HOW TO CULTIVATE SELF-RELIANCE.

One of the *first rules* for the man who wishes to cultivate Self-Reliance is the rule given in Lesson Two of this work, viz: *"Keep your mouth shut."* This does not mean merely compressing the lips; it means the action of setting the teeth together, just as you would do in biting something. This braces the biting muscles and gives the face that set, square-jawed look which is so characteristic of the man of grim determination—*the man of strong will.*

This setting of the teeth is closely connected with the pugnacious instinct. In prehistoric man his teeth were weapons of defense and attack, and with him the setting of his teeth together was the preliminary to attacking his enemy. Something of this old fighting spirit or instinct still survives with us, when we set our teeth close and shut our mouth. We feel ready to do—the spirit of fight or attack is aroused. I still speak of attacking things *"tooth and nail."*

The *second rule* is, develop your instinct of *Self-Assertion;* concentrate on such words as *Boldness, Courage, Defiance,*

Strong, Powerful, Resolute, Imperious. Try to imagine yourself as possessing these qualities. Five minutes' drill per day in this way will remake your character. You will feel a thrill go through you as the repeating of, and the concentrating upon, these words arouses the powerful instinct of *Self-Assertion.* Try to carry something of this feeling into your daily life. Learn to look at people with a steady gaze—the gaze of quiet confidence. Always remember to employ tact when asserting yourself.

The *third rule* is, never indulge in self-depreciation*—the *"I'm no good"* sort of feeling. It does you an immense amount of harm, both physically and mentally. Nothing tends quicker to lower your vitality, your stamina, than self-depreciation and self-condemnation. It is the worst enemy the will-power student has to fight, but it *must* be fought if any success is to be won.

THE WILL IN ACTION.

Whatever part you wish to play in life, you must act the part NOW. Suppose you join a Dramatic Society, and are called upon to take your part in a play. The book of the play is handed to you, and forthwith you commence to study your part. As you dwell upon the character you are to play you gain a conception of how he will act in certain situations. You study how your man will talk; how he will walk; his manners. You will carry this conception with you on the stage. If your conception is wrong the stage manager will draw your attention to it, forcibly, if need be. While the play is being rehearsed you will find yourself, even at your work, living in the character and times of the man you are to play. *For the time being you are your part—your character.*

Now life is a stage on a larger scale; you *must* take a part—*there is no escape.* There is this difference, however, the number of parts to choose from is almost infinite. *What part will you play?*

What the writer is seeking to impress upon the student is the fact that whatever part you wish to play in life you must *act* the part. And first you must know *definitely* the character you wish to represent. It is no use saying: "I wish to play

*"Self-depreciation and self-condemnation is the rock upon which many a man and woman has been wrecked. Study Lesson Thirty-one, "Concentration Applied To Health And Disease, "The Psychology Of Faith And Doubt."

the part of a wealthy merchant"; you must know what kind of merchant; his business. When you know this you have something to go on; you will then study the line of action necessary to reach the end you seek. You will employ the aid of books, of friends, strangers, experts; you will make use of everything and everybody to aid you to be your typical merchant; you must work and toil as this man worked, yet avoiding, as far as possible, the mistakes he made; you must practice his habits of self-denial, his industry, his hopefulness, his perseverance, and you must commence NOW.

All that I said above in reference to the Dramatic Society applies to your part in life. You must dwell upon the character you are to play; you must conceive how he will talk, act, and work. *Life itself will be the stage manager and point out where you are wrong.* It will teach you to avoid anything that offends in the character you are representing, for, fortunately, you are not compelled, as you are in the Dramatic world, to represent the follies and weaknesses of your part. Experience will teach you how to avoid these and how to copy only such qualities and characteristics as are worthy of being copied. And now let the student of success study how to act the part, and he shall find the great secret of success.

AUTO-SUGGESTION.

It is customary with certain people to dismiss, as unworthy of serious consideration, any reference to *Auto-Suggestion.* This is owing, partly, no doubt, to the influx of late years of a mass of so-called *"Occult" literature* by surface writers. Some absurd statements are made in many of these books, and this has naturally tended to disgust a number of people who feel that they cannot come in contact with these subjects or their teachers without becoming contaminated.

A little reflection, however, will show you that there is not a man, woman or child but uses *Auto-Suggestion* in some form. Take the question of health. How often do you catch yourself saying or thinking, "I'm not well today—I'll take it easy"; or, "I'm out of sorts—my liver, I suppose"? Such statements are forms of *Auto-Suggestion,* for the body tends to fall in line with the thought.

To *Auto-Suggestion* (self-thought) must be ascribed many of the ills from which mankind suffers. It is the mainspring of man's habits; it dominates his thoughts and actions; it can ruin him body and soul. For you are what you *think;* your constant thoughts make or mar you, for much of your thinking is really a talking mentally to yourself—telling yourself what you are, what you are going to do, what things you will not do, etc. All this is *Auto-Suggestion;* everybody is using it more or less unconsciously every day of their lives.

Now *Auto-Suggestion,* when used consciously, can make you a different being, but mark—it must be fully meant. No amount of repetition of phrases such as "I am well," "I am happy," "I have every confidence in myself," will do you much good unless you *act the part* and *strive* for it—*believe* it. Your mental attitude towards *Auto-Suggestion* must be one of true *Faith* and *Belief.* When you use *Auto-Suggestion* unconscious you *always* believe it and *act* upon it, and that is the reason why it often works such mischief in your life. If you believe in it *consciously* it will make a success of your life.

Every man or woman, therefore, who desires to make something of himself should see that he uses *Auto-Suggestion* consciously and only in the interest of his life as a whole. Keep repeating to yourself every day, "I *shall* succeed; I'm determined to succeed." *Say it until it is a belief with you; a creed.*

Dean Farrar used to say of prayer: *"You will have either to give prayer up or your sins."* In the same way you will have either to give up affirming as above, or the affirming will force you to seek the means that will lead you to success.

THE ART OF INFLUENCING OTHERS.

The Art of Influencing* others is of great importance to the student of Will Power, for it is one of the means he must employ on the road to success.

The first thing that will engage your attention is the manner in which you will convey your suggestions; this, of necessity, will vary with the occasion. As a general rule, you can only convince others if you are convinced yourself. The writer is not speaking here of arguments; you may be convinced you are right when nevertheless you are wrong. It is the *tone* of conviction, the tone of quiet confidence that carries weight in influencing others. If your tone is hesitating, if

*The student should also study Lesson Twenty-five "Personal Magnetism Obtained by Concentration."

your language is badly chosen or ill-arranged, you cannot hope to influence others. It is essential also that you feel within yourself a sense of power while speaking, a feeling that you *can* influence the person to whom you are speaking. Once you gain this power you will find it an effective weapon in influencing others.

You must also be on your guard, when seeking to influence a person, against using unconscious language, for this will reveal *you*. A slip in expression, an unconsidered word, will betray you to a keen observer more than all your well considered phrases. It is for this reason that you should be careful of what you say and do when alone. If you wish to appear polished and refined when in society you must be polished and refined when alone. If you wish to talk correctly when in the world outside, you must talk correctly when in the privacy of your own home. If you wish to be self-reliant and controlled when engaged in your work, business or profession, you must be self-reliant and controlled when by yourself. If, then, you desire to influence others, *the preparation must be done in private.*

If you wish to get the thoughts of the person with whom you are speaking you should look steadily at his face, and at the same time keep perfectly still so as to receive any impression possible. Every one tends to reveal his thoughts in this way, and that is why I advise students to gain control over their facial muscles.

If you wish to induce emotions in others, you can do this by counterfeiting the expressions which are manifested in such emotions. Again, if it suits your purpose to let any one imagine they are influencing you, the same plan may be adopted. Thus while your face may express surprise, enthusiasm or interest you are conscious all the time that you have yourself well in hand.

THE VALUE OF EXERCISE.

A well-developed and active muscular system tends to maintain a certain tone of the nervous system that favors an alert and confident habit of mind.

Every student of Will Culture and Mind Training should see to it that he takes a certain amount of physical exercise each day, for health of the body is an important factor in these studies. Therefore I shall give here three exercises which can be thoroughly recommended—their daily practice, which only takes a few minutes, will do much to keep you in good trim.

Exercise One. Stand erect with the arms hanging down by your side. Gradually withdraw the arms from the side, the arms and hands fully extended, and raise them in a circular sweep as high as they will go (drawing in a full breath while doing so) until the finger tips meet above your head. Separate the hands after a few seconds and gradually let them fall back to their first position by your side, expelling the breath gradually while doing so. Repeat the raising and falling of the arms ten times.

Exercise Two. Stand erect, the arms stretched straight in front of you with the finger tips meeting. Throw the arms backwards, gradually, as far as they will go, at the same time throwing the chest well forward and drawing in the abdomen. Bring back the arms, gradually, to first position. Repeat ten times. Remember to inspire when throwing the arms backwards, and expel the breath when returning to first position.

Exercise Three. Stand erect. Now bend down until your finger tips touch the floor (or as near the floor as possible). Next clench your hands tight and draw them up to your chest slowly (as if raising a heavy weight), straightening the body until erect. Keep the hands in this position (at chest) for a few seconds, then let them fall loosely by your side. Repeat ten times. Expel the breath when bending, and inspire when rising again.

ADVICE ON DIET.

Eat what agrees with you, and, as far as possible, stick to fixed meal hours. Note, it is not the quantity you eat that does you good, but the amount you digest. To secure perfect digestion masticate your food thoroughly. See that you get the *taste* of what you eat; you *will* do this if you masticate properly.

Mastication serves another useful purpose besides that of preparing the food for digestion; it informs you when you have had enough. You will soon note this if you masticate properly; you will probably find that you will not want to eat nearly so much as you are accustomed to eat; you will *feel* you have had enough to satisfy your needs.

TO SUM UP.

Eating right is a very simple matter, and consists of:

First—Don't eat until "good and hungry."

Second—Don't eat when angry, worried, or when you cannot enjoy your food.

Third—Chew all solid food until it swallows itself.

Fourth—Get all taste out of liquid or mushy foods by sucking or sipping.

Fifth—Stop eating when the appetite begins to say "enough."

Sixth—You will lose weight at first, even if you are thin to start with, but in a little time you will find your normal weight and stop.

Seventh—Don't think about the number of chews or sips, but only of the enjoyment of the taste.

Eighth—Don't imagine that meat is necessary to strength. No meat meals give better strength and endurance results.

Ninth—Remember that a week, or two weeks, of careful attention to learning how to eat, as above, will put you in the habit of it so that you will not have to trouble yourself about it after a while.

Tenth—Remember that dietetic righteousness means less expense and more solid enjoyment of the food; and, also, that it makes it easy to be righteous in other ways.

These are ten good commandments of right eating, and unless you respect them, and observe them, you are a dietetic sinner, and do not know what is good for you.

WILL POWER IN BUSINESS.

Cultivate decision—learn to think quickly and to act quickly. Decision gives you the power to say *"No"*; not the curt "No," but the "No" with weight behind it, which always tells strongly in business.

Cultivate manner and courtesy. Nothing tells so strongly in business as a frank, genial manner, but *it must be natural*. It must have its springs deep seated, or instinctively we know it as false. Especially be courteous to business men and women; they can often put things in your way and give you valuable hints, ideas and information.   Discourtesy on your part will put a bar to all this.

Cultivate repose of manner.   The conjurer acts quickly without appearing to do so—imitate him.   Repose of manner will enable you to get through a great deal of work with less strain.

Have the road to success, in your particular business, clearly mapped out.   Have a distinct aim and work for it.   To this end you will specialize in your business; you will learn all you can about it from experts and *technical* and business journals; you will make use of everything to help you in your aim; you will be on the lookout for aid from your fellow men and from every quarter;   you will constantly seek to do things better. Do not merely *wish* for things to come your way; take the necessary means to *make* them come—be determined that they *shall* come.   Cultivate faith in your power to achieve things; like every other power, this power will grow with use, and as it grows it will increase your ability to do things.

Do not be discouraged if success seems tardy; so long as you can measure *some* progress you need not be dispirited. Sometimes this progress may not be shown in your business in actual figures, but if you feel that *you* have made progress in business knowledge and in better ways of doing things you have every cause to hope.   The man who is progressive as a *man*, who is mentally alert and possesses staying power is bound to win in the long run.   This type of man wearies success with his persistency and makes it yield to him.

The man who takes an interest in his business has the greatest chance of succeeding.   *Interest creates energy.*   On the other hand, the man who does not really care for his business, yet cannot get out of it, should make every endeavor to grow interest in it.   He can make a study of it—often this reveals possibilities he has not dreamt of.

The business man should look forward to his evenings— many business men make them the key to their day.   If you know that when evening comes a pleasant time is before you, it greatly adds to your working power during the day.   Plan, therefore, to make your evenings pleasant; there are many ways to do this; see to it that they are ways that will cause you no regrets.

Never study business problems requiring pluck and enterprise late at night unless you feel full of life and energy.

Many a business man loses heart when he faces a business problem at night. The reason of this is that both body and mind are generally fatigued then, and when this is so the mind always paints the future in dark colors. Everyone knows how different a business problem appears when we have slept well and enjoyed a good breakfast. We feel full of vitality, full of willpower, and we can ride over difficulties that at night appeared insurmountable.

When you go to bed, go with the determination to have a good night's rest. The power to sleep can be cultivated. Consider—*what is it that in the day-time tends to make you drowsy?* Answer—*the monotonous; the dry, dreary and uninteresting.* If you *must* think when you go to bed, think of things which do not interest you; think something monotonous or rhythmic in character—*never think of anything interesting.*

Finally—never make a practice of hurrying over your meals. Time saved in this way is time lost, for you will have to meet the bill some day, with heavy interest added.

WILL POWER IN STUDY.

Be on your guard when you feel you are enthusiastic over any new study. Many a student uses up all his enthusiasm in the week or the first month; he has none left for afterwards, and so the study which at first seemed so fair and rosy is allowed to droop and die. The reason is this: If you touch one end of the scale of feeling you are bound to come to the other end. Remember that the negative of the emotion of *Exhilaration* is the emotion of *Despondency.* Cultivate, therefore, *balance and poise,* in study as in other things, if you desire to make steady progress.

Every student, especially if studying for an examination, should practice rigid economy with regard to the time at his disposal. The following hints will be found useful:

First—Prepare a chart of your studies with the time you can give to each. Allot the most time to the subjects in which you are weakest. Note what part of the day you feel in the best mood for study and reserve that part for your most difficult subjects. Never study a subject for any great length of time—one hour is ample—pass on to another subject after a slight interval of rest. Experiment until you find which period of rest you find the most serviceable.

Second—When it is necessary to copy out rules or paragraphs from a text-book, underline these and leave them to be copied when you do not feel *"up to the mark"* for study. Never waste in copying the hours when you feel mentally alert; utilize these precious moments for your stiffest tasks.

Third—Test your mood when you feel disinclined for study. It may be just a lazy fit, and if so will pass off if you settle down to work in earnest. Authors know that *they* must test these moods, for often their brightest ideas will come after they conquer the disinclination for work.

Fourth—When you feel you *cannot* study, that is after thoroughly testing the feeling, do not force yourself to study—you will simply waste your time if you do so.

Fifth—Value your odd minutes—do not think them useless. A recent writer declares that if a man will give one hour per day to any study for five years, he can make himself an authority on the subject.

Sixth—Do not attempt to grapple with a difficult point in your studies during the last few minutes of your allotted time. Try to leave your work with an appetite; that is, with a feeling of pleasure. In this way you will return to your studies with greater zest.

For Summary of Lesson Twenty-two, see Page No. 207.

SUMMARY.

In this Summary is indicated the essential parts of Chapter XXII, Chapter XXIII and Chapter XXIV. These Chapters contain Lessons which every student of *Will-Culture* and *Mind Training* should thoroughly grasp.

Note.—That Chapter XXII, Lesson Twenty, and Chapter XXIII, Lesson Twenty-one, are mainly theoretical, descriptive or analytical; whereas Chapter XXIV, Lesson Twenty-two, is entirely practical.

HABIT.

SUMMARY OF LESSON TWENTY.

Nature of Habit. Remember that Habit is that tendency of the mind to repeat its processes with their characteristic movements.

Fixed Habit. Note the outstanding features of Fixed Habits—Automatism and Facility. Remember that in acquiring habits of skill you are apt to use more muscles than are requisite. Analysis of the muscles required will save you much in time and labor.

Habit Formation. Concentrate on the start of a good habit, and embrace the aid of good impulses to strengthen the start. In forming habits of skill see to it that the initial movements are correct in every detail.

Bad Habits. Do not fight a bad habit—concentrate on its opposite (Vice—Virtue). Do not dwell on your lapses—forget them. Note that minor bad habits are all performed unconsciously; to cure them, become conscious of them.

Special. Make a list of your good habits and bad habits. Seek means to strengthen the former and to eradicate the latter.

WILL CULTURE—MIND TRAINING.

SUMMARY OF LESSON TWENTY-ONE.

Volition. A volition is always a conscious act; it seeks a definite end; it is never satisfied until its end is reached. Alien ideas antagonistic to this end are not volitions; they have come unsought and are not identified with you.

Emotions and Instincts. These are two of the principal factors that influence Volition. Note the order of the events i ι an emotional state; also the three classes of Emotions —-the *Perceptual,* the *Ideational* and the *Organic.* Note that Instincts are independent of education and are distinguished from reflex actions. The section on the Emotions and their correlate Instincts is very important.

Desire and Motive. Note that the strength of a desire lies not in itself, but in the totality (or Universe) of your desires. Remember that a motive induces you to act, whereas a desire often ends in inaction.

Suggestion. Seek to understand the part suggestion plays in *your* life. Note the things and persons that influence you and the ways in which they influence you; this will put you on your guard and strengthen your will-power. Note the power of a suggestion when in agreement with your convictions. This should be noted by all who wish to treat a subject scientifically; convictions must be treated, and tested, impartially.

EDUCATION OF THE WILL.

Summary of Lesson Twenty-two.

Types of Will. Read carefully this section in Lesson Twenty-one until you understand your type. Endeavor to cultivate the Ideal type.

Motives and Success. Analyze your motives, for this will reveal their strength. When you have secured yourself against conflict of motives you add greatly to your chances of success.

Emotions and Impulses. Learn how to check emotions, and how to simulate them. Note that impulses demand instant recognition, *i. e.,* they must be gratified instantly, or checked instantly. If you encourage them they are sure to result in action.

Qualities to Cultivate. Fight Indolence by testing your moods for work. Cultivate Hope by having faith in yourself. Cultivate Cheerfulness, for this will increase your energy. Practice the smile exercise, and note its effect on your moods. Cultivate Politeness and Courtesy from models, *i. e.,* study the people you meet who have these qualities.

Self-Reliance. Test the value of the tight shut mouth. Cultivate Self-Assertion, but remember to use it with tact. Never indulge in Self-Depreciation.

Will in Action. Get a thorough grasp of this section. Understand your part (aim) in life and play the part *now.*

Auto-Suggestion. Remember that Auto-Suggestion is used universally, but mostly unconsciously. To use it consciously, with faith in its powers, is to add enormously to your power of will.

The Art of Influencing Others. We are all called upon to influence others, therefore all should learn the means of doing this. Note the importance of what you are when alone in the influence you will have on others. *Also study Lesson Twenty-five on Personal Magnetism.*

Exercise. You should practice some form of physical exercise each day, for it tends to keep you in good health. Remember that ill-health greatly lessens will power.

Diet. Do not be a faddist in diet. Eat what agrees with you, but see that you masticate thoroughly what you eat. Remember that thorough mastication is the best guard against over-indulgence in eating, especially meat.

Special.   As the sections on Will Power in Business, and in Study, are of special application and sufficiently condensed in themselves, I shall not summarize them.   I know that the students to whom these sections specially appeal will carefully digest them.

The Master Key

CHAPTER XXV.

LESSON TWENTY-THREE.

MEMORY.

GOOD AND BAD MEMORIES.

"I've an awful bad memory." "I cannot remember anything." How often one has to listen to such expressions stated in perfect sincerity. It comes as a startling fact to such a person if you tell him that there is *no such thing* as an absolutely bad memory. *Yet this is so.*

There is hardly a man or woman but possesses a good memory for a certain class of facts. The woman who cannot remember anything will keep you, if you are foolish enough, listening in your office for hours to a recital of her domestic woes and worries. A man of similar type will astonish you with a category of all the ills that beset a business man. Working men with no memory are often walking encyclopedias of sporting details. Schoolboys who cannot learn their lessons can often tell you the names and characteristics of all the leading foot-ballers or base-ball players.

The writer need not prolong such examples, for we are all familiar with them. It is interesting, however, to analyze this seeming *paradox*—people with a memory that remembers nothing, and yet are able to talk for hours on a subject in which they are interested. What is the explanation?

I have just given it: *these people are interested in the subjects they talk about.* But after all this is only a partial explanation. The fundamental reason is that, *these people are constantly going over these matters in their minds. Repetition and Interest*—there you have the explanation of the paradox.

The lesson for you to take from the above is this: Put

210

down on paper the department in which your memory is good; that is, the class of facts you can remember with ease; next put down the departments in which you say you are weak. Let us call the first department *Class A*, and the others *Class B*. Put down on your paper the time you give each day to *Class A*, the frequency with which you draw upon its facts, either by going over them or telling them to others; state also your degree of interest. Now do the same with *Class B* and compare results. Is it any wonder *Class B* is defective?

The fact is, we all have better memories than we think we have; further, we all act in some class of facts in harmony with the fundamental laws which regulate memory. The trouble is that we do this unconsciously; that is, in ignorance of these laws. It is the purpose of the writer to make these laws clear to you; their application will then rest with you.

WHAT IS MEANT BY MEMORY?

Memory has been defined as the power to recall prior experiences; this involves the theory of retention. But memory means more than retention and the power to recall an experience, for the memory of things often comes to one unasked— you do not seek to recall them. It is better, therefore, to look at memory as both active and passive. In the former, recall is a conscious determinate act; in the latter, association tracts in the brain, under stimulation, bring without your asking or seeking, the past once more into consciousness. Memory is, therefore, seen to be to some extent dependent upon Will and to some extent independent of Will.

Memory has two further aspects—the physical (bodily) and the psychical (mental). On the physical side we have *Retention—the theory that "prior experiences produce residual dispositions which determine subsequent experiences,* and on the psychical side we have to consider the factors that aid Retention and so enable us to bring back former experiences to mind.

It is well for the student to understand that *Memory is not a Faculty;* that is, a distinct localization of brain area. Memory is really a complex of faculties; we have not a memory, but memories, as distinct as our several needs. In other words, there are as many memories as there are classes of things to remember.

NATIVE RETENTIVENESS.

Why is it that some people have much better memories than others? Training and varied interests partially explain these differences, but the principal reason is congenital. All are born with a certain capacity for retention, and, therefore, it is easier, much easier, for some people to retain what they see or hear, for instance, than it is for others.

This Native Retentiveness,* so far as our present knowledge goes, cannot be improved by any training. We have no grounds for saying that this will always be so,† but there is no system of training at present known that can increase one's Native Retentiveness. It is well for students to recognize this. The system of memory-training that offers you a perfect memory is offering you something unknown to psychologists; it is offering you something that is not in harmony with our present knowledge of psychology.

All that you can do with your natural power of retention is to see that you use it to its full capacity. Your control over it is simply directive. You can train it, by proper methods, to its full capacity, but you can get no further; you cannot add to it, but you may diminish it by neglecting your health. Training and good health are the only aids to securing the most man's Native Retentiveness has to offer.

HAS THE MIND PIGEON-HOLES?

One of the theories that used to be common, in connection with memory, was that every idea had its special pigeon-hole, or store-house, in the mind. If you wanted to recall the word *"Abracadabra"* you must turn to pigeon-hole No. 242326, so to speak. Today certain people point to the fact that according to laboratory research there are three thousand millions to nine thousand millions of cells in the brain; if ideas are not stored in the pigeon-holes of the mind, then surely they are stored up in these millions of brain cells.

. *Both theories are fallacious.* Ideas are not stored away to be recalled at will; they have no existence except when before our consciousness. There are no such things as permanent ideas.

---

*That power of retention peculiar to every individual from birth.
†Some psychologists are inclined to think that there is a possibility or probability that as you multiply associations you may thereby increase the plasticity of the neural (nerve) processes; the writer has, however, no knowledge that this is so.

Every idea that enters the mind must travel along neural brain paths. The effect of this is to leave what is termed a disposition—*the idea persists* (not exists) in these neural traces; let these brain paths, or residual traces, be stimulated again and the idea will tend to come again into consciousness.

You have no conscious knowledge of Retention; you only infer that there is such a thing because of the fact that you do recall past experiences. By Retention, therefore, you simply mean the possibility or probability of your being able to recall facts.

IS IT POSSIBLE TO FORGET?

It used to be held that it was impossible to forget anything you had once experienced. Within certain limits this *may* be true, but *Cerebral Physiology* is now able to prove that you can forget an experience, and forget it completely, *i. e.*, it is impossible for you ever to recall it again.

Physiologists are able to prove that the hemispheres of the brain have *zones, allocations,* or *localizations* commanding definite movements or responses. Should these zones be injured in any way, the movements dependent on that particular brain area *will be impaired*—perhaps rendered impossible.

Thus, certain of these *zones* control sight, others hearing, taste, speech, writing, trunk movements, head and eye movements (conjoint), thigh movements, knee movements, ankle movements, toe movements. Now if any of the nerves connected with these zones are destroyed, their respective movements are impossible. Thus, if the nerves in the sight zone are destroyed sight is impossible, or if only some of them are destroyed your power to remember words from their visual presentation may be destroyed. Similarly, lesion of other nerves will destroy your power to speak, to write, to move your arm, leg, toes, etc.

You will see now how it is, since memory is dependent on neural processes, that it is possible to forget. Further, it will be apparent to you that memory is not a distinct faculty, but that you have as many types of memories as you have different senses for acquiring knowledge.

Students are warned not to confound the *"localization of brain-functions"** with the absurdities of Phrenology. Phre-

---

*Those areas, or parts of the brain, which control the senses, and various bodily movements, as above.

nologists map out the brain into an aggregation of organs corresponding to Concentrativeness, Acquisitiveness, Language, Wit, etc.; all these are complexes, and depend upon the co-operation of a vast number of fundamental processes.

MEMORY IN RELATION TO EFFICIENCY.

It is a common fallacy to suppose that if you had a memory that would retain all you see or hear you could become a genius, or something akin to that. But this is a mistake. Some of the most extraordinary memories have been possessed by idiots, or by people of very slight intelligence. Some idiots have a wonderful memory for words—words totally unrelated; on the other hand, men of the highest intelligence, tested with the same list of words, have proved utter failures, as far as retention is concerned.

Some writers go so far as to say that instead of an extraordinary memory being a boon it may be a hindrance. The mass of material at its command tends to confusion of thought and renders a critical survey practically hopeless. *Further, people who can remember almost everything they read are very often unable to draw conclusions from their reading.*

It has been proved that men of very poor elementary, or congenital memory, may yet be a mass of erudition. Some of our greatest scientists and literary men cut very poor figures when subjected to so-called memory tests. You, as a student, must never forget that your mind is a complex and also a unity. Where you may appear to be weak in one faculty you may be strong in another; it is the conjunction or working together of the weak and the strong *"faculties"* that make for mental efficiency. Hence, though your congenital memory may be weak, you may still be able to do splendid work through strong reasoning and critical powers.

Experiments go to prove that mental efficiency depends not so much on our ability to remember everything as on our ability to see essentials and to cast the unessentials to one side. This is dealt with more fully under the section, "The Art of Forgetting," in *Lesson Twenty-three.*

Students whose congenital memory is poor should not be discouraged; they are not barred from the heights in Literature, Art, or Science; given a keen interest in any subject, such a student may yet excel the person whose elementary memory is extraordinary.

MENTAL ATTITUDE.

Mental Attitude is one of the most important sections in all memory training, and yet it is the one most commonly neglected. It is of fundamental importance to every memory student, and once it is grasped *a great stride towards "learning" will have been effected.*

It is of the utmost importance in learning "by heart" to have an objective. Ask yourself *why* you wish to learn any particular thing; on your answer will depend to a very great extent the measure of your success in learning. Take the case of the schoolboy, who says, *"I cannot learn Euclid;* it's a lot of bosh." Now is he likely to learn when his attitude to *Euclid* is such?

Such considerations prove that in learning *you must see a reason* why you should learn; you must *see utility* and also further fields of application to which your learning can be extended. Once you see this clearly your interest is aroused, *and then acquisition is easy.*

In almost every case your interest in the subject *will save you.* If you only care enough for results you will be almost certain to attain them.

It has been found, experimentally, that where a student has doubted his ability to learn a list of meaningless syllables the number of repetitions necessary to learn the list are much greater than where the same student receives a list which he thinks within his powers.

Students should be careful never to doubt their ability to learn a particular subject; in so far as you doubt your powers, so will you limit them. Never say "I cannot learn this"; say rather, "I *can* learn this. I will never rest until I master this subject; *I'm determined to master it."*

The *Will Power and Faith* you put into your learning will determine, to a great extent, your success. Keep your intention constantly reinforced by the *"I will master"* attitude, and you will help your memory enormously.

It is the negative attitude which plays havoc with thousands of students. *Logic, Psychology, Metaphysics*—these are called difficult subjects, hence students rarely do well in them.

Difficulty is ever present with them in studying these subjects, hence their mental powers are never really given a chance.

Try to look forward to your tasks with joy and eagerness. Do not allow any negative thoughts to interfere with the learning process by having *"faith in yourself"* and you will soon be able to trace satisfactory results.

THE INFLUENCE OF IMAGINATION ON MEMORY.

Imagination plays an important role in memory. Much of what you think you remember is nothing but the work of imagination. You can test this very simply.

After witnessing any event, write down as soon after the event as possible a description of it, with as much detail as you can remember. Put your description away, and a week after write another description of the event, giving all the details you can, as in your first description. Compare now the two accounts and you will find that your second description will omit either many of the details of the first or it will describe details which had no part in the event.

A few trials, as above, will convince you that you really only remember the outstanding or striking features of an event —the omissions will all be supplied by the imagination. It is this that makes the memory of witnesses so unreliable; much of what they say they saw or heard they never saw or heard; it is simply the work of their imagination.

Schoolmasters and teachers are familiar with this phenomenon. A story is read out to the children and they are told to write down what they remember of it in their own words. When the papers are collected they are often a revelation to the schoolmaster; the main features of the story may be given, but along with them will be details entirely foreign to the story. The same thing is illustrated in dramatic psychological experiments (see section on Attention, etc.).

Students who wish to keep a record of anything they have seen or heard should see to it that such records be made at once —even the lapse of a few hours may render the record untrustworthy. Whenever an event or experience is revived in memory it will be found that something has been lost or added. The reason is, whenever you revive a memory image it comes back to you with new associations, and these either add to, or take away from, the original experience.

FACTORS THAT INFLUENCE RETENTION.

How is it that we remember some things with ease—without any effort at all, in fact? It must be that certain things, by their very nature, have a direct influence on retention; *i. e.,* our native retentiveness is impressed by these things in a way that tends to make recall almost certain, or at all events, extremely probable.

It has been found that the chief factors which influence retention are—

First—Emotional Factors, such as Pleasant Experiences, Painful Experiences, Terrifying Experiences, Ridicule.

Second—Vividness and Striking Contrasts.

Third—Recency, or freshness of the impression.

Fourth—Degree of Attention.

Fifth—Things with many associates.

Sixth—Rhythm.

Seventh—Health.

Factors *First, Second* and *Fourth* illustrate the importance of a well-formed impression as the basis of a rational memory.

Thus, *Painful* and *Terrifying Experiences create a powerful impression* which time seems powerless to eradicate, especially the latter experiences. Pleasant Experiences and Ridicule tend to persist by the associations which cling around them. Vividness and Striking Contrasts tend to persist by the force of the impression they make upon the mind. Recency influences Retention simply because it is new to the mind; it does not tend to persist unless it falls under some of the other heads.

The degree of Attention is an important factor in retention. The better our attention the better are our chances of remembering. Things with many associates, such as holidays, weddings, social events, tend to persist because of their complexity, and because any one of the associates may call up the others. Rhythm is an important aid to retention. Its effect is strongly marked in poetry and music. Children are strongly influenced by it.

Health is an important factor in retention. Since memory has its physiological expression in the power of the organism to preserve traces of received impressions, it is self-evident that the fresher and more energetic the general vital process the better may things be learned; that is, the sensuous percepts will leave behind more permanent and deeper traces.

ASSOCIATION OF IDEAS.

The subject of Association is of fundamental importance; the student must, therefore, try to understand what is meant by *Association of Ideas*.

If you analyze any idea that comes into your mind you will find it hardly ever comes alone; it is generally attended by its "*associates*." For instance, if the word holiday comes into your mind you do not think of it to the exclusion of other thoughts—you think of *some holiday*, what you did, the people you met, what they did, etc. The reason of this is because all your thoughts are connected with other thoughts forming part of prior experiences.

Association is not a psychical process; a psychical process is a part of your experience which exists only while it is being experienced, but associations persist even when you are unconscious of them, for they are simply "*an acquired connection of dispositions*" which are formed in conscious experience. Thus, if you met Mr. Blackstone today for the first time, and meet him again a week after, and then recognize him; that is, remember having met him before, it is evident that some part of your past experience in meeting Mr. Blackstone has persisted—*this persistency is termed an acquired disposition.*

Now, when you recognize Mr. Blackstone you do not say to yourself, "that Mr. Blackstone," or if you have forgotten his name, "that is a gentleman whom I have met before." The first thing that presents itself to you is the simple recognition, and then comes with this knowledge some incidents (time, place, etc.) which accompanied your former experience of meeting Mr. Blackstone.

Analyze any "*recognition*" or "*recall*" and you will generally find clustered round it associates of some kind.

THE FACTORS WHICH REGULATE ASSOCIATION.

The ways in which Associations are formed are principally by Similarity and Contiguity; next comes Unity and Interest, and Repetition.

Similarity. Things which are similar, by which is really meant partially identical, tend to persist together, so that to think of one is to think of the other.

Contiguity. Things that have been experienced together tend to persist together; to think of the one experience is to connect it with the accompanying experience. In contiguity we have also the presentation of experiences; that is, their order. The tendency is for presentation to be reproduced in their original order, but it has also been found that Associations have a backward as well as a forward tendency, for if you learn anything by heart it then takes fewer repetitions to learn backwards.

Unity and Interest. Where there is unity of sense and interest, associations are numerous—unconnected words have no unity, hence they are difficult to remember. Interest is closely connected with feeling, and feeling with emotion; hence associations are very numerous where our interest is keen, our feeling pleasant or painful, and our emotions strongly stirred.

Repetition. Associations are firmly established according to the number of times they are repeated or thought of in mind. The writer has dealt with this fully under *"The Effect of Repetition."*

THE NATURE OF RECALL.

It used to be held by some Psychologists that ideas cannot come into consciousness unless accompanied by their *habitual* associates. This is not true, and it is here that most memory systems go astray, for ideas will flash into the mind of themselves without any associates. You can easily verify this for yourself. If you try an experiment such as the letter experiment (see section under *"Aids to Remembering"*) you will find that sometimes it is not the associate fixed upon that recalls the fact that you must post a letter—it will suddenly come into your mind in the most unlikely place, without any associates that analysis can trace. This is called *Spontaneous Revival.* It is Spontaneous Revival that constitutes Worry—the worrying idea keeps coming into the mind in all places and at all times.

Frequency and Recency are the great determinates of recall, yet sometimes they miss fire, or seem to go astray, for ideas sometimes part company (*Divergent Revival*) with their habitual associates and come into consciousness with strange associates. Highly emotional states are largely responsible for this.

One cannot think the same when depressed as when they are filled with joyous, happy feelings. There are three ways in which ideas are principally revived: first, by *Explicit Revival;* second, by *Explicit Reinstatement;* third, by *Implicit Revival.*

In *Explicit Revival* ideas come in the form of mental images, and cause one to experience similar sensations to their original presentation; one lives the past over again. In *Explicit Reinstatement* ideas come to you with their original motor associations; you speak the words, go through appropriate gestures, walk about, etc. In *Implicit Revival* you recall the past indistinctly; you fail to remember many of the details which accompanied the former experience; there is always a *"fringe"* which defies your efforts to pierce.

Implicit Revival plays a great part in our experience; it forms the greater part of all our recalling—it brings the past back to us in a more or less shadowy form, and bids us call upon our imagination to fill the gaps that are missing.

HOW TO RECALL A FACT.

Now that the student has learned something of the nature of recall, he can understand better the *modus operandi* in recalling a fact to his memory.

In trying to recall a fact, the first thing you must do is to pay a visit to its associates. The following is an example:

Recalling a person's name. The general rule for recalling a person's name is, think of as many things as you can associated or connected with the person. Thus you will think of his appearance, dress, walk, where he lives, his occupation, his friends. If these fail to bring his name to memory, you will think of where you saw him last, what he was doing, what he said, and so on. You thus go over everything connected with the man in the hope that some of the associates will bring his name to mind.

In some cases, when you are trying to recall a person's name, you remember that it begins with a certain letter.* In

*It has been proved experimentally that the initial and final letters are the dominating factors in recognition. The bearing of this on recall is, therefore, manifest. Further, in the case of names of people and places, the initial letter being always a capital is thereby given a prominence which serves to impress it upon the mind. A common practice results from this. Many people often speak or think of Mr. Brown (to quote a specific case) as Mr. B, or simply B. Hence, when they forget his name, and try to recall it, almost invariably the initial of the name comes first to their mind, and they proceed from this to form associates.

this case it is usual to associate this letter with the other letters of the alphabet. Thus, supposing you were sure that your friend's name began with the letter B (the name to be recalled being *"Beattie"*) you would associate B with the vowels and consonants in alphabetical order, as Bac, Bad, Bag; Bec, Bed, Beg, and so on, until, possibly, when you commenced the combination of B and T with the various vowels the B and the T would send the name flashing into your mind. Sometimes while you are busy associating the initial letter with other letters, suggestions of other words will appear. Thus, in trying to remember the word *"Beattie"* you will suddenly say: "The name I want has something to do with *striking*." Then after a while the word "beating" suggests itself, and almost immediately as you repeat it, the name *"Beattie"* will stand out clear.

In trying to remember the name of an author many people find it helpful, where they know the title of one of his works, to try to picture what the book is like, how it is bound and lettered, its price, the nature of its contents, where they saw it last. In this way some association with the author's name is often found.

If the above methods fail, it is best to leave the matter for a time and go on with some other work. Many people adopt this plan with success; they find that spontaneous revival comes to their aid, and in the midst of totally unrelated ideas and circumstances the man's name flashes into consciousness.

In recalling facts connected with study, students are advised not to worry over the unremembered facts. To think and think of facts in this way in a vain attempt to bring them back to memory is to set up wrong associations which will certainly cause you trouble on some future occasion. It is much better to go over the ground again than to indulge in guesses. Review your work, strengthen the associates of the facts you wish to remember, and you will get much better results.

Many people cultivate *"trust"* in memory with remarkable success. They say to themselves, "Now I shall remember that next time I want it," and they find that this trusting of the memory yields excellent results.

It is well, too, in trying to recall, to think of any motor associations which accompanied the facts you wish to bring to mind. Some people find that if they walk about or talk aloud that associates are aroused which help them to recall the facts desired.

People who belong to the auditory type of memory (see next section) find it a distinct help in recalling to close their eyes; the brain is then shut off from visual impressions and auditory images have a better chance of coming back to consciousness. Visuals sometimes adopt the same plan.

Students should experiment and find which method of recall is most natural to them, and stick to that method in future. The next section will help to that end.

MENTAL IMAGERY.

In all our remembering or recalling, we mostly think in imagery. If you begin to think of a Horse, you see it in mind; your mental ear hears the noise it makes as it gallops along, and your mental eye sees it galloping; you perhaps imagine, also, touching it at the close of its gallop—all this you image in mind. Similarly you associate lightning with the sight of the flash, its swiftness and the noise of the thunder; but you never think of it in terms of touch, smell or taste. Now it has been found that all of us have our own peculiar method, or type, as it is generally called, of imaging in mind, and in trying to remember we principally employ one type to bring into consciousness that which we seek to recall.

There are three main types of imagery—the *Visual* type, the *Auditory* type, and the *Motor*, or *Motile* type. The *Gustatory*, the *Olfactory*, and the *Tactile* types are less used, but nevertheless play their part in influencing recall. The *Visual* type has a good memory for form and color, the *Auditory* for sounds, the *Motile* for movement of every kind, the *Gustatory* for the taste of anything, the *Tactile* for the sensations of touch, and the *Olfactory*† for smells of all kinds.

This subject of mental imagery is of the greatest importance in the cultivation of memory, for it tells you which methods, according to your type of imagery, are the best to employ in anything which you wish to learn—to make your own.

People with strong visualization, in recalling anything, always see it. If it is something they have read they can see in mind the letters and words, their appearance, the look of

†With some people the sense of smell has a strong associative power, and feeling-tone. A particular scent not only brings back to these people scenes and incidents in the past, but also the emotional elements which accompanied these.

the page, etc. The *Auditory* type remember by sound; all the time they are reading their mental ear is hearing the sound of each word, and it reproduces these when they seek to remember what they have read. The *Motor* type remember by movement.* In drawing they follow the movement of the pencil; in silent reading they are inclined to move their lips and even to whisper words. In reading aloud they are apt to gesticulate, to sway their body, and to pose into various attitudes.

It must not be imagined that we are all divided into these distinct types in the sense that we use one type, and one only. This is erroneous; the generality of people use a complex of all these types in remembering, but the fact remains that in every person one of these types predominates, and therefore it is important to know which type plays the greatest part in our life.

HOW TO KNOW WHICH TYPE OF IMAGERY PRE-DOMINATES.

Apart from the special apparatus of the psychological laboratory, it is not easy to determine, with any preciseness, the type of imagery predominating in an individual. There are several experiments, however, which give what may be termed a good idea of each type of imagery.

EXPERIMENT NO. ONE.

On the next page are three lists of words marked respectively *A, B, C*. Read list *A* aloud, three times, at a fixed rate and then put it to one side. Take now a sheet of paper and mark it *A*, and write down as many words as you can remember. Next, read list *B* silently, with your mouth closed and lips compressed to avoid any movement. Read three times and then write down what you remember, marking your list *B*. Now get a friend to write down a list of twelve words, as in list *C*, and let him read these over to you three times (you yourself must not have seen the list; the words must be different from those in list *C*, which is merely an example), and

---

*The Motor Type remembers written words, and drawings (made by themselves) by the memory of the sensations involved in writing and drawing. Motor-memory forms a large part in games like Golf, Billiards, Tennis, Cricket, etc.; also in playing musical instruments.

then write down what you remember, marking your list *C*. Note, in recalling the words of each list you are not to strive for a long time trying to reproduce the words; you should not take more than a minute or two.

List A.	List B.	List C.
Coat	*Girl*	*Poker*
Song	*Fluty*	*Shrill*
Race	*Fight*	*Circle*
Sour	*Perfume*	*Putrid*
Rough	*Hot*	*Uneven*
Noxious	*Sweet*	*Delicious*
Shop	*Landscape*	*Zigzag*
Salt	*Shriek*	*Child*
Shrill	*Lightning-Flash*	*Smooth*
Cold	*Bitter*	*Drum*
Running	*Lukewarm*	*Taste*
Smell	*Aroma*	*Stench*

Now compare your lists and see which list gives the best results in recalling. If *A* gives the best results you are probably of the *Motor Type;* if *B,* you are probably of the *Visual Type;* if *C,* you are probably of the *Auditory Type.*

Note: It is important to note the bearing that Immediate and Primary Memory may have on your results in recalling the words in the above lists. See section on "Time-Rate in Reading, and its effect upon Memory."

EXPERIMENT NO. TWO.

Practice the above methods in learning poetry. Take verses of equal length and equal difficulty. Read one verse aloud, another silently, with the lips compressed, and the third get a friend to choose and read aloud to you. See which method enables you to recall the best by writing out as much of each verse as you can remember after three readings. Continue experimenting as above until it is fairly clear which method gives you the best results.

EXPERIMENT NO. THREE.

Go and watch some event, such as a football match or a baseball game, a race, a play; or look at a landscape, a street scene, a crowd. Write a description of any of these sights and then carefully analyze them; note which things impressed you most; that is, things seen, or heard, or movement of any kind. Re-write the scene a week after and note which class of facts you recall best.

Note re Visual Memory. First, one of the best tests of visual memory is as follows: "*Try to spell long words backwards.*" If your visualization is strong, you will be able to *see* the word standing out clear before your mind's eye, hence, to read* it backwards should not be difficult.

Second, visuals have strong powers of local memory. Thus, if you look at a public clock and note the time, afterwards when you recall the time you passed the clock, the image of the clock will stand out clear, marking the time.

MISTAKES COMMON TO THE VARIOUS TYPES OF IMAGERY.

First, if your Memory is Visual you are liable to make the following mistakes:

(a) To confuse letters which are much alike in appearance.
(b) To mistake words which appear alike, but sound different.
(c) To grasp the appearance of words as wholes, thus overlooking errors in spelling.

Second, if your Memory is Auditory you will make the opposite mistake to that made by visuals under (b). You will also be liable to make more errors in consonants than in vowels.

Third, if your Memory is Motor you are liable (a) to confuse letters articulated alike, such as b-p, t-d, ch-j, f-v; (b) to speak while learning or thinking.

Note what errors you are liable to make in reading or in writing and see which head they fall under. This will help you to decide as to your type of Imagery.

NOTE.—Students are warned not to decide as to their type of Imagery after making only *one* of the tests in this section. They should decide only after a thorough trial of *all* the tests.

THE INFLUENCE OF REPETITION.

Repetition is of fundamental importance in memory. Viewed genetically, it falls under the law of habit. Just as

---

*That is, the letters separately.

the oftener we do a thing the easier does its performance tend to become, so by frequent repetition in learning anything, the easier is the tendency to retain it.

If we view Repetition analytically, we find that both physical and psychical processes not only tend to become easier to do, or remember, by frequent repetition, but they entail a less expenditure of nervous energy, and conscious force.

The value of Repetition is greater in subjects that lack interest to us; where there is unity of interest ideas tend to persist better, and, consequently, repetition is not needed so much.

The student can economize in Repetition. If this student is careful to give his first repetition the full force of attention, paying strict heed to every detail required or involved, he will greatly aid the repetitions following. Students should, therefore, pay great attention to the first repetition and see that they put concentrative, conscious force into it, and not repeat in parrot fashion. Repetition without conscious attention has little reproductive value.

Note: The first reading in the learning process is more important than any single subsequent reading. It is important to note, also, that concentrated attention during the learning process reduces the number of repetitions necessary for immediate reproduction.

Repetition is made much more effective by the way you divide it up or distribute it. The more extended the distribution of repetitions, the easier is it to learn, and the better able you are to reproduce what you have learned. Thus, experiment has proved that better results are obtained by spreading the repetitions over a long period than over a short period. Thus supposing you have twenty-four repetitions; if you divide this into eight repetitions for three days, four repetitions for six days, or two repetitions for twelve days, the last division will give the best results. The reason of this is that the older associations are more strengthened by repetition than those of recent date. There is also less fatigue, with fewer repetitions.

Students should note the above; it illustrates in a remarkable way the value of odd minutes—the time which they often think is of no account. Students of languages will get excellent results if they arrange their vocabulary learning on this plan. Students reading for examinations will see the necessity for constant revision. Daily revision will give better results than weekly, weekly than fortnightly, fortnightly than monthly. Notes intended for revision should be as precise as possible so that a whole book can be subjected to revision in a day or so. The side notes in good text-books are models in this respect.

RATIONAL LEARNING AND ITS SUBEQUENT EFFECT ON RE-LEARNING.

If you have once *really* learned anything, say a poem, a portion of a play, a formula, etc., you have done something which will never be obliterated unless accident or illness intervene.

"It has been observed that, even twenty-two years after a piece of poetry has been learned, a saving of seven per cent may be effected." That is to say, it will be easier for you to re-learn this piece of poetry than it will be to learn a poem new to you.

You should test the above by experimenting on a poem learned to repeat during your youth; you will find that even where it seems to have entirely faded away, it will require very little effort to make it yours once more. This should prove to you the value of rational learning over "stuffing"* the mind. Once make a thing your own by thoroughly understanding it and it only requires an occasional "touching up" to make it a permanent possession.

TIME-RATE IN READING AND ITS EFFECT ON MEMORY

The rate at which you read has an important bearing on your power to reproduce what you have read. Experimental data is not sufficiently advanced to enable psychologists to speak with precision on the relation of time-rate to the rate of forgetting, but it is fairly well established that fast readers are the best *immediate* reproducers. The reason seems to be in the fact that in fast reading the mind is pinned to its subject and not drawn aside by irrelevant thoughts.

---

*NOTE.—There are two kinds of stuffing—bad and good. Bad stuffing of the mind ignores the laws of memory; the bad stuffer is generally ignorant that he is ignoring these laws. Good learning works in harmony with the laws of memory; it recognizes that knowledge is sometimes required for an immediate end, or special need. The lawyer stuffs when he reads up for a case. The politician, public-speaker, or lecturer bulges his memory for a special occasion. The knowledge these people acquire is useful, perhaps, solely for their special object. Afterwards they may never need it, and hence are content to let it fade from memory.

Much, of course, depends on the type of mind. Many scientific men and literary men who are accustomed to weigh well what they read, are slow readers. On the other hand, men of quick understanding and effective perception are all fast readers.

Note: In connection with the above, students should distinguish between Immediate Memory and Primary Memory. If a passage is read out to you, and you are asked to write it out at once, you will be using Immediate Memory. If you are required to write out the passage some hours after, you will be using Primary Memory. Some people have a strong Immediate Memory, but a weak Primary Memory, and vice versa.

Students are warned that there is no relation between the quick grasp of a subject and mental efficiency. A quick grasp is too often associated with a tendency to forget as quickly. Hastily learned, hastily forgotten is common to many minds, especially the type that stuffs itself for examination work.

This fact should not be taken as a warning against fast reading. Students should cultivate reading as fast as they can with due regard to pronunciation, and an appreciation of the sense of what they are reading. To guard against the proneness to forget after a time which so often accompanies fast reading, students should make permanent their reading by frequent repetition, and by making notes of the essential points in everything they read.

Business men and professional men should cultivate fast reading and a quick grasp of the matter read. It is often of vital importance to apprehend quickly; in many situations in life it marks the turning point in a man's career, *for decision cannot always wait on convenience.* Cultivate, then, the type of mind that says in a quick, decisive tone: *"What does that mean?" "Do I understand that?" "Is that clear to me?"*— You will find it a friend in need in many a trying situation.

THE RATE OF FORGETTING.

The Rate of Forgetting has been the subject of much experiment by a student of a certain memory teacher. He experimented with a set of meaningless syllables, and he found that after having learned them sufficiently to repeat them by the end of an hour he had forgotten two-thirds, and at the end of a month he could only repeat one-fifth of his list. Other experimenters on the same lines have found much the same results.

While the above experiments are interesting, they cannot be accepted as establishing a precise rule for all forgetting; all that they seem to prove is that the rate of forgetting is at first very rapid, gradually decreasing until a rate is reached which appears to be stable, i. e., the further loss is insignificant.

The experiments seem to prove the necessity for constant revision until associations are thoroughly established, when the periods of revision can then be extended.

Students should note that the first few minutes, then the first few hours following the learning process, show the most rapid loss of memory. If you attend a lecture, or have just received a music lesson, or any other form of instruction, and wish to write down any important points to remember, you should make your notes at the earliest opportunity.

THE DECAY OF MEMORY.

Since memory has been proved to have a physiological basis it is evident that *Decay of Memory* must be looked for as you grow older, and the organism wastes away or deteriorates.

Note: Generally speaking, there is no sign of decrease in memory power before 50 years of age. After this, the decrease is very gradual, right onwards to extreme old age. Students should note that even in old age the decrease in memory power can be controlled to a great extent by systematic exercise of the memory.

It is a significant fact in memory decay that the things which give the most trouble to learn are those that go quickest from memory. Now the hardest things to learn and to recall are proper names and nouns generally; they give one the most trouble to acquire and they are the first words you forget when your memory begins to decay. You remember *verbs, adjectives* and *pronouns* much longer than you remember the names of persons and things.

The reason of this lies in the fact that you can image things, but not their qualities. In thinking of persons and things you think in mental imagery; in thinking of the qualities of persons and things you must employ language, and in so doing you of necessity are much more complex, for to describe a thing requires the use of a number of words, hence associations are stronger and the impressions made on the neural brain-paths are more numerous and deeper.

Students should, therefore, pay special attention to names in learning; they should try to create a deep impression and practice constant revision until the names are firmly fixed in memory.

Note: Students who find a difficulty in remembering the names of persons will find the following helpful. Make it a practice, whenever you call up in mind the face and general appearance of a person, always to associate the *name* of the person with the mental image. If you make this a constant practice, you will find that the difficulty of remembering a person's name will be greatly diminished. Remember that the mental image is easier to recall than the name; hence in recalling, give emphasis to the *name*.

THE ART OF FORGETTING.

THE PARADOX OF MEMORY.

Facility of Forgetting, and of driving out one train of ideas by a new train is almost as essential to a well trained intellect as facility of retention.

To remember it is necessary to forget; this has been termed the paradox of memory. If you wish to make advancement, you must know how to forget; it is the stepping-stone to all progress. This is recognized in business. Said a great business man once: *"I have no use for the man who remembers past achievements."*

Many men deal every day with a mass of facts, most of which it is useless to remember. A mind that could remember all these things would be a mind encumbered, *not equipped.* All real memory, therefore, must involve selection and rejection if we are to advance in knowledge.

It would seem as if our organism looked at memory strictly from a utilitarian point of view; what it thinks is of no use to its progress it ruthlessly casts to one side. Even the things which seem to contradict this view may be reconciled if we look at them from a biological point of view. And do not we ourselves seem to act in this same utilitarian spirit; what we have no use for, or where we cannot see utility, we speedily forget.

Now since you cannot remember everything, it is evident you must decide what you wish to remember. If you wish to succeed you must know what to forget. *"Men of strong character acquire unusual facility in refusing attention to the things they desire to forget."*

The general Rule for Forgetting is: *Disregard non-essentials and concentrate upon essentials.* Do not waste time trying to remember everything. Make utility your standpoint; utility as applied to your profession or business, to your hobbies or amusements, to your social life, moral life, or religious life.

Note: The ability to see the essential in anything is that which distinguishes one man from another. To acquire this power you must constantly ask yourself questions. Thus, in study, the student's attitude must be: What are the really vital parts in this text-book, grammar, etc.? If he cannot discover this himself he must get expert advice. In games of skill or playing musical instruments (piano, violin, etc.), the beginner makes a great number of unnecessary movements, calling into play muscles antagonistic to each other. Expert guidance is absolutely necessary here to know which movements are essential to the development of skill.

But there is another side to this subject of *Forgetting.* *Themistocles,* when *Simonides* offered to teach him the art of memory, replied: *"I would rather learn to forget . . . . I* remember what I do not wish to remember, but cannot forget what I wish to forget." How are we to proceed to forget ideas which we do not wish to remember—ideas we do not seem able to forget?

Students should note that the ideas we find troublesome to forget are generally those involving emotional factors; that is, experiences that give us pain, or cause us annoyance whenever they rise into consciousness. The following rules will be found helpful in such cases.

THREE RULES FOR FORGETTING.

Rule 1.—Give the idea you wish to forget lack of attention.
Rule 2.—Give the idea you wish to forget lack of repetition.
Rule 3.—Substitute for the idea you wish to forget some opposing idea.

Students will note that Rule 2 readily follows from Rule 1. When you attend to emotional, or annoying experiences of the past, you tend to repeat these by going over the ground, time after time. Students should refuse to give these ideas

attention or repetition; the instant they come before consciousness the mind should be turned aside to thoughts of an opposite nature.*

Students† must remember that they cannot oppose directly
memory images of past experiences; such ideas must always
be opposed, as above, by substituting for them ideas of an
opposite nature.

---

*Permit me to give an illustration. A gentleman, at one time, was
troubled by the following experience. Every time he pulled his shoes on,
there came to his mind the memory of a lady friend who died while in
the act of pulling her shoes on. He opposed the morbid ideas accompanying the memory image as follows. He imagined himself full of
strength and vigor. He put this thought of vigor into the act of putting
on his shoes; the operation was performed as quickly as possible, and
gradually the former memory image, with its attendant morbid associates, gradually faded away, and ceased to trouble him.

†Students should read in connection with this section, "How to cure
Bad Habits" (Habit and Will-Power); also the whole of the section on
Thought-Control.

The Master Key

CHAPTER XXVI.

LESSON TWENTY-FOUR.

CULTIVATION OF MEMORY.

HOW TO IMPROVE YOUR MEMORY.

FUNDAMENTAL LAWS FOR THE CULTIVATION OF MEMORY.

The prime law for the cultivation of memory is—*Concentrate your attention on that which you wish to remember,* for concentrated attention is the foundation of all memory cultivation; it intensifies mental images, keeps your thoughts pinned to the subject-matter, and stimulates thinking. According to the power of your attention (native retentiveness apart) will be the power of your memory.

To secure readiness in recalling facts you must go over them from time to time. *Repetition* is, therefore, of fundamental importance in memory cultivation. The great difficulty in using repetition is to make it conscious. You must know *what* you are repeating and *why* you are repeating it. This applies with special force to the first repetition. *Mechanical repetition is of little avail.*

This brings the observing student to another great law. If his repetition is to be conscious he must have an aim and this involves *interest.* If the student's interest is to be strong and of real use his *aim* must be clearly defined. But this is not all. The aim should be of such a nature as to make its attainment desirable and the way to that attainment agreeable and pleasant. Lacking the latter it is much more difficult to remember. *Aim and interest* must work hand in hand if your memory is to be reliable.

Another fundamental law is, that what you seek to learn must be of use to you. *Utility* is of the greatest importance for the permanency of memory. Unless you can see utility in

233

what you learn you are almost certain to forget it unless it falls under some of the heads noticed in *"Factors that influence Retention."* This explains why so many of the students, after leaving school, college òr university, forget the greater part of what they have learned; they have no use for it, and therefore it fades away.

The law of utility leads the student to another law of fundamental importance. Simple facts tend to die; complex facts tend to stay with us. The reason for this is obvious. Complexity means a great number of associations, hence the greater chance of some one of these associations leading to the remembrance of the fact we wish to recall.

This brings us to what is sometimes called the most fundamental law of memory—*Association of Ideas.* This I have already dealt with in a previous section.

Another great law is what may be termed the law of *understanding.* When you clearly and thoroughly understand a subject, it does not give you nearly so much trouble to remember it. Examiners make use of this law. They know that a great number of students get up a subject in parrot fashion; they, therefore, vary their questions so as to give them a different complexion, with the result that the parrot student is floored.

AIDS TO REMEMBERING.

Students should stand out as much as possible against using *mnemonics* as an aid to remembering. In the first place they are irrational, and in the second place they are burdensome and cumbersome and tend to decay quickly.

Note: Students should recognize that *mnemonics* are only of use where *immediacy* is concerned. A lawyer getting up facts or details for a case, a student getting up various facts or figures for an examination, a professional man, or business man preparing matter for an interview, or a public speaker preparing headings for his speech, may use *mnemonic* devices to aid him at such times; but it will be found that as soon as the time or occasion in question is over the facts mnemonically grasped tend to fade very rapidly from memory. To the student who wishes to make his knowledge a permanent possession, *mnemonics are of very little use.*

Mnemonics are applied by many Memory Systems more especially to figures, dates being the principal application. Psychologists condemn this practice. This is clearly an excessively poor, trivial and silly way of thinking about dates. The way of the historian is better. He has a lot of land-mark dates already in his mind. He knows the historic concatenation of events and can usually place an event at its right date in the chronology-table, by thinking of it in a rational way, referring to its antecedents, tracing its concomitants and consequences and thus ciphering out its date by connecting it with theirs.

Nothing can be said against the practice of what are termed *"ingenuity methods"* in committing figures to memory. Thus suppose you wish to commit the following sets of figures to memory: (a) 884422; (b) 123654; (c) 93003936.

You can divide (a) into (88) (44) (22). Here all that is necessary to remember is that the first two figures are 88, the next two figures half of 88 and the next two quarter of 88, or half the second two figures. In (b) you can group as follows: (123) (654). Here you remember that the first group follows in numerical order from 1 to 3 and that the second group continues in this order if you start with the last figure of the group. In (c) you can group into (930) (039)—the reverse of the first group—and (36) which you can remember as 3 less than the last two numbers of the second group.

Note: I have purposely made the above examples as simple as possible, to enable the student to grasp the principle in such methods.

Similar methods are applied in learning lists of unconnected words. Thus Psychology, Sigh (similarity of sound in the first syllable), Potato, Pearl, Prince (each word commencing with the letter P), Sewing, Drinking, Playing (each word ending with "ing"), and so so. It is clear that all such methods are after all merely methods of better or closer attention.

It is a great aid to remembering a fact to be able to link it to some other fact already in your mind. This is rational remembering and gives much better results than the mere attempt to commit the fact to memory, by repetition or mechanical aids. It is the *thinking* that impresses the fact upon the brain substance, for numerous associates are formed thereby and the tendency to recall is made more probable.

Suppose you wish to remember to post a letter on your way to business, or to bring something home as you come from business. You can say either (1) "I must not forget to post my letter," or "I must bring so and so home with me," or (2) You can arrange matters so that every here and there as you go to business, something will recall the fact that you must post your letter, etc.

Thus, you can say: *"When I pass Robinson's shop I'll remember I have a letter to post," and so on.* You are much more likely to remember by the second plan than by the first, for each of the places you fix on as an associate will tend to bring the fact to your mind that you have a letter to post.

Children rely on mere repetition to remember. This does not give such good results in the case of adults; you cannot get away from the *sense* of what you are learning, hence "adults should chiefly attend to logical relations of things, to ideas, to argument, and to courses of thought."

It is much easier to learn poetry than to learn prose, for the rhyme and rhythm of the former are powerful aids to memory. If, therefore, you can introduce or see rhythm in anything you wish to learn, you strengthen the associative ties and render recall more likely.

Learning Poetry. The learning of Poetry has been the subject of much experimental work. It has been found that passages up to two hundred and forty lines are learned more economically by the *"Entire Method"* than by the *"Sectional Method"* (see next section—*"The most Economical Method of Learning"*). Students are advised not to devote more than from thirty to forty minutes, at each sitting, to the learning of such passages. Long poems, i. e., of more than two hundred and forty lines, should be divided into sections, each section being, as far as possible, as thought-whole, i. e., closely connected in thought and matter—a natural division of the poem. The student will have to exercise great care in binding together the various sections. It is recommended to number each section, and to give to each a name or phrase expressive of the leading ideas or thought contained in such section.

It is sometimes a help in remembering to get someone to read to you the matter you wish to learn, for in the reading they tend to give stress to certain parts, and these, as you saw above, form associations and help you to remember. This method is specially applicable to persons of the *auditory type* of memory.

It is a great help towards remembering a subject to be able

to talk about the subject to some congenial mind. I drew attention to this in your numbered exercises. The endeavor to explain a subject reveals your limitations, and these you can attend to when alone.

Students should never read a good book without a pencil in hand. Mark the passages, or parts, you wish to remember, and afterwards make notes of these.

THE MOST ECONOMICAL METHOD OF LEARNING.

There are three main methods of learning:

First, the sectional method.

Second, the whole, or Entire method.

Third, the Mixed method.

In learning by the *Sectional method*, the matter is divided into sections, and each section is learned before proceeding to the next.

In learning by the *Entire method*, the matter to be learned is read through from beginning to end, and repeated in this way, until it is learned as a whole.

Note: The Entire method is quicker than the sectional, for no redundant associations are formed. The piece is grasped as a whole, and everything is seen in its proper relation. In the *Sectional* method, associations are formed between the last word and the first word of the *same* section. This hinders the reproduction of the matter as a whole. The student should note that even where the sectional method seems to involve less fatigue in consequence of fewer repetitions, it has been found that the matter learned is not so well retained.

In learning by the Mixed method, an attempt is made to avoid the disadvantages attaching to the other methods. The student has seen that the Sectional method encourages wrong associations; it will be equally apparent that the Entire method is apt to discourage a learner, and also to induce fatigue. The Mixed method *seeks to avoid these defects* as follows: The matter to be learned is divided into sections; each section must be read through on the principle of the Entire method, but as soon as the end of the section is reached a pause must be made, before reading the section over again. The pause should be sufficiently long to be felt as a distinct break, before the passage is repeated again. This rests the brain; that is, minimizes fatigue, and no unnecessary associations are formed.

Students are advised to map out the learning process, as follows: Read through carefully, for a few times, from beginning to end, the whole of the matter to be learned. Note, in your reading, how the matter may be divided up into sections, so that each section forms a logical division of the whole. Pick out the difficult sections, and learn these by the Mixed method, and, as soon as possible, return to the Entire method.

LEARNING BY HEART WITH THE MINIMUM OF FATIGUE.

In *Experimental Psychology*, various experiments have been carried out to test individual differences in memory, the best methods of recall, etc. In order to make the conditions of wide application, a series of meaningless syllables is chosen, generally of three letters, such as gar, lem, ped, meb, etc. There are three methods that have been extensively used in testing the reproduction of such a series, viz.:

First, the Learning and Saving method.
Second, the Prompting method.
Third, the Scoring method.

In the *Learning and Saving Method* a series of meaningless syllables is read over and over until the list can be repeated. The number of repetitions requisite to learn the list is noted, and after a certain interval (by which time many of the words of the series will have been forgotten) the list is gone over again and the number of repetitions requisite for its reproduction noted. A comparison of the repetitions shows the saving effected by the second reproduction.

In the *Prompting Method* the series is read over for a certain number of times, but not sufficient to reproduce the list. Note is taken of the number of promptings necessary to enable the pupil to reproduce the series.

In the *Scoring Method* the syllables of the series are learned in pairs, the second syllable in each pair being strongly accented. The series is read over a certain number of times—not sufficient for complete reproduction—and then the first syllable in each pair is exposed on a screen, and the pupil is required to give the corresponding syllable to complete the pair. When he answers correctly, it is counted as a score, hence the name of the method. I have found that the Scoring method is not so fatiguing on the student as the other methods, and, also, gives better results.

A good exercise in this method is to write the words, as shown here, and then read the pairs over six times, accenting the second word in each pair.

Coat—Song.
Race—Sour.
Rough—Noxious.
Shop—Salt.
Shrill—Cold.
Running—Smell.

Next cover the right-hand words, and see if you can reproduce them as soon as you expose each of the left-hand words. When you can reproduce them perfectly, reverse the process—cover the left-hand words and expose the right-hand words.

You can apply this adaptation of the Scoring Method with excellent results to your studies—Languages, Poetry, the Sciences, History, Geography, Law, Philosophy, Short-hand, Bookkeeping, etc., all that is necessary is to make your notes as concise as possible and then skeletonize them. Thus, suppose you have a note as follows: *"Ethics is the study of the Ultimate Good of Man."* You arrange it thus:—Ethics—study, ultimate good—man. Leave the word *"Ethics"* exposed and see if it suggests *"study"*; then expose *"ultimate good,"* and see if it suggests *"man."* Afterwards expose the word *"Ethics"* only and see if it suggests the other words.

Students should also test the principle of the scoring method by applying it to the lists *A, B, C,* on page 224.

Students will find the above method gives much more satisfactory results than the associative methods of the memory systems. The latter demand a certain arrangement (differing in the order of presentation) and often find it necessary to introduce other words, foreign to the subject-matter, to complete the chain or series.

Note on Learning Languages. In learning Rules and Vocabularies, the student is advised never to work at them for longer than 15 minutes at a sitting. This was the plan of study adopted by the great linguist, Sir Richard Burton; after 15 minutes of concentrated attention, he found the brain lost its freshness. The same applies to all kinds of purely mechanical learning—short periods of study give the best results. Musical students should note the bearing of this.

THE MOST USEFUL MEMORY AND HOW TO CULTIVATE IT.

Which is the most useful Memory? There is not the slightest doubt that the preponderance of opinion would answer—*The memory for everyday affairs.* You wish to re-member where you put things, where you saw things, where you read things, and what you read (i. e., general reading, apart from study), where you heard things, the names and addresses of people, appointments, and one hundred and one things of this nature. This is the memory you want, not so much the memory for dates, the Kings and Queens of England, the horses that have won the Derby, or who won the Oxford and Cambridge boat-race. Give me the memory for everyday affairs, the *"where did I leave my umbrella"* type—this is the cry of the vast majority who seek to improve their memory.

Now, how are you to get this memory? If you will analyze any case of forgetting which falls under the above heads, you will find that *Inattention* lies at the root of them all.

You go into a shop, put down your umbrella and ask to see certain articles which you have come to purchase. After you have got what you want you leave the shop, and likewise your umbrella. Why? Simply because you put it down in a *semi-conscious state,* your mind being intent on what you had come to buy. Is it at all strange that you forget in such cases?

A lady puts her purse down when she returns home; next time she wants it she cannot find it anywhere. Why? Simply because she put it down without a thought, *her mind being intent on other matters.*

Now, what is the cure for this type of forgetfulness? The cure is simply this—*you must cultivate the habit of paying attention to what you are doing; you must make your acts con-scious acts.* The lady who puts her purse down must be *aware* of the fact; it is a simple matter for her to say to herself, as she puts her purse down—"I will put my purse here, on this table, and I will know where it is when next I want it." The man who locks up at night, and who wonders when he reaches his bedroom whether he really locked the front door, will do the same on succeeding nights unless he makes the locking of the door a *conscious* act. You cannot remember doing a thing, if while you are doing it your mind is elsewhere. You *must* attend to what you are doing if you *really* wish to have a reliable memory.

If you wish to remember what you see, or hear, or read, you must pay attention while seeing, hearing, or reading, and you must impress upon your mind that you wish to remember these things. It is here that *Will Power, Concentration and Mental Discipline* play their important role in memory.

If you wish to remember to do anything in an hour's time, or a few hours' time, or a day, a week, a month ahead, you must make provision beforehand, either by making a note of the thing to be remembered, or by associating the fact in some such way as the letter experiment in *"Aids to Remembering."*

Business men who wish to remember to do a certain thing as soon as they reach their office can cultivate this type of memory in the following manner. *Determine before you leave home that on reaching your office you will do a certain act—* any trivial thing will do. Suppose, for example, you say: "When I reach the office, I will immediately unlock the safe." With this as your objective you arrange that as soon as you come near to your business premises the fact that you must unlock your safe will come to your mind. Similarly it must come to you as you enter the building, as you go up the elevator, as you enter the office.

I have taken the business man as a type for the cultivation of this type of memory, but its application can, of course, be extended to any type. Let any man or woman try this experiment for a week and they will soon see its utility. Extend the exercise by determining to do some particular act (such as lifting or touching an ornament, taking down a particular book from its shelf) as soon as you reach home, associating the act with stages in your home-coming as above, and you will be surprised how your memory for this class of facts will improve.

WORDS OF ADVICE ON MEMORY.

Students are requested to pay particular attention to this summary and to carry out the instructions. The head-lines or titles of each note direct your attention to the principal sections in memory cultivation, as mentioned in this Volume. .

Defects. Note where your memory is weak and concentrate on that weakness.

Health. Remember that good memory depends on good health; look after your health as the first consideration in memory training.

Mental Attitude. Read this section until you understand it thoroughly. Learn the value of Will Power and Concentration, and use them in your work. Cultivate, also, trust in memory.

Imagination. Understand the part that Imagination plays in memory; to understand is to be on your guard.

Retention. Note the factors that influence Retention and seek to know what bearing they have on *your* memory.

Association. A thorough understanding of Association is necessary and also of the factors that regulate it. Analyze a train of thought and see how one idea suggests another.

Recall. Understand the nature of recall and the methods to employ to secure recall.

Mental Imagery. Experiment until you find to what type of imagery you belong, and employ this type in learning by heart.

Repetition. Understand the value of Repetition—where it is most successfully employed and how to distribute it to the best advantage.

Time-Rate. Cultivate quick reading and a quick grasp of the subject-matter read.

Forgetting. Cultivate the Art of Forgetting by concentrating on essentials only. Précis writing is a valuable aid to this end; it also cultivates your thinking powers.

Learning. Learn rationally; employ mnemonics as little as possible and *only* where immediacy is involved. Remember that rational learning is not mechanical learning; it is the acquirement of knowledge by thinking—analyzing, synthesizing, and correlating experience.

Economy. Experiment with the Scoring method and other methods of learning laid down in the work, and note which yields you the best results with the minimum of Fatigue. Be economical in study, as in means.

Attention. Understand the value of paying attention to everyday matters as noted under *"The most useful Memory."* Re-read the sections on *"Attention"* and *"Observation,"* *"Attention, Observation, Interest and Fatigue."*

WORDS OF CAUTION.

Students are cautioned as to how they regard the effect of exercise in *Memory Cultivation.* The learning of a number of verses per day will not improve the Memory as a whole—it will only improve it so far as the learning of poetry is concerned. The same applies to any other department of learning.

Students are cautioned not to attempt to learn by heart too much at one time, and to refrain from learning, when they are tired. The effect of *Fatigue* on *Memory* is marked, and in extreme cases renders recall an impossibility.

THE KEY TO MEMORY CULTIVATION.

The key to memory cultivation *is Interest,* for Interest—*First,* multiplies associations; *Second,* makes retention easier and more permanent; *Third,* makes the mind inventive and progressive.

Students are advised to study carefully *Lesson Seventeen* on "Interest"; also the paragraph on "the road to success" in the section on "Will Power in Business," in *Lesson Twenty-two.*

The Master Key

PERSONAL MAGNETISM.

OBTAINED BY CONCENTRATION.

This silent, invisible soul force known as *Personal Magnetism* is the power that has been conserved to the use of the strong minded; and when concentrated, and projected by the will with a combative, subduing or controlling intent, it becomes the magic wand that rules the social and commercial world, for it triumphs over obstacles and brings success in business, social and domestic life.

It is that subtle, unseen influence that enables many people to control those around them. A person of ordinary intelligence and strong mind having this *mental power* well developed is able many times to control those having no knowledge of mental science.

The present stage of social and commercial life is one of combat—*man pitted against man*. The invisible weapon used in this battle, or struggle for supremacy, is *concentrated mental force*.

The student who has developed will-power can, without doubt, *influence* his fellow beings to do that which he wills them to do. It is this unseen element that often *causes* men and women to do things in business, social and domestic life that their ordinary common sense and reason would reject; yet *under the magnetic personality of another* they do it without thought, impressed that their acts are the outcome of their own natural inclinations.

The business and social world is ruled and influenced by this psychic force known today as *Personal Magnetism, Concentration, Will Power, Suggestion, Thought. Force, etc.*

Those persons who have this sublimated life essence well developed, and under strict discipline of the will, are enabled to influence, rule and sway their fellow men by the concentration of this force. To the learned in *Psychology*, or those who have studied *Mental Science*, it appears nothing more than the intelligent application of one's power of mind.

There is constantly emanating from every person his own particular personal magnetism. It is this particular invisible element which enables the faithful dog to scent and trace his master through a crowded thoroughfare, the hunting dog to follow and run wild game to its lair. This same *Magnetism* enables the bloodhound to run the criminal to earth. *Personal Magnetism is the medium by which and through which persons are either attracted to or repelled by each other, its nature being the key of success in our dealings in this world.* Success in worldly affairs does not always depend upon intelligence or education, as is demonstrated to all who have observed the success of the man or woman of a magnetic personality, but depends entirely upon their mental or psychic forces.

All persons, to a greater or lesser degree, possess these latent forces, but a few have developed them to their fullest extent.

Take the *Magnetism* of a fascinating young lady, which is invested with a subtle, indefinable charm, so subtle, intangible and alluring, that the effects of its far-reaching influence is felt by all with whom she comes in contact. *Personal or Vital Magnetism* radiates from the loving parent's heart, emanates from the powerful public speaker, as it does from the teacher whose strong Magnetic personality gives her discipline over her pupils.

This invisible influence goes forth unseen, but ever felt, in the gentle tone and kindly ministrations of the skilled nurse. This subtle influence is felt by the very presence of the trusted physician, whose magnetic look and reassuring words give to the poor, suffering and afflicted soul new energy, life and hope.

Magnetism breathed and pulsated in every word, look and action of the marvelous *Patti* enthralling and charming the soul by her magic spell. And so the masses are swayed, charmed and fascinated by this selfsame *Magnetism*, which is looked upon, by those unacquainted with the art of Concentration, as a wonderful gift by Providence to a few favored ones.

All of our great leaders in Congress sway and bind their audiences, either consciously or unconsciously by conforming to the law of this supreme soul force. History records many illustrations of the absolute certainty and power of a magnetic personality.

Our late President, *William McKinley,* who was just, tender and wise in his kindly ministration of the affairs of the nation, by his firm and diplomatic manner, so well known to his associates, exerted this influence, which radiated from his powerful personality, ever leading the people lovingly and safely; always winning their confidence and retaining throughout his executive life, their undying affection and unquestioning, loyal obedience.

The gracious influence of his strong personality was always forcibly felt in the brilliant glance of his manly eye, scintillated in his welcome smile, glowed in his friendly word and thrilled those who felt the hearty and firm grasp of his hand.

In every sphere of life the cultivation and development of Magnetic qualities are of the highest importance, as this force is latent in every human soul, a sacred gift and priceless jewel, whose assiduous cultivation always bestows benefit.

This magical power belongs to the inward man or soul whose spiritual strength, faculty or efficacy is best stirred into action by intense concentration and earnest intention, combined with spoken words in which there is a wonderful hidden virtue whereby you *can influence another.*

Indeed the virtue of man's words are so wonderful when pronounced with a fervent constancy of mind or soul.

The three Evangelists relate how Jesus "Appeased the troubled waters and roaring deep." Matt. 8:23-27. Mark 4:35-41. Luke 8:22-25.

Jesus, who was asleep in the hinder part of the ship when there arose a great tempest on the sea, the waves beating into the ship so that it was now full, arose and rebuked the winds and the sea; and there was a great calm. Christ spoke first to his disciples, calming their fear and agitation with a word, His magical address of—*"Peace, be still";* to the furious elements which caused a great calm was a revelation. The men marveled, saying: "What manner of man is this, that even the winds and the sea obey him?"

Christ again turned to them and more deliberately rebuked their lack of faith. *"And He saith unto them, Why are ye*

*fearful, O ye of little faith?" Jesus rebukes a fever (Luke
4:39),* which rebuke was not unheard or unheeded: for not
"willingly" was the fever or *"condition"* made *subject* to man's
vanity." (*Romans,* 8:20.)

The unseen forces of nature which were constituted at first,
as man's servant or hand-maid, rise up against him, and become
the instruments of his hurt and harm, trouble and sorrow,
when he remains ignorant of their nature and use.

But even in the moment of their wildest uproar and devasta-
tion they recognize and yield to the voice of the man who
can concentrate for he is the rightful *master,* and gladly return
to their allegiance to him, and in this, to their proper place of
service to the human race.

The student who gives this book a close perusal will learn
that man is not by nature a creature of circumstances, and
should always endeavor *to be master of the event,* ever re-
claiming and reasserting his Psychic or Magnetic possibilities.

The question of *Personal Magnetism, Will Culture* and
Mental Discipline is naturally one which concerns the bulk of
people, for it only means the practice of the spirit of helpful-
ness extended to every creature with whom you are brought into
contact. One of the greatest powers with which human beings
are endowed is sympathy, or love, and there is by no means
too much in the world. Sympathy postulates a recognition
of the unity of all with the one, that brotherhood is not a
matter of sentiment but a great fact in nature. Sympathy,
however, is not that sickly sentimentality that gushes over,
losing balance; it is essentially something strong, something
inherent with power. Wherever there is a great love flowing
out to one's fellows that character is strong, and commands the
homage of all, for everyone admires strength. Some writers
have endeavored to surround *Personal Magnetism* with mystery, but there is no need whatever. Every human being
is surrounded by an envelope composed of fine *etheric matter,*
or *aura,** which Dr. Kilner has now rendered visible to the
majority by means of chemical screens he has made. This
human atmosphere is composed of various colors, and character readers who can see it find no difficulty in giving a pretty

*Those interested in the different *astral auras,* which surrounds men
and women, should read *"Man Visible And Invisible,"* by *C. W. Lead-
beater.* This work contains 22 color plates showing the different *astral
auras* which emanate from every human being like a soft *luminous
phosphorescent* light.

accurate delineation of a character from it. It is this finely constituted envelope which stands out round an individual which is sensed by others as soon as their and his *auras* impinge upon each other. The. interpenetration of each will cause many people to make up their minds at once as to whether they like or dislike a stranger. They cannot explain why, but they have certain feelings which either attract or repel them from one whom they have not met before.

It is thought by some writers that only those in robust health possess *Personal Magnetism*, but there are plenty of individuals with a superfluity of vitality who do not attract others towards them. The more unselfish a life is led the more will one generate and diffuse this essence. To secure it, therefore, the way is obvious. Concentrate daily upon its increasing in the system*; picture your highest and best thoughts and wishes raying out all over the world to all men, though you can commence at first with those nearest to you.

Take an interest in your fellow beings; seek to be of service, remembering that *"I serve"* is the motto of all great souls, and *service* the keynote of all of the greatest characters known to history. The more you do the more you are able to do, and to help should be regarded as a privilege. The reason why those with this *catholic spirit* possess so much *Personal Magnetism*, and are thereby able to influence people, is that such an attitude allows of a free flowing of a *Magnetic Personality*. The man who lives to himself shrivels and contracts all his vehicles; he becomes self-centered to the exclusion of all better feelings and promptings, and it is a scientific fact that no man or woman can live only to themselves. The exclusive spirit must be abandoned, the barriers erected by a spirit of narrowness to keep the world out must be broken down if one wishes to be popular or successful.

It follows from the above that sex attraction is very similar. *Were the question of love between the sexes relegated to the higher part of the nature there would be less marital friction, divorces and domestic trouble.* Through bringing marriage

*One of the prominent *Psychological Exercises*, very much in favor in New York and London, among those who have taken up these studies with the one idea of mental and physical betterment, is to lie down, relax (the position of the body has much to do with the free flowing of certain currents through the spinal cord), and direct all the concentrated attention possible on the nervous system, holding steadfast the thought of health and strength, the breathing meanwhile being deep, rhythmic and long.

down to a purely animal and commercial level it has been de-
based, and those concerned have only sensed the outermost
sheath of the individual. Good looks count with some as the
only consideration, character being a minor matter, yet character should come first. When you have come across one
whom you think will make a good partner for life, let a mental
image of the person be made, when alone, and concentrate
intently on it. Ask the higher mind to say whether this person
is suited to you or not. Consult your good judgment. In some
cases the answer has come like a flash—much depends upon
the advancement of the person in practical psychology, but if it
does not come then drop the idea and try again next day and
the day after that, and several days, if need be. It must not
be forgotten that to make a conscious contact between one's
lower and higher vehicles is not a thing to be accomplished
with one or two attempts. There are business men today who
undertake no important matter without first submitting it to
their higher judgment, and in going over this work the observing student will notice that a great deal has been said with
regard to training the judgment. Above all, look for the highest and best only in everyone with whom you desire to enter
into friendly relations. By practicing the highest you know
you will call forth in the majority of cases a corresponding best.
One hesitates to use the word *"soul,"* because it is capable of so
much misunderstanding, but where the highest part of the
nature feels an irresistible attraction towards another person
there is not likely to be any cause, dissention or disappointment.

The eyes may be made a medium for the reading of another's innermost nature, and one will know intuitively sometimes whether a person can be trusted; to do this with absolute
certainty, of course, means a high state of mental development
on the part of the experimentalist. In the same way one may
convey one's wishes to another by expressing them through
the eyes, as well as through the voice. *Integrity, Scientific
Concentration* and *Mental Discipline,* coupled with literal *Faith*
and *Confidence* in *one's self* are the *talismans* used in all cases,
and *without* these essentials the student will have little or no
success. Naturally one would never wish to impose his will
upon another, because they are not acting harmoniously; for
wherever there is inharmony of any kind there is loss of power,
magnetism, and a tangle of vibrations.

You cannot do any creature a wrong without risking your

own stability. You can hoodwink others, *but never your inner consciousness,* and it is this knowledge which jars through the whole of the vibratory system of all the mental forces.

Some psychologists claim that however long a man may live every impression made on his consciousness remains there indelibly fixed, and at his death passes before his dying eyes.

To be thoroughly *vitalized and energized,* to possess *"executive ability,"* and thereby attain the function, or power, of executing and performing things, that count in life, there is no more effective method of attaining it than by *Concentration* and *"faith in one's self."*

For a few minutes, daily, *see and literally realize,* that is, believe yourself as the recipient of the great stream of vitality, health and success that fills the ether.

Believe that it is pouring into your body at every point, and, that you are *absorbing* it like a sponge taking up water. As you inhale *believe* that you are drawing vitality and strength in great waves into your being. Next realize it as being distributed all over the system to every part. If there is a weak spot or organ in your body concentrate on it at given times and affirm that vitality is centering there, that extra blood is coming from various parts of the system and that life power is intensely active there. That you, by concentration and faith, are attracting life and vital force to a weakened organ or function. It is a law of psychology that in whatever part of the body the thought is centered increased circulation takes place, and with the life-stream carrying more force to the part obstructions are broken down and carried away. Disease has been removed by this means, and a regular circulation established in parts where it has been impeded through the accumulation of morbid material. This explains cures made by Christian Science. The writer looks forward to no distant day when Practical Psychology shall have acquired such stability of character and utility as to entitle it to universal reception, when its advantages shall be looked to as the main auxiliary of good health, sound morals, rational philosophy and true religion.

The Master Key

Part Five

CHAPTER XXVIII.

LESSON TWENTY-SIX.

THE ART OF PUBLIC SPEAKING.

CONCENTRATION APPLIED TO SPEECH MAKING.

The art of public speaking is one thing—eloquence is another. Often one hears successful examples of the former far removed from the latter. True eloquence is only gained by study and *intelligent concentration*. The mere ability to speak fluently is not uncommon, but far more important than the mere flow of language is the power of putting forward convincingly, in a concentrated manner, the view and opinions which the speaker desires to impart to his audience. When to that ability, which is only to be gained by Scientific Concentration, is added the gift of polished and fluent diction, the added attraction of real eloquence, then one has the orator, although there are singularly few in the present age who can truthfully lay claim to that distinction.

By the very nature of things real eloquence must be a diminishing quantity, and the dominating factor driving to that end is the growing cult of unemotionalism broadening widespread down through the Universities and Public Schools to the great middle-class. Today the appeal is to the intellect, to the reason of one's audience.

The growing change in the fashion of our speaking is nowhere more plainly evidenced than in our Courts of Law. Advocates are practiced and professional speakers paid on each occasion to achieve by their powers of speech a particular end. It must be a foregone conclusion that they will endeavor to, *concentrate* on and *use* the methods of speech which experience

251

shows to be most essential. Only those who frequent the Courts can properly realize how seldom one hears the least attempt to employ the effect of mere language. Sheer earnestness sometimes carries an advocate before a jury into the appearance of a resort to eloquence, but such a state almost always is unintentional and unpremeditated. It is only in the ordinary public political meeting, and when there is a tendency for the intellect to be subordinated to the loyalty of party feeling, that enthusiasm can be raised by the emotionalism of eloquence.

The growth of a cynicism and the repression of emotion are having a striking effect on public speaking in this country. The oratory of half a century ago is dead; the tearing eloquence of the old stump speaker has given place to the seasoned skill of the unemotional orator. Now and then we find in some local politician a lonely survivor of that greater age.

In politics there have been great orators of every party; there have been, as there are, great statesmen and great men of all shades of political opinion, but ever and always, for turgid eloquence, one must look to the more democratic schools of thought; for the very caution produced by the knowledge and experience which breed Conservatism must of necessity check and control exuberance of language. Serious speaking with a purpose, however, tends every day more and more to pass into the hands of a few professional speakers. Politics are rapidly becoming machine-made and standardized; and political speaking, as the years go by, comes more and more under the influence of the party machines and party organizations, and of the recognized political speaking clubs. Politics —one of the few things men are serious about—form almost the only object of public meetings. To the written, rather than the spoken word, do we increasingly intrust the advocacy of all other subjects. Such other public speaking as exists— debate at the meetings of public bodies hardly reaches that level—may be broadly described as "after-dinner speaking." To be earnest on such an occasion is a mistake: a serious speaker is a bore, and usually so regarded. In this we are far in advance of our cousins across the Atlantic. Here, after dinner the Heaven-born orator holds forth at length, and, strange to say, he gets listened to. If the amateur orator is not to hand, a professional speaker is hired. We hire a musician or an expert in funny stories, and a long toast-list is only less anathema than a succession of long speeches. The result is that a type of speech has been evolved which is a type more difficult of attainment than any other. As a rule it needs careful preparation, which nevertheless it must not indicate in any way. It must be brief; it must be witty; it must be clever; it must be delivered fluently, without a trace of hesitation; it must be to the point, and it needs to be as light in its persiflage as the *souffle* which has preceded it. To some such a speech comes naturally. To the majority of men it comes only by experience, only by careful thought. It is because the most successful form of speech in this country, is the product of study and practice, that the opportunity is open to anybody who will take the trouble to acquire the reputation of a clever speaker. I know I am laying myself open to contradiction, but in my own experience the most successful after-dinner speeches have been those in which the speaker has employed genial and extravagant raillery of others who have been present, in such a manner that whilst all present have been amused, the person dealt with has felt no trace of resentment. To deliver such a speech needs more preparation and care than is entailed in the delivery of a serious one. Unfortunately, speeches of that kind are seldom, if ever, reported. Imitation is not recommended; but study of speeches made by great orators is advised, that the student may discover the why, and how, and the wherefore of their success, for in and through that study will come the knowledge of the essentials of success in public speaking. Given that knowledge, practice, concentration and experience will then produce the effective and successful public speaker.

THE SET SPEECH.

I am not a believer in "the born orator." Of course, some people have a much readier vocabulary than others. They can, as they go along, invest their thoughts with appropriate expression with the utmost ease and readiness. They can move smoothly forward while others drag painfully along. Yet, but unless there has been plenty of concentration, plenty of good hard study, plenty of good clear thinking, and plenty of good honest preparation, the speech of your "born orator" will simply be grandiloquent emptiness. Whenever I hear a man say that he is going to trust to "the inspiration of the moment" I know that I am going to listen to a speech that isn't going to add very much of value to the discussion.

Therefore, here as elsewhere, let it be understood that the essentials are concentration and hard work. The man who is going to make a good speech must first of all immerse himself in his subject. He must read all there is to be read about it; he must concentrate on it and think about it; he must talk about it. And particularly must he master completely the view of the other side. Naturally, if he is accustomed day by day to make speeches on public affairs, his mind will become stored with information on current topics; and, therefore, the amount of detailed preparation required will be less. But even here I always feel a cold shudder run down my back when I see one of the speakers of the evening jotting a few notes down on the back of an envelope during the Chairman's opening remarks.

So far, I am dealing with the set speech. The debating reply is different, and calls for different qualities. And of these more later.

The first thing to do, then, if you are to make a set, and prepared speech on a given topic, is to concentrate on it, and also read all there is to be read about it. The next thing is to talk about it whenever you are in the company of a fellow human being willing to listen to you. The exchange of views which conversation affords is invaluable. The truth fo the old proverb that "two heads are better than one" is never better exemplified than in the preparation of a speech. The members of my *classes* and my intimate friends have rendered me enormous assistance in the preparation of speeches—though I can't doubt they occasionally voted me an insufferable bore.

Very good. Having made a careful study of all that has been said or written upon the subject, the next thing is to think out the framework of the speech. You will consider the lines along which you will go, the points you will make, the conclusions you will enforce. Jot these down in a series of heads, and then sit down to *write the speech out*. Whenever time offers write the speech out fully. If we could all find time to do that—even the most practiced platform performers amongst us—our speeches would be so much better phrased, so much more closely knit together and reasoned, so much more worthy of the audience which has taken the trouble to come to hear us.

Having written the speech down, concentrate upon it and see what can profitably be struck out. In all probability it is too long, contains too many points, and will bewilder rather than educate or convince. Most speakers, even the most experienced, try to cover too much ground. The real art in speech making lies in selecting for enforcement just those *three or four significant* points upon which everything else depends And in the exercise of that art comes success.

Now comes the work of translating the written speech into *"speaking notes."* A very great deal will depend upon the way this is accomplished. If you can spare the time you should make two or three separate sets of *"notes,"* each succeeding set more condensed than the former. Use quartosized sheets of paper, write on one side only, and write boldly and clearly. Your *preliminary* "notes" should really be the text of the speech, with all the less important words omitted. Your *final* "notes" need not be much more than the barest outline of the points you intend to make. Mark each note off by a line drawn across the paper. You will find it is a good plan to use red ink as well as black. I often use red alternately with black for my "notes." I find it more easy for the eye to pick them up when thus written.

Concentrate on the striking phrases of your speech and learn them by heart. You will then deliver them far more effectively and forcibly. Study your notes over again and again until the eye becomes so accustomed to them that it can take in the whole pageful at a glance.

But while I lay great stress upon the necessity for hard work and care in the preparation of your "notes" I would beg of you to try and depend upon them less and less as your speech-making proceeds. You may easily become so much a slave to them that you will lose all capacity for spontaneous statement. You may find yourself incapable of expressing any thought save that set down on your tablets. That will cripple you seriously and render you hopelessly unable to take an effective part in a debating reply. Your mind will become petrified by too much reliance upon your "notes."

Undoubtedly the presence of your "notes" on the table will prove a most effectual preventive of nervousness in your early day. But, as I say, do not become too much enslaved to them. If you have a quick and retentive verbal memory* you may

*Study Chapter XXV., Lesson Twenty-three, *"Memory"—"Good And Bad Memories"*; also study Chapter XXVI., *Lesson Twenty-four, "Cultivation of Memory."*

learn your speech by heart. *People would be astonished if they knew how many efforts of spontaneous coruscation have been laboriously committed to memory beforehand.* There are many exponents of the value of learning by heart. It is positively uncanny to watch a public speaker of this kind talking away—and talking very well, indeed—at high speed and without a note before him. I always admire this performance. But I can't help thinking that much of the wonder of it really belongs to great industry, concentration, and quick and retentive memory. I do not speak disparagingly of all that. Quite the contrary. It is entirely in keeping with my general proposition that here, as elsewhere, concentration and hard work is the only road that leads to success.

DELIVERY OF A PUBLIC SPEECH.

But now I turn to the delivery of the speech. *First of all,* put your "notes" frankly on the table in front of you. Don't roll them up in your hand as though you were ashamed of them—keeping them behind your back, save for a furtive and hasty glance at them when you begin to get flurried and nervous.

It is most amusing to watch the attitude of many speakers towards their "notes." It is quite clear that they are shamedfaced about them. They obviously think it an evidence of weakness to have to come armed with notes at all. I don't know why. They try ineffectually to roll them up in the palm of the hand, but only succeed in depriving themselves of easy access to them. Put them frankly down on the table and have done with it. Better still, get a flat box, say two feet high, put that on the table, and put the notes on the box. If you *must* have a reading-stand let it be a flat one; the sloping music-stand is a trap for the unwary. (*Demosthenes* himself would have looked ridiculous gathering up his scattered notes from the floor.)

Begin quietly, incisively and slowly, and above all *be natural and unaffected. Don't strive after effect and don't "mouth."* Simply talk, but talk slowly and *impressively.* Try not to look severe or nervous if you can help it. A pleasant manner will put you into touch with your audience quicker than many eloquent periods. Move forward slowly and give each word its due weight. If you think any point hasn't gone home, repeat it. And don't be afraid to pause frequently to let your points sink in. Speakers as a rule do not realize the value of the pause. They know all about the subject themselves and they fall into the mistake of imagining that their audiences are similarly equipped. *The fact is the speaker is really a teacher in an adult school.* He must adopt the method of the teacher—without, of course, being pedantic. And he will be well advised if he takes very little indeed for granted.

I remember some time ago speaking for an hour to an audience on the subject of Psychology and Mental Discipline, with all the simplicity of method of the old school-teacher. In my audience was a very distinguished and justly renowned lawyer. He left the meeting with me and made a comment, the justice of which I at once recognized. He said, "Do you suppose the people understood what you meant by '*Moral Clairvoyance*'"? The phrase was one I had used several times, and without explanation. I assumed that my audience knew what it meant, as I did. They did not; and my assumption left the contingent parts of my speech more or less unintelligible.

Remember that the voice will play a leading part in the success or failure of your speech. As I say, begin quietly, and always keep plenty in reserve. Above all, never shout. If you want to emphasize, let it be by intensity rather than loudness. If you know how, you can make a whisper far more startling than the loudest whoop. If you ever have the good fortune to hear this kind of a delivery you will at once know what I mean. With this kind of a speaker his most moving passages are no louder than the main current of his discourse. But unconsciously he puts an intensity—I know no other word for it—behind the passages he feels most, and the effect upon his audience is instantaneous. Intensity is replied to by intensity. I remember a peroration of a certain speaker of this type that impressed me very much at the time, and I have often thought of it since. He had been recounting what he hoped to do in the field of Social Reform with the income which would be placed at the country's disposal by the Budget of 1909-10. The audience consisted of a couple of thousand working men in one of the poorer parts of South London. He concluded something like this: "In my country, when the people look out of a morning and see the mist rolling away above the mountain tops, they say, 'It is going to be a fine day.'" Leaning forward with a smile upon his face, and with marked but quiet emphasis and great deliberation, he said: *"Gentlemen, it is going to be a fine day."*

I have often recalled the scene. Just a small man, a small but very musical voice, and a hopelessly commonplace sentence upon which to sit down. And yet a scene of enthusiasm the like of which I have rarely seen equalled at the close of any speech. I recall the incident now for a purpose. If you must perorate—and for the life of me I don't see why—let it be simple and unaffected. And if you must perorate in poetry, let it be not more than four lines, learn them by heart, and study their delivery well beforehand.

GESTURE IN PUBLIC SPEAKING.

And this brings me to the question of gesture. I don't think you should study gesture. Let it take care of itself. Of course, there is no need to stand stock-still like a lay-figure. If you do that you will rob your speech of much of its effectiveness. But, on the other hand, don't set out to accompany your words with appropriate gesture. If you do you will not disguise the staginess of it all, and your opinions will be discounted. Just be natural, and before you know where you are the probability is that you will find yourself clenching your fist and smiting the table quite sufficiently for the peace of mind of your audience. If you must go in for scientific training I would rather you took courses of lessons in voice production than in histrionics.

Gesture will always depend on the temperament. You may learn a few swings and movements with the arms, hands and head, but they won't help you much.

The only gesture in my opinion which enhances the value of a speech is the natural and unconscious gesture.

Be careful, when you undertake to make a speech, to ascertain precisely how long you are expected to speak, and who and how many other speakers there will be. There is nothing more disconcerting than to come with a carefully prepared speech of half an hour's duration and find that you will be allowed five minutes. Indeed, I know nothing that will tax the resources of the practiced speaker more shrewdly than this will. In such a case as this he will probably be well advised not to take the notes of the speech he intended to make out of his pocket.

Under no circumstances should you assume a self-depreciatory air. It is curious how many people open a speech with something like this: "I haven't the faintest idea why I have been asked to speak to this Resolution. I can imagine no one less qualified to do so than myself." *Now that's all nonsense.* If you really felt that you ought to have sent an apology. The fact is you are nervous and self-conscious. But you needn't tell everybody. They'll probably find it out soon enough.

But don't let nervousness disconcert you. Quite the contrary. Indeed, if you have never been nervous on the public platform you have never made a really effective speech. If you have no susceptibility in your nature you can give up public speaking. You may be clear, lucid, forcible and even convincing. But the man who follows you and can touch the hearts as well as the heads of his audience will—even though he be nervous as a kitten—have beaten you on the show of hands. All our great orators confess to their moments of nervousness even after many years of platform experience.

As regards the substance of your speech let me say a word. Let the diction be as simple as possible, and don't wander off into long and involved sentences. If you do the probability is that you will tire your audience without completing your sentences. Remember, you have neither Mr. Gladstone's marvelous command of language nor his magnificent power of clear, consecutive thinking; neither have you Bob Ingersoll's eloquence and wit. Let your illustrations be homely and apposite; and if you feel the need to lighten the texture of your discourse with an anecdote, do for goodness' sake let it arise naturally. Don't start out determined to drag in a particular story. That is most inartistic. Humor is admirable if not overdone. But unless you are a professional humorist don't start out determined to be funny. And unless you are fairly experienced and know your audience, be sparing with the oratorical question. If you start out with "Why am I here tonight"? you must not be surprised if some one impishly replies, "The Lord only knows." You will find the oratorical question grows upon you. Only the other night a roguish lodge member explained at the dinner table the number of times he could have "laid me out"—to use his own expression—by replying to the oratorical questions I had put in a speech at a meeting from which we had just come. He appeared to contemplate ruefully his lost opportunities.

Be very careful how you handle interruptions; and remember they are quite as likely to come from a friend who is trying to help you as from an enemy. Many speakers are not able entirely to practice what they preach in this respect. Instinctively they treat all interruptions as hostile. It is a great mistake. They must have offended many an honest friend by this failing.

Never argue with an interrupter. If you don't think you can give him a *Roland* for an *Oliver* in the shape of a short, sharp retort, let the interruption go unnoticed. *If you can get home with a really clever and apt retort, do.* Your stock will go up at once as a speaker. American people greatly relish a prompt return. Many a man owes more to a nimble-witted reply to an interruption than to many labored orations. But you must always be good-tempered. Never sneer, *and never hit below the belt.* If you are not prepared to tackle an interrupter, who evidently means to disconcert you, politely ask him to defer his questions until your speech is ended, when, if you can, you will be glad to answer him. This may not satisfy him, but the sense of fair-play is so strong in the average American audience that he will see the wisdom of accepting your suggestion.

But now a word or two on the debating reply. Excellence as a debater is, in my opinion, the last word in public speaking. You may excel in a set oration given a certain amount of time for preparation, a certain amount of practice, and certain fairly commonplace qualifications. But to excel in debate is quite another story. You need great concentration, great experience, great assurance, great readiness; and it is here you will break down if you become *too much the slave* of your "notes" on other occasions. You will have become so accustomed to lean on your "notes" that you will go to pieces without them. For, of course, in debate you can only scribble down a few points from the preceding speech or speeches, and here the powers of concentration and discrimination are invaluable. Most practiced speakers listening to a speech can follow it in such a way as to reply more or less effectually to it point by point. Some few can at once analyze it as a whole, expose its fallacies, lay bare its false premises, and ridicule its weak conclusions. They can, in a word, riddle the whole fabric of a speech with a single shaft of scorching criticism.

I am afraid it is no use trying to teach some how to become a good debater. You may have great experience as a speaker and then fail in the thrust and parry of debate. You need, as I say, to be as quick as lightning, cool and collected to a degree, and as ready with your tongue as a comedian.. To reply to a big debate in the United States Senate, to reply effectually, and to wind your speech up on the stroke of eleven —even though the time at your disposal may vary between twenty-five and forty minutes—is unquestionably the most severe test of all-around capacity to which any public man can be subjected. And I am always filled with admiration when I remember how well the task is almost invariably performed.

DONT'S FOR PUBLIC SPEAKERS.

Don't rely on the belief that you are a born orator. Hard work and concentration is the only precursor of success here as elsewhere.

Don't fail to study with great care the other side of the proposition you propose to present.

Don't expect to say anything worth listening to if your only preparation is to scribble a few notes on the back of an envelope during the time the Chairman is introducing you.

Don't shout, don't wave your arms about like a windmill, and don't upset the water bottle.

Don't ever get a "cheap" laugh. Don't call an interrupter an ignoramus or a fool. Neither of these is precisely the soft answer that turneth away wrath.

Don't scratch your head or rub your nose more than you can help.

Don't fumble with your watch-chain, and don't pull your waist-coat down more than two or three times.

Don't quote poetry unless you know it by heart, and then quote very little of it.

Don't perorate. Or, if you do, let it be short, simple and unaffected. Remember the ridiculous is always on the heels of the sublime.

Don't ever expect any sane audience to listen to you on any subject for more than an hour. Except on very special occasions you should never speak more than from a quarter to half an hour.

Don't go on after you have finished. Sit right down. Many a first-class speech is spoiled because of the inability of the speaker to *sit down*.

Don't, if you mean to succeed in politics, get the reputation of being funny. That will be fatal.

Don't talk too fast. Your audience is probably where you were *when you began to read the subject up*.

Don't deliver the speech you intended to deliver if called on after ten o'clock p. m.

Don't reply to a vote of thanks with more than *"Thank you very much indeed."* No matter how enthusiastic the audience may have been over your speech, *it doesn't want another —just yet*.

Don't lean against the table with your legs crossed. Don't stand with one foot on your chair. In fact, let the chair alone.

Don't attempt to out-shout a noisy meeting. At the first lull in the storm get in a quick, quiet, arresting sentence, and follow it up quietly and rapidly every time you see an opening.

Don't get fidgety if the Secretary leans over and whispers to the Chairman. And don't show annoyance if any members of the audience should get up and go out.

Don't forget the speech you timed for half an hour will usually run into forty minutes.

Don't do more than take a very occasional sip from the glass of water on the Chairman's table. And don't do that when the action, taken in conjunction with the statement you have just made, is calculated to raise a laugh.

Don't, if a time-table has been arranged, allocating a certain amount of time to your speech, under any circumstances exceed your limit. It is most unfair to the others.

Don't fail to appreciate the significance of the emphasis when the Chairman calls upon you briefly to support the motion.

Don't, when your speech has already run into considerable length, mistake a gentle but well sustained tapping on the floor with feet, walking-sticks and umbrellas as necessarily a mark of approval. It is more likely to denote impatience.

Don't assume that a silent, attentive audience is unsympathetic. It may be paying you the highest tribute when it refrains from breaking in upon your remarks with applause.

Don't leave your notes on the Chairman's table when the meeting is over. You may want them again.

Don't, if you can avoid it, hand any manuscript down to the reporters' table. Let somebody else do it for you.

Don't fussily correct every small mispresentation of your view in the press. Remember the art of severe condensation is not an easy one.

Don't forget that in the heat of controversy it is very easy to impute wrong motives.

Don't let your enthusiasm for a cause lead you to believe that the advocates of the other side must necessarily be evily-disposed persons.

Don't forget that a man may vehemently oppose your view and still remain a Christian gentleman.

Don't forget that you are not the Chairman. It is he, and not you, who is responsible for the conduct of the meeting. Defer to him in everything.

Don't be personal under any circumstances.

Don't try to explain away an indiscretion by blaming the reporter.

Don't, if at a public meeting, ever go on the assumption that no reporters are present. It won't help you afterwards to explain that you were not aware that reporters were present. That, I consider, is the feeblest form of excuse.

Don't lose your temper. Whatever befall, keep smiling.

The Master Key

LESSON TWENTY-SEVEN.

CONCENTRATION USED IN COMPOSING A PUBLIC SPEECH.

Given one's subject the first thing to consider in the composition of a speech is the composition of one's audience; the subject may be the same, but *the selection of words* needed must vary with circumstances.

This can only be determined by concentration. The flowing periods and well-turned sentences, for instance, which might delight an audience at some anniversary banquet would, to use a common phrase, be "over the heads" of the members of a working men's club, and when a speech is over the heads of an audience one may be quite sure that those who have come to hear will either go to sleep or depart in scornful wrath before the orator or lecturer has reached his peroration. The speaker should use no phrases, no words, which cannot be easily understood. I often wonder how much ordinary audiences can grasp of certain speeches and addresses which I read in the newspapers, so involved are their sentences, so hidden away in a mass of superfluous detail is the single shining truth which they are intended to place before those who hear them. Not that I favor the idea of speaking down to one's audience; the man who thinks that the intelligence of his hearers is vastly inferior to his own is usually a very unintelligent person himself. There is plenty of intelligence in every American audience, but very often the language in which it is addressed might be Greek. Clearness of style is as essential in the preparation of a speech as clearness of utterance in its delivery. In *Matthew Aronold's* words, "Have something to say, and say it as clearly as you can. That is the only secret of style."

In political life it is an axiom that what is known as "the

platform manner" is as unsuited to the United States Senate as the style favored by that assembly when it allows speeches to be made, is unsuited to the feverish times of a general election.

It is in everyday life that you must lay the foundations of success in the art of speaking. Set your ideas, your impressions, your feelings in order. Think of certain facts and weave them into a story. Imagine situations and think how they can be told to an audience. Mental work is not enough. You must speak aloud when you are alone, in your house or in your garden. You must forge a mass of phrases for yourself, rehearse them, keep some, discard others, and always go on manufacturing new ones. Speak aloud, think aloud—those are two golden rules!

In ordinary everyday conversation many people, and they are by no means unintelligent or badly educated, neglect the way to express their thoughts. Their vocabulary is limited to a certain number of words which they utter a number of times, varied by a certain number of stock phrases. The would-be orator must extend his vocabulary, and this can only be done by reading the works of the masters of literature.

To get accustomed to the sound of your own voice—that somewhat alarming thing to beginners—it is a good plan to read aloud, say twenty lines at a time, of some familiar author, very carefully and very slowly, giving every syllable in every word its due value and correct pronunciation. Nervousness is a disease which tortures those afflicted by it. Many men whose intelligence and zeal have destined them for the most brilliant careers remain obscure, solely because they are unable to control themselves in public sufficiently to give expression to their thoughts before their fellow men. But it is a disease which can be cured by concentration and perseverance. Rehearse your speech aloud, to yourself first of all; then call in some good friend to hear you; thus you will get accustomed to the sound of your own voice. When you go on the platform, look at your audience before your turn comes to speak—you will seldom be the first—and firmly concentrate your mind upon your audience and what you are going to say.

Most great orators have suffered from nervousness at the outset of a speech, but the feeling quickly wears off, and, of course, in oratory, as in everything else, practice helps towards some degree of perfection.

Speak slowly, punctuating your remarks rather freely. Everything has its importance in your opening sentences; the more your audience understands them the more it will be interested in what follows.

The great art of speaking distinctly is vital to success in every walk of life, and it cannot be cultivated at too early a period of one's education.

Good diction is a *sine qua non* to those who desire to speak in public. With real orators, who are rare, indeed, certain qualities of the first rank may compensate for their defects, but the more these qualities are lacking the more it is necessary to learn everything that can be learned in the art of speaking, and even those orators who are the most richly endowed by nature cannot apply themselves too assiduously to perfect themselves in their art. Study diction in order to speak well. Speaking is one of the functions which we use most often. Why should we neglect it, even if we have only one person to listen to us? Admitting that we have no moral or material interest in winning his sympathy or in convincing him of the truth of what we are telling him, it is surely only polite that he should be saved the trouble of stretching his ears or straining his attention to hear what we are saying.

The student should study diction in order to read well. Reading aloud is an excellent way of passing an hour of the evening in the family circle. Thus are introduced, as friends of the house, poets, philosophers, historians, novelists. Some may prefer the musicians to these magic-workers, and you can admit the preference, but at the same time agree that many years of study are necessary before the violin or the piano are tolerable, before even the most indulgent home-critics, while good diction is comparatively easy, or at least sufficiently good to read clearly and enable us thereby to communicate to our friends some of the beauties which we ourselves are enjoying.

Distinctness of utterance can only be acquired by cultivation, by taking pains. The learner should be advised not to be afraid of opening his mouth; the voice need not be loud, so long as the words are enunciated clearly. Clipping of consonants and slovenly slurring over of syllables should be avoided; the suppression of the final "g" is surely reprehensible, as great a crime, as the dropping of the aspirate. To speak with distinction is given to few, but to speak dis-

tinctly is an accomplishment as easily acquired by the dullard
as the genius.   Surely it is not utterly outside the range of
possibility that the art of speaking distinctly may beget the art
of speaking with distinction.   Distinction is latent in some
of us, but distinct utterance is patent.   It is interesting to take
Shakespeare's lines on the *"Seven Ages of Man,"* and to see
how well they can be applied to the foregoing remarks on the
necessity of clear enunciation.

First the Infant.—When our children cry, we may grumble,
but we have at least the satisfaction of knowing that their lungs
are sound, and good lungs give promise of ripe soil whereon
to grow the power of fine oratory in the future.

Then the whining Schoolboy.—The boy who answers clearly and readily is invariably preferred to the one who does not.
Many a punishment is escaped by the boy who dashes boldly
at some horribly intricate piece of *viva voce* work, while he
who mumbles and hesitates is lost!

Then the Lover.—Surely the man who woos can only win
by speaking up, while he who stammers out the tale of his love
remains a bachelor to the end!

Then the Soldier.—To him, indeed, distinctness in giving
words of command, or in issuing verbal instructions to sub-
ordinates, must be of the very first importance.   *Skobeleff*
used to say that unless an officer could speak to his men they
would never follow him.   Many a battle has been lost by the
misunderstanding of verbal instructions, the result of faulty
diction.

Then the Justice.—The judge who puts the case to the jury
with clearness of diction and distinct enunciation is always an
honor to the bench, even if he be a little shaky in his law;
but he who mumbles and mouths his charge tries the jury
as well as the prisoner.

The Sixth Age.—You will always find that, however shrill
the piping treble of the old man, it will be clear as a bell, if he
were taught to speak distinctly in his youth, and early attention to the elementary rules of distinct utterance will maintain
resonance of tones in the voice of one who is playing his
part in *"the last scene of all, that ends this strange eventful
history."*

Cultivation of the art of speaking distinctly is the very
first principle of all oratory.   Without it "winged words"
are of no avail, and the periods over which we have spent so

many hours of study are best left undelivered—save, perhaps, in the form of MS. for the reporters.

It is not necessary to shout—your slightest whisper will be heard if you articulate properly, and if you remember that in every audience there is probably one old lady who is slightly deaf of one ear.

You will not be able to read well or speak well unless you breathe properly. The secret of breathing properly is to keep the lungs well filled with air, not expending more breath at any given moment than is absolutely necessary, and refilling them at every possible opportunity.

After distinct articulation and correct pronunciation comes expression, without which all reading or speaking must be unintelligent. Expression depends largely upon proper attention to modulation of the voice, to emphasis on the right word or phrase, and to pause.

By modulation of voice I mean the passing from one key to another, showing changes of sentiment, changes of thought. To acquire modulation, it is a good thing to practice reading dialogue and dramatic scenes, when you will easily see that the voice must be modulated to suit the different characters.

Emphasis means the marking by the voice of such words or phrases or sentences as you consider the most important. This you can do in various ways; by an increase of stress upon a particular word or sentence, by variation of tone, or by varying the time of the enunciation of the words. Correctness of emphasis must, of course, depend upon the intelligence of the speaker, for, if he understands his subject right through, he cannot fail to note the right words to emphasize. Incorrect emphasis will make a sentence ludicrous. For example, every one probably knows the story of the nervous curate, who, on reading the words, "And he said unto his son, Saddle me the ass, and he saddled him," read it thus, "Saddle *me* the ass." Being reproved by his rector, who pointed out that the word *ass* was the one on which emphasis should be placed, the curate, to be on the safe side, added yet another emphasis, and an amused congregation heard the passage read thus: "Saddle *me* the *ass,* so they saddled *him!*"

The value of pause is three-fold. It enables you to get breath, and, as I said before, to keep the lungs well filled with air; it gives your audience time to consider the full meaning of what you have been saying; and it serves for extra emphasis.

In this connection I will quote the words of *Froude,* in illustrating *Cardinal Newman's* power as a preacher.

Froude relates that on one occasion *Newman,* who was at that time vicar of *St. Mary's Oxford,* had been describing some of the incidents of *Our Lord's Passion.* "At this point," he says, "he paused." For a few moments there was a breathless silence. Then, in a low, clear voice, of which the faintest vibration was heard in the farthest corner of *St. Mary's* came the words, *"Now, I bid you to recollect that He to whom these things were done was Almighty God."* It was as if an electric stroke had gone through the church, as if every person present understood for the first time the meaning of what he had all his life been saying. I suppose it was an epoch in the mental history of more than one of my Oxford contemporaries.

Among actors of our time, none understood the value of pause more than the late *Henry Irving,* who never failed to give it extraordinary significance. It was said of his delivery of certain speeches that the very pauses had eloquence.

Next to distinctness, and almost equal in importance, is the art of speaking fluently and with conviction.

Cicero says, "There are three things to be aimed at in speaking—to instruct, to please and to affect powerfully." And again, "To be worthy of the proud title of orator, requires an ability to put into words any question that may arise, with good sense and a proper arrangement of the subject; further, your speech, when spoken from memory, should be ornate in style and accompanied by dignified action befitting the topic."

Let us turn once more to *Shakespeare,* and we shall find in *Hamlet's* advice to the players many wise hints, invaluable not only to the actor, but to the politician, to the lawyer, to the doctor, to the business man, and to all who take part in public, or, for that matter, private discussions.

Fluency, the use of suitable gestures, proper emphasis— all these are touched upon in this wonderful address, and all can be acquired by assiduous practice. The question of gesture, though perhaps a side-issue, is very important. In acting, the hand plays as vital a part as the brain. A clever, well-considered performance is often marred because the actor is too restless of hand or foot—perhaps of both! This is in a lesser degree often the case with public speakers.

Verify your references and quotations. A false reference in a speech has often as tragic consequences as a false reference

to a butler, and to a man of taste—there is always at least one
in every audience—a garbled quotation is as horrible a thing
as the individual who wears brown boots with a dress suit.
Your ideas may be wrong—none of us are infallible, not even
the youngest of us—and much may be forgiven to the man
with any fresh ideas, but carelessness in the preparation of a
speech is unforgivable.

And now let me insist, with all the force that in me lies,
that in speaking, or in preaching, or in acting, the only real
bond which joins man to man is *sympathy*, and without sincerity and *conviction* that bond of sympathy cannot exist.

"Cor ad cor loquitur"—heart speaks to heart. However
lost a cause may seem, it is never wholly lost as long as it is
defended with sincerity and conviction.

> "Si vis me fiere, dolendum est
> "Primum ipsi tibi."*

The barrister pleading for his client's life, the statesman
defending an unpopular cause in a hostile House or Senate,
the business man addressing a stormy meeting of shareholders,
the actor playing an unusually bad part before an exasperating-
ly critical audience, all these can triumph, if they but show that
they *believe* what they are saying, and, even if they fail, we
can say of them that they were *Faithful Failures*.

Having mastered his subject, the question of the best method to become acquainted with all the points of his speech must
be left to the individual. Some speakers, and they among
the greatest, learn their speeches by heart; others make a bare
outline of what they want to say within their minds, and only
give their thoughts concrete form before their audience; others,
again, improvise as they go along. The first system is the
safest, at any rate for beginners—write out your speech and
then learn it by heart. But it has its disadvantages. What often
happens is this: a man knows every word of his speech by
heart to his own satisfaction, but in the presence of an audience
something goes wrong; he may forget his opening sentence,
which is the keynote to what is to follow—and again I must
repeat, the opening is everything—then he stammers, and
seeks another phrase, but too often the thread of his argument is lost, and it is a long time before he gets on terms with

---

* "Those who would make us feel must feel themselves."

himself. Thus it does not do to trust too much to one's memory. A few notes consulted from time to time will save a speaker much tribulation, but the less often he has to consult them the better, for, in the reading, his gestures, his play of features are lost upon the audience, and the less he has to do with a bundle of papers the better. *The Roman Catholic Church,* for instance, teaches its priests to dispense with notes in the delivery of their sermons, and the *Scottish Church,* the parish ministers of which are elected by popular vote, does not encourage them. *"But he reads!"* has sometimes been the indignant comment on the merits of a sermon by a young candidate, from whom, however, many a mumbling curate might take a lesson in clearness of utterance.

Every speech, like every dog, should have a head, a middle and a tail, and it should be remembered by every orator, however practiced in his art, that he must, *"Above all, spend special pains on your peroration—you never know how soon you will require it."*

Be careful, too, to suit your wit to your audience; an ill-considered jest, harmless enough in itself, has cost its perpetrator very dear before now. There is the warning instance of the London barrister, who, in his courtship of a Scottish constituency, made a jesting allusion to the haggis. It was held that an insult to the national delicacy showed want of taste in more ways than one, and a vote of no confidence in the candidate was promptly passed.

Further, I would offer this advice to the young orator: When you are before your audience you must banish from your mind all the thousand and one details of the art of speaking. You must speak sufficiently *loud* to be heard, sufficiently *clearly* to be understood, and sufficiently naturally not to give an impression of finicky superiority. But you must forget all such details as I have laid stress upon in the foregoing pages— *emphasis, pause, punctuation, gesture*—these must come naturally, or your discourse will seem stilted and artificial and devoid of inspiration.

Do not exaggerate the importance of your own defects. The more you develop your good qualities the less will these defects displease. What your audience wants is to be interested, to be moved. But do not stop at merely pleasing it; try to give it something to think about and talk about long after the next day's newspaper is a back number. If you wish to be a real artist in words or in letters, you must never weary of study and concentration on these subjects. The more you learn the more you will wish to learn. In *Leonardo da Vinci's* phrase—*"The more we know, the more we love."* Finally, in the words of Abraham Lincoln, "Make your speech with malice towards none, with charity for all, with firmness in the right, as God gives us to see the right," and always bear in mind those noble words of *St. Paul*, "Whatsoever things are true, whatsoever things are just, whatsoever things are pure, whatsoever things are amiable, whatsoever things are of good report, if there be any virtue, and if there be any praise, have these in your mind, let your thoughts run upon these."

The Master Key

CHAPTER XXX.

LESSON TWENTY-EIGHT.

AFTER DINNER SPEECH.

PERSONALITY OF THE SPEAKER.

In a consideration of Oratory I shall include, not only the spoken word, but that intangible, elusive and dominant quality which we call the personality of the speaker. It is frequently referred to as *magnetism**, but however it may be described it is the mysterious power in an orator which charms and coerces his audience and causes it to applaud sentiments with which it may not have the slightest sympathy. As we read a speech of long ago, which seems cold and lifeless upon the printed page, we wonder how the audience in listening to it could have been moved to tears or laughter, to indignation or scorn, to outbursts of frenzied delight or to a display of grim determination. Was the effect produced by a peculiarly attractive quality in the voice, by an unusual mastery of expression, by some subtle power of understanding and interpretation, or was it indeed produced at all? In our perplexity we read some of the passages again, and finding that they only provoke a languid interest, conclude that contemporary judgment was wrong, or that audiences then were far less critical and far more demonstrative than they are in our own time. It would be an erroneous conclusion, however, because of our failure to realize how different is the quiet and tranquil atmosphere of the study from that of the banqueting hall, the legislative chamber, or the crowded public meeting. Imagine the eager throng, the upturned faces, the absorbed attention, the vibrant air and the tumultuous applause, all reacting upon the speaker

*See Chapter XXVII., Lesson Twenty-five *"Personal Magnetism Obtained By Concentration."*

so that he gave something of himself to his audience which cannot be recaptured and reproduced—and the miracle is explained.

Oratory has been defined as *"The art of making speeches; highly colored presentment of facts; eloquent or exaggerating language."* The definition is inadequate and misleading, since it only accentuates that meretricious kind of oratory which may dazzle with its rhetoric, but whose spell is broken when the last word is spoken. The people as they disperse gossip about the opera or the latest novel, or the next baseball contest, about anything and everything except the speech itself, which they have already forgotten.

The examples of the best oratory with which I am familiar are characterized by moderation and restraint instead of by exaggeration, and evidently depended for their effect upon under-statement rather than upon over-emphasis. The lurid and rhetorical and sensational style of speaking may please the thoughtless, but the really great orator knows the value of sober utterance clothed in noble diction.

The statement is frequently made that oratory has lost its power, and that, with the spread of education and the multiplication of newspapers and magazines and books, men and women have become so well informed that they no longer care to listen to speeches. May it not be, however, that instead of a waning interest in oratory there has been in recent years a notable lack of great orators?

Commenting upon speakers in the United States Senate a Washington correspondent for a large newspaper stated it was an usual happening to hear an eloquent speech at the National Capital. But eloquence, like genius, is a thing apart, and there were very few men in any generation who possessed the great gift. There was plenty of rhetoric, but eloquence was fire, and rhetoric even at its best was only fireworks. Three things were essential to good speaking; the first was elocution; the second was that the speaker should think only of his speech, and absolutely forget himself, and the third quality was readiness—resource in impromptu speaking. The really good speech, which it was a pleasure to read as well as to listen to, was impossible without previous preparation."

Never, I am satisfied, were people more eager than they are today to listen to one who has really something to say. and who knows how to say it, and never were they less inclined to be tolerant with the mere clever phrasing of platitudes and commonplaces. The present age is so practical, so direct in its methods, and so impatient for quick results, that the orator embodying the spirit of his time is apt to present his theme in such a bald form, and with such an entire absence of embellishment as to make it about as interesting as a business man's report of an unprofitable trade year.

The style of oratory has changed radically since the time when a speech was received with little favor, unless it was long, and abounded in classical quotations and familiar allusions. It was a style of oratory which was adapted to those who refused to be hurried, who disliked surprises, and who insisted that the speaker should approach his conclusions by easy and gradual stages. The winding path of oratory, disclosing now and again pleasant views, and thereby stimulating the desire for the final revelation, has given place to the broad highway along which the speaker travels, passing the milestones as rapidly as possible so that he may quickly reach his goal.

The aim of modern oratory would seem to be to discover the shortest possible distance between premise and conclusion. Long sentences and many-syllabled words have gone with the old stage coach and the slow-moving sailing vessel. We must talk quickly now, or our destination will be reached before we have finished our sentence.

There are many varieties of oratory, and it seldom happens that distinction is won in all the departments of this great art. The platform speaker, whose words are received with rapturous applause by listeners who agree with him, but who lack his facile speech, his sonorous voice, and his self-confidence, may prove to be a very pathetic and tragic figure if he endeavors to win favor in Congress by employing the devices which endear him to his constituency. The audience is more discriminating, less sympathetic, quick to detect a false note, and easily fatigued. Impassioned appeals fall on trained ears. The hum of conversation and the departure of members are not reassuring. Finally, the only thing the orator is conscious of is an insistent desire that he should sit down and commune with himself.

So much has been said of oratory generally because of its pertinence to after-dinner speaking, and yet that branch of the art occupies a very distinct and separate place; a unique place indeed, and one which seems to be little understood. Is it not strange that man who would hesitate to address a great gathering of people does not seem to have the slightest hesitancy in making, or trying to make, an after-dinner speech? He apparently believes that anything will suffice on such an occasion, and so, after expressing gratitude for the manner in which his toast has been proposed, and surprise, as well he might, at the good-will with which his name has been received, begins at once to flounder in a sea of trivialities and futilities, until, with one final gasp, he sinks beneath the waves, accompanied by the fervent prayer of all his victims that he may never recover sufficiently from the shock to feel encouraged to make another attempt. If asked at any time between the soup and the savory, men wholly unaccustomed to public speaking will readily undertake to talk on a subject of which they may have only the vaguest knowledge. They give the impression that their idea of an after-dinner speech is a series of pauses, united by a poverty of thought. They indulge in numerous tedious excursions, and only occasionally return to their theme as if it were something to be avoided rather than to be embraced. Nothing is more fatiguing than to be addressed by an after-dinner speaker who wanders aimlessly about in a labyrinth of words, becoming more hopelessly entangled with each sentence he utters until, finding no way to extricate himself, he brings his remarks to a close in a mere splutter of sounds.

TYPES OF AFTER-DINNER SPEAKERS.

What a great diversity do we find in the types of after-dinner speakers. .We have the man, for example, who makes the most thorough preparation, writing out word for word what he desires to say and memorizing it. His speech, however well it may read in the newspaper next morning, will be a failure when it is delivered, unless he can give his audience the impression that he is not simply performing a feat of recollection, but that he is actually developing his speech in their presence, and to some extent at least through the inspiration of their attention and interest.

Then there is the man who thinks that if he is only funny nothing more will be required of him. How few men really possess what *Lowell* calls *"that saving sense of humor."* It is a rare gift, which the gods have sparingly bestowed, and one who really has it is never compelled to bend his speech in order to bring in an anecdote which a succession of audiences have attempted to laugh at for many years. The merely funny after-dinner speaker usually tells irrelevant and incongruous stories to which he attempts to give a resemblance of reality by relating them as personal experiences.

There is also the sentimental speaker, so sentimental indeed that he almost weeps as he refers to the scenes of his childhood, or the University at which he matriculated, but which probably never gave him a degree, or alludes to the ties that bind him to a particular locality which in all likelihood welcomed his departure, but to the memory of which he clings with a fervor that seems to grow in intensity through the years.

The after-dinner speaker must not be forgotten, either, who simply has a voice, strong and robust, and who mouths his words, evidently thinking it is sound that carries conviction rather than clearness and strength of thought.

We have, too, the flippant and buoyant after-dinner speaker who goes carelessly to his fate imagining that when he is on his feet not only will ideas come to him, but also the appropriate language in which to express them. He suddenly discovers that he is without a prop of any sort, that there is nothing before him but a vast expanse of vacancy, and sits down weak and limp with the consciousness that he had nothing to say and that he said it.

We cannot afford to overlook the pompous after-dinner speaker who never rises above the dull level of mediocrity, and who exasperates all who listen to him by the bombastic way in which he utters trivial thoughts. He is enamored of himself, and so colossal is his egotism that he honestly believes he has a message to deliver which people are impatient to hear. Rebuffs do not make the slightest impression upon him. If his audience fails to appreciate his remarks he attributes the failure to ignorance and poor taste.

Of all after-dinner speakers the one who does not know when to quit is the most irritating. He recalls the little boy who was accustomed to say his prayers at his mother's side. He had prayed on one occasion for his father and mother, his brothers and sisters, his nurse and his favorite dog, and then immediately proceeded to pray for them all again, and, still not satisfied, began to plead for a third time that blessings might be showered upon him. His mother remarked that he had certainly prayed enough, and told him to jump into bed. He drowsily replied that he had forgotten the word to stop it with. When she said "Amen" his devotions promptly ceased. This is the trouble with so many after-dinner speakers—they have forgotten the word to stop their remarks with, and so they go on aimlessly and interminably in the hope that they will suddenly find it. They seldom do so, however, as there is no kind Providence watching over them.

There can hardly be a greater bore than the after-dinner speaker who mistakes the occasion, who talks about the beauties of a world-wide peace at a dinner given by the Navy League, or eulogizes the advantages of a vegetarian diet at a stock breeders' banquet. He talks with facility, and does not seem to understand the impatience of his hearers.

This is the age of short poems, short stories and short speeches. It is the age, therefore, of the after-dinner orator. If he produces any effect at all it must be instantaneous. He cannot console himself with the reflection that if he has an attractive exordium and a brilliant peroration it matters very little what goes between. When an address is limited to a few minutes it must be all excellent or it will be received with little favor. There is no time to get under way. One must capture his audience at once or he will lose it forever. The opening sentence or two determines his fate. A colorless beginning means a tragic ending. It seems incredible that our forefathers could have listened to speeches for an hour or two and wanted more. If a sermon is not finished within twenty minutes it is criticised today for its extreme length. We may not be less spiritual than the people were a hundred years ago, but we are certainly less passive. We are not inclined to sit with folded arms and to be talked to for any considerable time. Was it not *Mark Twain* who said that at the end of the first ten minutes of a sermon which greatly interested him he took out five one-dollar bills as his prospective thank-offering, but as the preacher went on and on he put them back into his pocket one at a time until, when the plate was finally passed, he languidly contributed a few cents? Many a speaker has lost the sympathy of his audience by the flood of words in which he has drowned his ideas. A great deal can be said in fifteen minutes if the speaker is interested in his theme and knows how to present it. Most addresses which continue beyond that time consist largely of amplifications and repetitions.   The after-dinner speech is something more than a mere vehicle for the use of anecdote and pleasantry, of pretty compliments and graceful acknowledgments.   The field for after-dinner speaking is indeed very great, the occasion affording such an excellent opportunity for the statesman and the social reformer and all men of earnest purpose to present their views in a concentrated form to an audience which is usually representative of a large and important section of public opinion.   It would be interesting to know how many libraries and museums and art galleries—how many splendid charities, how many social and political reforms can be traced to the suggestion of an after-dinner speaker.   When one has dined well how can he be indifferent to the claims of those who are less fortunate than himself?   Could a more congenial atmosphere than that created by an after-dinner audience be imagined in which to dwell upon the glories of peace and the advantages of international friendships?

Fewer speeches, shorter speeches, and a greater variety of speeches would add very much to the enjoyment of those who attend public dinners.   Reception is the bane of the modern toast-list.   The same themes have been assigned year after year until they have become so absolutely threadbare that only a genius can arouse the slightest interest in them.   They simply recall the past, and we frequently fall into a gentle slumber from which we are awakened by the announcement, "Ladies and gentlemen, pray silence for Mr. ———, who will propose ———," another subject with which we are perfectly familiar! A new theme would so vitalize an after-dinner audience that a dull speaker in presenting it would probably be received with rapturous applause.   I have a friend who has responded to the same toast so often that he assures me it has assumed for him a sort of tigerish form which pounces upon him at the most unexpected times and in the most unusual places.   It draws nearer and nearer as the evening for the dinner approaches, with hot breath and glaring eyes and fiendish looks, and hisses, "What can you say about me next time?   Think of something new.   I am tired of the old things which I have heard since men were sufficiently civilized to enjoy good fellowship."   It was once said by John Bright that it was his custom in making a speech to pass from headland to headland, as he seldom found time to loiter on the way.   That is what the after-dinner speaker must do in order to be effective. If he wanders very far, although, of course, he may occasionally pluck some stray wayside flowers of speech, he will probably lose his path and not be able to find it in the few minutes allotted to him. A good test for an orator would be to stop, as the story-teller does in the Far East when a dramatic situation has been developed, and refuse to proceed unless his hearers come to him bringing gifts. How many addresses, I wonder, would be concluded under such a stipulation! The after-dinner speech, to be enjoyed, must either have much humor in it or it must be so lofty in sentiment and so pure in style that men feel at once its beauty and power. Among its essential qualities are naturalness and spontaneity. Of the toast which is delicate in construction and equally delicate in suggestion—an exquisite creation—free from intellectual purpose or moral intention, dying with the night, perhaps, but filling it with joy, *Lowell has written:*

"I've a notion, I think, of a good dinner speech,
Tripping light as a sandpiper over the beach,
Swerving this way and that as the wave of the moment
Washes out its slight trace with a dash of whim's foam on't,
And leaving on memory's rim just a sense
Something graceful had gone by, a live present tense;
Not poetry—no, not quite that, but as good,
A kind of winged prose that could fly if it would.
'Tis a time for gay fancies as fleeting and vain
As the whisper of foam-beads on fresh-poured champagne,
Since dinners were not, perhaps, strictly designed
For maneuvring the heavy dragoons of the mind.
When I hear your set speeches that start with a pop,
Then wander and maunder, too feeble to stop,
With a vague apprehension from popular rumor
There used to be something by mortals called humor,
Beginning again when you thought they were done,
Respectable, sensible, weighing a ton,
And as near to the present occasions of men
As a Fast Day discourse of the year eighteen ten,
I—well, I sit still, and my sentiments smother,
For am I not also a bore and a brother?"

If an after-dinner speech sounds like a carefully prepared essay it will receive little consideration. It must not be prepared, nevertheless, in the presence of the audience. Can

anything be more depressing than to listen to a speaker who
chooses his words in public, selecting one and discarding it,
choosing another and rejecting it, and continuing the process
in the desire of finding a word that will adequately express
his thought?

ENGLISH AND AMERICAN AFTER DINNER SPEAKING.

While an after-dinner speech should primarily be entertaining, there is no reason why it should not also be informing, if the information is not delivered in a pedantic or ponder-
ous or dictatorial form.   Men do not come to dinners for instruction, but if something vital and significant is said they
are glad to listen, provided the speaker does not give the impression of trying to impart knowledge to very young people.
It is probably a mistake to have more than one response to a
toast.   The first speaker is apt to allude to the most interesting and suggestive phases of his subject, and those who follow find very little virgin soil which they can upturn.   The
spectacle is often presented of the same things being said again
and again in a slightly different form, until the audience, genial
and tolerant as an after-dinner audience may be expected to
be, shows unmistakably its fatigue and resentment.   A more
harmonious result is secured if all the toasts are proposed
by the Chairman, who should never allude to the subject-
matter of the toast except in the most casual way, but should
confine himself to an anecdote or two, a little banter, perhaps,
and a graceful allusion, leaving the toast to be dealt with as an
original theme instead of turning it over to the speaker, as
is often done, in such a marred and damaged condition that
he can never hope to recover its freshness and bloom.   The
success of an after-dinner speech depends almost as much
upon the chairman or the proposer of the toast as upon the
one who responds.   There is no one who is more dreaded by
the after-dinner speaker than the man who introduces him
at great length, and avails himself of the opportunity which
may never occur again of expressing his views upon all conceivable subjects.   It is unfair both to the speaker and the
audience to intersperse the toasts with a long musical pro-
gramme, so that one may be called upon at such a late hour
that the mood of expectancy, the most delightful mood an
audience can present to a speaker, has given place to a de-
fiant and rebellious attitude which signifies, "You must enter-

tain us at your peril, as we will not show the slightest mercy for stupidity, especially if it is long drawn out."

The accomplished after-dinner speaker is one whose wit sparkles, whose humor flashes, whose thought never droops, and whose digressions are always delightful. He takes his audience at once into his confidence and causes every one to feel that he is simply expressing their opinions. His voice sounds like a perfectly tuned instrument, so exquisitely is it modulated. His manner is so appealing that he can make the dullest subject glow with interest. Speakers of this type never use a superfluous word, but always the inevitable word without which there can be no real distinction of style.

It is true of after-dinner speaking, as of all other forms of oratory, that the speaker must be sincere himself in order to convince his audience. Too much stress cannot be laid upon this element of sincerity in all after-dinner speeches, which are intended to be something more than graceful little talks, which charm and delight, but which are really without substance, although they may be perfect in form.

One more or less familiar with after-dinner speaking in England and America is often asked wherein lies the difference. In a sense there is no difference. The true orator is regarded in exactly the same way in the two countries. It is not a greater fallacy to say the English are devoid of humor than it is to suggest that all Americans are orators. If this were true this country would have perished long ago in a war of words. There is one substantial difference, however, between English and American after-dinner speaking. The public dinner is regarded in America as more of an event, as a less casual and incidental thing than in England. Men who respond to toasts in England are, therefore, expected to have given a good deal of thought to their subject. The invitation to speak is often sent several months in advance of the dinner, so that very thorough preparation is naturally anticipated. A man is seldom asked to make an after-dinner speech in this country because of the distinguished service he may have rendered in any field of effort, unless it is· thought that he is an interesting speaker. Americans value such service so highly that they do not wish to feel embittered toward the man who may have rendered it by being compelled to listen to him when he does not possess a single qualification for public speaking. It happens, only very occasionally, however, that a man untrained in speaking may have his lips touched with the divine fire, or that hesitancy and the earnestness born of a great conviction will produce a more profound impression than can be achieved by the arts of oratory.

The real object of lecturing, however, is not to communicate information, but to try to plant germinal ideas in the mind, and to arouse curiosity, not to satisfy it. A lecture ought not to be the handing over of coined thoughts to be stored away in mental strong boxes; that is the work of the teachers, if, indeed, it is or ought to be any one's work at all. But what one desires to do in a lecture is to make a subject interesting; to tempt one's hearers to look into it themselves, to sweep away the dreary tissue of unnecessary and useless knowledge in which many books involve a subject, and to present, if one can, ideas in an attractive form. In this country people are suspicious of new ideas, but many people would find ideas more palatable than they think if only they did not know that they were new ideas.

Lecturing is really an attempt to kindle interest and curiosity, to unveil in a desirable manner the motives which lie behind effective action; if one takes the field of political science ·or economics—the same end as Psychology and mental science is in view; to trace the workings of the human mind, to show how people co-operate, and for what purpose. But if one call in rhetoric to one's aid, the aim of it must be stimulus; it is not the dry, concise, clear teaching of the class-room, with blackboard and note-book, which after all is but the clay for the bricks—it is an attempt to summarize and suggest lines of thought, to set the mental current moving, and to rescue people from what is the cause of many of our worst troubles, the curse of muddled thinking and the confusion of similar ideas. If a hearer, as a great teacher once said, goes away "with his note-book full, his head empty, and his complacency perfect," nothing whatever has been done; and a lecturer ought rather to aim at defining a few absolutely clear points, from which a hearer's mind can spontaneously advance, and to do this by emphatic repetition, which must never be mistaken for wearisome iteration. Thus a lecturer is well advised if at the beginning of his lecture he lays down very clearly what he is going to aim at; then proceeds to illustration; and finally shows at the end that he has a case, and that he has sustained his initial argument.

But, after all, a lecturer must form his own methods; it is of no use to model oneself in style or manner on some other lecturer. He has his own idiosyncrasies to consult. Some speakers have their own perennial difficulties in lecturing on literature, so that they cannot effectively quote a sentimental piece of poetry, because of a curious sort of *hysterica passio,* which tends to make them lachrymose. This is not an indication of real emotion; it is simply a mental symptom of the effects of a certain sort of sentiment upon the nerves.

Many speakers have it very strongly, and can never read an impressive passage aloud without a tendency to tears.

This can be overcome by concentrating on one's sympathetic nature with the object of driving out sentimentalism. This is an inconvenient failing, and it has really prevented many from lecturing on certain subjects to a great extent.

One ought to be very careful if one wants to lecture effectively about one's physical condition. If your voice is not a robust one, and if you are going to give a long lecture to a big audience it is advisable not to speak at all for an hour or two before, and to concentrate on your voice in the meantime, with the sole object of making it strong. And then, too, there is that perfectly unaccountable sense of nervousness which lies in wait for many a lecturer. It is perfectly unreasonable; one has done the thing a hundred times before, one does not care in the least what any one thinks of the lecture, one knows that it will be all right five minutes after one has begun; but many speakers always face a big audience with a certain tremor; and, what is still more odd, to face an audience with entire unconcern, as occasionally happens, is very nearly a presage of ineffectiveness, for the simple reason that nervousness is a sign of an emotional desire to do one's best and to affect one's audience. There was an old professor who I used to know, a trenchant talker, and more devoid of shyness than any one I ever met, who was yet a tremulous lecturer, so tremulous that he put his lectures at an hour when it was difficult for men to attend; and even when his audience, as sometimes happened, was reduced to a single person, he was still unable to adapt his phraseology to the situation, but continued to say, "Some of you may object to this theory," or "If there are any convinced Mendelians present, they may feel, etc." He had, too, elaborate stage directions at the side of his manuscript, such as "SHORT PAUSE," or the figure of a wineglass, with the

words "DRINK HERE" on the edge of the text. This is an
extreme instance, yet there are many men who are more or less
affected by the same terrors; while anything more disconcerting and hampering than to deliver a lecture with a haunting
nervousness from beginning to end cannot be imagined. Practice diminishes it, but cannot take away the possibility of it.
A great preacher who has preached thousands of sermons has
told me that he never enters a pulpit without a strong sensation of nausea; and another well-known preacher said once
in my presence that he always took a manuscript into the pulpit, though he seldom, if ever, used it, because thirty years
ago, preaching without notes, he forgot not only the thread of
his discourse but his text and subject, and indeed was not sure
for a moment who or where he was—an incident which, it may
be added, passed wholly unnoticed by his audience.

The main point, then, is that a lecturer should form a perfectly definite theory and method of his art, and discover by
preference and practice how he does his work best. The ultimate charm is a thing unattainable by any amount of practice,
because it depends upon concentration and personality. I was
amazed the other day, at a lodge which I often attend, to see
one of my colleagues, a silent, good-natured, not very emphatic
man, rise slowly in his place to address the meeting; I had
never heard him speak before, and did not know what to expect.
But there it was, the indefinable charm! He did not speak
easily or fluently; but he knew what he had to say, and he said
it clearly, gently, and persuasively in a fine intonation, and
with a friendly and modest mien. An absolute silence fell, and
when he sat down I felt I could have listened to him for an
hour with pleasure.

But if that is a natural gift there are many things which
are merely matters of practice—form, clearness, enunciation,
deliberation, courtesy, emphasis. These are all within reach;
and one thing is of high importance. A lecturer must never
yield to a temptation, which comes in the guise of modesty, to
deprecate his efforts, to apologize for speaking at all, to plead
that he does not do it willingly. After all, he would not be
asked to do it if he was not wanted. His subject should rather
be presented as a matter of urgent concern, with a gusto, and
a sense, conveyed rather than insisted upon, that the same statement cannot be obtained in so perfect a form elsewhere.

If to all this a lecturer adds the conviction of which I have spoken above, that his work is not the mere imparting of information, but analysis and synthesis, a clear defining of ideas, a bid for the universal attractiveness of the subject, if only that subject be understood, he may reach a high level of effectiveness; for the purpose of it all, as I have said, is to persuade and to start other minds on excursions of their own. A lecturer *succeeds* if his audience departs, saying, "I must look into that; there is more in it than I thought!" He fails if they go away with a sense of relief that they know all that is worth knowing on a particular subject, and firmly persuaded that it needs no further elucidation.

Broadly speaking, however, study, concentration, mental discipline, practice, natural endowment and character, are all indispensable to the making of a great orator.

Things the After-Dinner Speaker Should Guard Against.

It may be useful to suggest a few things which the after-dinner speaker should guard against:

Avoid speaking altogether unless you can make yourself distinctly heard.

Avoid talking in such a loud tone that those who listen suffer as much as they would from the near-by beating of a big drum.

Avoid apologies.

Avoid an assumption of knowledge which you do not possess.

Avoid any appearance of condescension.

Avoid any suggestion of imparting knowledge.

Avoid an anticipatory chuckle before you tell a story, for the story may prove to be pointless.

Avoid a climax which you cannot negotiate, as it is awkward to be suspended upon a sentence in mid-air.

Avoid statistics, as they usually provoke slumber.

Avoid undue humility, which is very different from becoming modesty.

Avoid quotations, because the memory is apt to be treacherous, and a quotation imperfectly rendered may destroy what would otherwise have been a very effective speech.

Avoid trying to be playful unless you know how to touch

a subject deftly and gracefully and how to return to it again and again without bruising or exhausting it.

AVOID rhetorical outbursts, remembering your hearers are on the earth, and that ten minutes is a short time in which to transport them to the skies and return them safely to the soil.

AVOID talking so long that the only impression you give is of the slow passage of time.

AVOID imitating the style of some distinguished orator, because your listeners will doubtless marvel how you could do it so badly.

AVOID waiting for applause; it may never come.

AVOID giving the impression that you think you have said something exceedingly clever.

AVOID reading your speech unless an issue as important as the fate of an army may depend upon your utterance.

AVOID being anything but simple and sincere and natural, for then you will talk of the things you really know, and men will gladly listen.

CONCENTRATION, ORATORY AND ELOQUENCE.

Oratory is like music; it *must* have tone and time.

An orator without judgment is a horse without a bridle.

Oratory is of little value unless it reaches the highest perfection.

Some orators captivate their audience by swaying its passions.

Sound logic is the sinews of eloquence.

Without concentration and solid argument oratory is empty noise, and the orator is a declaimer or a sopist.

In oratory, affectation must be avoided.

The art of Public Speaking is designed to instruct people and reform their manners; to support the laws, direct public counsels and to make men good and happy.

The really great speaker makes you keep your mind on the subject he is speaking of.

The orator who can concentrate on his subject, and send out a flood of wisdom and noble thoughts, has learned the secret of *concentration* and *mind power*.

Concentration, when used by the orator, is applicable everywhere, in all classes of human life; the rich and the poor alike experience the effects of its *magic influence*.

How often, in the court of justice, does the able lawyer by his *concentration* and matchless oratory free the character of the prisoner from suspicion, allowing him to go forth a free man?

To acquire the habit of *concentrating* on your subject is the *beginning* of the art of oratory and easy speaking.

If you wish to acquire the habit of correct diction, when speaking in public, learn to keep your mind *concentrated* on your subject.

There are grandiloquent orators, impressive and sonorous in their language, vehement, versatile and resourceful; well trained and prepared by faithful *study and concentration* to excite and turn the minds of their audience.

So great is the dignity and excellence of oratory that it transcends all eulogy.

Oratory by its *magic power,* obtained by concentration, not only lights up, but dazzles, the eyes of men.

What is more wonderful than the *magnetic influence* of the gifted orator, which has the power of holding an assembly of men and controlling their minds?

Oratory has justly been compared to the rainbow of *Iris,* because it overwhelms the souls of mortals with wonder.

Eloquence, founded upon *intelligent concentration and study,* in this day is a power. Let a man armed with concentration, a presence, sway over language, and, above all confidence, or the skill to simulate it; start out in the public arena equipped with these requisites, and ere many years have passed he will be in a high station in life, or in a fair way of rising to it.

Unless you have the art of clothing your ideas in clear, captivating diction, of identifying yourself with the feelings of your hearers, and uttering them in language more forcible, or terse, or brilliant, than they can themselves command; or unless you have the power—still more rare—of originating, of controlling their intellects, their hearts, of drawing them to your subject by the irresistible *magic of concentration*—of making their thoughts your thoughts, or yours theirs—never hope to excel in oratory.

The student of oratory will find *"True Eloquence,"* by Daniel Webster, Abraham Lincoln's *"Inaugural Address,"* and Charles Dickens speech, *"On Learners and Workers,"* which follow here, worthy of study and consideration.

DANIEL WEBSTER.

TRUE ELOQUENCE.

When public bodies are to be addressed on momentous occasions, when great interests are at stake, and strong passions excited, nothing is valuable in speech, farther than it is connected with high intellectual and moral attainments.

Clearness, force, and earnestness are the qualities which produce conviction. True eloquence, indeed, does not consist in speech. It cannot be brought from far. Labor and learning may toil for it, but they will toil in vain. Word and phrases may be marshaled in every way, but they cannot compass it. It must exist in the man, in the subject, and in the occasion. Affected passion, intense expression, the pomp of declamation, all may aspire after it. They cannot reach it. It comes, if it come at all, like the outbreaking of a fountain from the earth, or the bursting forth of volcanic fires, with spontaneous, original, native force. The graces taught in the schools, the costly ornaments, and studied contrivances of speech, shock and disgust men when their own lives and the lives of their wives and children, and their country, hang on the decision of the hour. Then, words have lost their power. Rhetoric is vain, and all elaborate oratory contemptible. Even genius itself then feels rebuked and subdued as in the presence of higher qualities. Then, patriotism is eloquent. Then, self-devotion is eloquent.

The clear conception, outrunning the deductions of logic, the high purpose, the firm resolve, the dauntless spirit speaking on the tongue, beaming from the eye, informing every feature, and urging the whole man onward to his object—this, this is eloquence, or rather it is something greater and higher than eloquence; it is action, noble, sublime, godlike action.

—Daniel Webster.

ABRAHAM LINCOLN.

INAUGURAL ADDRESS.

(Address at his Second Inauguration, March 4, 1865.)

FELLOW-COUNTRYMEN: At this season, appearing to take the oath of the Presidential office, there is less occasion for an extended address than there was at first. Then a statement somewhat in detail of a course to be pursued seemed very fitting and proper. Now, at the expiration of four years, during which public declarations have been constantly called forth on every point and phase of the great contest which still absorbs the attention and engrosses the energies of the nation, little that is new could be presented. The progress of our arms, upon which all else chiefly depends, is as well known to the public as to myself, and it is, I trust, reasonably satisfactory and encouraging to all. With high hope for the future, no prediction in regard to it is ventured.

On the occasion corresponding to this, four years ago, all thoughts were anxiously directed to an impending civil war. All dreaded it, all sought to avoid it. While the inaugural address was being delivered from this place, devoted altogether to saving the Union without war, insurgent agents were in the city, seeking to destroy it with war—seeking to dissolve the Union, and divide the effects of negotiation. Both parties deprecated war, but one of them would make war rather than let the nation survive, and the other would accept war rather than let it perish; and the war came. One-eighth of the whole population were colored slaves, not distributed generally over the Union, but localized in the southern part of it. These slaves constituted a peculiar and powerful interest; all knew that this interest was somehow the cause of the war. To strengthen, perpetuate, and extend this interest was the object for which the insurgents would rend the Union by war, while the Government claimed no right to do more than restrict the territorial enlargement of it.

Neither party expected for the war the magnitude or the duration which it has already attained. Neither anticipated that the cause of the conflict might cease with or even before the conflict itself should cease. Each looked for an easier triumph, and a result less fundamental and astounding.

Both read the same Bible, and pray to the same God, and each invokes His aid against the other. It may seem strange that any man should dare to ask a just God's assistance in wringing their bread from the sweat of other men's faces. But let us judge not, that we be not judged. The prayer of both could not be answered. That of neither has been answered fully. The Almighty has His own purposes. "Woe unto the world because of offenses; for it must needs be that offenses come, but woe to that man by whom the offense cometh!" If we shall suppose that American slavery is one of these offenses which in the providence of God must needs come, but which, having continued through His appointed time, He now wills to remove, and that He gives to both North and South, this terrible war as the woe due to those by whom the offense came, shall we discern there any departure from those divine attributes which the believers in a living God always ascribe to Him? Fondly do we hope, fervently do we pray, that this mighty scourge of war may speedily pass away. Yet if God wills that it continue until all the wealth piled by the bondsman's two hundred and fifty years of unrequited toil shall be sunk and until every drop of blood drawn with the lash shall be paid by another drawn by the sword, then, as was said three thousand years ago, so still it must be said, that "the judgments of the Lord are true and righteous altogether."

With malice towards none, with charity for all, with firmness in the right as God gives us to see the right, let us finish the work we are in, to bind up the nation's wounds, to care for him who shall have borne the battle, and for his widow and his orphans, to do all which may achieve and cherish a just and lasting peace among ourselves and with all nations.

CHARLES DICKENS.

ON LEARNERS AND WORKERS.

[Speech delivered at the Annual Meeting of the Institutional Association of Lancashire and Cheshire, held in the Free Trade Hall, Manchester, on December 3, 1858, at which Dickens presided.]

LADIES AND GENTLEMEN:—It has of late years become noticeable in England that the autumn season produces an immense amount of public speaking. I notice that no sooner do the leaves begin to fall from the trees, than pearls of great price begin to fall from the lips of the wise men of the east, and north, and west, and south; and anybody may have them by the bushel, for the picking up. Now, whether the comet has this year had a quickening influence on this crop, as it is by some supposed to have had upon the corn harvest and the vintage, I do not know; but I do know that I have never observed the columns of the newspapers to groan so heavily under a pressure of orations, each vying with the other in the two qualities of having little or nothing to do with the matter in hand, and of being always addressed to any audience in the wide world rather than the audience to which it was delivered.

The autumn having gone, and the winter come, I am so sanguine as to hope that we in our proceedings may break through this enchanted circle and deviate from this precedent; the rather as we have something real to do, and are come together, I am sure, in all plain fellowship and straightforwardness, to do it. We have no little straws of our own to throw up to show us which way any wind blows, and we have no oblique biddings of our own to make for anything outside this hall.

At the top of the public announcement of this meeting are the words, "Institutional Association of Lancashire and Cheshire." Will you allow me, in reference to the meaning of those words, to present myself before you as the embodied spirit of ignorance recently enlightened, and to put myself through a short, voluntary examination as to the results of my studies. To begin with: The title did not suggest to me anything in the least like the truth. I have been for some years pretty familiar with the terms "Mechanics' Institutions," and "Literary Societies," but they have, unfortunately, become too often associated in my mind with a body of great pretentions, lame as to some important member or other, which generally inhabits a new house much too large for it, which is seldom paid for, and which takes the name of the mechanics most grievously in vain, for I have usually seen a mechanic and a dodo in that place together. I, therefore, began my education, in respect of the meaning of this title, very coldly indeed, saying to myself, "Here's the old story." But the perusal of a very few lines of my book soon gave me to understand that it was not by any means the old story; in short, that this association is expressly designed to correct the old story and to prevent its defects from becoming perpetuated. I learnt that this Institutional Association is the union, in one central head, of one hundred and fourteen local Mechanics' Institutions and Mutual Improvement Societies, at an expense of no more than five shillings to each society; suggesting to all how they can best communicate with and profit by the fountain-head and one another; keeping their best aims steadily before them; advising them how those aims can be best attained; giving a direct end and object to what might otherwise easily become waste forces; and sending among them not only oral teachers, but, better still, boxes of excellent books, called "Free-Itinerating Libraries." I learnt that these books are constantly making the circuit of hundreds upon hundreds of miles, and are constantly being read with inexpressible relish by thousands upon thousands of toiling people, but that they are never damaged or defaced by one rude hand. These and other like facts lead me to consider the immense importance of the fact, that no little cluster of working men's cottages can arise in any Lancashire or Cheshire valley, at the foot of any running stream which enterprise hunts out for water-power, but it has its educational friend and companion ready for it, willing for it, acquainted with its thoughts and ways and turns of speech even before it has come into existence.

Now, ladies and gentlemen, this is the main consideration that has brought me here. No central association at a distance could possibly do for those working men what this local association does. No central association at a distance could possibly understand them as this local association does. No

central association at a distance could possibly put them in
that familiar and easy communication, one with another, as
that I, man or boy, eager for knowledge, in that valley seven
miles off, should know of you, man or boy, eager for knowledge twelve miles off, and should occasionally trudge to meet
you, that you may impart your learning in one branch of
acquisition to me, whilst I impart mine in another to you.
Yet this is distinctly a feature, and a most important feature,
of this society.

On the other hand, it is not to be supposed that these honest men, however zealous, could, as a rule, succeed in establishing and maintaining their own institutions of themselves.
It is obvious that combination must materially diminish their
cost, which is in time a vital consideration; and it is equally
obvious that experience, essential to the success of all combination, is especially so when its object is to diffuse the results of
experience and reflection.

Well, ladies and gentlemen, the student of the present profit-
able history of this society does not stop here in this learning;
when he has got so far, he finds with interest and pleasure
that the parent society at certain stated periods invites the more
eager and enterprising members of the local society to submit
themselves to voluntary examination in various branches of
useful knowledge, of which examination it takes the charge
and arranges the details, and invites the successful candidates
to come to Manchester to receive the prizes and certificates of
merit which it impartially awards. The most successful of
the competitors in the list of these examinations are now among
us, and these little marks of recognition and encouragement I
shall have the honor presently of giving them, as they come before you, one by one, for that purpose.

I have looked over a few of those examination papers,
which have comprised history, geography, grammar, arithmetic,
book-keeping, decimal coinage, mensuration, mathematics,
social economy, the French language—in fact, they comprise
all the keys that open all the locks of knowledge. I felt most
devoutly gratified, as to many of them, that they had not been
submitted to me to answer, for I am perfectly sure that if
they had been, I should have had mighty little to bestow upon
myself tonight. And yet it is always to be observed and seriously remembered that these examinations are undergone by
people whose lives have been passed in a continual fight for

bread, and whose whole existence has been a constant wrestle
with

"Those twin gaolers of the daring heart—
Low birth and iron fortune."*

I could not but consider, with extraordinary admiration,
that these questions have been replied to, not only by men
like myself, the business of whose life is with writing and with
books, but by men, the business of whose life is with tools and
machinery.

Let me endeavor to recall, as well as my memory will serve
me, from among the most interesting cases of prizeholders and
certificate-gainers who will appear before you, some two or
three of the most conspicuous examples. There are two poor
brothers from near Chorley, who work from morning to night
in a coal-pit, and who, in all weathers, have walked eight
miles a night, three nights a week, to attend the classes in
which they have gained distinction. There are two poor boys
from Bollington, who began life as piecers at one shilling or
eighteen-pence a week, and the father of one of whom was
cut to pieces by the machinery at which he worked, but not
before he had himself founded the institution in which this
son has since come to be taught. These two poor boys will
appear before you tonight, to take the second-class prize in
chemistry. There is a plasterer from Bury, sixteen years of
age, who took a third-class certificate last year at the hands
of Lord Brougham; he is this year again successful in a competition three times as severe. There is a wagon-maker from
the same place, who knew little or absolutely nothing until
he was a grown man, and who has learned all he knows, which
is a great deal, in the local institution. There is a chain-maker,
in very humble circumstances, and working hard all day, who
walks six miles a night, three nights a week, to attend the
classes in which he has won so famous a place. There is a
moulder in an iron foundry, who, whilst he was working
twelve hours a day before the furnace, got up at four o'clock
in the morning to learn drawing. "The thought of my lads,"
he writes in his modest account of himself, "in their peaceful
slumbers above me, gave me fresh courage, and I used to think
that if I should never receive any personal benefit, I might
instruct them when they come to be of an age to understand
the mighty machines and engines which have made our country,

*Claude Melnotte in The Lady of Lyons, Act iii, sc. 2.

England, pre-eminent in the world's history." There is a piecer at mule-frames, who could not read at eighteen, who is now a man of little more than thirty, who is the sole support of an aged mother, who is arithmetical teacher in the institution in which he himself was taught, who writes of himself that he made the resolution never to take up a subject without keeping to it, and who has kept to it with such an astonishing will, that he is now well versed in Euclid and Algebra, and is the best French Scholar in Stockport. The drawing-classes in that same Stockport are taught by a working blacksmith; and the pupils of that working blacksmith will receive the highest honors of tonight. Well may it be said of that good blacksmith, as it was written of another of his trade, by the American poet:

"Toiling, rejoicing, sorrowing,
Onward through life he goes;
Each morning sees some task begun,
Each evening sees its close.
Something attempted, something done,
Has earn'd a night's repose."

To pass from the successful candidates to the delegates from local societies now before me, and to content myself with one instance from amongst them. There is among their number a most remarkable man, whose history I have read with feelings that I could not adequately express under any circumstances, and least of all when I know he hears me, who worked when he was a mere baby at hand-loom weaving until he dropped from fatigue; who began to teach himself as soon as he could earn five shillings a week; who is now a botanist acquainted with every production of the Lancashire valley; who is a naturalist, and has made and preserved a collection of the eggs of British birds, and stuffed the birds; who is now a conchologist, with a very curious, and in some respects an original collection of fresh-water shells, and has also preserved and collected the mosses of fresh water and of the sea; who is worthily the president of his own local Literary Institution, and who was at his work this time last night as foreman in a mill.

So stimulating has been the influence of these bright examples and many more, that I notice among the applications from Blackburn for preliminary test examination papers, one from an applicant who gravely fills up the printed form by describing himself as ten years of age, and who, with equal

gravity, describes his occupation as "nursing a little child."
Nor are these things confined to the men. The women employed in factories, milliner's work, and domestic service, have
begun to show, as it is fitting they should, a most decided determination not to be outdone by the men; and the women of
Preston, in particular, have so honorably distinguished themselves, and shown in their examination papers such an admirable knowledge of the science of household management and
household economy, that if I were a working bachelor of Lancashire or Cheshire, and if I had not cast my eye or set my
heart upon any lass in particular, I should positively get up
at four o'clock in the morning with the determination of the
iron-moulder himself, and should go to Preston in search of a
wife.

Now, ladies and gentlemen, these instances, and many
more, daily occurring, always accumulating, are surely better
testimony to the working of this Association, than any number of speakers could possibly present to you. Surely the presence among us of these indefatigable people is the Association's
best and most effective triumph in the present and the past, and
is its noblest simulus to effort in the future. As its temporary
mouthpiece, I would beg to say to that portion of the company who attend to receive the prizes, that the Institution can
never hold itself apart from them—can never set itself above
them; that their distinction and success must be its distinction
and success; and that there can be but one heart beating between them and it. In particular, I would most especially en-
treat them to observe that nothing will ever be farther from
this Association's mind than the impertinence of patronage.

The prizes that it gives, and the certificates that it gives,
are mere admiring assurances of sympathy with so many striving brothers and sisters, and are only valuable for the spirit
in which they are given, and in which they are received. The
prizes are money prizes simply because the Institution does not
presume to doubt that persons who have so well governed themselves know best how to make a little money serviceable—because it would be a shame to treat them like grown-up babies
by laying it out for them, and because it knows it is given and
knows it is taken, in perfect clearness of purpose, perfect trust-
fulness, and above all, perfect independence.

Ladies and gentlemen, reverting once more to the whole
collective audience before me, I will, in another two minutes,

release the hold which your favor has given me on your attention. Of the advantages of knowledge I have said and I shall say, nothing. Of the certainty with which the man who grasps it under difficulties rises in his own respect and in usefulness to the community, I have said, and I shall say, nothing. In the city of Manchester, in the county of Lancaster, both of them remarkable for self-taught men, that were superfluous indeed. For the same reason I rigidly abstain from putting together any of the shattered fragments of that poor clay image of a parrot, which was once always saying, without knowing why, or what it meant, that knowledge was a dangerous thing. I should as soon think of piecing together the mutilated remains of any wretched Hindoo who has been blown from an English gun. Both, creatures of the past, have been—as my friend Mr. Carlyle vigorously has it—"blasted into space;" and there, as to this world, is an end of them.

So I desire, in conclusion, only to sound two strings. In the first place, let me congratulate you upon the progress which real mutual improvement societies are making at this time in your neighborhood, through the noble agency of individual employers and their families, whom you can never too much delight to honor; elsewhere, through the agency of the great railway companies, some of which are bestirring themselves in this matter with a gallantry and generosity deserving of all praise. Secondly and lastly, let me say one word out of my own personal heart, which is always very near to it in this connection. Do not let us, in the midst of the visible objects of this nature, whose workings we can tell of in figures, surrounded by machines that can be made to the thousandth part of an inch, acquiring every day knowledge which can be proved upon a slate or demonstrated by a microscope—do not let us, in the laudable pursuit of the facts that surround us, neglect the fancy and the imagination which equally surround us as a part of the great scheme. Let the child have its fable; let the man or woman into which it changes, always remember those fables tenderly. Let numerous graces and ornaments that cannot be weighed and measured, and that seem at first sight idle enough, continue to have their places about us, be we never so wise. The hardest head may co-exist with the softest heart. The union and just balance of those two is always a blessing to the possessor, and always a blessing to mankind. The Divine Teacher was as gentle and considerate as He was powerful and wise. You all know how He could still the raging of the sea, and could hush a little child. As the utmost results of the wisdom of men can only be at last to help to raise this earth to that condition to which His doctrine, untainted by the blindnesses and passions of men, would have exalted it long ago; so let us always remember that He set us the example of blending the understanding and the imagination, and that, following it ourselves, we tread in His steps, and help our race on to its better and best days. Knowledge, as all followers of it must know, has a very limited power indeed, when it informs the head alone; but when it informs the head and the heart too, it has a power over life and death, the body and the soul, and dominates the universe.

The Raven

"Surcease of Sorrow for the Lost Lenore."

This *elegy* by *Edgar Allan Poe* is well calculated to call forth those qualities of mind, in the student, necessary to strengthen his powers of *Concentration* and *Oratory* as well as to develop the *retentive powers of memory.* To those who *can "Concentrate"* this poem brings to their mind and imagination *the dramatic, the weird, the raven*—symbol of despair— *the sorrow and sadness for the lost, "Lenore."*

It is generally considered the most remarkable example of a harmony of sentiment with rhythmical expression to be found in any language. While the poet sits musing in his study, endeavoring to win from books *"surcease of sorrow for the lost Lenore,"* a raven—*the symbol of despair*—enters the room and perches upon a bust of *Pallas.* A colloquy follows between the poet and the bird of ill omen with its haunting croak of *"Nevermore."* The "Raven" has been more *widely translated* and more universally recited than any other selection in all literature.

Once upon a midnight dreary, while I pondered, weak and
    weary,
Over many a quaint and curious volume of forgotten lore—
While I nodded, nearly napping, suddenly there came a tapping,
As of some one gently rapping, rapping at my chamber door.
"'Tis some visitor," I muttered, "tapping at my chamber
    door—
        Only this and nothing more."

Ah, distinctly I remember, it was in the bleak December,
And each separate dying ember wrought its ghost upon the
    floor.
Eagerly I wished the morrow; vainly I had sought to borrow
From my books surcease of sorrow—sorrow for the lost Le-
    nore,—
For the rare and radiant maiden whom the angels name Le-
    nore,—
        Nameless here forevermore.

And the silken, sad, uncertain rustling of each purple curtain,
Thrilled me,—filled me with fantastic terrors never felt before;
So that now, to still the beating of my heart, I stood repeating,
" 'Tis some visitor entreating entrance at my chamber door,—
Some late visitor entreating entrance at my chamber door;
      That it is, and nothing more."

Presently my soul grew stronger; hesitating then no longer,
"Sir," said I, "or Madam, truly your forgiveness I implore;
But the fact is, I was napping, and so gently you came rapping,
And so faintly you came tapping, tapping at my chamber door,
That I scarce was sure I heard you"—here I opened wide the
    door;
      Darkness there, and nothing more.

Deep into that darkness peering, long I stood there, wondering,
    fearing,
Doubting, dreaming dreams no mortals ever dared to dream
    before;
But the silence was unbroken, and the stillness gave no token,
And the only word there spoken was the whispered word, "Le-
    nore!"
This *I* whispered, and an echo murmured back the word, "LE-
    NORE!"
      Merely this, and nothing more.

Back into the chamber turning, all my soul within me burning,
Soon again I heard a tapping, something louder than before.
"Surely," said I, "surely that is something at my window-
    lattice;
Let me see then what thereat is and this mystery explore,—
Let my heart be still a moment, and this mystery explore;—
      'Tis the wind, and nothing more."

Open here I flung the shutter, when, with many a flirt and
    flutter,
In there stepped a stately raven of the saintly days of yore.
Not the least obeisance made he; not a minute stopped or
    stayed he;
But, with mien of lord or lady, perched above my chamber
    door,—
Perched upon a bust of Pallas, just above my chamber door—
       Perched, and sat, and nothing more.

Then this ebon bird beguiling my sad fancy into smiling,
By the grave and stern decorum of the countenance it wore,
"Though thy crest be shorn and shaven, thou," I said, "art sure
    no craven;
Ghastly, grim, and ancient raven, wandering from the nightly
    shore,
Tell me what thy lordly name is on the night's Plutonian
    shore?"
       Quoth the raven, "Nevermore!"

Much I marveled this ungainly fowl to hear discourse so plainly,
Though its answer little meaning, little relevancy bore;
For we cannot help agreeing that no living human being
Ever yet was blessed with seeing bird above his chamber door,
Bird or beast upon the sculptured bust above his chamber door
       With such name as "Nevermore!"

But the raven, sitting lonely on that placid bust, spoke only
That one word, as if his soul in that one word he did outpour,
Nothing further then he uttered; not a feather then he flut-
    tered—
Till I scarcely more than muttered, "Other friends have flown
    before,
On the morrow he will leave me, as my hopes have flown
    before.
       Then the bird said "Nevermore!"

Startled at the stillness broken by reply so aptly spoken,
"Doubtless," said I, "what it utters is its only stock and store,
Caught from some unhappy master, whom unmerciful disaster
Followed fast and followed faster, till his songs one burden
    bore,
Till the dirges of his hope that melancholy burden bore,
        Of—'Never—nevermore!' "

But the raven still beguiling all my sad soul into smiling,
Straight I wheeled a cushioned seat in front of bird and bust
    and door,
Then, upon the velvet sinking, I betook myself to linking
Fancy unto fancy, thinking what this ominous bird of yore—
What this grim, ungainly, ghastly, gaunt, and ominous bird of
    yore
        Meant in croaking "Nevermore!"

This I sat engaged in guessing, but no syllable expressing
To the fowl whose fiery eyes now burned into my bosom's core;
This and more I sat divining, with my head at ease reclining
On the cushion's velvet lining that the lamp-light gloated o'er,
But whose velvet violet lining with the lamp-light gloated o'er
        She shall press—ah! nevermore!

Then methought the air grew denser, perfumed from an unseen
    censer
Swung by seraphim, whose foot-falls tinkled on the tufted floor,
"Wretch," I cried, "thy God hath lent thee,—by these angels
    he hath sent thee
Respite—respite and nepenthe from thy memories of Lenore!
Quaff, oh, quaff this kind nepenthe, and forget the lost Lenore!"
        Quoth the raven, "Nevermore!'

"Prophet!" cried I, "thing of evil!—prophet still, if bird or
    devil!
Whether tempter sent, or whether tempest tossed thee here
    ashore,
Desolate, yet all undaunted, on this desert land enchanted—
On this home by horror haunted—tell me truly, I implore,—
Is there—is there balm in Gilead?—tell me—tell me, I im-
    plore!"
        Quoth the raven, "Nevermore!"

"Prophet!" cried I, "thing of evil!—prophet still, if bird or
    devil!
By that heaven that bends above us, by that God we both adore,
Tell this soul, with sorrow laden, if within the distant Aidenn,
It shall clasp a sainted maiden, whom the angels name Lenore;
Clasp a rare and radiant maiden, whom the angels name Le-
    nore!"
        Quoth the raven, "Nevermore!"

"Be that word our sign of parting, bird or fiend!" I shrieked,
    upstarting,—
"Get thee back into the tempest and the night's Plutonian shore!
Leave no black plume as a token of that lie thy soul hath
    spoken!
Leave my loneliness unbroken!—quit the bust above my door!
Take thy beak from out my heart, and take thy form from off
    my door!"
        Quoth the raven, "Nevermore!"

And the raven, never flitting, still is sitting, still is sitting
On the pallid bust of Pallas, just above my chamber door;
And his eyes have all the seeming of a demon's that is dream-
    ing,
And the lamp-light o'er him streaming throws his shadow on
    the floor;
And my soul from out that shadow that lies floating on the floor
        Shall be lifted—nevermore!   —*Edgar Allan Poe.*

Gray's Elegy

The Curfew tolls the knell of parting day,
  The lowing herd winds slowly o'er the lea,
The ploughman homeward plods his weary way,
  And leaves the world to darkness and to me.

Now fades the glimmering landscape on the sight,
  And all the air a solemn stillness holds,
Save where the beetle wheels his droning flight,
  And drowsy tinklings lull the distant folds.

Save that, from yonder ivy-mantled tower,
  The moping owl does to the moon complain,
Of such as, wandering near her secret bower,
  Molest her ancient solitary reign.

Beneath those rugged elms, that yew-tree's shade,
  Where heaves the turf in many a mouldering heap,
Each in his narrow cell forever laid,
  The rude forefathers of the hamlet sleep.

The breezy call of incense-breathing morn,
  The swallow twittering from the straw-built shed,
The cock's shrill clarion, or the echoing horn,
  No more shall rouse them from their lowly bed.

The Master Key

CHAPTER XXXI.

LESSON TWENTY-NINE.

RATIONAL AND MORAL EDUCATION ETHICALLY DIRECTED BY CONCENTRATION.

"The mind of man is ever restless. Prone to err. Small is its infinity for right *unless ethically directed.*"

Modern education is entirely founded upon the idea of determinism. In fact, its aim always is to make the individual accept ideas that will determine his future conduct. Education badly directed by faulty Concentration strengthens the motives of the senses and renders the individual *a slave* to his passions and bad mental habits. If education, by intelligent concentration, is ethically directed, it raises those moral barriers which, coming between the unhealthful idea and the act, prevent the accomplishment of evil. It is still from the psychological point of view slavery, but a *useful* slavery, *because* it contributes to our own happiness and to that of others.

We feel the chain that holds us when those who guide us make us take a direction opposite to that of our inmost wish, and we complain of this violence done to our feelings. We think ourselves free as soon as we are led in the direction we wish to go.

Guyau expresses this very well when he says, "A dog held in leash by his master would consider himself perfectly free if the master wanted to go just where the dog wished, and at the same pace." The young man who has not yet felt the attraction of virtue resists the counsels of a mentor, he is indignant at constraint and does not see that the advice given him, regarding mental discipline, is good for him even if it restricts his liberty. But when he gets *moral clairvoyance**

---

*The term, moral clairvoyance, as used here is not to be confused with the word clairvoyance when used in connection with modern so-called clairvoyants and mediums.

another desire—*a good one*—will waken in him; he will then pursue it, and although *always held in leash* by the idea that has taken possession of him, he will have the feeling that the chain is loosened; he will get the illusion of liberty, like the dog, which, guided by attraction, closely follows his master. If, in his enthusiasm, the dog goes ahead, he will think that he is pulling his master, and has become his conductor. At first slave of his passions, and bad mental habits, the individual, by concentrating on virtue, becomes slave of the moral idea.

It is consideration of the ethical goal to be reached, for the good of the individual and of humanity, that establishes the distinction between the two forms of slavery; that of evil and that of good; we too often forget the latter in psychological analysis. That is the reason why, in ordinary speech, we declare him a slave who obeys his impulses of passion, of egotism, and why absolute obedience to moral principles is considered liberty. "Become a slave to philosophy and you will enjoy real liberty," said *Epicurus;* and *Schiller* repeated, "The moral man is the only free man."

And to think that the majority of men and women imagine themselves free!

Too many are slaves of bad mental habits. It is not a question of our freedom, but of finding the straight path, like the traveler who seeks to climb the longed-for height. He will profit by his personal experience in looking for the road; he will ask his way from those who have gone before him, and when he has found it he will not say, "I should like to take it," *but will take it*. This was well put by an intelligent invalid who said, *"Will passively falls into the rut dug for it by right."*

Man does not willingly do evil. He rather goes astray, as *Socrates* so justly thought, and all rational and moral education has for its aim showing him the right road. If he does not take it, it is because he is not yet sure of the correctness of your directions; it may appear to him shorter, but not so pleasant; much becomes a matter of taste.

The determinist character of education is clearly shown when this education is applied to authority in all its forms; it would be absurd to speak of the liberty of the child that is brought up on beatings, of liberty of thought when an opinion is imposed upon a person by law or church. There are methods of *moral orthopaedia* which are still often used in communities where free will is claimed and the antinomy* between the two ideas, authority and liberty, is not apparently noticed.

Liberty does not become greater, psychologically speaking, when we yield to any suggestions whatever. It is enough to have been present at hypnotic or suggestive seances in order to know that ninety-seven per cent. of people are apt to come under these influences by reason of their credulity and belief, to appreciate the extent of liberty of judgments in man. Persuasion by more logical arguments does not leave greater liberty to the individual. It imposes nothing, it is true, and even expressly says, *"You are free, listen to me, follow the arguments."* But if the idea presented to a person is accepted by him, and this acceptation does not depend upon his will but upon his faculty of comprehension, it becomes imperious, tyrannical, and carries away the person by so much the greater force as he is the more convinced.

If, on the contrary, he resists the dialectics of the master, it is because he does not thoroughly understand the idea submitted to him; there is no room for it in his mind, which is already full; he remains the slave of his previous opinion. We all know how painful it is to come across this *resistance* in others' minds when we wish to do them a service by *making them share our views.*

Education by means of reason and persuasion is the only kind that the apparent liberty of the individual respects, the kind that submits motives to him and allows him to value them according to his intellectual powers.

Every method that resorts to authority is essentially bad, although it may have the advantage of producing a quick and useful result. *The end never justifies the means.* A real idea which may take us by the collar and make us obey in the manner of a whip may be more agreeable. It is not because the constraint of authority comes from others that we detest it, for the ideas that govern us also come from others, from our parents, from our teachers, like the instruction they have probably given us. What is bad in authority is that it does not develop our *moral clairvoyance* and our perspicacity.

What the student really needs in life is not will, which so many people pride themselves on having while they are only

---

*The contradiction, which arises when we carry the categories of the mind above material experience, and apply these to the sphere of the absolute is always prominent where the question of free will is concerned.

voluntaries; that is to say, slaves of their impulses. Intelligence, self-control, and properly directed concentration is what he wants. Intelligence and *will* properly controlled and directed are one and the same thing. Whoever has *grasped* this formula understands the entire question of determinism; for intelligence is a gift either of God or of nature, as you will; mere wishing does not make one intelligent. That is why it is as absurd to reproach a person for moral ugliness as it would be to consider his physical infirmities a crime.

We give a too *restricted meaning* to the word "intelligence" when we speak of those who have shown certain intellectual aptitudes as intelligent persons; it is necessary to specify in *what branch* of human understanding they have merited this distinction as commonplace as decorations.

The Latin word *intelligere* means "to understand." Now, every day one sees people who, though masters in the field of science, arts, and politics, do not understand, and are, from an ethical point of view, idiots or weak-minded. Alas, they lack exactly the most necessary intelligence—that which makes real men; they have only the kind, more brilliant in the eyes of the world, which makes savants, artists, statesmen, and often black-legs of genius! The aim of the education that we give to others, or receive from them, should be, above all, to form that moral intelligence which enables us to distinguish good from evil and to lighten through life our pathway, which is surrounded by pitfalls. All other kinds of intelligence are inferior to this. For those who possess them other kinds of intelligence may procure personal advantages, enjoyed by others, and thus contribute to the establishment of that contingent and always precarious happiness which comes from the benefits of civilization. One need scarcely be a wizard to prove that this *is not* real happiness. Brilliant but fragmentary minds often do so much moral harm that the gifts they bring do not pay for it.

We have schools enough of this kind, which give us general and special knowledge, and can turn us into excellent technicians in all branches of human activity; what the student needs is a school to make men. In writing these words, I see myself assailed, in thought, by a crowd of experts of existing religions, who cry, "But this school exists; it is the Church." I find myself a little embarrassed in the presence of good people who see salvation only in a religion of authority. I in no way refuse

their help and do not doubt their excellent intentions. I am
even convinced that actual practice of Christ's morality would
have brought this sought-for happiness to the earth.   This is
what *M. Jean Omer Joly de Fleury* said in his thundering speech
against the book *"De l'Esprit,"* "What men would be happier
than Christians if they only regulated their conduct in everything by the moral teaching of the Evangelist; what gentleness
of customs, what cordiality in the relations of society, what
regulations, what honesty, what justice in all our actions!"

Ah, yes, it would be very fine, but I humbly confess that I
am not surprised at the result obtained at the end of nineteen
hundred years.   I have a deep feeling that if Jesus Christ
revisited this earth He would cover His face at the sight of the
Christianity that claims to be His; perhaps His grief would
not be greatly increased by visiting those who were called in
his time Gentiles.   Respect for authority is passing.   I observed to an excellent *Jesuit* father, "You have the name of
being the cleverest of all religious orders; you even tell me
you do not fear law for your congregations, because this little
business was settled in advance."   "It is true," he replied, with
a satisfied expression, not dissimulated, "we have this reputation for *savoir faire.*"   "Well, do you know, I find you very
clumsy."   "How so?"   "Because your part should be to keep
your flock intact, together, and although you take all the care
of sheep-dogs, I see your sheep escape you and scatter afar."
"It is true," he replied with a slightly bitter smile, "many people do not love us, and among my own friends, although very
devout, I had to beg forgiveness for joining the order."

The good village priest has certainly a better influence over
his sheep.   I find many, nevertheless, who complain of preaching in the wilderness; there are still too many who have recourse to authority, threatening eternal punishment, without
adding the wit of the cure of *Cucugnan.*

This impotency of the Church over certain souls has been
clearly recognized by a nun, a sister of the *Sacred Heart,* who
said: "A great number of persons whom we bring up with
the religious idea turn away from us in the course of life,
under the influence of social contagion, and with dogmas they
abandon the morality attached to them.   If then we want to
influence these souls we must institute a path of rational morality."   Indeed, it is to those who cannot accept religious dogmas
that *rational moral education* will most appeal, founded upon

the experience of all and transmitted to all. This does not mean that Christians can do without it. Even while accepting a moral code divinely given, and revealed, and upon which their faith is founded, in order to apply it they must understand the utility of its precepts, and constantly concentrate upon them either, for their relative happiness on this earth, or to achieve eternal bliss. Thus they also are obliged to understand; they must have ethical intelligence which is the fruit of pure mental habits.

"Obedience to good thoughts is liberty."

This necessity for the control of reason is what *Channing*, and with him the *American Unitarians* generally, clearly saw. While remaining a Christian, he admits that revelation and reason, both given to man for his guidance, are necessarily in agreement, and can never be in opposition. Following his comparison, both are seen to be the same light differing as dawn and midday; one is the perfection and not the opposite of the other, completing and not overthrowing it. He accepts dogmas on condition that they receive the assent of reason.

Even for those unable to reach the point of this Christian rationalism it remains evident that morality may be founded upon reason, and that a perfect harmony may be established, from the point of view of the conduct of life, between those who believe in religion and those who seek support in philosophy. As a sign of the times, a society to study the inner meaning of the Bible has been recently founded.

I say that for the flight into life we must start from a platform able to support our spring. Christians suspend it from the heavens by chains of dogmatism; I do not deny that this can be used by those rare persons sufficiently gifted morally to truly live the Christian life. Those who do not believe construct this platform upon a broad base, upon firm layers of reason. I have no right to admit *a priori*, that this edifice is the weaker. Besides, there have been enough virtuous rationalists to have justified the daring expression of *"lay saints."* It is then entirely by the influence of persuasion, and by showing the path of the True, the Beautiful, and the Good, that we can influence others; and they should have recourse to the same means to educate us. Unfortunately, the result of this desired education is not always what we expect—indeed, it stumbles against many obstacles.

Like seed sown in badly prepared ground, the moral idea

is also abortive in minds warped by heredity and atavism. In a greater degree, fortuitous educative influences act surreptitiously, as unforeseen meteorological conditions act upon a plant and disconcert the sower. The word "education" is used in much too restricted sense when, always with the idea of liberty, one makes the objection, "Look at this; here are two young persons, both gifted, who have received at home, at school, and from the Church the same education, and yet one is a delightful fellow and the other a good-for-nothing." The latter is blamed, as if he voluntarily shut the ears of his understanding to the excellent counsels given to him.

We commit the same mistake as the gardener who would say, "Here are two plants that I sowed in the same bed, that I have cultivated with the same care; one is well developed and the other is a disobedient weed." Between two brothers, apparently so dissimilar, there may be less moral difference than we imagine, and some fortuitous circumstance might have been enough to invert the roles.

By the side of directed and desired education there are many secret influences which are acting from the first day of life and which may lead the individual into a wrong path. We feel these influences every day, however absorbed we are in our surroundings, exposed to the contagion of all these germs of vice which breed in the moral air that we breathe, and we become inoculated by speech, by reading, and, above all, by example. It is the same with education as with the precautions we take to prevent our children catching contagious diseases such as scarlatina or measles. Sometimes we think we have succeeded—until the day when one of them comes home with measles, while his brother, sitting by his side at school, escapes.

Doubtless the intentional education the student receives does a great deal for his subsequent development, but he must not forget the material and moral influence working unknown to him, and against which he must concentrate his mind. I have said that they may, from foetal life,* influence the character of the child, and lead it into the path of sadness or of sullenness. At the moment of writing these words I have received from a well known practitioner the following communication: "Two children that I know were born twelve months apart.

---

*See Chapter XXXV., Lesson Thirty-three, "Concentration Applied During the Period of Gestation."

At the birth of the first an excellent wet-nurse was chosen; the child flourished, was raised without trouble, and the parents wondered at this big, fresh, rosy boy, always laughing, and who was never heard to cry. The second arrived; the nurse had been so good that the parents decided they could not do better than confide the second child to her; but the exhausted breasts were not sufficient; the child made vain efforts and, often famished, cried with all his might; diarrhoea resulted, and the cries of the child were still shriller. 'You see,' said the parents, 'what a bad disposition this one has! He is brought up like his brother, he has the same nurse, and as the first was well behaved and gave us no trouble the second is just the opposite, fretful and sulky'; the conclusion being, what a wretched disposition!"

Do not let it be thought that this is a rare case, in which the parents were not intelligent; it is a typical example of that which goes on in different ways in families, in *creches,* in the best organized charity institutions.

Doubtless if a child has a case of well-defined sickness kind persons will be found to take care of it, but if it be sulky *without the cause being discovered,* let it beware. Children who cry are *not loved, nor are those who look sad or refuse to be petted.* Affection is naturally given to those who are chubby and, above all, smiling. It is hard for a mother to avoid preferences, even at the very time when a keener sympathy *should* particularly surround the one more poorly endowed. These preferences aggravate the state of mind of the little sufferers. Soon they wake to feelings of jealousy, and moral deformation increases. We are unjust towards those we should protect, because we forget that they *are what they are able to be.* We flatter ourselves on being charitable towards them when we have only thought egotistically of the annoyance they cause us. How much harder are we upon adults who no longer exercise upon us the charm of childhood!

In other ways, there are contagions working surreptitiously. A word spoken before a child at a time of psychological receptivity may destroy all our moral orthopaedia. Let us always bear in mind these many and powerful causes of deformation, and never throw a stone at him who has strayed from the right way. A delicate tact is needed in this reciprocal education; its base is in the plenary indulgence that the determinist idea admits of and in the constant worship by concentration of the moral ideal. The education the child receives from others is the first degree, the kindergarten. During the years when the intelligence is insufficiently developed, logical persuasion must not be rigorous, but a grain of authority will of necessity be mixed with teaching. We must add the least possible amount of authority; it becomes efficient only when later it is completed by advice that shows the pupil how to concentrate on the good. As soon as he feels its attraction he will look for it alone. At the advent of the age of reason the most efficacious education begins, the education of self.

But here let us understand each other. In the same way that there is no free thought, so there cannot be a really free education of self. It is impossible for us to will to think, to invent ourselves a new idea. We can develop only what has been acquired and enlarge the ideas with which we have been imbued. Education by others is the master's lesson; education of self by Concentration is the personal work in the individual; it works by the data of previous teaching. It is only a repetition, and if occasionally we add something not in the lesson, we use ideas taken from others or drawn from the *master* of us all, *experience*. The pupil does not voluntarily perform this work of development by the decision of a sovereign will; he can only give himself up to this increasingly serious study by reason of its attraction for him—attraction not given to him, but one he submits to from the very fact of previous cultivation. To study the piano with enthusiasm, to practice out of lessons, one must have felt attraction for it, and be fond of the work; thus can one calculate the advantages derived from it. Then, and only then, is our attention fixed upon the advice of our teacher, and we take pleasure in following it. But how many are never able to recognize the attraction and abandon the study! It is the same with mental and moral culture. Many are given the basis, as in music. But where are the zealous pupils who continue their education? Alas, the deserters are numerous! It is because they have not tasted its attraction. They are like the youngster who would rather play in the woods and who yawns when put at the piano, which he hates. *Isn't this often due to the fact that the teacher has disgusted the pupil?*

The education of self and mental discipline is then not voluntary or spontaneous. The student gives himself up to it only when he has discovered the attraction attached to this

work of inner perfecting. It only differs from education received from others in the fact that he teaches the lesson to
himself. Attracted by its charm, his attention becomes fixed;
thought received from others becomes clear, and is developed.
Our fortune is increased by accumulated interest, like capital
in a savings-bank, yet there are people who prefer to keep
their money in a stocking.

It is still another illusion to consider the education of self
as the result of a wish. Such education is passive in the sense
that it is created from a received impulse, which the student
follows only when it gives him pleasure. When an idea means
nothing to it, it loses its character as a force-idea, and the
movement stops.

Moral ideas are so naturally the result of experience that
they have been in existence ever since the beginning of human
thought; that is why we add nothing absolutely new to the
ethical capital we have inherited from past centuries. Obedient
to modern association of ideas, we express the same old
thoughts under different names; we choose pictures from real
life that ought to illustrate the idea, but on close inspection it
proves to be just the same old doll dressed in new furbelows.
New ideas, with a particular nomenclature, spring up only when
there is a fact that was unknown to our predecessors. This is
what happens in the field of science, or when experience, most
often fortuitous, opens new horizons to us. Thus the discoveries in electricity, the Roentgen rays, and radium have created
new words, labeling new conceptions; only a few years are
needed to make a treatise on natural philosophy old-fashioned.
Moral ideas, on the contrary, remain the same throughout civilization. If we eliminate from ancient writings a few allusions
that gave them local color, we shall find the ideas of *Socrates,
Epictetus, Seneca* and *Marcus Aurelius* absolutely modern and
applicable to our times. In this field of ethical thought men
remain the same. The everlasting struggle between the priests
of dogma and the rationalists was long ago summed up in
this speech of the Stoic slave, "Why *don't* we do from *reason
what the Galileans do from habit?*" He added a criticism that
would be pertinent today as it was in the first century of the
Christian era, when he accused the Christians of not leading a
life in conformity with their doctrines. I believe that *Epictetus,*
traveling now over our civilized world, would retract nothing
from that just remark.

It is precisely because man does not think as he wishes, but as he can, that education should try to enlighten him, to show him the road to that inner happiness which lives in the satisfaction of an enlightened conscience.

Whoever has been touched in his moral feelings by the lessons of his childhood will feel the powerful attraction of such a state of soul; his association of ideas will fall naturally into the circle, his thought will be fixed, beset upon this task of ethical perfecting. He will live with enthusiasm for what is good, whether he depends upon a religious belief that satisfies his aspirations towards another world or whether he tries to find his road by the light of reason. Rationalists have always been accused of pride. The reproach would be justified if they pretended to have found or invented the only truth for themselves. Their role is more modest; they have only gathered the heritage of previous generations and have taken from it what they could understand and love. We cannot ask of a man more than the consideration of ideas submitted to him; he has the right to examine them by the light of reason, even if it be defective, for it is the only lantern that he has in his search for truth.

Moral Clear-Sightedness and Self-Control.

The sole liberty that man enjoys is the power to react under the influence of an idea, the ability to obey either the motives of feeling—that is to say, of his passions—or the motives of reason. This obedience is willing, and that is why we call it free, but this willingness depends upon our innate and acquired mentality. To struggle against the temptation of the passions, we require, not liberty, but self-control, and a uniformity of moral views that would make the mental balance lean to the right side. It would be necessary for the little head, that we suppose at the end of the indicator, to have a clear mental and moral view, a distinct vision of what is good to concentrate our thoughts on, and of what is bad.

Education of *self* alone, in its broadest sense, is able to give one this moral clear-sightedness which in the determinist conception replaces the idea of *will*. The student must see the road before taking it. This education of moral conscience is made either by his experience of feeling and morals or by that of others. It begins by being receptive to the teachings of his educators, until his culture is sufficient to permit him the labor called personal. This continued culture leads him, not to liberty, but to the control of himself; that is to say, to a beneficent slavery in face of moral feelings imposed upon the spirit. One may here speak of the categorical imperative, not native, and reduced to an imperceptible core of conscience, but acquired and firmly based upon our understanding. Of this noble idea of moral determinism the wise *Guyau* was able to say, *"Who does not act according to his thought acts imperfectly."*

THE DETERMINATION OF THOUGHT.

In analyzing the determination of thought I have remarked that every mental representation of an act produces the immediate accomplishment of that act if it be not prevented by a contrary mental representation. This is a fact capable of verification, but requiring its expression to be perfected. That the idea may culminate in action, the mental representation must kindle a desire. The pure and intellectual idea has no motive power; it acquires this only by the addition of an emotional and passionate element. Then only does it become a force-idea, according to common speech, sentiment and passion. This is what so many great minds have not seen, accustomed, as we are, to admit a fundamental difference between reason and feeling, to disregard the tie that binds them. Hear what *Pascal* says, that mystical and neurasthenic genius who wrote so well, and who so often thought imperfectly:

Man's conversion is prevented by his idleness, his passions, his pride—in a word, by his self-love. We cannot expect to conquer this sentiment with an idea; a passion only yields to a passion.

Truly a passion only yields to a passion, a sentiment only yields to a sentiment; I could not put it better. But why did not *Pascal* see that all passions, with the exception of the purely animal ones are ideas become sentiments from being forced upon our understanding? The passion that Pascal wished to oppose to human passions, to ever-recurring egotism, was religious passion; that is to say, an idea that had become hot from having been hammered into his head.

It is true that man does not act directly under the influence of ideas; he is ripened by sentiments. The act must have an attraction for him, and if it is a question of a complex idea, of a moral conception, he must become enthusiastic before he can become its apostle. Sometimes the ethical idea presents itself to us as does classical feminine beauty; we remain unmoved towards the body of a goddess, towards the elegant poise, towards the Grecian nose; she does not awaken love in us. But let us know her thoroughly, and we shall recognize the qualities of grace, of mind and of heart. Beware, lest she strikes like the lightning, for she is more dangerous, and we may become her slaves. Thus it is that an idea takes possession of some people and holds them in its claws. In an article upon *Brunetiere,* a writer has shown the illustrious critic during his march towards Christianity as *"guided by his logic as a prisoner by his chain."* The expression is *correct;* it demonstrates the slavery many men are in concerning their own thought, and their personal logic, which is not always that of others. That of *Brunetitre,* through authority and tradition, *brought* him to Rome; that of many others *keeps* them away just as imperiously.

Many people have noticed that certain thoughts produced a particular emotion, the strange sensation of a full heart, of precordial suffering. They think they feel that inhaling and forcing pump, called their heart, but which in reality is only a bodily function intended to keep up the circulation, associate itself with their joys as with their griefs, and in their unthinking language they immediately relegated feeling to the heart and ideas to the head. The fancy is poetic, and as such merits preservation, but the student, while studying psychology, *must* not take comparison for reason. Sentiments are *not* born in the heart, which has quite other functions; they are *awakened* in the mind, under the cold form of mental representation or picture.

Isolated, this idea could not produce the emotional storm, but immediately associations of ideas surge up, reawakening ideas already stored in our memory, and physical preparations are set going, revealing psychic emotion. An isolated string of an instrument can vibrate alone and produce a little sound; vibrating between other strings, properly stretched, it transmits its movement and we get harmony, which gives us more than its single sound. It is the same with the life of the mind. Innumerable ideas may follow one another through our brains; they are isolated strings, vibrating in succession; they produce no emotional movement. This is what generally happens in scientific work, in spite of the abundance of ideas busy in our mind.

We remain cold in spite of intense intellectual work. We read a letter, and nothing among this succession of ideas at first disturbs us. Suddenly we think we detect a reproach in an expression intended to be good-natured; we blush and our ·hearts beat faster. This is because the idea that sprang up awakened new ones; the shaking of a string transmitted itself to others, and the sound gained in volume.

It is by this awakening of previous mental representations, already become sentiments because they are habitual, and touching our pride, that the phenomenon of emotion is produced. It begins by an idea, to which others link themselves; it ends in physiological disturbances—pallor, blushing, tears, heart-beatings, catching of breath, stomach trouble, insomnia, neurasthenia, etc.

There is the same difference between the cold intellectual idea and warm feeling as between the simple tangible sensation and the sensation of grief, which is also accompanied by analogous physiological phenomena. Excitement of the peripheric nerves becomes painful when it passes a certain limit, and this physical feeling varies in different individuals. If there are intense pains which induce in all people analogous reactions, there are others confined to certain persons. It is the same with emotion; an event to which our neighbor is indifferent throws us into the height of agitation, and we recognize it to be untimely and disproportionate to the cause which produces it.   It is because we not only obey the actual mental representations, the momentary logical arguments, but obey before everything else the yoke of our previous feelings, the ideas ranged at the bottom of our personality. They also have been intellectual in their time, and they have become sentiments because they satisfied our most secret aspiration. There is not between sentiment and reason that antinomy which poets, moralists, even psychologists, and, above all, those impressionable beings called "nervous," are pleased to point out. The heart has no *"reasons that reason does not understand."* What is true is that man does not think perfectly; he allows emotional storms to burst forth when cooler and prompter reflection, combined with self-control and mental discipline, would have prevented it. It is by this clear view of things that we check growing emotion, as we stop the vibration of a glass by touching it with our fingers. It would still be better *not* to allow it to start.

Many of my patients, whose chief trouble is emotional, come to me saying they are nervous and suffer from mental troubles apart from their reason and physical ailments. The truth is that their feelings form a group apart, and their reason exists beside them; between these two compartments there are air-tight partitions which do not allow their reason to introduce order into their feelings. I tell them, You deceive yourselves; there are no primary feelings; they are all bound to a mental representation of intellectual order, accessible to the criticism of reason. So, also, there is a logic of feelings. They should only penetrate your mind and remain there when they have received the permission of your reason. The tendency of this class of patients to separate these two fields equals the saying, so commonplace and so foolish, "It is stronger than I." This is *not* the spirit that leads to victory.

To our passions we can only oppose ideas, but they must be sufficiently clear for us to seize and carry them off; they then will become feelings (passions), and we will act automatically under their imperious injunction.

These directing ideas, which should serve as a guide, are not voluntarily chosen in what has been called "willing indifference"; our choice is determined by our sympathies; let us call it our moral taste. In the presence of the train of ideas continually filing past their eyes, many are like the prince that had to marry and to whom a number of young girls was presented. He is graciously told, "You are free; now choose." It is forgotten that only a certain number of the same social rank have been presented to him and that his choice is forcibly restricted. Whom will he choose? Why, she who best pleases him. Will he let himself be led by a pretty face, or by the money-bags of an ugly one? Will he act under the moral constraint of his father, who gives him liberty in words only? Well, that *depends* upon his mind, and prince though he be, he has *neither* escaped the effects of heredity *nor* the suggestions of his education.

There are people who are really lucky in this world. They are born among moral surroundings, have been brought up kindly, gently, by the affection of their parents, by teaching and by example; more important still, they have learned to *understand* these moral ideas and have grasped the advantages of beauty. Their education has been carried on with that ability which makes for sincerity, without forcing a choice upon them. Exterior constraints have disappeared, and the individual yields only to his personal sympathies; he feels himself free. Is it to be wondered at if he *becomes* wedded to these pet ideas, if he be guided through life by them? Other people have had the same advantages and have chosen badly; and like a dissipated elder son upon whom honorable marriage is urged, and who prefers loose women, they disdain virtue. Perhaps · they have been treated with greater severity; perhaps they are incorrigible, abnormal, incapable of appreciating real charm. Finally, others are not brought up with this care, but like those young men who, without knowing many women, still *find* charming wives, they become enamored of virtue *without* being pushed towards it. Thus, one may go astray in spite of all the favorable educative influences which seem to act upon him, while another *finds* the right path alone.

Education should compel nothing, for constraint *produces opposition;* it may suggest, present ideas, demonstrate the advantages of them, and create a liking for them without urging them with displeasing insistence.

In the education of themselves, some are like the marrying man who, arriving home, thinks over the girls that have been suggested to him, finding in one new charms, in another more serious qualities. They also are smitten with ideas submitted to their judgment. Alas, they are often unfaithful to them, but the choice made, this love must increase and the bond become unbreakable!

Education of ourselves when it succeeds unites us to an ideal of good. We may borrow these governing ideas from a set of doctrines, obey a religion that we admit to be revealed, those moral laws which *Le Play* called an "eternal decalogue." There are also many people who require authority, who like to bend before it, as well as to use it over others. Needless to say, *I am not one of them.*

We may also construct this ideal by thought, by an increasing attachment to conceptions which to us seem good, useful for us, for others, and for humanity. The ideal is the idea carried to infinity; we move towards the establishment of this conception like the mathematician who draws a finite line on the board and asks us to consider it infinite, by supposing that it continues forever.

There is nobody in the world, however disinherited he may be, who has not experienced the benefit of kindness from a mother, a friend, or some person or other—perhaps *only* that of a faithful dog. From that minute he has the *conception* of that virtue. It is easy for him to imagine somebody better than his benefactor, and beyond that other, still a better one. This "always better" leads us straight to infinity, to the ideal of kindness. In the same way we conceive the ideal of other virtues, if we concentrate our mind on virtue, whose beauty we recognize, and it is this gathered knowledge that will make the beacon of our ideal.

Alas, many often allow this beacon to go out, which they should so carefully preserve, and render brighter by adding the ideal of another virtue! There are virtues whose beauty some do not immediately recognize; thus humility is very little appreciated and chastity is ridiculed. It needs a certain maturity of mind to arrive at patience and indulgence; these are not the virtues of youth. The greatest fault of man is to lower his ideal, while it can never be placed too high. It is not a goal within our reach; it is a star in the firmament, of *"true faith in self,"* that guides our feet. Doubtless many often go astray; they forget to look at the star that should guide them, but it is always there, and so they should look up! Do not become discouraged, and, to make the task easier, do not take an object nearer you as guide, a will-o'-the-wisp which is disappearing, the light of a house about to be put out, a traveler who does not know the way. *"Faith in yourself is the Master Key."*

You cannot make terms with *virtue*, nor arrangements with *"faith."* This ideal seems lacking in the present generation.

Man's faith in himself disappears, *stifled* under a mass of superstitions; it inflames only a few isolated souls in whom education has developed tradition; it is associated with the dogmas of others, with faithful attachment to superannuated political forms, to an unchanging social order; it is the ideal of natures deeply conservative, *lost* in this troubled age where everything is given up to motive, where doubt *corrodes* man's ideas. The result is an indescribable uneasiness from this transitory state of mind, and for man's happiness he must return to a faith—in himself; that is to say, he must seek the kingdom of God within himself. A few thinkers retain a valiant religious optimism and hope that after many strayings the docile sheep will come under the crook. Their watch seems to me to be slow, like *Brunetiere*, that great but wrong headed man of letters. We must not forget the thousands of souls that reform has separated from *Rome*, those prosperous nations that have found in the education of themselves, in a religion of mind and self, their strongest support. We must have no illusion about the religious feeling of the masses ostensibly remaining faithful; the authority of the Church has only trained them to an apparent obedience. It has developed in them, not religious needs, but cultivated habits, without moral influence. It is easier to subscribe to these rites, to go to mass or to a sermon, to eat fish, or to fast than to *change* one's heart and become *better* today than one was yesterday.

What man needs is faith in the inward powers of his own soul and, an attachment increasingly greater to ethical views, contributing to give him happiness and physical well being upon this earth; not that happiness dependent upon circumstances, but inner happiness entirely resulting from a complete unison between conduct and the ideal aspiration.

Some, who would have us think them very pious, speak disdainfully of this utilitarian morality that consists of the search for happiness. Now, those who rail would be unable to name an act of their lives that was not performed under the influence of this ineradicable desire. A moral that was *not* utilitarian would run a great risk of being a moral *without* utility and without force. Criticism of this independent morality would be just if personal interest *were* its guide. One must be blind to found morality upon egoism, but that is a word the sense of which we must agree upon before we wrangle about it.

Faith In Self "The Master Key."

Who can tell the delights of, *"faith in self."*

A faith, for faith is *"The Master Key,"* which turns *reason into sense, and belief into things hoped for.*

Man should live by, *"faith in himself;"* and this faith is the kind that draws down satisfaction, health and success into the life of all. But we must not mistake; this kind of a faith is here but in its infancy.

This is the faith that comes "with purified reason."

Through this medium one beholds and loves the world in its order and beauty; by its means souls follow after and feel success, health and guidance in their lives. With them *"the tree of knowledge grows beside the tree of life"* which is *"faith in self."*

When the soul hath the full measure of complement of happiness; when the boundless appetite of that spirit remains completely satisfied, that it can neither desire addition or alteration, that is truly *"faith in self."*

Man's will and intellect must be passive to receive by faith *"things hoped for."*

Discontent is a *"mingled web of faith and doubt"* in the soul.

Faith in self is only obtained after *"many a death of doubt,"* inward and outward.

Faith in oneself is a luminous star that leads the honest seeker into the deeper truths of mind and soul.

"Obedience to good thoughts is liberty."

In this nineteenth century, when men are splitting hairs about predestination and the scheme of salvation, imputed righteousness and the like, let us deal with themes such as follow here. God in His world—Divine Immanence; God in man—the kinship of the Divine and Human; God in Christ —the Incarnation; God in Himself.

"The world is in God, rather than God in the world." He could not write His image so that it could be read, save only in rational natures. Whenever we look upon our own souls in a right manner, we shall find an *Urim* and *Thummim* there." *"Faith is that which unites man more and more to the center of life and love."*

"The *foundation of heaven and hell is laid in men's own souls."*

"The gospel . . . is life whereby faith comes to dwell in us, and we in it."

"Belief in self attracts life and spirit which, flowing out from the source of all life, returns to him again as into its original, carrying the souls of good men up with it."

"It is only life which can fully converse with life."

"The waste, silent solitude," found by those who "make their whole life desolate of faith in themselves," *has nothing uplifting about it;* it really proceeds from "the stillness and fixedness of melancholy" of their own oppressed, cheerless nature.

"Know Thyself."

That the past centuries have been a time of *"stum* and *drang"* for the soul is evident; the painful, often blundering, search after what is true and real and would bear the stress of life is going on on every hand; conventions are being broken down, and in numberless cases the soul has felt itself nakedly face to face with the magical words of the lowly Nazarene— *"Know Thyself."*

The above illustrates the tone of my teachings, and their epigrammatic force.

The Master Key

CHAPTER XXXII.

LESSON THIRTY.

INDIVIDUAL MENTAL EFFICIENCY.

The mental efficiency of an individual is in direct proportion to the *quality* of his mental powers and the *control* he possesses over them.

Improvement in mental hygiene depends upon a knowledge of the causes which produce mental troubles, and mental defects, and the application of proper means which will bring about in whole or in part the eradication of mental disorders.

In many, inherent mental characteristics or lack of characteristics do not manifest themselves until middle life. Perverted mental states then begin to show themselves by the gradual or sudden manifestation of peculiarities in thinking, speech, feeling and conduct.

It is thus the various kinds of mental defectives and individuals with *mental anomalies* are produced. There are certain periods in the life of those predisposed to mental disorders where a mental breakdown is likely to occur unless some means of prevention are used. These danger zones are, for men between the age of thirty and sixty, for it is during this time that the strain and stress of life is more keenly felt. For women the danger periods are at the on-coming of womanhood, pregnancy, child-birth and the change of life.

During the life of those who are predisposed to *dementia,* nervous and mental breakdowns, environmental conditions may be so bad that they not only pave the way for *"nerve storms,"* but they really precipitate them.

As the mentally defective individual grows older, life's deteriorations and perversions manifest themselves, and if he is utterly destitute of *Mental Discipline,* and ignorant of the

326

causes which develop mental disease and mental defects he is unable to properly adjust himself to his environment.

While in this condition he comes in contact with his fellow men, and his fellow men judge him as being a mental wreck, and call him insane.

Dementia is a form of insanity caused by a lack of self-control and bad mental habits.

It will be to the student's interest to note that almost one-third of the admissions to the detention hospitals are mental unfortunates suffering from *dementia* or allied diseases due to bad mental habits formed by faulty concentration.

Specialists in mental and brain disorders know that many who suffer from diseases are the authors of their own misfortunes; and not always they alone, but their relatives and their fellow men.

The reader must not be impressed that the above applies only to those nervous patients who, since the discovery of *neurasthenia,* crowd the physician's office.

The writer's dictum does not refer to invalids alone; it applies to many who are perhaps too confident of their own mental balance. It applies to physicians equally as to patients; to educators of all kinds as well as their pupils.

When one considers the life of the mind, it becomes no longer possible to divide humanity into two classes, the sick and the well. Neurasthenia, of which one hears so much nowadays, is not a disease that attacks the patient like rheumatism or consumption; it is a psychic form of mental weakness that the patient owes to his natural and hereditary defects, to his badly directed education of the causes of mental disorders, and, again, to the vicious influences which act upon him during his entire physical and mental development.

It is not a weakness of nerves such as the word *"neurasthenia"* implies; it is, above all, mental debility, and *psychastenia"* is the word to express it.

When hereditary and constitutional influences seem to predominate, the debility is accounted illness; it appears essentially physical because it manifests itself by functional troubles, by intellectual blemishes—the fore-runner of mental and moral decay.

It·is to the physician that these disinherited, these degenerates apply; for them the world has no sympathy only when their suffering is at its height.

They are closer to us than you imagine, you who are prone to judge others severely and take pride in your own mental poise; remember that no man is a hero either to his physician or to his valet, or to those who know his private life. Each man has some defect due to heredity, none are perfect. Education itself plays an immense part in forming these pathological mental conditions; it spoils the judgment of those who call themselves normal and who imagine themselves in a position to cast a look of contemptuous pity upon their less fortunate brethren.

In the *Carnavalet Museum* in *Paris* is an autograph of *Alexandre Dumas, the younger,* that is worth a whole treatise on philosophy.

It says: *"How does it happen that while children are so intelligent, men are so stupid?"*

The witty author adds: *"Education must be responsible for it."* Yes, education is chiefly to blame; no other hypothesis is possible. It is indeed to various educational influences, in the broadest sense of the word, to the influence of environment, that we must ascribe this gradual mental and physical decadence we so often encounter.

The fact is, people do not learn how to think. Bad habits of thinking pass insensibly into actual mental disease. Again, a busy man who is capable of doing a great amount of thinking may not know, due to faulty education of what brings on mental and physical ill health, when the danger line of a mental breakdown has been reached.

He does not know his mental strength; he overworks his brain and brings on an abnormal mental state which quickly produces physical symptoms of a nervous breakdown.

The fact is, men do not learn how to think. Schools impart to students, even more zealously, knowledge of which they can only use the smallest part; it burdens their memory, and only serves to temper their intelligence with a commonplace stereotyped logic, which they think will equip them for the struggle of life.

This hot-house culture does not develop their judgment; on the contrary, it clouds it by giving the student ready-made opinions to digest, without teaching him to appreciate their accuracy.

Many today are prone to copy their neighbors when it is futile or even bad to do so; they respect traditions in all departments without submitting them, for an instant, to criticism and reason. Thinking seems to be very tiresome for some.

The physician who every day is called upon to interview the mentally diseased experiences painful surprises in finding how warped are the minds of individuals who are proud of their intelligence, and belong to recognized social and what are called governing classes.

I have no intention whatever to speak here of present-day difficulties as if the world had just started to go wrong. No; weakness of judgment and *mental anomalies* have always existed since the world begun—and this fact well justifies the epigram of *George Eliot, "We are born in a state of moral stupidity."*

Judgment is what is needed in life—a clear knowledge of our mind and defects, enabling us to foresee the immediate and future consequence of bad mental habits ond wrong thinking. Men have this foresight when it comes to protecting their material interests.

What intelligence do they not display when in the pursuit of these benefits. But when it comes to the question of *Mental Hygiene* and *Mental Discipline,* or to the question of their moral life, their conduct and the consequence of their acts, they lose their power of judgment.

Life has only one aim, to be lived, and it is an art to live it well, to draw from it the sum of happiness for which the world desperately strives, from the voluptuary, who so easily loses his way, to the religious or philosophical idealist who, in a radiance of light, sees love in his path.

Many believe that peace and happiness does not belong to earth life and soothe themselves with the hope of eternal bliss in the life beyond, which will at last compensate them for the injustice of destiny from which they suffer.

I do not believe in this terrestrial discouragement. Among the vicissitudes of life too many are avoidable—those for which we are responsible—for us to have the right to fold our hands and reserve our hopes for celestial joys. There are without doubt calamities that befall mankind, that trouble his life; and which he is powerless to exorcise; but they will always befall poor humanity. Shall they necessarily destroy his inner happiness? No. While one sees many people who are afraid to live, who despair at the smallest failure, and who are unhappy, there are souls who bravely endure many ills, including poverty, the death of those who belong to them, and the ruin of all their hopes. Multiplied misfortunes fall upon their shoulders, but their faith and inner happiness remains unshaken; they do not take refuge in a disdainful stoicism which would be a loss of feeling, but in a hidden content, which is their greatest possession.

The overcoming of mental deterioration, improvement of mental health, the eradication of mental disorders and the development of moral personality is only possible by the education of self. Every step man takes along this road contributes to his happiness and involves those who, willing or unknown to themselves, come under his influence.

For the improvement of mental health mental habits are important considerations.

Poor hygienic surroundings, incorrect habits of thought and feeling, and false modes of living often makes life uncomfortable and tedious and in many cases actually brings on a mental attack.

Every individual has in the course of his life many trials and tribulations. He is the possessor of uncomfortable feelings, secret longings, troubled thoughts, ardent desires and internal mental conflicts.

Those who have learned the value of *thought control* and *mental discipline* bring these mental troubles under control and dispose of them by casting them out of their mind. Bitter thoughts, worries and bad mental habits are brought from the dark recesses of the mind, are carefully considered, and then placed where they belong, a certain amount of weight or importance being given to each annoyance.

One of the best methods of overcoming one's troubles, as stated elsewhere in this work, is to forget them, banish them away to the deep sea of nothingness. It is not necessary to incite your mind to think always of your misfortunes. Some people sleep six hours at night and let their mind dwell uninterruptedly upon their *"worries"* eighteen hours a day. In their sleep they dream about what has previously occupied their mind. One would think they would sometimes wish for a moment of rest from their ever-active morbid thoughts. The heart, that slave, known as a bodily function, which is forced to pound along without compensation during the entire life of a nervous, worrying individual, should inspire their pity, but at least it has no feeling; like a wild animal tamed, it is not conscious of its constant drudgery and misery.

Is it any wonder nervous people have heart trouble when this organ is kept under a constant strain due to internal mental conflicts.

Nervous people are always thinking of their troubles. When they are sad and miserable they cry out and lament their lot. When they are happy they cloud their present joys by selfish regret for the past and a morbid fear for the future.

The brain of those who make up that large class of cases, the maniac-depressive group, literally exhaust their mental health. What surprises the observing medical man is not the fact that there should be so many suffering from delusions and *dementia*, but that the brains of this class, who suffer from mental deterioration, should be able to resist the continual procession of morbid ideas and nervous emotions which they produce by their fevered and disordered mental activity. Those, of this class, who must live and earn a livelihood should interest themselves in others and affairs other than their own, as this tends to lesson the importance of their own trials and mental conflict, no matter how serious these may be.

Another healthy means by which some find relief is to tell a sympathetic friend their troubles, and in this manner their trials deteriorate into comparative insignificance, and they come forth victoriously from their mental combat. Many who suffer mental ill health are, however, powerless to overcome their troubles.

Their controlling desires and mental defects get the better of them, and they are unable to set them aside.

Their strength to equalize and balance mental troubles is not sufficiently strong, and, finally, after a long struggle, their beliefs and torments burst forth in the shape of false delusions, or they imagine that they hear voices.

Sometimes they suffer from hallucinations claiming to have seen strange things, and it is thus they become insane.

There are on the streets of every city today people suffering from physical diseases who should be in some hospital. There are, also, on these same streets, thousands who are suffering from serious mental troubles and mental habits of a constitutional character.

This large number of mental inferiors, eccentrics, mental

wrecks, and others suffering from different border line types of mental diseases, while allowed freedom and considered harmless, would, for obvious reasons, be much better off if sent to some sanitarium or hospital where mental ills are treated.

There are over two hundred and twenty-five thousand insane people in the United States today.

Almost the number that goes to make up the population of such a city as Cleveland or Pittsburgh.

The number of insane confined in state institutions on December 30, 1910, was almost two hundred thousand. The cost of taking care of this vast army of mental unfortunates is over thirty million dollars annually. It is a conservative estimate that there is one out of every five hundred population that is a mental wreck or a mental defective. Again, it is a conservative estimate that one out of every six hundred of the population of the United States is today a victim of epilepsy, which is a chronic physico-mental disease characterized by irregular attacks of unconsciousness with or without convulsions.

As I have stated before what many need today is teachings in mental hygiene.

The mental unfortunate, who is always troubled with the delusion of looking for slights from relatives and others, and who is constantly on the lookout for offense when there is none given, later may, in the absence of those balancing factors, known as mental discipline and self-control, become the victim of permanent persecutory delusions; that is to say, he will imagine that he is being persecuted by others.

The things which make logical thinking so difficult for many are preconceived ideas, dogmas of all sorts, false settled convictions, solidified, in a word, and obtruded upon them by those with whom they live—their relatives, so well meaning but often so clumsy and ignorant, friends and advisers, whom they have chosen unwisely, the class in which they believe, and socially all with whom they come in contact, to whose contagion they unwittingly lay themselves open.

As the child imitates its parents, so they copy their neighbors and listen to their advice when it is even bad to do so; they respect traditions in all departments without submitting them for an instant, to criticism and reason.

Thinking appears to be very tiresome, while seeking thought

control or mental discipline is checked by their pursuit of religious dogmas.

Increasingly mental defects and abnormal thinking, which have remained unchecked, and which have not been intelligently analyzed nor controlled by their possessors, may come to the surface at a later time in their life in the form of mental disorders and false beliefs.

It has thus been shown that the individual who tolerates abnormal thought, and cultivates bad mental habits, passes unconsciously into a state where he actually suffers from mental disease.

Jealousy, selfishness, doubt, fear, suspiciousness, undue sensitiveness, morbid meditation, brooding, seclusiveness, worry, despondency and excesses, if unchecked or uninterrupted will run riot and make a mental and moral wreck of their victim.

False education, conventional fallacies concerning health, the lack of practical mental and physical training, lack of mental hygiene, the endeavor to perform tasks beyond one's capabilities, alcohol, animal sensuality, idleness, dishonesty, the acquisition of useless and false beliefs all encourage unhygienic mental habits and pave the way for serious mental diseases and nervous breakdowns later on in life.

Unchastity is always followed by mental defects. In view of this, those who unite to work in common for the improvement of morality should not be so severely criticised.

In speaking in public on the subject of chastity, a term so rarely written today that it has an archaic air, one often hears remarks mingled with the scornful laugh of some none too well mannered young lady.

One can see the discreet but yet mocking smile of many honest women; you detect also at times the heart broken sob of the girl who has seen her dream of happiness crumble away.

Why this quasi-unanimity of revolt when one dares to recommend self-control in this domain? Because, we are told, one must not interfere with the right of man to love.

Is it not a natural law, a primordial, ineffaceable instinct?

Far be it from me to condemn love even when it is reduced to the merest animal sensuality.

By a false belief many force themselves not to see the influence that amorous passion has upon the mind; it seems as if they were ashamed of it; others realize very clearly the slavery in which they live. The Pharisee still constitutes the virtuous man in society. Judging from appearances, one might think humanity were all asexual.

Man lowers himself beneath the brute when he gives himself up to libidinous thoughts; on the contrary; he raises himself by ethical thought to a more beautiful conception of love when he puts feelings of real affection first, and when the union of souls completes the bodily union.

I should not care to make man a mental eunuch, avoiding, by continual asceticism, the slavery of passion. I understand chastity to mean, according to the dictionary, "abstention from illicit pleasures, and reasonable control in pleasure allowed."

I do not speak here of that complete and definite abstinence which is unnatural, and I know that,—"*Too many men take vows of chastity to keep them.*"

However, this much I have to say that the man or woman who indulges in unchastity is known by all medical men as a mental and moral pervert. *No man or woman can steep their souls in the dregs of sensuality and retain their mental equilibrium.*

The Master Key

Part Six

CHAPTER XXXIII.

LESSON THIRTY-ONE.

CONCENTRATION APPLIED TO HEALTH AND DISEASE.

THE PSYCHOLOGY OF FAITH AND DOUBT.

Fundamental mental states of belief and faith for health *generates* health; while fundamental mental states of fear and doubt for health *generates* disease.

In short, positive mental states of faith and doubt are for or against health.

Fear and doubt of self to become immune to disease are active generators of mental *poisons and physical toxicants;* while worry is a destructive element ever tending to destroy mental discipline and over throw the mind.

I have emphasized *faith* and *doubt* in the origin, cause, cure and prevention of physical and mental ailments, because in the past they have always been associated with some particular religion, moral teaching, or system of Christian healing.

Right here I desire to *separate* the study of *mind and thought* as well as *faith and doubt* from any particular cult, creed or brands of religion.

It is my object, as far as my efforts are concerned in this work, to uphold *"faith and belief in one's self,"* as the *emancipators* of men and women *from the bondage and servitude of doubt and fear.*

Many are vying with others about New Thought, Christian Science, religious beliefs and spirit healing all of which are premature, unscientific, superstitious, misleading, incompe-

tent, incomplete, oriental and very disastrous in their misleading influence upon the minds and morals of their adherents.

I would admonish the student *to beware* of "philosophical
fads," "healing cults," "ism," "Spirit Healers" and the claims
these people make in their literature.

Let the student approach the subject with his feet tread-
ing on a foundation of common sense and reason.

Let him get away from the shadow of mysticism and superstition which has darkened the path to reason for centuries.

Let the student approach the subject of mind from the
standpoint of the trained psychologist.

Let him examine all the actual facts respecting the effect
of thought, and the various mental states on the physicial body
during both disease and health.

Let him learn from observation and experience just how
thought and mental states affect the functions of the human
body in disease and health.

Concentration, belief and auto-suggestion is like unto a
two-edged sword; it cuts both ways. Therefore, man needs
a knowledge of its nature and possibilities as much to protect him from all of his own adverse concentration, auto-suggestion and morbid meditation as he does from that of others.

The student should study the *psychology* of *faith* and *doubt*
in such a way that he can obtain conclusions and be able to
comprehend them.

He will then understand the universal law of thought and
mental therapeutics. He will know the *Psychology of Faith
and Doubt.*

*   *   *   *   *   *   *   *   *

Every human being prefers health to disease; prefers happiness to misery, suffering, insanity and an early death.

When we look with pity upon those around us, that are
heavily laden with afflictions and begin to realize their pain and
poverty, their sorrow and despair, we then begin to understand the truth of that line by Shakespeare which follows:

"There is no darkness but ignorance."

Sorrow, bodily disease and mental ailments are, in almost
every case, traceable to the individual being ignorant of the
cause of their troubles, and the fact that, by the intelligent
application of concentration, he could become immune.

Bad health is the fruits of a material and not a psychological education.

The real student will study the psychology of *"fear and disease," "faith and belief in self"* as taught herein.

It is only ignorance of the origin and cause of disease and pain that makes sickness and misery so prevalent.

Many persons are loud in their lamentations and wonder why God has sent these afflictions upon them, while they bring them upon themselves, by an improper use of their mind, or mental forces.

This is the great fundamental error and the cause of many nervous diseases, sorrow and despair, as very few have any true knowledge of the science and art of living any more than they have of—*"the psychology of faith and fear."*

The puzzling and perplexing problem of disease finds it only rational solution in the relation that exists between mind and body.

The question is often asked why so many souls pass prematurely out of the physical body through the agency of disease? Why is it that you seldom hear of a natural death? Why have so few persons a perfectly sound and normal body?

There is but one logical answer: The human body is developed and strengthened by positive thoughts *concentrated on health, reinforced by a perfect faith in oneself for health.*

This regulates to healthy action the functions and organs of the body. People are now experiencing a *decided reaction* against the overly learned materialism of past years.

It is mental efficiency, scientific concentration, mental discipline and mental hygiene combined with literal *faith and belief in one's self for health,* that courts and attracts physical well being and mental equilibrium; while their opposites *are harbingers* of physical diseases and mental ailments.

No observing or intelligent person will deny that a despondent or gloomy condition of mind affects the health.

The body is the outgrowth of the mind, representing the nature and condition of the life forces within it. In the right control and direction of thought lies a mighty factor in the curing and healing of disease and pain; for we must deal with causes and not effects.

A mind perfectly controlled and directed in the proper channels of strength and health-giving thoughts will produce and maintain a normal healthy body.

The human mind is a loom—constantly weaving. Our thoughts are the warp and woof of that fabric which the mind weaves. If the thoughts out of which the fabric has been woven are concentrated, positive and health-giving, we have strong healthy bodies free from disease and pain; but if our thoughts are negative and we have no faith, then our bodies which are the fabrics woven from this impure and defective warp and woof, will be afflicted with disease and ailments.

As stated above if our thoughts are negative and we doubt our ability to ward off disease, this mental attitude effects the body and its various functions in health and disease.

Our manner of thinking; the thoughts which are entertained in the mind or soul, shape and form the destiny of man; bringing to him sickness or health, poverty or wealth, affliction or happiness.

What has been thought either by ourselves or our mothers determines what we are or what we will be. The mother*, by her condition of mind, molds and forms the characteristics and traits of her child as stated in a following chapter.

Children are always stamped with parental individuality. Therefore, every one sails this great sea of life, subject to concentration, heredity and environment. Our surroundings from which we receive external impressions, or suggestions, furnish us with thought material. If we receive into our mind good material for pure health-giving thoughts, we have strong healthy bodies. If we accept or select that which is bad, and makes doubtful thoughts, we have weak and diseased bodies, and are surrounded by afflictions and misery.

From the right control and direction of thought the soul receives happiness while the body receives health. Thought influences build and control every organ and function of the physical body.

Mental discouragement and depression are accompanied by a disinclination for exertion and a sense of bodily fatigue.

A combination of symptoms and complaints follows disappointments and worry, and the removal of the cause is followed by an immediate disappearance of the effect.

A depressed or wearied condition of mind inhibits life and energy, and a constant dwelling of thought on some real or imaginary trouble wrecks the mind and destroys the human

* See Chapter XXXV., Lesson Thirty-three, *"Concentration During the Period of Gestation."*

body. Worry sends to a premature grave or the insane asylum all who harbor it as a constant companion. The extent to which it kills is appalling to contemplate, and one should drive it out of his mind as he would a thief or an unwelcome guest from his house.· This can be done by concentrating on peace and calmness.

It is the duty of every man to suppress his evil and morbid tendencies, and encourage those that are good and noble.

We all know that in every human soul, as in the smallest bud or flower, are encamped the opposing hosts of good and evil—of disease and health.

Every human soul at birth is launched upon the mighty sea of right and wrong, of disease and health, of joy and grief, of life and death. And it is only by a knowledge of the science of being that we are able to avoid the rocks and tragic depths of earthly life.

Physical disease and discomfort are most always traceable to mental causes, many being mental in origin. The material body always responds to mental impressions.

There is an abundance of evidence reaching from the remotest ages to the present time, to support or demonstrate this fact.

"A merry heart doeth good like a medicine,
but a broken spirit drieth the bones."
—(*Prov.* xvii:22.)

A quiet, pleasant and composed condition of mind resting upon a foundation of *belief in self* maintains a healthy body.

Sleep knits up the raveled sleeve of care.

Joy and happiness do the system far more good than drugs. Narcosis (sleep produced by narcotics) leaves the system depleted and weakened. While the sleep of those with a peaceful and contented mind restores and builds up the wasted energies of the body.

Disappointment and gloom fill the physical body with disease and pain, sapping life's vitality and energy.

Hatred and revenge poison the blood and he who entertains revengeful thoughts brings a curse on himself.

Anxiety and fear, or an irritable condition of mind, induces hysteria, insomnia and other nervous symptoms.

Those who are confident in their ability to ward off disease and sickness, thereby placing the life forces on the defensive, can expose themselves to contagious diseases without any fear of contracting them.

This is especially true of the professional nurse and physicians who are so accustomed to being among the sick that they have no fear of exposing themselves to the most contagious disease.

It is this fear and expectancy of contracting a disease, and which fills the mind of most people when they enter a sick room, or are in any way exposed, that invites disease and makes the body susceptible by weakening those forces, which, if properly governed, will throw off the most contagious disease known.

Every intelligent human being is making a pilgrimage in pursuit of health and happiness. This is true of the sinner as well as of the saint; of the humble as well as of the exalted; of the disinherited as well as the prosperous. This innate desire of the human heart for perfect health and happiness is universally recognized as its legitimate, inalienable and divine right, for these aspirations and yearnings are common to all mankind.

But how can true happiness and success in life be obtained? This is the great rock in the turbulent stream of life upon which poor humanity splits. Opinions upon this subject are at great variance. Some fancy health and happiness lie in wealth. Others that peace and happiness come of knowledge, while others court ignorance to obtain it. Some seek and expect to find it here, and others are waiting patiently its acquisition in the great hereafter. As a natural consequence, of course, disappointments are many, and history swells with the record of broken hearts.

A final analysis of the universal struggle for peace, health and happiness leads to a definite conclusion upon the subject and which cannot fail to interest every intelligent person. As the common aspiration is the acquisition of health and happiness, no reasoning person would seek it where it is not to be obtained, but, without a true knowledge of the path which leads to it the earthly wayfarer is left to fancy and speculation and becomes a creature of circumstance, hence the mistakes, disappointments, sickness and sorrow of life. The person who imagines that health, peace of mind and happiness lie solely in the possession of wealth is not liable to be particular as to the means by which it is obtained, and when once the coveted treasure is in his possession he believes that all the problems of life are satisfactorily solved. If before he began his struggle for ill-gotten wealth he could only have realized that dishonesty and selfishness are fatal to health and peace of mind he would never have resorted to such methods, but in his ignorance of what leads to true happiness and health he blundered.

Selfishness never brings the slightest degree of that comfort and consolation which are essential to good health and happiness. A man with a true knowledge of the origin and cause of unhappiness and disease would never be jealous or covetous, for these are selfish vices, and selfishness always brings pain instead of pleasure. A man who knows that the pleasures and allurements which earth has to offer her children do not in themselves insure health or happiness, would never be proud and seek satisfaction in ostentatious display of any kind, for he would know that comparisons are extremely odious, and it would simply visit upon him the enmity of his fellow men instead of that good will in which he could find peace, comfort and happiness. Neither would he seek political or social preferment merely for the sake of power, for he would understand that all true greatness lies in service to others and not in the glittering garb of authority. A man wise in the science and art of being would not seek health or happiness in sensuality, for he would know only too well that those who have sought it in the lusts of the flesh have indulged their appetites to satiety in vain, for the flesh profiteth nothing, and its true mission is for man's service and not his mastery.

Every human being should understand the great fundamental, life-giving truth and principle, that perfect health (a physical condition) and true happiness (a mental condition) are the outcome and depend upon the right direction and control of the mind or mental forces within the body.

Health and success in life are the outcome of man's individualism, and depend entirely upon his knowledge of and his mastery over his own mind or soul.

If man encourages and cultivates perverted mental conditions, by entertaining a *doubtful, apprehensive* condition of mind, pain and disease follow *as surely as the cart follows the ox that draws it*. If man encourages and cultivates a confident self-possessed condition of mind and entertains pure, health-giving thoughts, health, happiness and success *will fol-*

low like a shadow that never leaves him, for they are the fruits of a pure, well-balanced and controlled mind or soul.

It is soul satisfaction, obtained through *"true faith in self,"* which alone constitutes happiness and health, and is entirely independent of all material or outward considerations or circumstances. There is not the slightest doubt of the correctness of this conclusion, and all human experience must inevitably sooner or later lead to it.

> "What man is there that is fearful and faint hearted? Let him go and return unto his house, lest his brethren's heart faint as well.   —(*Deut.* xx:8.)

Confidence, faith in yourself and a strong mind bring health and peace, while despondency, doubt and fear sink the soul deep into the slough of misery and despair. *Inquietude and discontent will never bring success or happiness,* as they contain all the elements of a *doubt of self, a self-consciousness of error. By an understanding of self-hood man is able to gain such control over his mental forces that he is able to repel or drive back those demoralizing mental conditions which are so disastrous to health and happiness, and maintaining in their stead those normal mental conditions which bring peace, happiness and comfort, combined with wealth, success and position. Every human being has these dormant powers (*mental forces*). All that is necessary is that they should, by knowledge and application, get them under such absolute control that they can at any time assume a defensive attitude against those things which wreck and ruin misguided humanity. Mental force, or thought-power, is one of the strongest elements of nature, and when under the strict discipline of the will and properly directed and controlled produces a normal body and maintains it in a state of healthy equilibrium.

But when this force, through fear, ignorance and expectancy, becomes demoralized, disease enters the system, which has become highly susceptible to it, and it invites instead of checking and repelling. It is fear and doubt of one's ability to ward it off that makes disease contagious. It is fear and expectancy that causes epidemics. The confident, fearless and

---

*"The waste, silent solitude" found by those who "make their whole life desolate of faith in themselves" has, nothing uplifting about it; it really proceeds from "the stillness and fixedness of melancholy" of their own oppressed, cheerless nature.

strong-minded who are able to assume a positive mental attitude are invulnerable. *The wreath of curses which encircles the brow of humanity today is man's belief in his own weakness.*

By encouraging the self-consciousness of weakness evil consequences are invited. The ignorant man by doubting his own ability, and believing in the strength and ability of others, assists them. He weakens himself by conceding to them that power which he does not claim for himself. The individual who is envious of the rich and who is at all times lamenting his own poverty, and attributes his misfortune to an inexorable fate, is one who makes the rich richer and the poor poorer, *for those things which are believed to be true exercise an all controlling influence over conditions of life.* The unfortunate who actually believes that he is destined to be poor and that it was preordained he should during his life always meet with reverses and misfortune, will by maintaining this condition of mind preclude all possibility of helping himself or being assisted by others; and until he changes this mental attitude of viewing his surroundings and harboring the belief that everything and everybody is against him, he will remain unfortunate and poverty-stricken to the same degree in which he indulges this belief.

It is this lack of self-confidence and assertion, this self-confessed weakness and want of character which curses so many people with poverty, disease and distress. The most deplorable evil that can overshadow the life of any man, or his family, is his own *self-condemnation.* The person who encourages this self-confessed weakness will never succeed, for he shapes his own failures, invites poverty, misery and disease, makes himself a sorrowful creature of circumstances, the solicitor and receiver of evils which his own ignorance has invited and heaped upon his head. The unfortunate who has by his own self-confessed weakness become a slave to abnormal mental conditions, and hence a victim of disease, poverty and despair, can never release himself until he learns that he is not by nature a creature or victim of circumstances, but that he has latent powers or mental forces within him which, if understood and used, will dispel all evil hallucination, and in its place establish an abid-

---

*Read Chapter XXXVI, Lesson Thirty-four. "The Secret of Abundance." And Chapter XXXVII, Lesson Thirty-five. "The Art of Getting Rich."

ing hope, self-confidence, perfect physical health, peaceful repose of mind and self-respect.

Self-respect, esteem for faculties, traits, ability and gifts possessed should be inculcated in every mind, and this should become a part of man's education in the great school of life, and the fruits and rewards of their right use—also the terrible consequence of their abuse—should be conclusively shown and taught.

There is apparent in many persons an extreme of modesty or rather a lack of self-assertion entirely inconsistent with the normal nature of the human mind, for it contains all the elements of self-condemnation and a morbid self-depreciation, which implies a lack of reverence toward the Almighty Creator, who has endowed all intelligent beings with the divine gifts of self-respect, esteem and whatever talents or ability they may have.

Every human being should be thankful for the gifts which have been bestowed upon him, and for the use or the abuse of which he alone is responsible.

All power and energy to create or destroy comes from the mind or mental forces. This force or power should at all times be under the control of the will, which is the executor of the intentions, impulses and emotions of the mind or soul.

The will, *when properly governed*, produces thought force that builds a normal mind and body. It is this force which forms and shapes the destiny of man. As everything within the universe is subject to natural law, it becomes apparent to all who have been close observers of the mentality of man, that the power to create or destroy health, strength and happiness has its existence in the human mind. *A man's belief or condition of mind is all that can control him.*

If he assumes by self-confessed weakness that he is impotent or that his body is susceptible to disease and pain, he will as the result of this assumption most certainly realize it.

If he believes that he has inherited some disease or that he is always to exist in poverty, his belief will bring unto himself these things. Job, the Patriarch, exemplified this when he said:

> "For the thing which I greatly feared is come unto me, and that which I was afraid of is come upon me."

This is common sense and reason, and fully justifies every

intelligent man and woman in seeking a perfect comprehension of the principles of *scientific concentration and thought control.*

This knowledge is most certainly indispensable to every intelligent man or woman. All of their influence in and relation to the world; their health, their finance, their friends and enemies, are the concrete expressions of their mental conditions. It is this knowledge which leads to power, health, wealth and happiness. The present is an age of transition from old and obscure conditions and doctrines, into better and more enlightened ones; an age of destruction for many of the old and inconsistent dogmas which have been fostered by superstition and ignorance. Ignorance of the nature and possibilities of the mental forces within the physical body causes man to falter and waver, whereas he should always be confident, rising above his circumstances and conditions. "Ever master of the occasion."

> "For he that wavereth is like a wave of
> the sea, driven and tossed by the wind."
> —(*James* 1:6.)

The mental or life forces of man influence and affect everything within the range of human thought; everything within the horizon of intellectual effort, and from which emanates the theories, customs, hopes, fears, hatreds, superstitions, vices and virtues of the human race. Most everyone has experienced the emotions of the heart, felt the thrills and ecstasies of love, the maddening fires of hatred and revenge, and knows how envy and desire defeat the better judgment and overcome the will—how weak the forces of reason are when passion pleads. Man should know how grand it is to be master of these ruling forces, and guiding passions; but he will remain a sport and prey to passion until he has a true knowledge of *Concentration, Self-Control and Mental Discipline.*

> "He that is slow to anger is better than
> the mighty; and he that ruleth his spirit
> than he that taketh a city."
> —(*Prov.* xvi:32.)

Observation will verify the statement that it would be impossible to enumerate the vast numbers who are suffering from perverted mental conditions. Pitiful victims are they, whose lives are made miserable from the effect and influence of their own beliefs. They believe themselves necessarily subject to disease, misfortune, poverty, calamity and despair, until these unfortunate conditions actually develop as the direct result of their morbid mentality.

"As a man thinketh in his heart, so is he."—(Prov. 23:7.)

"Heaviness in the heart of man maketh it stoop; but a good word maketh it glad."
—(*Prov.* xii :25.)

Many of our learned men persist in encouraging these demoralizing and morbid mental illusions.

Morbid apprehension, mental depression and irritability should be systematically antagonized by hope, confidence, faith in self and mental tranquillity.

The Master Key

CHAPTER XXXIV.

LESSON THIRTY-TWO.

CONCENTRATION APPLIED TO FEAR AND DISEASE.

EXPECTANCY AND ATTENTION.

The physiological effect of drugs is not always according to their known, or proved, properties, but according to the anticipation or expectation of the patient. Every medical man knows from his own practice that if a patient is given a decided suggestion or receives an impression that a fictitious medicine he is about to take will act in a certain way, marvelously good results sometimes follow; as in the administering of such substitutes as bread pills or sweetened water. A great many people are under the impression that pills always act as a laxative, and if given bread or even an astringent in pill form an operation of the bowels will follow.

The plan of substituting something for a narcotic mixture, without which a nervous patient thinks himself unable to sleep, is as we all know, continually resorted to, and is an instance of the beneficial employment of the imagination, and the effect of expectancy upon the mind or mental forces. This also well illustrates what great influence and power the mind has over the organs and functional duties of the body, causing unusual and extraordinary physiological effects and conditions, as illustrated in the following instance. A lady who, while sitting upon the upper deck of the steamer City of Mackinac, when crossing Lake St. Clair, became so badly frightened by the grating of the paddle wheel over a sunken crib that she gave vent to a series of screams, and begged for some one to save her. This was the first time in six years that she had uttered a word, influenza having partially paralyzed her vocal organs, and medical science had failed to cure her.

Since this occurrence, however, she has recovered her full powers of speech. Most every one, especially physicians, know of some particular instance illustrative of the effect of mind upon the body (which always responds and registers mental impressions and psychological conditions) such as the case of a physician, who when about to administer chloroform to a hysterical woman who was to be operated upon for the removal of two tumors, discovered that the chloroform vial was empty, and that the inhaling-bag was entirely free from odor of the anaesthetic. While waiting for the return of the person sent to the drug store for a new supply, he thought that in order to familiarize the patient with the process he would place the inhaling-bag over her mouth and nose. He did so, and instructed her to breath quietly and deeply. After taking a number of deep inspirations she suddenly cried out, "Oh, I feel the effects of it already, I am going"; and a moment later her eyeballs turned upward, and she became completely unconscious. As she was found to be perfectly insensible to pain, the physician suggested that the surgeon proceed with the operation. He did so, and removed one tumor without disturbing her in the least.

When about to begin operations for removing the remaining one she partly came to. The inhaling-bag was once more applied with the Suggestion that she was going to sleep again, when the patient immediately lost consciousness and the operation was performed successfully without pain or knowledge to the patient. This woman, it is said, had taken chloroform three years before. Recollection of her previous experience, combined with expectation and the application of the inhaling-bag, were sufficient to cause her to self-induce precisely the same psychological condition that a liberal application of an anaesthetic would have produced.

The power and effect of the imagination is wonderful, and there is no question but that sickness and even death itself is often caused by it, as is readily seen in an instance given by *Dr. Hack Tuck.*

The victim was a Frenchman, who had been condemned to death for committing some crime, and his friends, wishing to avoid the disgrace of a public execution, consented to his being made the subject of an experiment. It was stated to the condemned man that it had been decreed that he must be bled to death. The executor then bandaged the victim's eyes, and, after his arm had been slightly pricked, a small stream of warm water was made to trickle down it and drop into a basin, the assistants all the while keeping up a continuous comment on his supposed weakening condition. *"See how pale he looks. He is getting faint, his heart is beating slower and slower, his pulse is almost stopped,"* with numerous other remarks of this sort. In a short while the miserable man died with decided symptoms of *cardiac syncope* from a hemorrhage, without having really lost a single drop of blood, a victim of his own imagination.

That decease and kindred states are induced by *auto-suggestion* (self-thought) and can likewise be induced by suggestions from without, there is no doubt.

Let a man's friends repeatedly tell him that he is looking bad, and that he does not seem able to be about, that he should take care of himself, or he will be down sick with this or that complaint, and it is almost a certainty that unless he is positive in his belief in himself for health, and can concentrate his mind against the suggestions, he will temporarily deteriorate in health.

As in the case of the farmer who was given suggestions of this sort for a joke. After being assured by a number of persons that he looked bad and was not able to be around, really did take to his bed and went through an unmistakable attack of fever. Although he was in good health previous to the suggestions given him. This of course was a wrong and unwarrantable joke, yet these same effects are often produced by well-meaning persons, who have the habit of always commiserating their friends and acquaintances for not looking well.

"Disease can be, and often is, caused by morbid suggestions, either auto or spoken."

"Disease can be, and many times is, cured by healthful suggestions, either auto or spoken."

This is an indisputable fact known to all advanced psychologists, and those who have a knowledge of the nature, possibilities and susceptibilities of the human mind and its relation to the body in both health and disease.

Any person who has ever given attention to the subject will acknowledge what immense power the mind or mental forces—acting in conjunction with or apart from the will—has over the physical body.

This power of mind over matter is exercised both in health and disease, but is particularly evident—perhaps because it is more closely observed—in the latter condition.

It is a fact well known to seamen that sufferers from sea-sickness almost invariably become quite well in moments of great danger, when the ship is found to be imperiled.   People will often lose all sense of pain by their mind becoming occupied with some affair of great interest.   It is a well established fact that alterations of tissue, irregularities and functional disturbances have been the direct result of a morbid concentration of mind or attention to certain particular organic structures.   Idleness is a well-known factor in producing all kinds of ailments, real and imaginary, of mind and body; perhaps because the idle man, from sheer lack of interest in life devotes too much attention to his own organism.   Imagination, combined with the *"direction of morbid self-consciousness,"* to certain organs or functions of the body will produce results which have been noticed by many pathologists.   In hypochondriasis, the patent, by fixing his attention on his internal organs, creates not merely disordered sensations, but disordered and abnormal action in them.

With some people there is liable to be irregular action of the heart.   This is brought on and greatly increased by the persistence of attention, causing deviation from the normal condition of the functions and which frequently lapses into structural disease from the effect of this faculty of morbid attention being for a lengthened period concentrated upon this organ and its action.   *Hypochondriasis,* being a mental state in which the patient feels and notices the action of his internal organs, and is always *morbidly conscious of them,* has a decided tendency to grow worse, because this morbid attention becomes more and more *concentrated and fixed or directed* upon *functions which ought* to be performed automatically and unconsciously, and unless some powerful *mental regulator* or *mental stimulant, such as scientific concentration,* is applied, organic disease actually sets in.

That the dangers of these perverted or morbid mental conditions are brought within the range, not only of possibility, but of probability and of actual fact, is indisputable, as there are many people of both sexes who never hear of a disease without fancying that they have it, and by pure imagination develop the symptoms of serious illness.

The illness of some prominent statesman or distinguished person, the progress of which is daily recorded in the papers, will sometimes become almost epidemic, and specialists of the particular disease could give some interesting information of the increase of imaginary and real symptoms and affections during the illness of such prominent person. That fear and expectancy is conducive to and will produce disease has been abundantly proved during epidemics of typhoid, smallpox, cholera, yellow fever and other contagious diseases. Laymen who dabble in medical science, and students at the beginning of their course, are apt to imagine that they have one or another of the diseases they had been studying—heart complaint being perhaps the most common; and of this disease many do frequently develop some of the subjective symptoms.

A prominent physician's wife, who was an eye-witness to an operation made upon a woman for the removal of a cancer, shortly afterwards complained of symptoms of cancer. Her husband paid slight attention to her complaints at first, but later the symptoms became so pronounced he called a specialist for diagnosis, and it was then discovered that she was actually suffering from a cancer whose location was precisely the same as that of the woman whose operation she had witnessed. Further investigation proved that the sight of the cancer and attendant operation had made such a decided impression upon the woman's mind that she had never been able to drive the sight of it from her imagination; she being always apprehensive that she would become afflicted in the same manner. There is little doubt but that this morbid condition of mind upon her part did actually cause her to become infected with the same disease.

If parents did but know it, many a child has had *planted* in its consciousness by concentration, the seeds of consumption. The thought that one's family had been victims of the white scourge rises to the mind from time to time, and the possibility of this passing through several generations, in conformity with the almost universal belief on the subject, is frequently *sufficient* to give a tendency to the disease.

Hereditary disease finds its only rational explanation in the morbid perverted mental condition which ever shadows the child who is a victim of a morbid self-consciousness that it must necessarily, as the result of nature's decree, inherit its parent's affliction and die an unnatural and premature death.

This is a nonsenical and absurd idea, furthered and fostered by ignorance of what that mental condition of mind, which nature requires to be maintained by every human being should be in order to promote health and strength in the physical body. This mental perversion invites and develops disease, and also greatly aggravates and prolongs disease actually existing.

Fear and expectancy (*perverted mental conditions*) invite and promote disease, while confidence and faith (*positive mental conditions*) in one's ability to ward it off, is a defense against its advance, and renders one immune against the most contagious diseases known. It only requires a superficial knowledge of electricity to understand the absolute abortiveness of the various electrical apparatus and appliances as remedial agencies; yet, whilst positively inert, they are undoubtedly the means of accomplishing much good by reason of the suggestive effect upon the imagination of the wearer.

Cholera-belts, camphor-bags, and divers so-called "*preventives,*" such as carrying a potato, buckeye, etc., in one's pocket, unquestionably act in a corresponding manner.

Consequently, though these and similar contrivances *are inoperative* in their anticipated results, it would be a mistake to say they do not serve a useful purpose and are not beneficial to mankind. By *inspiring confidence* and keeping alive hope and faith, they often enable people to go unharmed in the midst of contagion, or help them to overcome disease, for there is no more effectual depressant, *no surer harbinger of disease, than fear and expectancy.* Much of the immunity from infection enjoyed by physicians and professional nurses is due partly to the preoccupation of their minds with professional duties, which leaves no room for selfish terror or fear, and partly to the confidence begotten by long familiarity with the sick room and disease.

Expectant attention (mental conditions and processes) is a mighty and wonderful force. The extent of its power and influence upon our physical and moral nature, for health, for disease, for good or for evil, is beyond the comprehension of any person who has not been a close student of the mentality of man.

This knowledge enables one to gain perception and possession of the great fundamental principle—"The Principle of Being."

The Master Key

CHAPTER XXXV.

LESSON THIRTY-THREE.

CONCENTRATION APPLIED DURING THE PERIOD OF GESTATION.

The effect of the *concentration* and *realisation* of the female at the time of conception, and, during the *nine months of gestation* upon the unborn child in the *uterus*, has escaped most authors of works treating on the subject of *Psychology*.

The fact of impressions passing to the child before birth, as in the case of birth-marks, may be turned to good account especially if the mother has some knowledge of *concentration*. In such a case she could prepare herself *by holding in her mind a mental image of the kind of child she would like.*

The longer such a preparation had been in operation the more likelihood would there be of the character of the *fetus* being affected. The question of *reincarnation* need not enter into the problem, and will not be considered here.

What I wish to emphasize is that with *concentration intelligently applied,* by the prospective mother, *pre-natal culture is a possibility;* for up to the time of birth the mother could, with full assurance of obtaining results, *concentrate her mind* on the nobility of feature, form and character she desired for her child.

Did you ever note the scowling face of some children; it's a true reflection of their mothers' mental state during pregnancy. *It will be remembered that the Greek mothers contemplated statues of beautiful women or powerful men, or the gods and goddesses, so as to influence their unborn children, this being done knowingly.* There is nothing to prevent a similar practice being returned to today, but with the knowledge we now have of the power of thought and *intelligent concentration* in the moulding of form no less than character the physical degeneration on which so many writers and speakers have touched during the last few years can be remedied very much.

There is wonderful power in the mind when directed by concentration and realization. This is fully demonstrated in the action of the psychic or mental forces from whence there are impressions and wonderful effects produced by the female during the period of gestation. By many these effects have been attributed to diverse superstitions.

The effect of concentration is evidenced, as stated above, in pregnant women, who stamp upon their child the image of things intensely desired or mark their offspring in some particular manner. This image or sign imprinted by the appetite, faith, realization, fear, or desire of a mother, on her young, does certainly confirm the fact that her mental state during this period has a decided influence upon the child.

For, let a woman, during the period of gestation, intensely desire cherries, strawberries or, any particular fruit, but touch her face or other part of the body with her fingers, and without doubt the child will be stamped in the same part of its body with the sign or image of the fruit desired.

We find a most remarkable instance of concentration and observation in the history of *Jacob*. It is as follows: *Jacob* agreed with *Laban* that he would still guard his sheep, provided that *Laban* would give him as a reward for his services all spotted lambs and goats that should in the future be added to his flock.

Laban consented to this proposal, and *Jacob* became immensely rich. It is worth the trouble to insert the passage relating to this transaction, as an application of the mysterious doctrine of concentration even in animals.

When Jacob would no longer watch over the sheep and desired to go away with his wives and children, *Laban* said unto him. *Genesis* 30:27-43: *"I pray thee, if I have found favor in thine eyes, tarry, for I have learned by experience that the Lord hath blessed me for thy sake." And he said, "Appoint me thy wages, and I will give it." And he said unto him:*

"Thou knowest how I have served thee and how thy cattle was with me. For it was little which thou hadst before I came, and it is now increased unto a multitude: and the Lord hath blessed thee since my coming: and, now, when shall I provide for mine own house also?" And he said, "What shall I give thee?" And Jacob said, "Thou shalt not give me anything. If thou wilt do this thing for me, I will again feed and keep thy flock: *I will pass through all thy flock today, removing from thence all the speckled and spotted cattle, and all the brown cattle among the sheep, and the spotted and speckled among the goats; and of such shall be my hire."*

"So shall my righteous answer for me in time to come, when it shall come for my hire before thy face: every one that is not speckled and spotted among the goats, and brown among the sheep, shall be counted stolen with me." And Laban said, "Behold, I would it might be according to thy word." And he removed that day the he-goats that were ring-streaked and speckled, and all the she-goats that were speckled and spotted and every one that had some white in it, and all the brown among the sheep, and gave them into the hands of his sons. And he set three days' journey betwixt himself and Jacob; and Jacob fed the rest of Laban's flocks."

"And Jacob took him rods of green poplar, and of the hazel and chestnut tree: and pilled white streaks in them, and made the white appear which was in the rods.

"And he set the rods which he had pilled before the flock in the gutters in the watering troughs when the flocks came to drink, that they should conceive when they came to drink.

"And the flocks conceived before the rods, and brought forth cattle ring-streaked, speckled, and spotted. And Jacob did separate the lambs, and set the faces of the flocks toward the ring-streaked, and all the brown in the flock of Laban; and he put his own flocks by themselves, and put them not unto Laban's cattle. And it came to pass whensoever the stronger cattle did conceive, that Jacob laid the rods before the eyes of the cattle in the gutters, that they might conceive among the rods.

"But when the cattle were feeble, he put them not in; so the feebler were Laban's, and the stronger Jacob's.

"And the man increased exceedingly, and had much cattle, and maid-servants, and men-servants, and camels and asses."

This proves clearly that the sheep and the goats could be made to bring forth their young changed in color and appearance corresponding with the pilled rods which were placed before them by Jacob as they drank from the waters.

In these days, the theory that the features of the offspring of a human mother can be affected by an object upon which the mother gazes, is pronounced absurd; and yet this theory, in the very nature of things, is as fully established as the fact that the mental qualities of many children differ totally from those of their parents. *The fact that the sheep and the goats, upon seeing the objects which Jacob so skillfully placed before them, brought forth their young differing in appearance from themselves, has a very deep significance. Either Jacob knew what the result of this strategem would be from experience, or it was revealed to him in a dream, for we read, Genesis 31:10:*

"And it came to pass at the time the cattle conceived, that I lifted up mine eyes, and saw in a dream, and behold, the rams which leaped upon the cattle were ring-streaked, speckled, and grizzled." With the water which they drank, and in which at the same time they saw their own reflection, they transmitted the image of the speckled rods to their young.

The writer has not the space here to enter into a more extended reproduction of facts and evidence to further show the benefits to be derived from pre-natal culture. However, the fact that the female progenitor, both human and animal, is capable at the period of gestation to transmit to her offspring the image and likeness of surrounding objects upon which the mind has been concentrated has a surer foundation than is commonly believed to be possible.

We are only at the beginning of the science of pre-natal culture, and the eugenists of the future, and those of today who talk so knowingly of sex-hygiene and eugenics must pay more attention to mental influences and mental impressions than they have done up to the present if they wish to gain ground.

The Master Key

LESSON THIRTY-FOUR.

THE SECRET OF ABUNDANCE.

THE POVERTY CURE.

Poverty is as much a disease as pleurisy, only the former attacks the *mind* and the latter the *body*. You never knew an energetic, spirited and pushing man really poor. The poor in purse are almost invariably poor in mind. Of course, one must not include in this category people who prefer leading a simple existence, with no hankering after servants, motor cars, large establishments and a thousand-and-one et ceteras which characterize modern life. There are many who, with a humble cottage and plain fare, scarcely have any use for money, their wants being so few. By poverty I mean a state in which men can scarcely get enough to eat or cannot pay their way as they would like. Going a step higher, I should include among those whose ambitions rise above their means—but I am not concerned at present with this class. My present aim is to stimulate those who are in want of means to sustain life comfortably; to show them a way out; to revive that hope which once they had in abundance, but which contact with the world has well-nigh utterly obliterated.

The cure of poverty, it must be admitted at the outset, is no light task, but it is curable in nearly every case. It does not seem to have occurred to people (except a very few) that no one need be poor. The saying about the poor being always with us seems to have been taken as an utterance that applied to all countries and ages, and the problem of the unemployed, which every civilized nation has to face, lends color to the idea. As a matter of fact if we take Nature we see that she is almost wantonly extravagant. Look at the millions of seeds

357

produced in flowers which cannot possibly grow up.   Note the myriads of tiny cells which constitute the spawn of fish; mark the lavishness and prodigality with which vegetation covers our fair earth, and you will recognize that there is nothing miserly or stinting about Dame Nature.   This is really a lesson for man, if he could but see it in the right light, and I, like many writers on the subjects of *faith and confidence in one's self*, have been endeavoring to the best of my powers to scatter broadcast during the last few years the conception that no intelligent, able human being need be in dire want.

One of the objections frequently raised by those opposed to a sensible socialism (not the view put forward today by socialists) is that there is not enough money to go round, and it has been affirmed that the earth could not produce sufficient food to maintain the inhabitants if the number grew beyond a certain proportion.   These good people forget that not a tithe of the treasures of the earth have been extracted, and that science would have to be reckoned with where the question of food supply was concerned.   I merely instance this objection because it stands in the way of reform with many people.

First, the well-fed moneyed class consider that the state of things is irremediable, and then the poor man imagines that conditions as we know them today are part of the natural order of things, and that if he were not in poverty somebody else would be, and that it might as well, perhaps, be himself who should suffer, and so he loses whatever grit he has in him, and he becomes what many would be inclined to call "philosophic," but which I should prefer to designate "resigned."

I trust I have effectually removed this barrier, and now comes another and important one which bars the way to plenty—the *belief* that the ability to make money is only given to a few people who are really clever; or that there are a class of people who may be termed *"lucky."*   I think I have shown in this volume that there is no such thing as luck or chance. We must admit that people differ mentally as well as physically, but it is frequently more in degree than in kind, and it is often the case with those who have had a defective bringing up or a scanty education that they are prone to exaggerate their weaknesses.   This exaggeration acts very prejudicially, and is at the root of much of the poverty amongst the people.

To cure poverty you *must believe* what is an absolute fact —*that you are of use in some way;* that you have something in you, that the impression of your acquaintances that you are a very commonplace person is merely an impression *caused* by your own conduct. In turn this impression has re-acted on you till you begin to believe firmly where before you had only a suspicion. It will show in your conversation, stamp itself in your walk, your features, your manner all round. You advertise your littleness wherever you go by your appearance, and servility clinches the unfavorable opinion formed of you by a prospective employer.

All that is written above should be read and re-read till it *burns* into the mind as the cure of poverty has been revealed.

To get a better opinion of yourself *think*. I know it is the most difficult task that could be set all poor folk. Had they learned to think they would not have been poor. They would rather do anything than think. Many will plead that they are not cut out for thinking;—they have had no education— *Shakespeare* hadn't, but it did not prevent his becoming a genius. Few self-made men have had any education, and many men highly educated are as poor as crows. We live in the busiest age on record, and the hands or brain of every human being are urgently needed. If you went to an employer of labor and told him you had an idea which would save his expenses by a third, or increase the efficiency of his business, do you suppose you would not gain his ear, if you approached him in the right attitude? Improvements are capable of being made in everything you can mention. Once you have learned to *concentrate* your mind and *think* you have solved the problem of poverty, and for this reason: You have opened up unsuspected avenues of thought, suggestions that will mean money to you in the long run. You have the same stuff in you as *Milton, Goethe, Edison,* but it never occurred to you, did it? It only wants rousing, bringing into activity. Every man is a gold mine to himself, and instead of letting others exploit him he should exploit himself.

It is never too late to begin, unless you've turned eighty, and with some men this age would not be an insurmountable barrier.

With a better opinion of yourself and the habit of thinking and controlling your thoughts so as to concentrate them you will begin to make plans; judgment and tact—that rare virtue—will show themselves; means will come to you to overcome difficulties and you will come into possession of that priceless gem—*initiative*. You will see the necessity of being thorough in whatever calling you may take up, so that an employer can *rely* upon you. Once gain the confidence of an employer and poverty and you will rarely meet. Make it a point to know your business from top to bottom; concentrate your mind on your duties willingly, with a light heart, for you are building for the future.

Get into close touch with the very poor and you will find that they invariably consider that only people with *marked* ability can *"get on."* You can have ability just as well as any one else. It is not the prerogative of kings; the poorest and humblest man may cultivate it, but, mark well, *thinking* is the basis of it, for by it you dispel ignorance, the greatest curse from which mankind suffers today. Willingness to learn is a sign of the successful man, and as ability is gained the other dread ally of Poverty—*Fear*—(they always go together, therefore by destroying the one you destroy both) will loosen its hold of your heart-strings, and hope will take up its abode.

At this point you should take stock of yourself. You will now have valuable assets, and the next step is to make the most of them. Are you working with system? Are you utilizing your time well? Are you getting the best and highest out of yourself? Do not be content till you do. Whatever plan you may have commenced give it a fair trial. Too many cases of failure have arisen from giving up too soon and not sticking with bulldog tenacity. To the man who sets his teeth and vows he will go through, whatever the cost Fate, gives way.

It is a well-known fact in psychology that an idea, even though devoid of truth, a mere delusion, if held sufficiently long in mind, becomes at length to be regarded as a truth. A knowledge of this law is of incalculable worth to you. Test it now if you are poor. Apply it to your own case. *Banish* for the time being the canker of care, the paralyzing effect of worry and doubt in yourself. Probably you have been indulging in the luxury of these mental visitors for days or weeks, so you can afford to dispense with them for ten or twenty minutes. I know full well the great sacrifice I am asking you to make, for you have an idea that by turning over these worries separately you are deriving a species of sympathy which is very comforting. You have, perhaps, poured your woes into the ears of friends, some willing and others the reverse. You have afforded the only solace that life holds out, just as some people are only happy when they are miserable. When you are miserable the state is *so infectious* that your friends avoid you when circumstances permit.

We are all familiar with the class of persons who are always finding fault and picking holes or criticising others or things generally, deriving immense satisfaction and comfort from the discomfort they cause. Probably they have seen no harm in this habit of supplying sympathy to themselves. As a matter of fact, their greatest enemy could not have inflicted a greater injury upon them. What practical good has it done them? Has the habit solved their problem? What it has done in reality is to have weakened their make-up to an incredible extent; it has literally poisoned the spring of Success. It has magnified their weakness, and their want of self-reliance. Every time you sympathize with a weakness you strengthen that weakness, and render yourself less capable. You paralyze sources of action, destroy initiative, prevent the inception of new ideas, and clog the mental machinery, the one factor which is to *lift you out* of the slough of poverty. It deepens within you the feeling that you are hardly dealt with, that other folk are helped and are "lucky," while everything goes wrong with you—I know the feeling, which is better understood than expressed. Get among the unemployed and they will tell you how by a bad trick another fellow *"did them out of a job,"* or how a chap who can't do his work a patch as well as you can has been in regular work for years. Cease whining, cease envying. The men who have kept their places have had some qualifications, for there is not much room for sentiment and favoritism in business. The man who holds a post because he is *"in"* with the foreman, or an official, is on very insecure ground, for changes are frequent, and removal of the foreman may be followed by the dismissal of the incompetent employee. If he does hold his position, however, it is no affair of the other fellow. Every man is concerned with himself alone. It is his business to see that *he* is thoroughly efficient in whatever his calling may be, quick, diligent, reliable, ready to be shown or to learn. Such a man is *certain* of regular employment; he can employ himself, in fact, for as soon as a man has confidence in himself he is fit to be his own employer.

Each time an unkind, mean, angry thought passes through your brain, each time you criticise others, pass judgment on them, discuss their failings with others you are nursing the poverty habit, and for this reason: Poverty is a condition of inharmony; prosperity is a condition of harmony; all criticism, etc., creates inharmony, and it and harmony cannot exist in the mind at the same time. One inevitably neutralizes the other; inharmony antagonizes, and the antagonism being destructive in its character mental force, which is only generated in sufficient quantity to meet the demands made upon it by the body and mind, is *wasted*. This waste of energy might be turned into another channel and produce force which would enable problems to be solved and ideas carried to completion.

Further than this the entertaining of such thoughts cause physical changes in cell tissue, manufacturing by some of those marvellous processes of chemistry poisons which break down the health, and no one who is poor can afford to dispense with good health.

Men who are in poverty and rags do not trust themselves or they would never have been in poverty. They have placed their trust in other people, hoping that *they* would make it all right. If they did not, then fear rushed in, and away went their hope, followed in hot pursuit by self-respect. I do not care how low down a man may be, where he may be placed, however sordid, however apparently hopeless his position, he can remedy it; but the cure must begin by trusting in himself. He has the same force, the same powers at the back of his mind, as all of us. All that is needed is to use them, and a thing can only be used by bringing it into the daily life. By idealizing surroundings and the daily life as outlined above you are insensibly led *away* from poverty and its inevitable degrading surroundings. An actual *"new life"* is lived, and in casting off the influences of the old the mind takes on new aspects— *hope and trust* are born into the nature, and ambition and determination are not far behind.

There will be the belief that circumstances are beginning to change. Poverty and doubt pulls down; hope raises. No one wants to engage a man soddened with the quality of misery or pennilessness; it would "get on the nerves" of many an employer, and when the staff was reduced the man stamped with these qualities would be the first to go.

A man of this type never does good work; he has no "heart," therefore his work is more or less mechanical, and this is soon noticed. We cannot expect employers to be philanthropists. Often they are driven on by the scourge of competition, and cannot help themselves. A bright face is often quite as much a tonic to them as it is to others, and brightness often goes hand-in-hand with intelligence and interest in one's work. A bright disposition often brings about an alert state of mind, frequently leading to keener observation, and inventions are frequently made by workmen of this type. Bright intelligence also often leads to smartness of movement, dexterity in one's calling, and the quick eye of the employer, who is always surrounded by the *"clock-watchers"* and *"stallers,"* soon detects the stuff a man is made of. When an employee really begins to take an interest in his work then he is on the right path.

But it does not necessarily follow that a man in poverty need be an employee. If he will faithfully follow the instructions given in this volume he may devise means by which he will free himself from his cramping environment. Not a quarter of the inventions possible have been invented, not a tithe of the riches in the earth has been suspected, not a thousandth part of the possibilities of existence has been touched up to the present, and all these possibilities are open to *you!* But you must think! When an idea comes along do not dismiss it as wild and improbable, but try and make it as clear as you would the idea of a house you would like to live in. When *Professor Morse* offered to sell his telegraph apparatus to the *American Government* in 1845 for a hundred thousand dollars the offer was refused. Today the *Morse* system is capitalized for two hundred and twenty-two million dollars.

"*Professor Alexander Graham Bell* offered to sell his telephone patents to the *Western Union Telegraph Co.* for $60,-000, but the officers of the company said it was only a toy and had no commercial value. This same toy, according to the annual report of the *American Telephone and Telegraph Co.,* just issued, earned $160,000,000 last year and. has now more than 5,000,000 telephones in use throughout this country."

Of course, I do not imagine that you will initiate a colossal scheme like the first two, although any man, who is not a congenital idiot, may become a genius if he wish. But this illustrates the idea I am endeavoring to make plain—that provided we are fair to ourselves and try to develop more of what is in us we are *certain* to enlarge our mind, or expand our consciousness. Many and many a man fails to improve his surroundings through lightly casting aside an idea which only needed a little more maturing, a little more hatching, to blossom into a really good thing.

It is not education we lack—we have too much of what goes under that name, and the fact that the vast majority of wealthy men were *never conspicuous for their learning* enforces the assertion, but a lifting or a shifting of our conception, a different standard of value of ourselves, and once that different attitude towards ourselves is adopted the way is comparatively smooth.

A hint may be gleaned from the case cited above: *don't get in a rut.* All poverty-stricken men travel in them.

Don't do a thing in the way your forefathers did it, if it can be done in a better manner. Always be on the lookout for improvements, and cultivate the habit of observation. A *Russian* proverb says, *"He goes through the forest and sees no firewood."* By the cultivation of *concentration* and *observation* the wits will be sharpened, and the mind more alert, quick to take advantage of an opportunity, quick to apprehend, and the best aid to that indispensable qualification to all success—executive ability.

Cut yourself off from your newspapers for a time; that is, unless you can discriminate. There is a large number of daily newspapers published in this country, Sunday papers, some of them, printed on cheap paper, and news to match. Analyze any of them and it will be seen that they consist for the greater part of full reports of every crime committed in the United States, and the bulk of the cases occurring in other parts of the world. The most sordid details, the most abject, pitiful, sickening and disgusting items are given as fully as the law of the land will permit. The shady, poverty-sodden side of humanity, with all its weaknesses, its vices, its wickedness, its meanness, craftiness is set forth with such a superabundance of minuteness that not only could a criminal career be learned by it, but it would even induce many weak-minded people to emulate the men figuring in them. Revolting incidents from the divorce court, the hashing up of trickery and chicanery of the world—in a word anything and everything which will not only depress, but will drag the mind down, are to be found in the wretched specimens of the gutter-press. Wallowing in the filth is it any wonder that a man's tastes become debauched, that he loses an interest in good literature, or that he keeps his poverty chains about him?

Never mind being out of date with your news for a few weeks or months.   When a crab is going to cast its shell it hides in a crevice where it can lie undisturbed until the new shell has taken the place of the old one, when it can once more go forth.   So with a man who would cast off his old mind.   While the shedding process is going on let him feed his mind with the best food obtainable—good literature is plentiful and cheap enough, in all conscience.   But I would advocate dispensing with cheap newspapers in the ordinary sense, or read only the best with comments on the world's happenings or thoughts.   The daily paper has got to be looked upon as a sort of necessity by some people, and it is a good sign when it proceeds from a keen interest in one's country, or progress of mankind, but even this can stand aside for a short time, as can the religious press for much the same reason— they all tend to weaken the optimistic faculty in man.   Naturally man is a bundle of hopes, but as one after another is damped by wet blankets hope begins to give up, and then indifference, misery, and finally hopelessness sets in, from which the grave kindly rescues many.

The sensational, and sentimental drama, and sickly poetry are two other sources which contribute to this weakening process.   They hold before the eye with dramatic force the conflicting emotions which surge in the human breast, its passions, its foibles, as well as its noblest impulses, and while it may be a veritable mirror of life it is not what many would have.   It is a fresh probing of wounds some souls would fain heal, an awakening of sad memories they would prefer to bury forever; an ever-recurring reminder of the dark side of existence, which they would cast from them forever.   When we read heart-rending accounts of misery, see plays poignant with grief, we discuss them with friends, or, if we keep silent respecting them, some one will discuss them with us, so that we keep alive within us and sear into our very soul the pains from which we have struggled to free ourselves.

In conclusion, the cure of poverty is the result of real growth, mental and emotional.   The nature which is poor in love, in sympathy, in goodwill, belief in himself and his inherent powers is poor in pocket.   To stint and stunt the nature is to stint and stunt the money-making possibilities.   If you feed on poverty thoughts there is no use for money; it could not be appreciated, and however much might be obtained it would do no good, but would dwindle away.

Many are familiar with the old saw: *"A fool and his money are soon parted."* Most of us have known cases where very poor people, accustomed to live from hand to mouth, having come into money, have soon been in the same plight. The proper use of money can only come to those who have evolved to a point where they can use it intelligently. *Money can never make brains in a man, but brains can make money, and all the wealth of the world is the result of brains.* A lump of gold would not have any value were it not for the brains which first enabled it to be wrought into something—coin or jewel, etc. The most precious substance in the universe today—radium—would not have been a penny a ton a century ago because brains had not discovered any use for it, and the same thing applies to everything. Evolve yourself and you make yourself of use; there is a need for you; you fill a position which only you can fill. It may take you some time, but what you gain is yours for all time. The enrichment of character means that new layers of yourself have been reached, and everything brought into manifestation must express itself, or, in other words, must act so that the added growth will open up opportunities you cannot foresee at present, and poverty will no longer affright.

As *like attracts like* so the poverty mind attracts poverty; and so long as the mind remains of that type so long must poverty be expressed in the environment. A locomotive made to run along on steel rails does the thing for which it was made; it cannot fly in the air or travel on water; a clock fulfils its functions by indicating time, but no one would expect it to record changes in the atmosphere. So with *mental states.* It is no use having ideals if the mind has not reached those levels where the ideals can be used. The mind that would have comfortable circumstances must always keep at a higher level, because by so doing the within thus created would find the without inadequate, *or not corresponding,* so the without would follow the within. Or a simpler illustration would be the pouring of a jelly into a mould. If the mould were misshapen or plain, so would be the shape of the jelly; if the mould were artistic or beautiful the jelly would have to pattern itself likewise.

When you grow a mind in which sufficiency, or plenty, *is the dominant thought,* in which the notion of poverty would appear so *grotesque,* so foreign to your nature as to be unthinkable, then you have created a mould, and the substance which will fill it—your circumstances or environment—*must follow the pattern. Truth gives rise to truth; a lie breeds lies; a rose produces a rose, not a thistle; good thoughts cannot produce bad actions;* everything fulfils the law of its being; an effect must be like its cause. *Sow thoughts of prosperity, by having faith in yourself, and you cannot reap anything but prosperity, but the thoughts must ever be of this type; to think now of poverty and then of prosperity will only yield indifferent results, for one neutralizes the other, as I have shown more than once in this book.* Reflect well over this truth: Poverty will not pass away until you create something better to take its place, and every man *can* create this *"something better."* Take courage; go in and win.

TWELVE AFFIRMATIONS FOR THE ELIMINATION OF POVERTY.

The following sentences will, if repeated with *understanding,* daily, bring about the change in consciousness which will eradicate completely doubt and the poverty habit.

The weakest man living has the powers of concentration folded *within his organization;* and they will remain folded *until he learns* to *believe* in their existence, and then tries to develop them.

To prepare for the life of opulence absolutely full of the power that draws wealth, *I must stand by the person I am.*

I *must* uphold my aim, by *believing* in myself, and never slacken one link of the good opinion I have formed of it.

Also know: each outreach of thy soul bears deep the seal of *cosmic impulse aeons.* That thing heart-hungry, every fibre thrills to reach, hath sought thee down the ages hungering, too.

You will never reach the place where you have all you want to spend except by *commanding yourself* to spend, and to want to spend, *less* than your income, whatever that may happen to be; for having all you want to spend is *a state of mind,* not a matter of hundreds, thousands or millions of dollars income.

It is literally true that you are what you think, and *when* you think, therefore think abundance always.

Every man gets just as much gold out of the world as he *puts into it.* All things are thought-made. Every man must *think his own gold into being.*

To him who believes he can, *everything* is an opportunity.

Depend only upon yourself, *believe* in yourself, but work in harmony with all things. Thus you call forth the *best* that is in yourself and secure the *best* that external sources have to give.

"The destruction of the poor is their poverty." The soul instinctively and rightly repels the idea of skimpiness.

Like the whirlwind and the waterspout I *twist* my environment into my form, whether it will or not.

Success from the most material to the most transcendental idea combines its power into a triad: *desire—expectation—preparation.*

"As a man believes, so is he." Even desultory thinking is *creative* and brings results. Premeditated and orderly thinking for a purpose *matures that purpose* into fixed form, so that you may be *absolutely sure* of the result of your dynamic experiment.

The Master Key

LESSON THIRTY-FIVE.

THE ART OF GETTING RICH.

OPPORTUNITY IN A NEW LIGHT.

REAPING AND SOWING.

More and more is it being recognized that there is scarcely a single phase of existence which is not the result of the *immutable laws.* At one time it was believed that only the physical kingdom was under its sway; later it was seen that in the moral world *cause and effect*—heredity as it was termed —was paramount. Because the working of the law cannot be readily observed it does not follow that it is non-existent. The law of gravitation has always existed, although it was thousands of years before it was discovered, so in the same way there are many laws in the universe today of which we never dream. Psychology in the West is too modern a science to permit one to dogmatize as to its limitations, but in every realm of inquiry experience is teaching man that what he once regarded as *chaotic* is in reality an *ordered sequence;* that chance and luck are merely names invented to cover our ignorance of the underlying factors at work. Every thinking man and woman is forced to the conviction that justice rules the world; any other conception is impossible, yet were luck or chance (*the absence of which does not necessarily imply the presence of fate*) an actual force in the universe, justice would be incompatible with it. *Think this well over before proceeding any further, because its acceptance admits such immense possibilities.* A belief in it opens up a new world, and the *"unlucky,"* the downtrodden life's *"failures,"* the friendless, the outcast— all see in it undreamt of possibilities. Getting rich is as much under the domination of an immutable law as are the tides, and in this most wonderful of all the centuries it will become manifest by the demonstrations of those who employ it. All successful men and women *obey this law,* though they do so *unconsciously,* for it is impossible to work outside it.

*No success is the result of chance,** though people will point to a single incident which served to raise an individual from poverty to affluence.

A man can only reap what he sows, and the stumbling across the opportunity has been prepared by the man himself previously, though he is probably unaware of it. The true inwardness of life can only be apprehended by the man who cognizes its operations upon *all* planes, and here and there such men have sprung up, shedding light upon what have hitherto been regarded as insoluble problems. As time goes on this class will increase, and more and more will the universality of law throughout Nature be proved. Within the last decade or two the science of metaphysics has been brought down to a practical working code for the everyday life of the man in the street, and every teacher of *Practical Psychology and Scientific Concentration* could show from his own experience or that of his fellow-students the truth of this. It is the application of this science with which many are concerned, and the application to the problems of daily life of a law which is unerring, and which places prosperity within the reach of every man or woman.

In Nature there is a constant tending of things from better to best, a proceeding from simplicity to complexity, but a complexity which means wider scope, more adaptability. We name this tendency Evolution, and it must not be restricted to the narrow sense in which it is generally used. Nature ever aims at perfection, an evolving, or expounding, so that more life may be expressed, and however slow this process may seem to the impatient reformer, who expects with a single act of congress to abolish poverty, crime, and injustice instantly, it is nevertheless very sure. Man can, however, delay the march forward; he can fall out of the ranks for the time being and rejoin later, but he *must* sometime or other obey the law of his being. A man of iron constitution may treat his body with impunity long past the period a more delicate man could, *but later he has to pay the penalty.*

See, Faith In Self—Belief In Chance, Page 402.

The purpose of evolution has not been recognized fully yet, so man has blundered along and created for himself *poverty and vice, disease and old age,* and thereby learned a much needed lesson—for all experience is but a lesson. He is beginning to wriggle out of it, and when he really desires a change he will get it.

Co-operation with nature is the point to aim at, for by so doing he achieves his true goal. There is one fact from which there is no getting away: *progress is eternal,* and man can help in this progress if he wishes.

There does not seem one epoch in the history of the world when the inhabitants of it were more *"alive"* than today. *Mental activity and industrial activity were surely never more intense!* Scarcely a plot of the earth's surface remains unmapped, and few regions that are at all hospitable but have been *"annexed"* by some government or other. We have vast continents in an undeveloped condition, and the wealth of the world continues to increase at a rapid rate. If there are more for the trade of the world there are more opportunities than ever there were. Life is far more complex; the wants of today have been a thousandfold increased as compared with those of our forefathers. As lesser evolved nations follow in the wake of *The United States and Europe*—and that they will is a foregone conclusion, *look at Japan*—more and more wealth will be created.

It is outside my purpose to consider whether all this leads to more happiness among humanity; the point is that where a century ago there was *one opportunity* today there are *a hundred* consequent upon our more complex civilization. This complexity is the outcome of the forces of evolution at work, and rightly interpreted, like pain and disease, are important factors in the advancement of man's conquest over his environment. Opportunity* is not that which comes once or twice in a man's lifetime, but something which may be created at pleasure. This superstititon has perhaps played more havoc with the human race in all ages in regard to getting on in life than that of any other. Quite a host of proverbs foster this delusion, such as, *"Every dog has his day." "There is a time in the affairs of men, which taken at the flood, leads on to*

---

* *See Opportunity, (The First Opinion), and Opportunity, (The Second Opinion), Page 388.*

fortune." Few men can say that they have not missed opportunities; we all do frequently, and it is galling when so many
men become despondent and lose heart when they realize that
they have allowed a splendid chance to slip through their fingers, especially if, as sometimes happens, it is apparently
through no fault of their own.

*The superstitions in which they have been cradled, which
obsessed their parents and great-grandparents, which con-
front them nearly every day of their lives among their fellows,
thundered at them from the pulpits, emphasized in the literature of all nations and times, objectivised in the columns
of the newspaper, in the records of crime and suicides, but
above all, in one's own daily life—it is perhaps not surprising
that the bogey of opportunity should bear the semblance of
reality.* How many men have not fallen under the glamor of
this gigantic illusion; when tired out with writing dozens of
letters or tramping many weary miles and meeting with repeated failure to secure a berth, they have exclaimed, "It's
just my luck"! You see, *the idea is so ingrained in one's
make-up,* part of one's nature, that it seems very real. If I
could convince you of its emptiness these pages would not
have been written in vain, yet I do not hesitate to assert that
opportunity is not a thing which fate provides for man, but
something created by man himself. The limits of space do
not permit the proof of this assertion being shown step by
step, but that man is *master of his fate* has been proved by hundreds if not thousands of students of *"Concentration"* and
"Faith in Self" in America, the home of the movement which
is spreading over East and West rapidly, and destined in the
not far distant future to revolutionize all our preconceived
ideas of the world, man's place in it and his destiny. *This
emancipation from the ogre of circumstances is not instantaneous;* it is a matter of growth, because it is based on law,
outside which neither gods nor men are able to step.

We live in a veritable age of advancement, surmounted
as we are by the triumphs of science and industry, but we
are merely in the kindergarten of the powers of which men
are now learning something. *Create your opportunities, but
how?* By having belief in yourself. Remember that, *"to him
that hath, faith in himself shall, be given; but him who hath
no faith in himself, even that which he hath shall be taken
away."*

This truth, *"have faith in yourself,"* has been lost sight of except by a few, and they have not sought to force it upon a humanity which was not ready to receive it. Even today, with some, it is a matter of experiment, more or. less. The ideas set forth here may not be fully appreciated by many, and for them the time has not arrived for the practical using of their thought-force. Even otherwise intelligent literary critics have shown a deplorable want of knowledge on the most elementary laws of practical metaphysics; luckily for their bumptiousness their opinions are in cold type, so that the world will be able later to measure their ignorance by the demonstrated powers of thought. A sign of the times is the thousands of students of Concentration.

HE CAN WHO THINKS HE CAN.

He can who thinks he can. Here is the burden of this *Chapter*, and were it expanded to a thousand pages it could only reiterate the fact. Now let us see if there is any connection between what precedes this section. We have on the one hand a busy world, daily expanding, on the lookout for men with brains, willing to pay handsomely for them. Such princely salaries were unknown in by-gone days, because then there were not the possibilities there are today. There are plenty of third-rate men—the market is glutted with them, but on all hands it is admitted that men *can not be found* to fill the responsible positions which are waiting to be filled.

Why is it the age of young men? Why are young fellows ousting men of experience in large and important business houses? Because the spirit of progress is in the air. New times *demand* new methods, and when men attain a certain age their minds like their bodies ossify, become incapable of admitting the wave of new ideas which is spreading over the world. Old age affects temperament, and does not favor the permeation of ideas quickly, except here and there, where a mind well up in age is tuned to a certain pitch to catch the vibrations.

The root of the problem lies in one's mentality. Most men take themselves as they are. They believe that they are limited in certain directions and therefore they never attempt to transcend those limitations. It stands to common sense that if a man has not a good opinion of himself no one else will have. The world takes a man at his own valuation, and if he labels himself a nobody the world is scarcely to be blamed for believing it. A man is *fettered* in circumstances because he is fettered in mind first.

The mental outlook determines the physical one.

One's circumstances are always the visible result of one's thought. All actions are the outcome of our thoughts, therefore our environment is self-created.

Some men like to *think* they are the victims of circumstances, as it saves them a lot of trouble; they can then *remain* quiescent, and put forth no new effort. When things go wrong, *as they inevitably must* under such circumstances, they turn round and say: "It's just what I expected—everything's against me."

Man has usually been hypnotized by the belief that he is the result of his environment—the sport of fate—what wonder when this is the attitude adopted that he *cripples the aspirations* which would lead him to better and higher things. Such a view of life *must* affect his progress, because *a man is that which he believes he is.* While this distorted view is held he fetters himself, because he is then incapable of formulating ideas which would give him financial freedom. Everything which enters the avenues of the senses produces impressions, and it is within man's power to *refuse* admission to any set of impressions. An undesirable element may crop up in his environment, but he may forbid its entering his mind, and so long as he prevents undesirable thoughts or things—*both are much the same*—from entering his consciousness he cannot be affected by adverse conditions. The mind cannot follow two trains of thought at the same time, and at the centre of the mind man is perfectly free to initiate or originate any thought he likes. It is only on the *periphery*, as it were, that he is at the mercy and impressions and thoughts of others, and so long as he centres his usual consciousness on this outside so long must he expect to be lacking in originality, force, judgment, and resourcefulness, without which prosperity cannot successfully be wooed. The *periphery* of the mind is made up of the scum of the current thought of the day of Tom, Dick and Harry, of the common garden man, who thanks his stars he is like the rest of his fellows. The owner is pleased to call it *his* mind; it is the unconscious receptacle of any thoughts of a similar nature.

Man alone possesses the power to *either accept or reject thoughts*, and it is by virtue of this fact that we have such a multiplicity of objects around us. It is the presence of the marvellous inventions and the extraordinary advances made by modern science that demonstrates this unique power. Only one greater power can be possessed by any creature—*the ability to create thought*. The man who can initiate thought is the man who has the world at his feet. Analyze the conversation round you daily and you will never by any chance hear an original thought, because everyone thinks from the outside of his mind, not the centre. Yet that centre exists, and it is the receptacle of the most precious gem the world can imagine. Its presence is unexpected because it has never been developed.

It has been taken for granted that a man was what Nature made him, that the brain he was born with could not be enlarged in its powers. Yet every day this view is demonstrated to be false. *Dull boys have become brilliant men; lads, the sons of laborers*, showing no marked ability even when manhood was reached, *have startled the world* by their achievements in science, art, commerce or literature. Their fellow men have regarded them as being geniuses, as being born with the faculties which have made them famous.

Many a poor farmer boy has given the true source of the powers displayed, and genius is *only a capacity* for taking pains; so in the same way every man may be clever in some direction or other if he only desires to be. Some men who have been absorbed in some pursuit have found that it did not yield the success they sought. It is possible in such cases to so develop their thought that ways and means will suggest themselves for improving to the fullest the gifts they have created by their own efforts.

"He hasn't got it in him," is a common expression applied to some men, *yet these same men when driven to extremities have risen above circumstances.*

The policy of ninety-nine men out of a hundred is to drift. When they have learned their calling they take no more interest in it, and at that point stagnation begins. *A man cannot stand still. The order of Nature is eternal progress,* and as man is the highest product of Nature he is a participator in this onward march. He can delay his evolution if he wishes, as already stated, but he cannot prevent it. On the other hand, he can hasten it immensely by understanding the laws. One expression of this eternal progress is the demand for the best. Even poor people want the best, whatever it be. One of the causes assigned for the falling off of *Canadian* trade with *England* is that the goods are not packed as tidily and nicely as those of *American* and other competitors. There is a sense of beauty arising in even humble quarters among people one would suppose to be quite indifferent. The public is more exacting in its demands, and what was good enough for our forefathers is not good enough for us. Criticism was never more rife among every section of the community than today; no one and nothing can escape it, and the quickened intelligence is spreading among all classes. The tendency of the age is a desire for more freedom, a wider life, a broader outlook. *There is desire for more power. Discontent is evident on all hands.* There is a dissatisfaction with things as they exist at present, and the world is filled with organizations to remedy evils of every kind.

Enough has been said to show the existence of a factor which is pushing man on, and it is a law that the *presence of a desire is evidence of the provision of means to express that desire.* The desire to be prosperous is a *perfectly legitimate one;* those who in the old days *"took the vow of poverty"* no doubt accomplished the development they sought along other lines, but poverty under present-day conditions is a very different thing, and there is nothing to recommend it. The glamor and romance which once surrounded it have disappeared.

In a world which is, as has been said, daily increasing in wealth and must continue to increase, until every square yard of the earth that can be tilled or exploited has rendered its service to man, there is no necessity for poverty. No one need be poor, nor need anyone be governed by circumstances. Every man may make his own.

The primary step to be taken is the creation of a desire or wish to reach some point; without this riches will not trouble anyone. While there is, as stated above, considerable discontent in the world with present conditions there is a large class of persons who regard contentment as the one virtue to be cultivated above all others. They try to believe that happiness and contentment are synonymous, because somebody somewhere and at some time said or taught so. That is sufficient. They tell each other of this, and by dint of assiduously endeavoring to believe it contentment is sanctified.

*In this way some of the greatest humbugs and illusions of
the ages have acquired an odor of truth and respectability.*
Contentment is one of them. When a man is quite content he
is on the down grade. He has ceased to grow. So long as
growth remains in animal or plant stagnation is impossible.
The meaning of growth is desire to express the individual or
nature, and once that end has been attained there is a gradual
decadence, simply because there is nothing more to express.
Nature will not tolerate lumber, and the man who believes he
has exhausted his powers is removed from the scene of his
operations. *He signs his own death warrant.* It has frequently been remarked how business men who have retired
and had no hobby have not long survived their new existence.

The creation of a desire is not difficult, but there must be
clearness in the desire and persistency in holding it, because if
the desire is *nebulous* and *spasmodic* the man will not work
understandingly, and the prosperity will be very haphazard.
He must outlive the good he has in view, and if this is adhered
to it will materialize.

As mind exists for the expression of the man, so once a
man has created by his thought an environment, that environment must surround him sooner or later. No power on earth
can keep it away from him. He may delay its consummation,
because he will have to outwear the causes he has set going,
but every cause must be exhausted some time. As soon as a
man has realized in his consciousness the goal he aims at people
and things instrumental to his success *will be magnetically
drawn to him,* for like attracts like on every plane. Many
instances of this could be cited were space sufficient. By the
creation of new desires new thoughts and ideas will spring into
being, and by nursing these ideas *"ways and means"* will
occur, and the man will say, "I wonder I never thought of
this before." When *Edison* wishes to get light on a problem
he just sits still and thinks quietly until the knowledge comes.
Intuition is a real force in every human being, but thanks to
the "practical" attitude taken everywhere it has been almost
stifled. The genius and the inventor get flashes now and then
which illuminate them for the moment, and any man or woman
could do the same if he or she cultivated the power. Concentration, as students have told me, has made them over again,
and the individual of little intelligence need not despair, for
the whole of the consciousness cannot manifest at once.

Consciousness is like an iceberg—the portion which is seen, corresponding to the ordinary consciousness, is only a tithe of the real size of the berg, which is hidden away in the depths of the water.

Many a man who has passed forty or fifty, who has not led an active mental life, gets it into his head that he is too old to pull his brains together, that it is all very well for a young fellow. Suppose, for instance, he decides to improve his education, and commences to take up the study of some subject. He is brought into touch with new terms, strange words, and lines of thought quite foreign to him. He finds his mind muddled, to use his own words, and he gives the study up, disgusted. He either comes to the conclusion that he is not cut out for study, or that he is too old to begin to learn.

Both suppositions are wrong. Any teacher will tell him that it is the universal experience that when new subjects are taken up the mind rebels because it is against that law which proclaims that the path of non-resistance is always the easiest. Water will always select a channel before ground strewn with obstacles, and a man who has always done a habitual act with the right hand will experience great difficulty and awkwardness if he uses the left. *Every thought marks a channel in the brain, or effects a certain area, and when a new channel is to be dug there are many difficulties to surmount.*

A little patience and persistence will enable any man to take himself in hand, and he may take up the study of anything he chooses.

Going back to what has been said, he will see that his mind is undisciplined, that it has *"bossed"* him up to now, and that naturally it resents being taken in hand, and compelled to go along a certain line.

Once desire has been awakened the mind will cast about for some means to achieve the end it has in view, and provided it is not damped by race-thought it will mature plans which will inevitably bring to pass the goal sought. When it is remembered that every one of the millions of cells of which our body is composed has a consciousness all its own, quite independent of that of the body—often termed by some schools of psychologists the *"group consciousness,"* and that each atom before it disintegrates, has the power of handing over as a legacy to the incoming tenant its own rate of vibration, it will be understood why all of us possess different natures. It will also explain why the things we would do we are unable to accomplish—at first. Thanks to the law of change, which permeates every part of Nature, there is no characteristic possessed by any human being which cannot be absolutely transformed, which accounts for the startling changes seen in some people. Even the *"eternal hills"* are never a moment at rest. Particle by particle changes, molecule by molecule, *undergoes transformation,* and in the interior of the earth the same changes are taking place. Life and motion are the same thing, so-called rest being but a change of motion. It is useful to remember these facts of exact science, because they are so pertinent to the matter we are dealing with at present.

As every force acts along the line of least assistance, the forces of mind inevitably flow along those channels which have been *carved by habit,* and habit is but another name for race-thought, plus environment and education. When one applies common sense to *Concentration*—and this is its very basis—the miraculous elements with which it is credited assume their proper proportions, and any thoughtful man is bound to accept the main propositions of the *new Psychology.* New channels can always be made, and as the old ones are not used they dry up, as it were, or become obliterated in time, and thoughts flow just as easily along the used ones. Keeping this in view and the fact that the surface of the brain has always areas which are like blank phonographic records, the student will understand the need of application.

The direction of a desire will be unconsciously guided along some line for which there is some taste. There is not a human being who has not some taste or tendency. If these appear to be general, and you cannot make up your mind which you should cultivate to the exclusion of the others, do not worry about the thing, but sit alone at intervals and have a good think with yourself. Try and cultivate a receptive attitude, and often you will find an idea will flash into your mind that will appeal to you instinctively as being worth noting. By dismissing it, or allowing the thought to be turned out by an obtruding thought is to render its reappearance less probable, so that you should *determine that* you are going to *"think it up"* for all it is worth.

Practical reverie of this kind is a necessary factor in prosperity building, for many suggestions undreamt of will occur spontaneously. Your brain, attuned to certain vibrations, will intercept similar vibrations, of other minds by a well-known law of psychology, just as telegraphic or wireless messages are intercepted at times.

Having nursed your desires and found your own line, you will find that after all questions as to ways and means are not so difficult. When this stage is reached a course of reading of biographies of successful men should be undertaken. The material for this class of literature is easily accessible nowadays, and some "points" will soon be picked up. The presence in nearly every case *of belief in oneself* will suggest to the reader that this is an essential—almost the first essential.

Some writers make belief the starting point, but I have always doubted the wisdom of this plan, as belief is one of the hardest things to induce, without a motive, and desire supplies this. *Want of belief* has stood in the way of achievement in so many times, even in the case of earnest students that anything which will make it more easily obtained is worth considering. Going carefully over what has been said, one will become increasingly familiar with the line of thought, and it will gradually work itself into the consciousness until it becomes part of his very being. What has so long been wanting has been a reason for things, and existing systems of thought training have not provided this. The point which the universe has reached in evolution at present enables any thoughtful observer to apprehend the why and the wherefore in a manner which would be utterly incomprehensible to our forefathers, who could only deduce from what they saw around them. The wider and grander interpretation of the *cosmos* was only possible to men of the twentieth century, because the unfolding in the past had not proceeded at so rapid a rate as in this "wonderful century," when things are accelerated in every direction.

Belief being a matter which is within everyone's power to increase as he will, provided he only goes about it the right way, the student need not lose heart, because he does not achieve results rapidly. Remember that it is the same with thought as it is with food: it is not the quantity supplied to the organism, but the quantity which is assimilated that counts. *Confidence is begot in oneself by carrying out whatever policy one decides upon; in other words, belief is of a twofold nature —thought and action.* It is only by doing things that one comes to actually believe, and ability to achieve increases with

every action performed. Begin to think better of yourself, for
it is generally the people who have a poor opinion of themselves that never get anywhere. Their belief works itself out
in their character, their demeanor, showing itself even in
physical characteristics, such as the walk, position of the head,
the carriage, the expression. Cast to the winds those enslaving
old saws which used to console the failures of the past, and
rob them of initiative. Knowing something of the times in
which they were coined, they were the natural outcome of
the age, the expression of the mental life. Authority is
responsible for the *self-condemnation* and disbelief in one's
self which has spread over so many people.

Make a new start. Learn to trust in yourself. You may
make mistakes at first; but the more you cultivate your intui-
tions and rely upon them the greater will become your reliance
in your own power. When a voice speaking in *England* or
France can be heard in *America* without any visible means of
connection it is not taxing your credulity to ask you to believe that space is filled by thought vibrations of various types,
and that one is automatically switched on to the type which is
thinking along the same lines. The success of all experiments
in wireless telegraphy or telephony depends upon harmony between transmitter and receiver. Both being tuned to the same
key the waves of ether carry the vibrations set up by the
transmitter to the receiver, which is keyed to respond to those
particular vibrations.

Now I will split up, for purposes of illustration, the
thought-atmosphere into layers of differing density. The
heavy, sluggish layers may be regarded as representing the
thought found in the majority of the people. This layer will
be composed of ordinary dull-as-ditchwater thought, and when
a man is content with an uncongenial environment his thoughts
sink down to this level. When he is inclined to be retrospective
this murky sea of thought surges round his brain. He unconsciously absorbs and stores away in his mental storehouse
masses of this destructive thought. The more he stored away
the more frequent would be the habit of chewing the cud of
bitter reflections, and his brain-machine would respond more
readily to the vibrations of this lowest level of thought. This
would produce a state of mind where he felt that he must let
loose the accumulated mass of thought, to gain relief, and he
would *"yearn for sympathy."* To whom would he unbosom

his troubles? Should he go to the successful man, the prosperous merchant? No, because he would be unappreciative; he would fail to *"understand"* him. The optimist would cheer him up, and he would feel that it was not exactly what he wanted at that moment. A callous man could not give him the aid he sought, so he would seek solace from some one who had experienced the same difficulties he had passed through. How common are such instances?

"Birds of a feather"—*"Like attracts like."*

He who would be prosperous *must avoid* the unlucky, the unfortunate, for the sympathy they receive in this direction but *fetters* them more closely, as it keeps their mentality on the low plane it should have risen above.

Raise the thoughts by determination not to succumb to the temptation of dwelling upon actual conditions. These were the result of previous thought, *and so the future is being woven of the fabrics of the present*—your thought, for, as the student must again be reminded, all action is preceded by thought. By the initial impulse you *raise your mentality* to another higher plane, and every time you succeed in doing this you strengthen your thought by the accession of analogous thoughts, thoughts from the minds of men who have scaled the heights of prosperity. You catch or intercept their thought currents, strengthening and solidifying your own mental structure. Unused brain areas will now be brought under contribution. Having created new permanent channels it will not be found difficult to maintain them, *and belief in yourself* will have been achieved—the one great task which renders the accomplishment of all else comparatively simple.

I will now consider some additional factors in the *Law of Prosperity*, and in the forefront of these must be placed *Concentration*. Every time the mind wanders off bring it back. Avoid abstract ideas when exercising for the acquirement of this faculty. Concrete examples should be taken, which the everyday life offers. It is infinitely easier to *concentrate* on that in which we are interested.

Let that subject be your work, whatever it may be. Let your work be representative of yourself, and your best self at that. If you are an employee concentrating on your work it will be more thoroughly done and you are unwittingly fitting yourself for a higher position. It will insensibly lead to your taking a live interest in your work, and if this is done it will make you a better workman. Doing a thing because it is your livelihood, and doing it because you love to do it, are two widely different things, and he who loves his work never finds time hang heavily upon his hands. He rarely gets tired, and hence extracts a joy from his daily duties which the artificial pleasures of theatre or ball do not yield to their devotees. It follows that equability and calmness will be built into the nature, and, incidentally, the health will be improved; good health will be needed, unless one be left a fortune, and even then riches without it will not benefit one much. Besides, the doing of a thing well fits a man to undertake more responsible work, and if his present employment does not offer this he will find the opportunity later, or create it himself.

A good memory is a necessity, and concentration is an important aid. Mind-wandering, or the dissipation of mental energy, which is so commonly found in the unsuccessful in life, is more effectively corrected by concentration than by anything else, and one secret of concentration is interest—a real, living, intense, whole-hearted interest. This is a quality which is generally very colorless in the man who lacks riches. If he has any live interest it is not of a constructive type, but takes his mind along channels which do not accomplish anything. As a rule a man who is wholly absorbed in a subject has a good memory as regards that particular topic.

He retains a mass of facts and figures which applied to another subject would make him an expert. So he who would acquire the *Art of Getting Rich* must cultivate his memory. A promise once made must be fulfilled, for the old-time excuse of a bad memory may pass occasionally, but it will not always be accepted. More money is lost through a bad memory than is supposed. Many a good order which would have led to larger ones has been lost through failure to call upon a customer or send him some data required. We in the West are always too ready to promise because we do not wish to displease our friends, but one should be very chary in giving one's word, when there is not much probability of carrying out what you have pledged to do.

Do not imagine that it is a good plan to improve a bad memory by relying upon it for a mass of details which it has no right to contain. Modern life gives us myriads of facts and things to remember with which our forefathers never had to trouble themselves, with the result that there is a far greater

tax upon the power of recollecting. There is no particular
virtue in loading up the memory with trivialities, things which
the mind cannot use for any purpose, therefore these small
things should be delegated to a notebook. Have no fear that
the mind will be weakened thereby. Rather will it leave it
the freer to attend to the really important things, for, after all,
the really important things one does in a day's work are few;
the bulk of the time of many is spent in "pottering about."
Even the day's work of many a so-called busy man could be
boiled down to a couple of hours, through a want of system
and method, and a paying of time and attention to insignificant things quite out of proportion to the necessities of the.
case. With the use of a notebook commences order, system,
the delegation of duties to their proper quarter, the saving of
time which can well be devoted to the working out of problems
which bear on the fact of your advancing, and the conserva-
tion of mental energy which would otherwise be exhausted. A
prominent cause of failure in modern life is the worry habit,
and this is induced as much by a multiplicity of details as by
anything else.   The man who would solve the problem of
riches must be of a calm temperament, but the man who worries has a mind alien to this requirement.

With the relief of the mind from little matters the memory can readily be trained to respond, and to yield up whatever is required of it.   Then the full meaning of that oft-
quoted phrase: *"His word is as good as his bond,"* will carry
weight with it. No man can rely upon himself alone altogether.
Put a man in the *Sahara* desert and he might remain there all
his life and never be a cent more in pocket. Put him, on the
other hand, where there are a number of men, and it is certain
that some one will want his help or counsel in some way. Man
is naturally a gregarious animal, and he is a dissatisfied one,
too.   That is, he is always wanting something which he thinks
will minister to his comfort.   It is this very never-content
attitude which evolves him, and as he may plan or theorize to
secure more of these comforts he has to invoke the aid of his
fellowmen in some shape. Man, being a bundle of wants, is
the safeguard of his getting on. Through it new industries
spring into existence every day, new luxuries or necessities,
according to the view taken, arise, and the demand must be
met. The man in request will be he who anticipates the wants
or demands of his fellows. History teems with examples of

men of this type, and the evocation of faculties which perfect the judgment will show what is wanted and how best to supply it. It is the man with ideas that the world wants, and whatever he asks will be given him.

It is a common thing to hear an unsuccessful man say: "If I only had scope I would not be where I am now." As a matter of fact the position he was in furnished all scope necessary, *but he had failed to recognize or utilize it.*

When a man fails to win out in a position he has been in for years, the cause is not in the position, but the man.

Experience confirms this every day. Two men will carry on the same kind of business in the same street, and, to all appearances, conditions will be equal for both. After some years one will have built up a good business and the other will be where he was, marking time, as it were, or have lost ground. The fault is not business being overcrowded, for one business is as good as another.

When *Baron Rothschild* was importuned by an anxious mother as to which business gave the best results, he replied, *"Selling matches is as good as any other, provided you sell plenty."*

It is method which tells, the way of looking at things, the mental attitude, in short. If a man can really believe he can make a business a success he will do so, but he has to be steeped to the ears in this belief. Once he gets on fire with the notion, the obstacles which meet him become very minor matters. The feeling that he can make the thing *"go"* brings forth all that is in him.

Unsuspected suggestions will occur to him; for one thing he will clear out of the time-honored ruts which his forefathers always followed so assiduously. He knows that there must ever be wants of some kind, and there is no logical reason why he can not supply those wants. He is not, of course, bound to stay in a business or a position he does not like, but the fact that he finds himself where he is shows that he is not fit for a bigger position. Once he is ready for a more responsible position he will gravitate towards it, provided he has the desire to; but the fault with the majority of people is that once having reached some point which they have always regarded as their objective, they have not placed a further goal in its place, so no further headway is made.

The business chosen, then, is almost immaterial: the cardinal point is the manner in which it is carried on. Many of the most successful businesses of the world have been created in the first instance by a winning personality, and where there is not much capital to commence with this is an invaluable asset. The laws of attraction and repulsion, which are seen even as low in the scale of Evolution as minerals, reaches its culmination in man. The man who repels his fellowmen is not the man who is likely to make a big success at anything. Even a genius or clever inventor cannot dispense entirely with his fellows. Help or co-operation of some sort is necessary, and it is only when a vast organization has been built up that the personal influences may be discounted. Exclusiveness, aloofness, reserve have been the stumbling-block of many really clever men who could have marketed their ability had they gone about it the right way.

It is not always that there is no scope, but that a man may be in a calling he has no taste for. In such a case he can make the best he can of the circumstances, and when opportunity occurs leave it. No man can be a big success in any vocation which he dislikes. Everything in connection with it is done perfunctorily. He cannot put his heart and mind into it, therefore his *best* is lacking, and only when the best is put into a thing does it yield its highest results.

If all men followed the *nomadic* life that is still practiced by some tribes in the *East* there would be small room for initiative. The wants of the tribe would be few; food, shelter and clothing would be sufficient. Thanks to modern civilization a thousand avenues are open to the man of today—art, science, commerce, in their innumerable combinations. Every day new industries spring up, new minerals or materials are discovered, new uses for old things spring to light, and the future will be still more remarkable in this respect. All this means countless opportunities, and the glib talk of there being no equality of opportunity is sheer nonsense. The man at the bottom is not there because he has not had any opportunities, but because he is not fit to be anywhere else.

It is futile to talk of abolishing slums by legislation so long as slum minds exist.

Poverty is no hindrance to riches, often it is the greatest aid. If you doubt this statement look at the lives of the rich men of the world—the *multi-millionaires.* How many of them began life with wealth, education, influential friends?

The world is changing its thought; in the past, those who believed in *The Art of Getting Rich,* were among the isolated few, and were looked upon with suspicion by the many; in the present, the great majority desire to take advantage of *"Opportunity"* and most of these believe it is possible.

This change of thought is due to the fact, that earnest men and women, are fast *eliminating* the term *"impossible"* from their vocabulary.

Many are now convinced that life is not made for poverty and disease; they now believe that these are but a temporary creation of man gone astray.

They do not believe that this world is a *"vale of tears,"* nor that we must suffer in the present in order that we may gain bliss in the future. We do not gather figs from thistles, neither can a life of poverty and disease be the direct cause of a life of pleasure. It is an immutable law that like causes produce like effects, and many are beginning to intelligently use this law in shaping their life and destiny.

The source of all riches is within. There is no more difficulty in becoming rich than there is in becoming clever in a business or profession, only some men find the secret more easily than others.

Adverse circumstances never yet held down a man who was determined to rise. The more insuperable the difficulties the more powerful has the man become who has emerged from them.

All the enemies a man has to contend with are of his own creation. One by one he can vanquish them if he will.

What man has done man can do.

What is the one desideratum in the acquirement of wealth? Talent? Not exactly. Some very talented men have been very poor. Education? No, there are *plenty* of educated men miserably poor.

Trust in ourselves must come first. After that all is secondary. This is the common asset of every wealthy man. Luck, fate, chance, opportunity have no claim to consideration. All men and women, with very few exceptions, *are hypnotized by them. Opportunity,* surely, you may say, plays some part?

Contrast the two following *opinions* respecting *"opportunity"* on the next page. The opinion expressed in the *first* you are probably familiar with, but the opinion expressed in the *second* is not so well known:

OPPORTUNITY.

THE FIRST OPINION.

Master of human destinies am I,
Fame, love, and fortune on my footsteps wait.
Cities and fields I walk: I penetrate
Deserts and seas remote, and passing by
Hovel, and mart, and palace—soon or late
I knock unbidden once at every gate.
If sleeping, wake—if feasting, rise before
I turn away. It is the hour of fate,
And they who follow me reach every state
Mortals desire, and conquer every foe
Save death: but those who doubt or hesitate,
Condemned to failure, penury, and woe;
Seek me in vain and uselessly implore—
I answer not, and I return no more.

OPPORTUNITY.

THE SECOND OPINION.

They do me wrong who say I come no more
　When once I knock and fail to find you in;
For every day I stand outside your door,
　And bid you wake, and rise to fight and win.
Wail not for precious chances passed away,
　Weep not for golden ages on the wane;
Each night I burn the records of the day,
　At sunrise every soul is born again.
Dost thou behold thy lost youth all aghast?
　Dost reel from righteous retribution's blow?
Then turn from blotted achives of the past,
　And find the future's pages *white as snow.*
Art thou a mourner? *Rouse thee from thy spell;*
　Art thou a sinner? *Sins may be forgiven;*
Each morning gives thee wings to flee from hell,
　Each night a star to guide thy feet to heaven!
Laugh like a boy at splendors that have sped,
　To vanished joys be blind and deaf and dumb;
My judgments seal *the dead past with its dead,*
　But never bind a moment yet to come.
Though deep in mire, wring not your hands and weep;
　I lend my arm to all who say: "I can."
No shamefaced outcast ever sank so deep
　But yet might rise and be again a man.

In the *first* opinion *opportunity* is shown as coming, or knocking but once at every mortal's door, and if you follow it you will reach every state mortals desire, save death; but if you hesitate you are condemned to failure, penury and woe. You seek *opportunity* in vain; it answers not, and returns no more if you fail to take advantage of it.

In the *second* opinion it is shown that *opportunity* stands outside and *knocks every day* at man's door, and bids him wake and rise up to fight and win. *Opportunity* is also shown as lending its arm to all who say, "*I can,*" and that you *can rise again and be a man.*

Needless to say that the writer *believes literally* in the opinion of *opportunity*, as set forth in the *second opinion*, and that those who have *faith and confidence* in themselves take advantage of opportunity whenever it comes.

Sincere, honest desire is the star that leads one to opportunities; while *"faith and belief"* in one's self enables the confident man or woman to take advantage of *"the opportunity,"* at any time.

Right here, faithful student, I again ask you to read all of this chapter over again, for the ideas being new will require some repetition before they can effectually bring you to take action. But you may object and say, I am only an average sort of a person, I am not gifted with any special ability. This is because you have not *"discovered"* yourself. You have got it into your head that having grown up you are what you were as a child, plus the result of experience and environment. But you are infinitely more than this, as I have already shown. *Your abilities are latent, like the strength that lies coiled up potentially in the muscles of everyone.*

It is action which brings forth the strength. So it is putting into practice the abilities that you will evoke from yourself that will enable you to reach the goal you have in view. Ability is undeniably required in building up a fortune, but this ability may be cultivated. You were perhaps put into some business because either your father was in it before you, or you thought you would like it. At twenty or thirty one does not always know what one likes; sometimes one does not discover one's life-work till forty and after that age—and then one thinks that as one is doing that kind of work it would be better perhaps to go on doing it for all time. How is it possible to find out what is in one, when that attitude is taken? *"The*

Great Within" has never been suspected except in the case of our great men, yet in this is a literal and figurative gold mine for every human being. Millions pass through life never suspecting that as one of the wise books of the *East* says:

"Within thyself must deliverance be sought."

Hero-worship *Diminishes Heroes;* every man is *potentially a hero, or a great man,* in some direction or other, but it usually requires a crisis to make the fact patent. No sane man dare place a limit on man's powers, for, as a matter of exact science, *no limit* has ever been found.

The oldest, and, at the same time, newest of sciences—psychology—has never had a fair trial. Its consideration has always been a purely academic one, never dreaming that it had another side, and that it was one of the most practical and matter-of-fact sciences of which we had any conceptions.

By trusting in yourself you provide those conditions which will reveal and bring forth your ability. No two human minds are the same, and if you regard yourself as commonplace your mind has taken you at your own estimate until all you think and do is commonplace, lacking resource, initiative, originality. The habit of trusting in yourself, of *believing* you are capable of much more will enable the mind within to give you new light on problems around you, and that indefinite thing—*ability,* will grow day by day.

It may sound strange to learn that *man has power to create any circumstances he desires,* but it is nevertheless a fact, and is being demonstrated constantly by students who have taken up practical metaphysics. Generally the fault is that a man does not know what he really does desire. This week or year it is this thing, next year it is something else, hence he rarely realizes his ideals. The man who would be wealthy must let this thought dominate his whole being. He must satisfy himself that he really does know what he desires.

Too many people entertain a vague feeling that they would like this, that, or the other: this attitude must be altered.

They must examine themselves carefully and find out what they actually do want first. It would be foolish to say: *"I should like to be rich,"* without having something to be rich for. If a *Hottentot* were given a cheque for one hundred thousand dollars it would not raise him in the slightest; if it were given to many a civilized man it would spell physical and moral ruin. No, a man who would be rich must have evolved sufficiently in order to have a use for those riches. If he has no leanings to culture, to travel, to surround himself with the beautiful, to express outwardly what marks his growth inwardly, or no wish to benefit those of his fellow-creatures who have not reached the same point he has, then the pursuit would be abortive and unmoral, for all men are brothers; all have a common origin, and whatever raises one without in some measure raising his fellows re-acts prejudicially. The unrest of the modern world is struggling to voice this fact.

The smarting sense of injustice to one section of the community through its inability to protect itself from the rapacity of another section becomes daily more articulate, more pronounced.

Examine your motives with the keenest scrutiny, and once convinced of their honesty take the plunge. Begin to develop yourself systematically. Cultivate an unconquerable ambition, an indomitable doggedness that you *will* accomplish the end in view. The desire must be one that·is not to be swept away with the first obstacle that presents itself. The word *"impossible"* must be erased from the tablets of your mind. Your goal must stand out as clearly as the outlines of a city behind which the pale moon is rising, *silhouetted* against the heavens. Blurred ideals, ideals lost in a diffusive mistiness never materialize because of their want of cohesion, of definiteness, of persistency.

The Law of Wealth.

How will the riches come, you may ask? Never mind for the moment. You have made up your mind that you are going to climb the path to prosperity: leaving the working out to your interior forces. As has just been said there are innumerable walks in life which the one-sided, narrow existence of our forefathers rarely dreamt of. It may be through invention, through the employment of a gift which has long lain in the recesses of the mind unsuspected, through what *you* may call "accident" or "luck," but, remember: *whatever you create mentally is absolutely certain to express itself outwardly.* This is the Law; you doubt it? Look at any man who is not well-to-do. Is he accustomed when considering finance to think in six figures? Does he not as the head of the household, often say: *"We can't afford this; this is too dear?"* Is he not ever seeking to economize along this line or that, or complaining, if in business, of the heavy rates, and the increasing cost of things, and the keenness of competition which will eventually drive him out of the place?

I do not assert that every man who is not wealthy talks like this, but I do say that all who *think* poverty *express* poverty. Getting into close contact with the poor will show that they never hold large ideas concerning money, and usually consider themselves incapable of organizing and conducting large concerns. They depreciate themselves, and therefore never rise above the average in regard to money. You will rarely hear them speak of what they intend to do in the future. Seldom will they go beyond a "wish," which usually is expressed thus: *"I wish I could find a lot of money."* Most successful men become so with no knowledge of the Law—it is done unconsciously, therefore one does not often hear of their saying beforehand what they intend being or doing. *Andrew Carnegie* and one or two other self-made men have put this on record, but I do not remember coming across any other instances. What I am seeking is the case of practical dreamers, who are naturally few and far between. I could cite instances of students who have put the *Law* into operation and benefited accordingly, but the best example which will be known to most people is the conception found in fiction in the character of *Svengali.* You will remember that when he was in the direst straits and could not pay his rent he would say: "One day I shall be rich: I shall have a carriage, a big fur coat, and even princes will pay me homage." He held to this ideal in spite of the squalor which seemed as though it would always surround him. He had an *unquenchable faith* in himself, and dreamed daily of the future that he planned.

This is the system upon which one should proceed. Ignore present conditions utterly; live in an atmosphere of plenty, whatever be your actual environment. You create your future from the present, just as the present is the outcome of the past. Do not postpone, even in thought, the advent of riches. Act as though you were already wealthy, that you had achieved the goal in view, then the wish which takes foundation will have passed into *expectancy,* which is a very different attitude, something far beyond even hope.

From what has been said it follows that *one must practice constructive thinking,* which is a very different thing from ordinary thought, a haphazard, happy-go-luck way of thinking. By constructive thinking you have a purposive plan where before you had no plan whatever, where the thought was merely drift, whatever presented itself to the mind. A thought repeated has a tendency to recur more readily according as the mind may be at liberty, or not disciplined. Discipline is always suggestive of something unpleasant, of duty, of something which runs in the face of the line of least resistance. A strong body results from use, from exercise, and even a robust and physically perfect body would lose its virility, its strength, by not being used. The case of the mind is just the same. The forceful, purposive mind can only result from ordered and trained thinking. The conception of training thought is a novelty to most people, but it is just as rational as training the fingers to play the piano like a *Paderewski;* the difference between the budding pianist, represented by the average man, and the artist, is a question of time. His skill is not a gift, the only gift he possessed was an *unshakeable determination* to master the task he had set himself, and an aptitude for hard work, and without these no man may hope to get rich.

There are too many people who are always seeking a quick-get-rich method, and are doomed to disappointment, for Nature never gives something for nothing. There is an increasing number who yearn for opulence, but who never raise a finger to obtain it, and it cannot be too plainly said that there is no magic, no mysteries in the lines laid down here, *merely a using of the materials every human being possesses.* The world is ever looking for the new, the latest, the great things, and it pays handsomely for them. Evolution being a progression, conditions are always undergoing modifications, and natural resources are more and more taxed. The mere fact of the invention of the *motor car* has led to the use of vast capital for the growing of rubber; the same cause has led another brain to attempt the solution of an adequate supply by the invention of a substitute for rubber, much cheaper. Such illustrations can be multiplied easily, and it is open to any man or woman to anticipate the wants of the world and provide them.

By constructive thought the faculties of the mind which have long lain dormant will be roused into activity, and in this rousing an expansion of the normal consciousness results. This gives an utterly new outlook upon life. As thought becomes constructive all the old poverty-stricken ideas will die out. Circumstances have always dictated the type of thinking. A man in financial difficulties, if he is of a sunny or careless type, may treat them lightly, or even *philosophically*, but from time to time his environment compels him to face the situation. This brings his mind in line with the orthodox thought, and in this way old thought is maintained. The habitual outlook upon life is kept intact; the self-made manacles are riveted the firmer about the victim who treads the old path, follows in the rut which the feet of countless millions have trodden. A standard is formed, and every thought is judged according to it; if it agree to it, well and good; it is accepted. If it deviate from the pattern it is thrown aside. A man rather prides himself on having concocted such a standard of value; it seems to him that it is a piece of originality; that it places him above other men; that he possesses judgment, discernment, tact, a discriminating mind.

He forgets that he has only taken another's model and labelled it his own. If a flock of sheep were passing a given spot and the first one jumped over an imaginary obstacle each of the others would do likewise. *So it is with men.* Here and there a member of the community breaks away from the rank, and then we term him a great man. It has been supposed that the number of such great men were limited, just as geniuses are, but as a matter of fact every human being is great. Every healthy mind has within untold possibilities, and the reason they have not evinced themselves is because their existence has never been suspected. For instance, possibly eighty persons out of every hundred who read these pages will smile in a superior sort of way when it is claimed that anybody can be rich who wishes. Why, they will exclaim, to amass wealth requires *brains, ability, cleverness*, and these are all wanting in the bulk of people. Quite true. These qualities are essential, but one is not justified in assuming they are the prerogative of the few.

Read the *biographies* of our merchant princes, of financial magnates of the world—your newspapers give you such cases almost daily—and note that they did not stand out brilliantly among their fellows at school. Some were among the densest, the dullest of their forms. In most cases no evidence of their being different from the common garden man was apparent for some years later. They simply had not *"discovered"* themselves, they did not know the stuff they were made of.

In the majority of examples they unconsciously stumbled upon forces which eventuated in their success.

Today, thanks to the new science of practical metaphysics, *man knows that he can attain the highest goal he can intelligently conceive,* and this through the medium of constructive thinking. Try to grasp this assertion. Think of the countless suicides which could be averted by such a belief, the immense happiness which could be brought to thousands of lives by its acceptance.

The fault with most people is that they *do not trust themselves.* They will seek advice from persons quite incapable of helping them instead of relying on their own interior powers.

To begin this constructive thinking try and find just where you stand. Take stock of yourself, mentally. Analyze your leanings, your tastes, the bend or trend of your mind. Do this only when you are in a normal state of mind—not when worried, angry, or nervous. No doubt several trials will be necessary to determine your line. Possibly you have been pursuing the right track but the wrong method. Alter the method. Take a successful man and note where he differs from you: in most cases it is executive ability. *Well, you can gain that. He* did not know the *Law, you* do, and hence you can do it more efficiently than he. Do you know your business from A to Z? Have you gone in for the latest or most up-to-date plant; do you pack your goods in the most approved fashion? Some countries have lost millions of dollars annually from bad packing, *Germany* scoring in this instance. Have you learned to hustle—not bustle? Have you overhauled your staff—assuming you have one? Are they reliable, capable? Have you all the details of the business at your finger ends? *Do you personally supervise it or leave it to a third-rate man?* Are you polite to customers? Do you organize a *"trouble department,"* placing a tactful man in charge who investigates all complaints, legitimate or otherwise, and settles the matter with the dissatisfied ones? These questions could be indefinitely increased— many will suggest themselves to you once you put your *thinking* cap on. It is then that you can determine if you are cut out for the calling you are now in, or if you could do better in some other line. Let your natural inclination have a hand in the debate with yourself, and you are not likely to get far out.

If you should find on going carefully into the matter that

you would have more scope in something which was more congenial remember it is never too late to change. Many of the most successful men in the business world today have followed callings very different from those to which they were brought up. Of course, one would not go to the other extreme, and attempt half-a-dozen lines at the same time. This has been a potent cause of failure, because the energies become scattered. Ideas which would bring to perfection the line on which a man chiefly depends are never realized, because before they are fully hatched they are tucked away in the mind to make way for some other problem which presses for solution at the moment, and afterwards the half-evolved idea either becomes forgotten, or the mind refuses to supply the missing threads which would make it perfect.

The importance of taking a real, live interest in one's work, whatever it be, has already been emphasized, and looked at in conjunction with the above it will be seen more clearly how success can be won.

Receptivity is not a frame of mind the average mortal cultivates; especially if he be a business man. He will tell you he has something better to do with his spare moments; that he barely has time to get through his work. *Yet the cultivation of receptivity is an absolute necessity.* It will be by freeing the mind of all worries, all plans, endeavoring to make it a blank for the time being that the most illuminative thoughts will strike—a literal, not merely a figurative expression—the mind. Where this frame of mind cannot be attained it will be found a good method to desire on retiring for the night that the answer to some question which demands attention should occur to you the next morning. Nearly always the subjective side of the mind, or the subconsciousness, will supply the information desired, and with a little more practice receptivity, which it must be remembered is the reverse of thinking, will be acquired. Then it is that you will find out whether you are on the right track in regard to your occupation.

Receptivity permits the entrance of thoughts which have long been struggling to express themselves in the ordinary consciousness. *Dickens* and other writers have put it on record how their *characters, conversations, incidents, and ideas* concerning their books leaped to their minds when in this mood —whence they could not tell, but modern psychology has, experimentally, demonstrated the source, analyzed the mechanism of the mind, and now can not only direct many of the operations, but can absolutely *create* any state of mind desired.

Run straight. When you indulge in sharp practices it is not the other fellow on whom you inflict the wrong, *but yourself*. It is the law that two thoughts of an utterly diverse nature can not occupy the consciousness at the same time. So long as you harbor a thought unworthy of an honest man you polarize your power of attracting, whether it be friends or money. *You can cheat others; yourself, never*, and he who essays to do so will sink back to the level of the crowd. Riches may, and often are, attained by unworthy means, but the man is the poorer, *for the Law is absolutely just.* There is no room in the universe for luck, for its existence predicates absence of law, to say nothing of injustice, and law is universal. A man who knows his inner forces, who expands his consciousness, who gains riches because as a part of the whole he is entitled to them, is oblivious to competition. He takes from the great storehouse of Nature, and no one is the poorer, rather by his efforts are others helped. To take advantage of a fellow creature, to grind and wring the uttermost farthing from a human being is to foul one's higher nature. For every cause there must be an effect, and like causes produce like effects, whatever be the plan, physical or moral.

One cannot handle pitch without being defiled, and ever to doubt the honesty of others is to *weaken* your own honesty. This is one reason why in this suspicious, critical age there is such a dearth of real happiness. To feel mean, angry, suspicious, is to invite those very qualities into your own being, to take their lodgment there and to undermine the character, and . the man without character can never be truly rich.

There are plenty of cases of miserable wealthy people who would envy the happiness of poor men, so far as money is concerned.

Every human being is his *own nemesis*, from whom there is no escape, and it is about time this *law were known* and much unnecessary misery saved thereby.

It is as well to know something of the *law*, so that the weak-kneed may think twice before going astray.

Many people are in indifferent circumstances because they have never supposed they would ever be otherwise. They have expected it to be natural that some folk—the favored few—

should be wealthy, and others—the masses, with whom they identify themselves, should be poor. Hence they have not looked into their own natures to bring to the surface all the riches lying there.

Character is only another name for a set of ideas which have become crystallized, therefore we see people who are colorless because the life-thought which should be pulsing through their being can not flow on account of the condition of the channels, which have never been kept open since childhood. In childhood one's fancy is elastic, and one thing can be believed as easily as another. *Romance and imagination* die away with the years of maturity, and in place of the spontaneity of youth there grow sets of ideas, the product of the senses, the result of ready-made thoughts. Opulence, luxury, freedom from care, abounding health, get to be looked upon as the prerogatives of specially-selected individuals. Living among commonplace people tends to set the stamp of commonplaceness upon one, and the way in which this spreads is seen (in one direction) by the slovenliness of speech which is so conspicuous, and the equal slovenliness of newspaper English. There has always existed a dead level, though each generation raises it higher, and the active propagation of one-eyed ideas, which are driven into the minds of the people by a power which the past knew not—the *"hardtimes"* advocate—is more thorough than it used to be.

The low standard of the marriage state is another sign of the times, and the *passing of chivalry* and romance, which is everywhere apparent, is a still further outcome of them. The connection between all this and *Art of Getting Rich* is the decadence or the failure to use the idealizing faculties which cuts one off from an important source of wealth because one cannot readily *differentiate* oneself from one's environment.

It can be done, however, only the task may require more effort on the part of the man. The mental stagnation which strangles all clear thinking effectually shuts out ideas which would be money-making, and hides man's true greatness from him. The antidote is clear; another set of ideas must be substituted, and here romance may be reinstated. Practical dreaming is as good a term to employ as any. Build air-castles to your heart's content, but unlike the mere dreamer do not regard your creations as mere dreams. The more frequently you go over the picture the more clearly will the details stand out.

Where gaps were seen in the early attempts suggestions for filling them will occur; until at length the entire structure will stand out in the mind's eye boldly and perfectly.

The bringing down of theory to practice will simply be a matter of time, for the power which has brought into existence the abstract creation has merely to be extended to the concrete one now.

One immense step will have been achieved by castle-building. You will know what to aim at. Leaving out of consideration the masses of the cities there are millions of human beings who drift all their lives.

Want of purpose, want of objective, indifference, are the chief characteristics of this class, who will do anything but *think.* Tenacity of purpose, earnestness, bulldog determination, patient persistence never characterize these people.

As has been said, there is no magic about the method here presented; it is the working out of *unerring Law,* so that the man who lives the strenuous life, full of hope, *full of faith in his own inherent greatness, cannot fail to become rich.* The outcome of such lines being followed is the creation of an inexhaustible storage-battery, always charged, which can always be depended upon.

As the man progresses, as success after success results from his efforts he becomes filled with a *certainty* that all causes must be followed by effects. Even his mistakes—for he will make these for a time—will teach him lessons which before he failed to understand.

That marvellous, but little understood asset of the human make-up, the *intuition,* will solve problems as they arise, if the right *mental attitude is taken.*

This attitude is the quiet turning of the mind in upon itself, shutting out the without so that the voice of the within may be heard. Many a successful business man of today owes his success to the *flashes of the ocean of consciousness* behind the ordinary work-a-day world, and the power to let it *"come through"* can be attained by anyone.

. All questions as to choice of calling, system, industry, thrift, investment, and the usual list of qualifications usually given to the aspirant for wealth, are in reality very minor, and need not be treated here.

TO RECAPITULATE.

It is now only necessary to *recapitulate* or cast into a concise form the propositions laid down in this *chapter*.   They might be stated in these terms:

First—*Both the world and man are in their babyhood.*

Second—*The purpose of life is to express more life.*

Third—*More life can only be expressed by man's desires being fulfilled.*

Fourth—*Every desire must inevitably materialize, unless neutralized by a counter-desire.*

Fifth—*Science has not yet found any limits to the power of man.*

Sixth—*The capacity for more power comes with the fullest use of present capacities.*

Seventh—*The only obstacle which can prevent man from entering into riches or anything else he wants is doubt of himself.*

Burn these statements into your brain.   Concentrate your mind upon them, whether in tram car, train, or walking, and fortify yourself by building up a strong inward confidence now and then, as opportunity offers.

There is no need to devote hours per day; it is the persistency which tells, and by cutting off the supply of pessimistic thought as served up for your delectation in the press, pulpit, conversation, pictures, and literature, and seclude your thought atmosphere for a time you will be the better for it.

To define riches is no light matter.   Tastes differ and opinions vary.   The *Vicar* of *Wakefield* was passing rich on £40 ($194.80) a year, but an individual with a large establishment and a high social position to uphold might consider $100,-000 scarcely adequate.

The writer would prefer to term that man rich who had sufficient to meet all his wants, which might be few or many, simple, or extravagant.

More effort would be required in the case of building up a big fortune than a modest competency, but the same principle would apply in each case.

The preceding pages are written in the midst of a *busy life*, and no pretence to literary style is made. The sole object in view the writer has kept before him has been to aid that ever-increasing class who, in a world of plenty, have not sufficient to gratify natural wants.

As to the moral side of the question the author contends that it is a duty every man owes to his country to have enough to keep him from want. By so doing he makes one pauper the less, and is in a position to help his fellows, for no man can truly rise without raising his fellows.

The new industries which have sprung into existence during the past two centuries, many initiated by single individuals, have found employment, some of it highly paid, to hundreds of thousands of people, in spite of what has been said of machinery ousting men.

Poverty has had its day as an *idyllic conception*. The world has had enough of it, and there are now other factors which will develop character in a much more satisfactory manner. Let those who still sing the praise of being poverty-stricken look the facts full in the face, and they will be almost bound to admit that in nearly every case it *dwarfs the man, crippling his finest feelings, and stunting his higher nature*.

Poverty is a crime—a crime against the state, and it is also as much a disease as any physical malady, and as such is curable.

The writer boldly asserts that no man or woman who applies the rules for getting rich can help becoming so; and the teachings can only be proved by being *put to the test*.

Reading is of little use. The pages *must be read and re-read* till they permeate one's being. No statement has been made which has not been demonstrated. If the student fails to demonstrate the truth of the assertions it is not they which are at fault, but himself. He is manipulating unchanging law, and his inability to demonstrate it is no proof of its non-existence.

FAITH IN SELF—BELIEF IN CHANCE.

"Faith in self is the—Key to Success."
"Doubt of self is the—Cause of failure."

Belief in chance is something, but *faith in self* is everything.

Belief in chance is sober, serious, grave, and respectable; *belief in self* is all that, and more too.

It is not second sight, nor is it the sixth sense, but it is *the life* of all of these things.

Faith in self gives one the *keen eye,* the *quick ear,* and the *business spirit;* it is the *interpreter* of all mysteries, the *surmounter* of all difficulties, the *remover* of all obstacles.

It is useful in all places, and at all times; it is *useful* in meditation, for it shows a man *his way* in the world; it is *useful* in business, for it shows him his way *through* the world.

Belief in chance may be power, but *faith in self is skill.*

Belief in luck, and chance, may have weight, *but faith in self is momentum;* belief in chance thinks it knows what to do, while *faith in self* knows how to do it.

Belief in chance makes a man respectable, *faith in self makes him respected;* belief in chance is wealth, *faith in self* is ready money.

For all practical purposes of life, *faith in self* carries it against belief in chance, *one hundred to one.*

Take them upon the stage of life, and put belief in chance *against faith in self,* and belief in chance will play a tragedy that will scarcely survive long enough to be hissed, while *faith in self keeps the house in a roar,* night after night, with its successful acts.

There is no want for dramatic talent which believes in chance; *there is* demand for dramatic talent *which has faith in self.*

Take belief in chance, and faith in self, before the bar of justice, and let them shake their learned fingers at each other's nose in legal rivalry.

Belief in chance sees its way clearly, but *faith in self is first* at its journey's end.

Belief in chance has many a compliment from the crowd, but *faith in self* receives the *fees* from its clients.

Belief in chance speaks loud and learnedly, *faith in self* logically and triumphantly.

Belief in chance makes men wonder that it gets on no faster, *faith in self* excites astonishment that it gets on so fast.

And the great secret is that *faith in self* has no weight to carry; it makes no false steps; it hits the right nail on the head; it loses no time; it takes all hints; and, by keeping its eye on the weather-cock, *is ready* to take advantage of every wind that blows.

Take them on the lecture platform.

Belief in chance has nothing worth hearing, *faith in self* is sure of an abundance of hearers; belief in chance may obtain a living, *faith in self will make one;* belief in chance gets a good name, *faith in self* a great one; belief in chance argues, *faith in self converts;* belief in chance is an honor to the profession, *faith in self* gains great honors from it.

Take them in business life. Belief in chance feels its way, *faith in self* marches promptly forward; belief in chance is ignored, *faith in self is obeyed;* belief in chance is sometimes honored with approbation, while *faith in self* is always blessed by preferment.

Take them in the *United States Senate.* Belief in chance has the ear of the senators, but *faith in self* wins their hearts, and *gets* their votes; belief in chance is unfitted for skilled employment, but *faith in self* fitted for it.

Faith in self has a knack of slipping *into a well-paying position* with as sweet a silence and glibness of movement as a billiard-ball insinuates itself into the pocket.

Faith in self seems to know everything, without learning anything.

It has served an *invisible and extemporary* apprenticeship; it wants no drilling; it never ranks in the awkward squad; it has no left hand, no deaf ear, no blind or lame side.

It puts on no looks of wondrous wisdom, it has no air of profundity, but plays with the details of place as *dexterously as a well-trained hand flourishes over the ivory keys of the piano-forte.*

Faith in self has all the air of commonplace, and all the force and power of genius.

GENERALIZATIONS FROM OBSERVATION.

If a man *possess* great talents, *he need not publish them;* they will generally publish themselves. •

The love of knowledge *inspires an interest* in all humanity.

Speak after the manner of a *self-confident* man, if you would that all true men *hear and give you credence.*   •

Our best opinions and thoughts *are the strong ones.*

Selfishness and doubt are the fruits of a weak mind.

Faith and belief, in one's self, are the *symbols* of success.

Fill thy mind with useful knowledge, and *thou shalt avoid* empty words.

He who talks more than his share of the time *always* shows weakness and egotism.

The disappointed efforts of mankind in every department of life generally *originate and terminate in* secret selfishness.

Instead of enjoying life those who are destitute of self-confidence *live a compound funeral all their days.*

Sometimes the faces of those who have suffered while living *from a terrible doubt of self* are, for the first time peaceful when they are laid in the grave.

Often when men speak loudest their inward courage is *weakest.*

Honesty, faith and self-reliance are the three sparkling gems in the crown of *true* manhood.

Good ideas often take wings and fly *beyond our reach,* while bad ones cling to us like barnacles to a vessel.

True reason *ripens not* in the torrid zone of passion nor amid the frosts of bigotry, which always congeal truth.

The higher, nobler thought *was never dishonest;* therefore the divorced *were never truly married.*

Evil becomes supreme monarch of the mind *when seated* on the throne of a *selfish* ambition.

The exercise of *faith in yourself for health and good common sense* are the *best remedies* known to prolong human life.

Calm reason never seeks to prevail by unreasonable arguments.

The mind of the truly good changes often; *the heart never.*

A selfish man *covets that which he does not need,* while a liberal man often *bestows on others that which he really needs.*

Many men unwittingly enter into copartnership with error and doubt to *work out their own destruction.*

Many men talk as easily as they breathe, and with quite *as little* thought.

Meditation in the *quiet calm of nature* is the poising of the mind's wings for flight.

Men fail, sicken and die, through feebleness of will.

All the potencies of man reside in the will.

Practicability, from a material standpoint, congeals the fairest blossoms of mental flowers.

It is the small-minded, weak man who *quenches* the fire of his own success by his doubts and skepticisms.

To avoid obsession by doubt keep the mind positive and the body strong.

Obsequiousness begets friends; *truth,* hatred.

Hippocrates said to his pupils: "The affliction suffered by the body, the Soul sees when we shut our eyes."

Search for good in everything, and, when found, speak of it at once to your friends and neighbors, that they may rejoice with you that it has been found.

Sordid desires are the creatures of indulgence that *enslave men* to habits of error and wrong.

The prevailing misery throughout the world consists in placing *too little value upon self.*

Genuine friendship will always subordinate self-will to the welfare of a friend.

If you treat a man like a brute, *he is justified in behaving like one toward you.*

Thoughts, like many persons, are often more valued for their dress and surroundings than for their true character.

Public opinion is but the mist arising from the great ocean of thought and anon descending, it may be, in quiet showers or furious storms.

Conventional politeness is often but the chalice in which time-servers are accustomed to *offer us the poison of hypocrisy.*

A man who is always ready with an answer *seldom gives* the best one.

He who is a disturber in his own affairs *will not prove a peacemaker* in those of his friends or neighbors.

A profoundly *calm, thoughtful person* may be often sad, but never lonely.

A true man may ignore the rules of modern society and the dictates of fashion, *and yet not always forfeit his claim to good common sense.*

Truth lies in a straight line, following which a man may always stand erect in the full dignity of his manhood; but falsehood and error ever take a zigzag, underground course, pursuing which he must *bend his better judgment, twist his higher conscience, and warp his manhood till he ceases to be a man.*

Self-praise, like a circle, ends where it begins.

Many persons *revolve around great centres,* while others turn only on very small pivots.

From every dilemma there is always *more than one way out.*

The largest trees have always been found in *uncultivated* soil.

Endeavor that your forethought be as *unbiased* and far-reaching *as your after-thought must be.*

A thought that *does not command* one's own respect and admiration very seldom *commands that of others.*

The human will, *with a silent concentration of thought,* has the same effect on man's *"opportunities"* as the *magnet's* action upon iron.

As iron is brought near the *magnet it is at once imbued* with a subtle principle, *capable of imparting it to other iron,* if brought within its immediate atmosphere, while it neither gains weight nor changes in appearance, yet we all know one of the most subtle *potencies* has entered into its substance.

All human bodies are charged with different degrees of *mental forces,* whose strength varies with the condition and health of the person.

Very much *if not all nervous prostration* is either over-production or lack of this fluid to sustain polarity, the loss of which produces imperfect health.

We often best enjoy that which we least understand.

A man's character can always be read *by the comparisons he makes.*

There are thoughts that often intrude, not as beggars, but as true gift-bearers.

None can understand the true *value of self-control* better than they who appreciate its blessings.

In youth many often woo and wed habits and errors from which in after-life they *strive in vain to be divorced.*

When men cease to bend the knee to mammon and become free from great possessions, they are in a more natural state of being.

Human faculties are nature's moulds in which ideas are given form.

Imagination is the mind's retreat, *when left in silence.*

Mental growth is, step by step, like the filling of a barrel, drop by drop.

The human mind is *nature's keyboard,* on which her harmonies and discords are sounded by the touch of, thoughts controlled, and, thoughts uncontrolled.

A well cultivated mind *makes* always a kindly critic.

Inordinate self-esteem makes a balloon of a man's head; all the rest of him is simply the basket.

An unstable mind is like the *meteor* in the midnight sky; it shoots through space, without orbit or direction, leaving but a momentary reminder of its existence.

A considerate man's first impression *is more reliable* than a hasty man's deliberate judgment.

Man *wisely* thinks ten times as often as he wisely acts.

Some minds are like those auction rooms which *have nothing* but second-hand furniture to offer.

Disappointments in life are the result of exaggerated hopes.

Great blessings often disgust *unappreciative and discontented minds.*

As we place rare jewels in a deep setting to enhance their beauty, so Nature sets man's mind in dark surroundings, that it may better *try his faith.*

The more egotism and treachery *become dangerous to,* and frequently *undermine* the cause of, freedom of all nations, the more does personal, material interest guide the acts and endeavors of men.

The man who in our era *is penetrated by a higher idea* and nobler sentiment appears to some people as a designing rogue, a visionary madman, or an enthusiast.

Instead of *love to man,* which as a paramount duty should lie at the foundation of all intercourse with his fellow-man, *mistrust* has become the first condition of judgment in the world.

Add to your knowledge—*"faith in self."*

Nothing possesses greater magnetism than *simple truth* well spoken.

All men should be good judges of human nature, *since all are actors.*

Merited rebuke from an inferior *has a double sting.*

Calm hope *gives* real moral courage.

Make use of time if you value eternity. Yesterday *cannot* be recalled; tomorrow *cannot* be assured; today only *is yours,* which, if you procrastinate, *you lose—which loss is lost forever.*

There is no better way known to man for *securing* mental and moral integrity than to encourage those habits, those methods, and those pursuits which tend to establish truth.

The things that appear delight us, but make the things that appear not, *hard to believe,* for the things that appear not to the natural eye are hard to believe.

The things most apparent to men are the evil of things, but the *good is a secret,* or hid in the things that appear, for it hath neither form nor figure.

Of this be quite sure. All that is rightfully yours *will come to you* in its own good time. *So reads the law.* "*Everything comes to the Man who in Silence can Wait.*"

It is the bright *oil of hope* which makes life's machinery run smoothly, and the fruit which generally gives the most happiness ripens on the tree of our best ideality and higher love.

Many of man's ideals of today *will be realities* on some golden tomorrow.

Hope is the mainspring of human action; *Faith* seals our lease of immortality; *Charity* and *Love* give the passport to the Soul's inmost, true, and lasting happiness.

Among the noblest sentences uttered by the martyred *Lincoln* was this: "*With malice toward none and charity for all, I seek only the good of my countrymen.*"

> Cross against corselet, Love against Hatred,
> Peace-cry for war-cry, *Patience is powerful;*
> He that *o'ercometh* hath power o'er the nations.

Do not be carried away by anger. As it is written, "*He that falleth on this stone shall be broken.*"

Opposition to peace is strife.

The first act of a living babe *is to wail a cry of pain;* the first expression of a dead face *is a smile.*

Does the babe *unconsciously shrink from the life before it;* and the smile *foreshadow* the peace *following* a life of toil? If so, life is a priceless boon, and the problem will be solved in eternity.

He who is *tolerant* with the intolerant, *mild* with the fault-finders, *free* from passion among the passionate, has conquered himself, and can truly say he has obtained *Mental Discipline.*

Truth always repays with priceless gems, the brave hearts who suffer for her.

Mental enlightenment, or thought-light, is the *product* of a well balanced mind.

The most ignorant mind has some form of thought or it would not be susceptible to improvement; *neither* would it be liable to defects.

We all feel *"enlightened"* when we come sympathetically into contact with a *calm superior mind,* and a flow of new thoughts is the result.

The process of mental culture goes on ceaselessly, with the sincere student, and thus his volume of thought-force improves, till *he pass out* of the sphere of doubt in self into that of *faith in self.*

Then the element *alters* and becomes more *homogeneous.*

Nature has no secrets from *her true votaries.*

He who would become one of her true disciples must first plant the *"tree of faith in self"* within his own mind and *culture it in silence* and patience.

In time it will yield to him the *true knowledge* of *success* and *failure.*

Thrice blessed is he who with a *lamp of truth,* in union with nature, has a natural inclination to develop his mind power without being driven to it by suffering and affliction.

Each must *carve out* his own way through life. Man can make his very contradictions harmonize with his *calm, quiet mind.* Try always to get better and better control of your thoughts. Go up higher and higher, ever trying to advance mentally.

It is far better to *try and try,* even if one make blunders, than never to have tried at all. When one is not strong enough to weather the gale, one must bow like a reed before it, rising again after the storm is past, more dignified, more grand.

Guard your weaknesses from most men; they are often either unworthy of your confidence, or in their friendship are very apt to abuse it.

Learn to know all, but keep thyself unknown, has been wisdom handed down the ages. Let your confidence and belief in yourself rest only on the heights of success.

To struggle on against all the world is *always unpleasant*, even if you be a thousand times right.

Do not strive to *pull against* the whole community where you live.

In silence and calmness listen patiently and do not argue.

You have *your freedom of thought.*

Isolation is best.

Better never to have been great than, having been so, *then fall forever to be so no more.*

A star that sets will *rise* again tomorrow; a star that falls rises *no more* forever. Search diligently for truth, no matter what the world may say. Press on, the golden *Star of Self-Reliance* is on the heights with its dawning lights.

On every height is found repose.

There come, to those souls who have no *faith in themselves*, times when they become *heart sick and weary.*

Alas! how many men of mature years are held back by doubt and self-condemnation because *they do not*, and have never, understood *what it means to have faith in themselves.*

The very best part of many men and women *lies buried* beneath their own fears and doubts.

Misunderstood, their fears hold them *down* with chains *forged* of *doubt and unrest.*

To all such a *change is necessary;* in fact, for the usefulness of their life, *a change is imperative.*

As the student acquires knowledge, he must learn how it has been acquired, and he is made to feel that no fact is worth knowing *unless with it he knows the way to prove it.*

Earnest student, *dare to be wise.* In silence *pursue the path of wisdom*, regardless of the world or what it may say, or any obstacle which it may throw in your way.

Be wise and *you will not only govern your own destiny but show others the way.* And you will possess a mind foreshadowing the future. By your prudence and foresight you will be able to counteract that which more gross or *untrained minds* have suffered to pass as fate or destiny, whereby their faculties are confined to a narrow line of operation.

I have—in THE MASTER KEY—given you the *Duality* of your being and *Salient* force.

DR. L. W. DE LAURENCE.

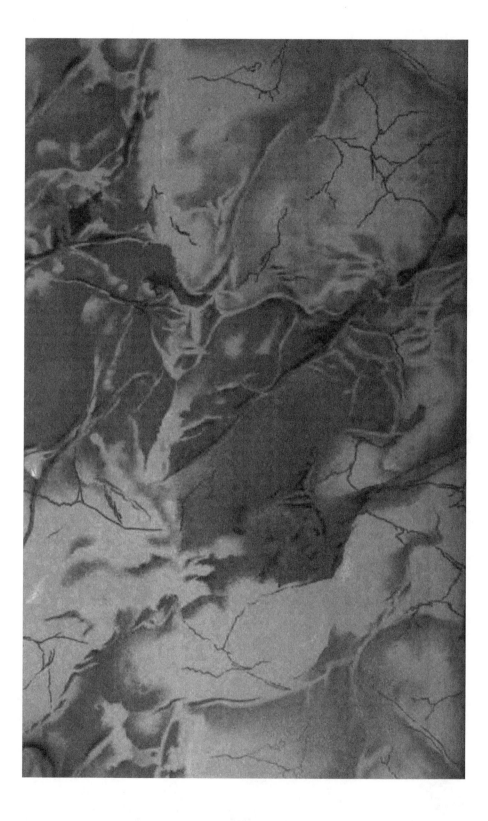

CPSIA information can be obtained
at www.ICGtesting.com
Printed in the USA
LVHW020811040423
743358LV00002B/320